ITALIAN FASCISM AND DEVELOPMENTAL
DICTATORSHIP

ITALIAN FASCISM AND DEVELOPMENTAL DICTATORSHIP

A. JAMES GREGOR

PRINCETON UNIVERSITY PRESS, NEW JERSEY

This book is dedicated to the memory of
GIOACCHINO VOLPE
and to those he loved

CONTENTS

PREFACE

Convention permits an author, in his preface, to speak in the first person. He is expected to outline his program, anticipate criticisms, and acknowledge his debts. I should like to attempt something of all that.

In the first place, this volume will attempt a summary outline of Fascist ideology and practice as that ideology and practice manifested themselves during the quarter century of Mussolini's rule on the Italian peninsula. I should like to think that it is the best brief outline of Fascism as an ideological and political system available in English. In the second place, there is an effort to relate Fascism to Bolshevism, both conceived as members of the class of mass-mobilizing, developmental regimes that have become so prominent in the twentieth century. Finally, some suggestions are made that attempt to lodge Fascism in the framework of a general comparative perspective. All these objectives, taken together, suggest that the book has assumed obligations that are very difficult to discharge effectively. No one is more aware of that than I. Nonetheless, I felt that the issues were of sufficient importance and interest to warrant the effort. I hope that there is enough in the following pages to justify the writing and merit the reading. Whatever failings afflict the text cannot be the consequence of a lack of concern or effort on my part, or the lack of assistance from scholars as interested and as dedicated as any in the profession.

This book is an obvious effort to satisfy the interests provoked by some of my earlier publications. In 1969, I published a volume devoted to the *Ideology of Fascism*. In that, I suggested that the clutch of ideas that made up the belief system of Fascism could best be understood as "developmental"—and that Fascism might well be identified as "the first revolutionary mass-movement regime which aspired to commit the totality of human and natural resources of an historic community to national development."[1] Given the obligations assumed in the exposition, however, there was little effort to trace Fascist intention as it manifested itself in Fascist practice. The present work, on the other hand, attempts to do just that. Although far less time is spent with Fascist ideas, I have undertaken to argue that Fascist practice was largely a function of Fascist ideas.

So much has been written about Mussolini's Fascism that I take to be mistaken, that I am convinced that the present effort has much to recommend it. The text, as a consequence, is clearly revisionist. As such, it is obvious that the exposition is interpretive. But, in my judgment, all accounts of complex social and political phenomena are similarly, and inevitably, interpretive. All such narratives are bound together by what Arthur Danto has felicitously spoken of as "project terms": terms that identify time-extended sequences of complex historical events as the working out of some conscious or unconscious, individual or collective, 'project.' Men undertake to accomplish certain tasks. Those responsibilities, whether successfully discharged or not, shape behaviors and lend sense and meaning to what might otherwise appear random, and sometimes pointless, movements.

There are many accounts of Fascism, for example, written with the conviction that Fascism was reactionary. Fascism's task was to administer a "preventive counter-revolution." Fascists either consciously, or under the pressure of objective circumstances, performed reactionary tasks. The project term "reactionary" is understood to expose the meaning of an indeterminate number of historical behaviors. The interpretation of Mussolini's regime is made the object of a "retrospective realignment of the past." Individual events are interpreted, and lent special significance, by including them in a reactionary sequence. Fascism was an instance of a reactionary regime, and the ideology and history of the regime are interpreted as providing confirming evidence of just such experimental naming.[2]

There are, of course, any number of project terms available that can serve as organizing concepts for alternative expositions. Some authors have conceived Fascism to have been nothing other than the result of Mussolini's efforts to "capture attention at all costs."[3] Others have sought to understand the behaviors of a quarter century as the working out of Mussolini's "love" for Italy.[4] Still others have attempted to understand the salient features of the period as a function of the psychological disabilities that plagued Mussolini as a consequence of the progressive deterioration that attended his putative syphilitic affliction.[5]

For the purposes of this account I have selected "development" as the project term that is most instructive. Which is not to suggest that I imagine myself to have captured historical reality. I am not sure what such a capture might entail. It seems clear to me that men can embark on any number of projects in the course of a lifetime. Fascists may have pursued a great variety of deliberate and unconscious projects over a quarter of a century. But it is not the business of social science or history to reconstitute the past in all its infinite detail, to catalog all the realized or faulted intentions, or to chronicle the precise sequence of events. Such an enterprise is doomed to failure. One must necessarily select from the richness of the past those elements conceived of as significant, and only projects lend significance to otherwise uninterpretable behaviors and events.

I believe that the identification of Fascism as a mass-mobilizing, developmental dictatorship affords a kind of preliminary understanding absent from any alternative identification. Correct or incorrect, it is that judgment that has governed my selection of materials and shaped the subsequent account. The result, I feel, is an exposition that provides an illuminating interpretation of Fascist ideological development and one that traces an intelligent and intelligible relationship between Fascist thought and Fascist practice. That commentators have failed to understand Fascist ideology is not only the consequence of their general ignorance of Fascist doctrinal literature, but of their inability, or unwillingness, to appreciate Fascist modernizing and industrializing intention.

Clearly, I have neglected a great deal. Limitations of time, energy, and the obligations of a specific exposition, have made that a necessity. Nevertheless, I feel the account provides an interpretation of Fascism that is not only instructive, but that relates Fascism to the Marxism in which it found its intellectual origins. Moreover, as I have suggested, it is an account that identifies Fascism as a member of a class of regimes that includes Bolshevism, Maoism, Castroism, as well as an indeterminate number of other regimes that mobilize masses under both unitary party auspices and the superintendence of charismatic and providential leaders, in the pursuit of modernization and development.

Even if this effort should fail in all of its stated objectives, it will provide, in outline, the ideas of several interesting Fascist ideologues—Sergio Panunzio, A. O. Olivetti, and Alfredo Rocco—almost unknown to English-language readers. It will also place the work of a more familiar figure, Roberto Michels, in the context of the Fascist ideological tradition.

Thirty years after its extinction, we really know very little of theoretical consequence about Mussolini's Fascism. For all the volumes dedicated to the subject, Renzo De Felice could recently insist that our understanding of Fascism "is still in a preliminary phase."[6] Confined by an ignorance born of an aversion to its ideology, afflicted by the prejudgments generated by moral outrage concerning its practice, possessed of the analytic and interpretive tools of what is, at best, an informal discipline, our understanding could only be "preliminary."

We are all, more or less, disabled by these shortcomings. We are all children of our time. In the effort to offset some of my own disabilities, I have attempted to treat Fascist ideology and practice with a studied measure of detachment. I am fully aware of Fascism's enormities, just as I am aware of the horrors of Bolshevism, National Socialism, Castroism, and Maoism, the injustices of liberal democracy, and the moral impairments of mankind in general. But I have never felt that these obvious facts assist us much in coming to understand, in any significant theoretical sense, complex historical and political events. Those who see some merit in the rehearsal of man's bestiality to man can make ready recourse to any number of other books that are more than prepared to satisfy their interests.

In terms of the substance of the account, there is a central argument that really requires more elaboration. I have argued that the thought of syndicalist theoreticians was of critical importance to the political maturation of Mussolini, and, through him, of similar importance to Fascism. Making that argument requires more space than could be justifiably allotted in this work; it is more adequately developed in my forthcoming, *The Young Mussolini and the Intellectual Origins of Fascism*. In the present work I have delivered enough of the argument to make a plausible case in its support. In this regard, Renzo De Felice wrote, more than a decade ago,

> The most important influence upon Mussolini's development, all the relationships and influences of the successive years notwithstanding, was that exercized by revolutionary syndicalism. Even after Mussolini concluded his socialist phase, the influence of revolutionary syndicalism revealed itself in the characteristic manner he conceived social relations and political struggle.[7]

Before bringing this preface to a conclusion, a word should be said about the style of the narrative. The reader will find considerable repetition in the text. In the effort

to establish the accuracy of the account, I have felt it necessary to restate syndicalist arguments with some frequency.
This allows not only evidence of continuity and development
over time to be brought to bear, but permits reference to
more documentation. Moreover, it is so often reiterated that
revolutionary syndicalism and Fascism were given over to
an irrational voluntarism and activism that had no relevance
to political practice that I have tried to draw the relationship
between Fascist and proto-Fascist ideology and Fascist
practice as clearly as possible. I felt this required a restatement of ideological arguments in relevant instances of Fascist
practice.

I realize that such a strategy may be tedious for many
readers. On the other hand, the conventional wisdom concerning Fascism's lack of ideological content, and the *ad hoc*
nature of its political practice, has taken on the status of
an all-but-incorrigible truth among Anglo-Americans. It may
serve some purpose to hear proto-Fascist and Fascist arguments several times, if only to redress the balance. By way
of further justification, I take some of the syndicalist and
Fascist arguments to be among the most original and interesting that have appeared among heretical Marxists. Restatement of these arguments in different contexts may high-
light their importance.

Finally, this work has profited from the gracious assistance of a number of people and several major research and
academic institutions. Maria Hsia Chang provided more
than invaluable assistance. She suffered my moodiness, often
spurred my flagging resolve, ministered to my fragile ego,
and provided advice and counsel. My colleagues, Peter Sper-
lich, Chalmers Johnson, Milos Martic, and Philip Siegelman
provided the warmth of friendship and the intellectual stimulation necessary for any such effort. Milorad M. Drach-
kovitch inspired the study with his encouragement and
Renzo De Felice by his example. The actual work was supported by the John Simon Guggenheim Memorial Foundation, the Hoover Institution on War, Revolution and Peace,

and the Institute of International Studies at the University of California, Berkeley. The University of California, Berkeley, provided the facilities and the environment without which I would be intellectually homeless. To all these persons, and all these institutions, I am enormously grateful. I hope this work can serve as a small token of that gratitude.

ITALIAN FASCISM AND DEVELOPMENTAL
DICTATORSHIP

ONE

THE AMBIGUOUS LEGACY

Political theory throughout history has shown itself to be a treacherous guide to political conduct. For centuries great thinkers have written about the origins, the nature, and the essence of life lived in common. They have written in an equally profound way about the political institutions that animate that life. They have sought to uncover the conditions governing the political organization of associated life, have speculated upon the trends and laws inherent in political combination, and have anticipated political futures and issued injunctions and proscriptions. They have advocated reform and revolution and have sought to justify their entire enterprise with appeals to the putative logic of history, divine imperatives, the identification of individual moral instincts, collective material interests and/or universal human dispositions. Out of all this, practical men were expected to tease out directives that might govern the specifics of individual and collective political behavior. Inevitably, such directives rely upon one of an immense variety of interpretations of oft-times enormously complex and obscure political theory. Unhappily, more frequently than not there have been as many interpretations of any given theory as there have been interpreters.

We all know that men have rummaged, for example, through the pages of Holy Scripture to put together justificatory arguments for almost every conceivable piece of political behavior, almost every form of political system or rule-governed interpersonal association. At one time or another, some thinker has contrived a "Christian" rationale for slavery, war, absolute or constitutional monarchy, anarchy, reformist socialism, revolutionary socialism, or fascism.

Somehow, we are all prepared to recognize the protean and effervescent quality of religious thought. And yet political theory shares some of the same features. The recognition of just these similarities has provided either grist for the cynic's mill or the substance of many a treatise on the sociology of knowledge.

In our own time and more to our present purpose, we have seen the theory associated with the name of Karl Marx invoked to justify those behaviors characteristic of both reformist social democracy and mass-mobilizing revolutionary movements. Marxism has been pressed into the service of that conduct which has led to the decimation of entire categories of unfortunates, or the instauration of vast labor camps in Stalin's Russia. Marxism has been understood to provide the rationale for the charismatic and hierarchical government in Castro's Cuba, the religious reverence accorded the thought of Chairman Mao, the postadolescent radicalism of middle-class student movements, the terrorism of urban or national-liberation guerrillas, and authoritarian regimes of every imaginable style. The rationale for each and every such posture has its own Marxist theoretician or group of Marxist theoreticans, often as much opposed to each other as they are opposed to the theoreticians of their "class enemies." There seem to be as many interpretations of Marxism as there are interpretations of Sacred Scripture. And there is little wonder.

If the Christian Gospels, for all their brevity, could be father to that vast array of interpretations mustered to the support of an indeterminate number of social and political behaviors, what might one expect from a body of theoretical literature that includes thousands and thousands of pages written over the course of half a hundred years? The new German edition of the works of Karl Marx and Friedrich Engels runs into two score volumes, most of them over six hundred pages in length.[1] Out of this enormous mass of materials men have attempted to fashion an interpretation that might provide one sure guide to political conduct. The majority of those who have undertaken the task have sought to deliver a faithful rendering of the thought of Marx. They have sought to express what Marx really meant, and what such orthodox meaning implied for political behavior.

That contemporary men have become increasingly skeptical about all such claims of orthodoxy is readily understood. We are not surprised that there continue to be those who believe they have discovered the true meaning of Marx, but we lament the fact that others should credit them with the accomplishment. There is so much in the writings of Marx and Engels that even the most minor talent can put together a plausible interpretation that seems, for all the world, to exclude alternative interpretations, which, on inspection, turn out to be equally plausible.

The writings of Karl Marx and Friedrich Engels are filled with profound insights, trenchant asides, heuristic suggestions, putative laws, empirical assessments, injunctions to behave, invocations, half-articulated predictions, unargued assumptions, vague generalizations, evident untruths, bits of foolishness, simple carping, question-begging, and sometimes circular reasoning. With judicious selection, anyone can contrive an account that, to one degree or another, might justify libertarian democracy, parliamentary government, peasant revolution, pacificism, internationalism, nationalism, charismatic government, and/or guerrilla warfare—all in the name of Marx.

As long as Marx or Engels was alive, each such interpretation remained subject to preemptive scrutiny. Thus Marx could pass damning judgment on socialist anarchism. Engels could dismiss socialist anti-Semitism, or peasant populism, or communist revolutions in preindustrialist environments. But after the death of Engels in 1895, no one remained to serve as the final arbiter in instances of contending interpretations. Upon his death, Marxism became father to a host of interpretations, some frankly revisionist, some claiming the mantle of orthodoxy, but all conceiving themselves to be faithful to the letter and/or spirit of Karl Marx's thought.

The situation in our own time is not fundamentally different than it was at the turn of the century when intellectual crisis first disturbed classical Marxism. Not only do Marxist theoreticians still generate a compelling number of mutually exclusive interpretations, but many of the issues around which these interpretations revolve are remarkably similar to those that agitated the Marxist theoreticians at the close of the nineteenth and the beginning of the twentieth century.

The Crisis of Classical Marxism

In point of fact, at no time during the second half of the nineteenth century could it be said that there was a single group of political thinkers who could be identified, without qualification, as orthodox Marxists. Classical Marxism, the product of the intellectual efforts of Marx and Engels, was apparently forever beset by misinterpretation. Both Marx and Engels regularly found themselves involved in acrimonious dispute with those who would debase their thought. Ferdinand Lassalle and Michael Bakunin—to mention only the most prominent—were considered by both Marx and Engels to have misconceived and distorted the most elementary insights of their theory. The record indicates that Marx and Engels spared few of the Marxists of their time. Josef Dietzgen for instance—the worker-intellectual whom Marx credited at one time with being the "one reader who really understood 'Capital' "—finally revealed himself to be little more than a "deviationist."[2] And the faithful Wilhelm Liebknecht, Marx's representative among the Social Democrats of Germany, lacked, in Marx's judgment, "the dimmest idea of revolutionary politics."[3]

Short of Friedrich Engels (and there is reason to believe that Marx's confidence may have been misplaced)[4] it would appear that Karl Marx failed to find a single contemporary who he felt could correctly interpret his ideas. At one point, Marx was so disappointed in the views that were being circulated in his name, that he insisted he "was not a Marxist."[5] In effect, even before the death of Engels, there was little that could pass as an orthodox interpretation of Marxism. It is quite clear that Marx had confidence only in Engels, and for twelve years after Marx's death it was Engels who continued to represent whatever Marxist orthodoxy there was.

In his turn, Engels bequeathed the responsibility for Marxist orthodoxy to Eduard Bernstein in whom he apparently had confidence.[6] Bernstein was a talented intellectual and a dedicated Marxist. There appeared to be every reason to believe that Bernstein would represent the integrity of Marxist thought as well as anyone.

As it turned out, less than a year after the death of Engels, Bernstein began a searching review of Marxism as a scientific theory. In a series of articles entitled *Probleme des Sozialismus*, published in *Die Neue Zeit*, Bernstein began a systematic review of the philosophical presuppositions, theoretical components, empirical generalizations, and research methodology of classical Marxism. In 1899 Bernstein published a volume in which his criticisms were made explicit. The disputes that had already been provoked by his articles in *Die Neue Zeit*, were inflamed by the appearance of his *Die Voraussetzungen des Sozialismus und die Aufgaben der Sozialdemokratie*.[7]

The fact is that although Bernstein's critique brought the issue of Marxism's theoretical integrity to the surface, others had already questioned it. The German Social Democratic party, even when it appeared most orthodox with the adoption of a Marxist program at the Erfurt congress in 1891, was nevertheless beset with grave theoretical misgivings. Theoreticians like Georg von Vollmar, for example, had already raised questions about the internal consistency, comprehensibility, and defensibility of some critical Marxist generalizations.[8] Bernstein, himself, could refer his audience

7

to Engels' introduction to Marx's *Class Struggles in France* as evidence of Engels' own moves in the direction of a significant reinterpretation of what might have been considered a rigid orthodoxy.

Until the years of overt intellectual crisis, many Marxists (whatever Marx and Engels may have thought of their efforts) had conceived Marxism to be a rigorously scientific theory of social dynamics, embodying "laws" that afforded insight into inevitable and ineluctable historic processes. These laws were understood to certify the immanent and violent collapse of the capitalist system. The proletariat—afflicted by grievous misery and constituting the vast majority of the population—would inevitably rise up against its tormentors and strike down the entire system. The outcome could be predicted with mathematical certainty.

There was much, of course, in the literature produced by Marx and Engels that made such estimations eminently plausible. Bernstein, on the other hand, argued that Marxism was composed of intellectual elements open to other interpretations, and, further, that Engels had given clear indication that whatever Marxism may have been at one time it had undergone significant changes in the immediate past.

Bernstein indicated that Engels, in his introduction to Marx's *Class Struggles in France*, had admitted that during their youth both he and Marx had been under "the spell of previous historical experience, particularly that of France." Engels went on to say that history had shown them to have been wrong, that their point of view of that time had been an illusion. Both he and Marx, for example, had believed a proletarian revolution to have been a real possibility at the time of the struggles of 1848 and 1850. They had then imagined that the revolution—precipitated by a small group of declassed intellectuals who would appeal to the real, but latent, interests of the masses—would inaugurate a socialist government. But it had later become obvious, Engels continued, that the "state of economic development on the Continent at that time was not, by a long way, ripe for the elimination of capitalist production."[9]

Engels argued that only comprehensively mature economic conditions, and the attendant appearance of a "genuine bourgeoisie and a genuine large-scale industrial proletariat," made socialist revolution a real historical possibility. Not only was Europe not prepared for socialist revolution in 1848-50, she could not be ready until a measure of social peace and national harmony could create the conditions under which the prerequisites of revolution could ripen and mature. Marx and Engels had been mistaken in making an appeal to social revolution in the mid-nineteenth century. Engels had come to understand, Bernstein argued, that only complete economic maturity, the fruit of peaceful industrial development, could create the conditions necessary for the advent of socialism. Only in an environment characterized by extensive industrial development could the proletariat emerge as an effective revolutionary class. Only after the unification of Germany, after the Franco-Prussian War of 1871, did industry begin to flourish in the Reich. Only with that development did the German working class organize itself into the "strongest, best disciplined and most rapidly growing Socialist Party" in the world. The strength of that party, and of the class it represented, Engels indicated, was revealed in the party's ability to attract votes. The working class had exploited what Engels identified as the newest and sharpest weapon in the socialist arsenal: universal suffrage. In his judgment, the use of the franchise constituted a "model to the workers of all countries." As a consequence, "rebellion in the old style, street fighting with barricades which decided the issue everywhere up to 1848, was to a considerable extent obsolete."[10]

Bernstein understood the Engels of 1895 to be saying that socialist revolution involved winning the electoral confidence of the masses, the vast majority of class-conscious proletarians, products of massive industrial development. Such a mass would increasingly collect around the Socialist party in industrially mature environments "spontaneously," "steadily," and "irresistibly," and "at the same time as tranquilly as a natural process." More than that, under such circumstances, Engels argued, the proletariat would attract "the middle strata of society, petty bourgeois and small peasants" in what resembled a democratic, multi-class coalition of popular forces capable of winning electoral victories that would be the preamble to socialism. "The irony of world history," Engels argued "turns everything upside down. We the 'revolutionists,' the 'overthrowers'—we are thriving far better on legal methods than on illegal methods and overthrow."[11]

Bernstein read all this as a significant change in the Marxist theory of revolution. His own long association with both Marx and Engels, his intimacy with Engels for the last five years of Engels' life, suggested to him that he had correctly interpreted the new perspectives. Socialism was to depend essentially on parliamentary and electoral strategies. Its victory was assured by the industrial development and the political democracy of the advanced capitalist states.

In Bernstein's judgment, Marx had left no precise theory of proletarian revolution. It seemed clear to him that, whatever the Marxist theory of revolution might have been, it had undergone significant changes in the course of half a century. Bernstein considered Engels' introduction to Marx's *Class Struggles in France*, written a few months before Engels' death, to be a definitive statement of the most contemporary Marxist view of socialist strategy and tactics, a reflection of the employment of what Engels called a "materialist analysis," which seeks to "trace political events back to effects of what [are], in the final analysis, economic causes."[12]

While it is clear that Engels did not foreclose the possibility, even the probability, of an ultimately violent confrontation between the bourgeoisie and the vast majority organized by the proletariat, it was evident that he urged socialists to be very circumspect in their use of violence in order not to impede the natural process of socialist succession.

But more than a change in the theory of revolution, Bernstein saw Engels' reform of what had been considered Marxist orthodoxy reflected in a more fundamental manner in Engels' letters to Josef Bloch and Conrad Schmidt—letters written in 1890, seven years after Marx's death. He held to be equally important Engels' letter to Heinz Starkenburg, dated January 25, 1894, in the revision of what had been considered classical Marxism.[13]

In his letter to Bloch, Engels had argued, for example, that "while the material mode of existence is the *primum agens* [of historic change] this does not preclude the ideological spheres from reacting upon it in their turn." He went on to admit, moreover, that "economic history," the very substance of Marxist theory, was "still in its swaddling clothes." Finally, Engels insisted that while "production and reproduction of real life" is the "*ultimately* determining element" in history, he rejected the "economic element" as the only determining element, for such a conviction would transform the critical proposition of historical materialism "into a meaningless, abstract, senseless phrase." All the elements of "intellectual life" Engels went on, "exercise their influence upon the course of the historical struggles and in many cases preponderate in determining their form. . . . There is an interaction of all these elements," he continued, "in which, amid all the endless host of accidents . . . the economic movement finally asserts itself as necessary. . . . There are," he argued, "innumerable intersecting forces, an infinite series of parallelograms of forces which give rise to one result—the historical event." All of which takes place as a natural process in which the will of each individual is merged in the statistical collection of all wills to produce that which no single individual, or group of individuals, specifically wills.[14]

To complicate the issues still further, Engels went on to accept the blame for sometimes laying "more stress on the economic side than is due to it," not having the time or opportunity to "give their due to the other elements involved in the interaction." As a consequence of these omissions on his part, and on the part of Marx, many Marxists had delivered themselves of "amazing rubbish"[15] when they attempted an interpretation of history.

In a subsequent letter to Schmidt, on October 27, 1890, Engels argued that the state could exercise considerable influence over economic development. The state, in effect, could influence the ultimate source of historic change. Similarly, statute law, no longer a simple reflection of economic conditions, could itself influence the complex chain of events that terminate in specific historical occurrences. Thus, Engels argued, political and ideological elements could react upon the economic basis of history and "within certain limits" modify it. In point of fact, Engels was prepared to admit that the most grievous "ideological errors" and simple "nonsense" could "react upon the whole development of society, even on its economic development."[16] All of which seemed to significantly alter the character of Marxism as a theory of historic development.

Bernstein took all of Engels' remarks to warrant a thorough review and reinterpretation of the entire collection of Marxist propositions.[17] Bernstein advocated a searching and detailed reconsideration not only of Marx's philosophical views, his methodological commitments, his economic conceptions, his empirical generalizations, and his predictions, but a reappraisal of the role of ideal and/or moral factors in individual and collective political behaviors.[18]

Bernstein's challenge precipitated a flurry of activity among the theoreticians of German social democracy. The commitment to classical Marxism, with the promulgation of the Erfurt program in 1891, was of too recent vintage to permit a casual reassessment of the entire fabric of the Marxist rationale. As has already been suggested, Georg von Vollmar had already advocated some of the same modifications, but his proposals had been defeated. Bernstein had raised the issues again and social democrats could not avoid facing them. Many questions, directly or indirectly related to these issues, had become increasingly emphatic during the 'nineties.

Few socialists could avoid the realization that the proletarian parties of the most advanced industrial nations of Europe had become more and more opportunistic. The indomitable Vera Zasulich, as a case in point, was aware that the English working classes, the proletariat of the most advanced capitalist nation of the world, had become increasingly accommodative in its demands.[19] Engels, himself, had noted that the English proletariat had allowed itself to become "bourgeoisified."[20] Bernstein had made much of just such considerations. What all this suggested was that the working class had become progressively nonrevolutionary, contrary to the orthodox interpretation of Marxist theory.

In a clear sense, both the English and the German socialists had, for some time, behaved in a reformist manner. For all their revolutionary talk, they shared an unmistakable disposition to search out conciliatory and negotiated solutions to social problems. Irrespective of that, German Marxist theoreticians sought to avoid a comprehensive inquiry into the world view that held their political party together, a crisis of faith. Neither Zasulich nor Engels appeared to waver in that faith. In fact, faced with the evident "bourgeoisification" of the proletariat, Engels seemed to invest his trust in a new generation of unskilled workers who would restore integrity to the propositions that informed classical Marxism. For her part, Zasulich restricted any misgivings she might have had to her private correspondence. It was Bernstein who sought to make a public issue of the discrepancies between the convictions of classical Marxism, as they had come to be understood, and the behaviors of the socialist parties of Europe. Those socialist leaders who, in practice, had given themselves over to "the inevitability of gradualism" continued to refrain from public profession of the modified faith. It was left to Bernstein to open the entire painful issue.

13

At first the German movement responded with unexpected passivity. Karl Kautsky published Bernstein's destructive analysis of Marxism's "catastrophism"—the conviction that capitalism must inevitably succumb either to a general crisis of overproduction or stagnate under the secular decline of profit—without comment in *Die Neue Zeit*. Bernstein argued that the proletariat had not become the vast majority of contemporary populations, a condition both Marx and Engels had believed necessary for the socialist revolution. He further denied that the living conditions of the proletariat in Europe or America had worsened, an event Marx and Engels seemed to have anticipated. As Bernstein's criticisms became more searching, resistance began to mount. The first to respond with acrimony were not Germans at all. Those who reacted most swiftly and most vituperatively were all non-Germans: Rosa Luxemburg, A. L. Parvus and Georgii Plekhanov. Kautsky suspended publication of Bernstein's articles in *Die Neue Zeit*, and suggested that Bernstein present his views for consideration at a party congress.

Bernstein argued that he was not forsaking Marxism. He insisted that he was continuing the work of Marx and Engels, that both these men, true to their commitment to science, had recognized that in some critical instances empirical processes had belied their assessments and faulted their predications. Bernstein maintained that Engels, himself, had licensed the review. Bernstein proposed a general reevaluation of the entire system in terms of contemporary developments. He argued that there was no economic catastrophy on the historical horizon. The classes in society had not been reduced to two irrepressibly antagonistic components, the vast majority of the proletarians against an exiguous number of monopoly capitalists. Society, as Marx himself had suggested in the third volume of *Capital*,[21] had become increasingly complex, with a proliferation of subclasses, economic categories, and professional strata, all with interests and concerns that bred an indeterminate number of political orientations and political demands.

Bernstein further suggested that the "anarchy of production," of which Marx had made so much, was significantly dampened by the increasing organization of whole segments of industry. Moreover, the working class had made substantial gains in terms of their standard of living and the acquisition of political rights. What was required was a studied reappraisal of the entire intellectual rationale of contemporary socialism. Finally, Bernstein doubted whether the social laws, to which Marx and Engels had alluded with such insistence, could be defended. Marx might well have spoken of such laws "working with iron necessity towards inevitable results."[22] And Engels may have insisted on the "general laws of motion . . . as the ruling ones in the history of human society," and on the course of history as "governed by inner general laws,"[23] but Bernstein maintained that these expressions could be most generously interpreted as infelicitous turns of speech, as expressions of enthusiasm, rather than as serious social science claims. He dismissed the possibility that social science possessed any such laws. At best, these statements were but heuristic suggestions, working hypotheses.

Bernstein advocated an abandonment of the pretense of having knowledge of any "inevitable laws of motion" governing human history that made revolution a predictable eventuality. He urged, instead, a recognition that German social democracy operated in a complex environment of increasing democratization. Such a recognition recommended a reformist program that would defend and enhance the gains enjoyed by the German working class in the modern world. He urged an abandonment of revolution mongering, the empty demagogic appeal to revolution. As a corollary, he suggested that socialists abjure metaphysical speculation as having no basis in reality or any import in strategic and tactical decision-making.

The first response to Bernstein's views made by Georgii Plekhanov, the father of Russian Marxism, was one of outraged betrayal. He conceived the arguments to be nothing

15

less than a "complete break with revolutionary tactics and with communism." He read them all as an appeal to "philistinism,"[24] and as soon as he regained his composure, he embarked upon a countercritique. Everything in which Plekhanov believed had been threatened by Bernstein's analysis. It was not only that the "philistine-tortoise" pace of social reform had been licensed as the tactical and strategic goal of socialism that repelled men like Plekhanov, it was the fact that Bernstein's critique threatened a total world view, an intellectual structure in whose integrity and coherence many Marxists had invested their faith.

Plekhanov's views had grown out of his reading of the enormous body of funded literature. He understood classical Marxism as a collection of scientific laws capable of anticipating futures in terms of lawlike inevitabilities. As early as 1895 he had given classical Marxism his own interpretation. In his *The Development of the Monist View of History*, he had committed himself to a Marxism possessed of a catalog of laws that revealed the necessities "underlying the historical development of society." "Every natural process," Plekhanov had argued, "is a process taking place in conformity to law. Changes in social relations which are unforeseen by men, but which of necessity appear as a result of their actions, evidently take place according to definite laws."[25]

By 1898 these convictions received still more emphatic expression in Plekhanov's essay, "The Role of the Individual in History."[26] Here he made evident his commitment to definite laws that make some specific series of events inevitable. When he addressed himself to human motivation, Plekhanov argued that men serve as instruments of historical necessity and cannot avoid doing so. "Since [man's] social status has imbued him with this character and no other, [man] not only serves as an instrument of necessity and cannot help doing so, but he passionately desires, and cannot help desiring, to do so."[27] In this regard Plekhanov could argue that he was paraphrasing Marx himself. In the *Holy Family* Marx had maintained that, "The question is not what

16

this or that proletarian, or even the whole of the proletariat at the moment considers as its aim. The question is what the proletariat is, and what, consequent on that being, *it will be compelled to do*. Its aim and historical action *is irrevocably and obviously* demonstrated in its own life situation."[28]

Plekhanov clearly took Marx to mean that although man creates his own history through individual and collective activities, "man's activities are the conscious and free expression of [an] inevitable and unconscious course." The course of history, he seemed to argue, is "in the last analysis" determined by "the development of the productive forces and the mutual relations between men," but, he concluded, "the final cause of social relationships lies in the state of the productive forces."[29] All of which leaves one with the conviction that the productive forces are the sole ultimate causes of inevitable historic sequences. In these sequences, the conscious will and volition of men play epiphenomenal and derivative roles.

This seems to be, for example, what V. I. Lenin understood Plekhanov to be saying. In 1894 Lenin wrote his "What the 'Friends of the People' Are, and How They Fight the Social Democrats."[30] In that early essay he argued that Marx had proven the necessity of the present order of things and that he had furthermore established the "necessity of another order which must inevitably grow out of the preceding one *regardless of whether men believe in it or not, whether they are conscious of it or not.* Marx treats the social movement as a process of natural history, governed by *laws not only independent of human will, consciousness and intentions, but, rather, on the contrary, determining the will, consciousness and intentions of men.*"[31]

In effect, some of the men who were to become the most acerbic critics of Bernstein had already interpreted classical Marxism in terms of social science laws that made human will and human intention by-products of more fundamental material processes that work with iron necessity to inevitable conclusions. And there was, of course, a basis for just that

17

interpretation. Everyone was well aware that Marx himself seemed to have licensed such a view when he reported, with evident approval, the comments of a Russian reviewer who characterized his dialectical method as one which treated historical and social change as a "natural process," the consequence of laws that were not only "independent of human will, consciousness and intelligence," but which, in fact, inevitably generated the appropriate "will, consciousness and intelligence."[32] It was this article, in fact, that Lenin cited to provide the warrant for his interpretation. If Bernstein had his preferred sources, Plekhanov and Lenin had theirs. If Bernstein could put together a plausible interpretation, Plekhanov and Lenin could fashion one no less plausible.

Like Plekhanov, the young Lenin believed Marxism provided revolutionaries with an inventory of lawlike assertions that outlined necessary historic change. This change took place as a consequence of economic development, the progressive emiseration of the proletariat who, ultimately, would constitute the vast majority of men, and who, finally, would make inevitable social revolution. Thus, in his objections to Bernstein, Lenin insisted that history was, in fact, governed by a necessity exemplified in objective sociological laws.[33]

It seems reasonably clear that Lenin's early notions concerning the inevitability of Marxism's political, social, and economic prognostications, were essentially those of Plekhanov. Men do, in fact, make their own history according to these convictions, but what men choose to do is determined by the material conditions in which they find themselves. "The conscious element," the young Lenin insisted, thus "plays . . . a subordinate . . . part in the history of civilization."[34]

The revolutionary critics of Bernstein that gathered around Plekhanov argued against Bernstein's interpretation of Engels' "ultimate Marxism," the competence of his statistics, his methodological strictures, and his tactical suggestions. Yet, for all their apparent confidence, for all their arguments, it was apparent that something was amiss.

It is clear that Marx had argued that the capitalist mode of production was beset by internal contradictions and that one of the most critical contradictions was that exemplified by what he chose to call "the law of the falling rate of profit." Marx argued that as capitalism matured there was a tendency for the rate of profits to decline, a decline which revealed the historic "transitoriness" of capitalism. This tendency of profit rates to decline with the increasing "organic composition of capital" (increments in capital investment in plant and technological innovation as distinct from capital distributed in terms of wages) revealed the intrinsic limitations of capitalism as a system of production. Within the secular decline of profit, cyclical crises provided only temporary relief. As the decline proceeded, crises would become increasingly severe.[35] In 1845 Engels had written that, even under the best of circumstances, the commercial crises that beset capitalism "would continue, and grow more violent, more terrible." And under such conditions the "majority of the proletariat . . . has no other choice than to starve or to rebel."[36]

Curiously enough, none of this implied catastrophism for Lenin. Neither did it imply a real decline in the life circumstances of the proletariat. Marx alluded, Lenin argued, to a *relative* decline in the standard of living of the proletariat. There were necessary processes which rendered the passage from capitalism to socialism inevitable. However necessary those processes were, their workings, given all the theoretical subtleties, remained obscure. What remained certain for those, like Lenin, who insisted on a revolutionary interpretation of Marxism, was that Marxist theory abjured reformism and pacific evolutionism. However paradoxical and opaque the interpretation, revolution was intrinsic to Marxism. To foreswear revolution was to abandon Marxism.

The death of Friedrich Engels marked the opening of a critical phase in the development of Marxism as a guide to revolutionary conduct. Among Russians it provoked a searching reappraisal of their commitments and an assumption of

19

theoretical positions that was to influence the subsequent development of revolutionary Bolshevism. Among Italians it was to precipitate the articulation of an equally revolutionary "syndicalism," a studied response to the crisis of Marxism that was, in a significant sense, to produce the ideology of Fascism.

The Crisis in Italy

Eduard Bernstein's critique of classical Marxism did not have the impact in Italy that it had in many other countries in Europe. In the first instance, Francesco Severio Merlino, in 1897, had already undertaken an extensive and critical review of the theoretical credentials of classical Marxism, and had raised many of the issues contained in Bernstein's account.[37] In 1899, Merlino organized and published the *Rivista critica del socialismo* which became, in substance, the vehicle of Italian reformism.[38] At almost the same time, Antonio Graziadei published his *La produzione capitalistica*.[39] Bernstein himself was later to identify Graziadei as an author who had anticipated many of his ideas.[40] Graziadei, like Bernstein, had denied that Marx's law of the declining rate of profit operated in the manner Marx had prefigured. Again like Bernstein, Graziadei insisted that capitalism had shown itself capable of ameliorating the life circumstances of the proletariat, and that, as a consequence, the transition from competitive capitalism to a cooperative social order was possible through reform legislation and social evolution.

The fact is that Italian reformism had already assumed relatively specific political postures without the searching theoretical critique advocated by Merlino and Graziadei. As was the case in Germany, Italian reformism was characterized more by its practice than by an intensive theoretical review of the fundamentals of classical Marxism. The followers of Filippo Turati, for example, had already begun to behave like reformists long before they had attempted to vindicate their political orientation with any sort of theoretical rationale. Only later, at the Rome congress of the socialist party in 1906, did Turati specifically identify the theoretical revisionism upon which Italian reformism was based. At that time Turati identified the "three dogmas" of revolutionary Marxism that reformism rejected: (1) the increasing emiseration of the proletariat, (2) the progressive concentration of wealth in fewer and fewer hands, and (3) the consequent proletarianization of the vast majority of men. Turati insisted that, irrespective of revolutionary dogma, the conditions of the proletariat had in fact been considerably ameliorated. Small industry had continued to grow and prosper, and wealth had found its way into more and more hands. Turati argued that these conditions constituted the warrant for reformist political tactics.[41] "Bernsteinianism" had made its appearance in Italy long before theoretical revision had become a necessity.

Like Italian reformism, Italian revolutionism had already begun to sort itself out of the classical tradition even before the advent of Bernstein's criticism. As early as 1895, Arturo Labriola and Enrico Leone had begun to put together a rationale for Marxist revolution as a reaction to the reformism that was gradually taking shape in the Italian environment. By 1898 the first halting statements of revolutionary syndicalism were being bruited.[42] By the turn of the century, the writings of Georges Sorel were becoming increasingly prominent and syndicalism in Italy began to take on theoretical substance. By 1901 Sorel had published his *L'avenir socialiste des syndicats* and syndicalism had begun its "return to Marx." At the Socialist Party Congress at Imola in 1902 there were thus two tendencies represented, the one, which sought a revision of Marxism, under the leadership of Turati, Ivanoe Bonomi, Leonida Bissolati, and Claudio Treves, and the other, which sought a reaffirmation of revolutionary Marxism, under the leadership of Enrico Ferri, Giovanni Lerda, and Arturo Labriola.[43]

Almost immediately after the Congress at Imola, Arturo Labriola founded the syndicalist weekly, *L'avanguardia so-*

21

cialista. At almost the same time that Lenin was outlining an intransigent Bolshevism, the revolutionary syndicalists of Italy were articulating the fundamentals of a revolutionary Marxism that was to significantly influence Italian life for a quarter of a century.

In 1904 the young Benito Mussolini, then a socialist agitator in Switzerland, began his collaboration with the *L'avanguardia socialista* and the revolutionary syndicalist current it represented. For the next five years Mussolini was to identify himself with the revolutionary formulations of Italian syndicalism.

Italian Revolutionary Syndicalism

In 1904 at the Socialist Party Congress at Brescia, the syndicalists, in reaction to the reformism of Italian socialism, succeeded in introducing an Order of the Day that sought to reaffirm the "intransigently revolutionary character" of proletarian political strategy, with an explicit rejection of any political opportunism that sought to reduce the Socialist party's activities to parliamentary and legalistic enterprise. The syndicalist submission went on to insist that proletarian revolution, coherently understood, required every form of resistance and struggle, including violence, against the bourgeois state.

In his commentary on the position assumed in the Order of the Day, Walter Mocchi (who, at that time, co-edited *L'avanguardia* with Arturo Labriola) argued that only in such fashion could the integrity of revolutionary Marxism be restored. Mocchi held that the function of the Socialist party of Italy was to organize the proletariat in preparation for the revolution that would transform the capitalist system into socialism. The proletariat, so organized, would be prepared to assume total control over the industrial system of the nation.

The *Ordine del giorno*, accepted by the majority of the congress, subsequently received the support of foreign socialists, Karl Kautsky, Paul Lafargue (Marx's son-in-law), and Jules Guesde among them. In effect, some of the most important standard-bearers of classical Marxism held the syndicalist position at the party congress of Brescia to have represented the position of classical Marxism. In the months that followed, this initial success was supplemented by practical success. The syndicalists organized the first effective general strike on the Italian peninsula. On the 17th of September, 1904, the workers of northern Italy called for a general strike—a call to which the rest of the peninsula, in substantial part, responded. For four days Italy seemed to be in the hands of the revolutionary workers. For much of the bourgeoisie, and for many socialists, the strike of 1904 was looked upon as a dress rehearsal for social revolution.

In 1904 syndicalism seemed possessed of recruitment potential and revolutionary capabilities. Young and aggressive intellectuals grouped around the first spokesmen of the movement. In the months and years that were to immediately follow, men like Ottavio Dinale, Paolo Orano, Sergio Panunzio, A. O. Olivetti, and Roberto Michels were to identify with the syndicalist intransigents and revolutionaries. Benito Mussolini was among their number.

All these revolutionary socialist intellectuals gathered around the standard of Georges Sorel, whose work was becoming increasingly prominent in Italy. In 1906 his *Reflections on Violence* was published in an Italian edition, with an introduction by Enrico Leone. In fact, after 1905 syndicalist literature in general became abundant in Italy. The authoritative works remained those of the "old men" of syndicalism, Arturo Labriola and Enrico Leone.[44] The master of the movement remained Georges Sorel. Guided by these standard works and influenced by Sorel, younger authors produced a profusion of books and articles that were to provide the intellectual rationale for Italian radicalism.

These first theoreticians of syndicalism directed their efforts principally against reformism in all its manifestations. For them the crisis of socialism was largely the consequence

23

of major departures from the theoretical substance of classical Marxism. As a consequence, they advocated a "return to Marx,"[45] a careful sifting through the body of materials left as an intellectual heritage by the founders of classical Marxism. Such an enterprise, they were convinced, would afford contemporaries a sure guide to revolutionary conduct, and reveal the fundamentally conservative disposition of reformism. They considered the political program of the official Italian Socialist party as conforming "admirably to the programs of all the conservative parties of Italy."[46]

This corruption of Marxism was conceived, in the first instance, to be the consequence of the Socialist party having allowed itself to fall under the leadership of "bourgeois elements."[47] While the syndicalists recognized that Marx had conceded that some declassed elements of the bourgeoisie might defect to the working class, they insisted that, in the final analysis, according to both Marx and Engels, the liberation of the working class must be the accomplishment of the working class itself.[48]

The syndicalists argued that the general outline of how this liberation might proceed was provided by Marx and Engels in the article, "The Civil War in France."[49] If Bernstein had his preferred citations—and Plekhanov and Lenin theirs—the syndicalists could appeal to Engels' introduction to Marx's essay, and to the substance of the essay itself to demonstrate their orthodoxy.

In the introduction, Engels had written that the Paris Commune provided revolutionaries with an anticipation of the socialist revolution itself. The Paris Commune had struck down the bourgeois state and had prepared to substitute, for the repressive machinery of that state, an organization of society based on the association of the workers in each factory and a combination of such associations in "one great union." Such a "free confederation" of workingmen's associations would everywhere substitute itself for the "oppressing power of the former centralized government, army, political police [and] bureaucracy."

This revolutionary transformation of society would then protect itself from the politicians—those who have always and everywhere acted as intermediaries between the people and the apparatus of government—by providing for institutionalized referendum and recall, and regular rotation in office, with all officials remaining working men and drawing, during their tenure in any office, no more than working men's wages.

The free confederation of working men's unions, which would substitute itself for the bourgeois state, constituted for Marx and Engels the "dictatorship of the proletariat." Engels maintained that this dictatorship—which only "social democratic philistines" abjured—was calculated to destroy the state which, either in the guise of a democratic republic or a monarchy, was "nothing but a machine for the oppression of one class by another."[50]

Engels' introduction to Marx's "The Civil War in France," written in 1891, clearly outlined, according to the syndicalists, a comprehensive strategy for revolutionary socialism. If the proletarian revolution was to substitute a confederation of working class associations for the political state, then the working class organizations, and not a political party, constituted the revolutionary "nucleus of the future society."[51]

The syndicalists could argue that not only had Marx, himself, characterized the syndicates, the *Gewerkschaften*, as the "centers of resistance against the pretensions of capital," but that he had identified them as agencies capable of accomplishing the ultimate ends of socialism, the "final emancipation of the working class . . . , the ultimate abolition of the wages system."[52]

In effect, the syndicalists could appeal to Marx to support their contention that the working class should not be organized into an essentially political party. The syndicalists argued that only the economic organization of the working class corresponded to Marx's most fundamental views concerning social dynamics and social revolution. The syndicalists objected to the organization of the proletariat into a political association whose principal preoccupation was parliamentary activity, electioneering, and social reform. They insisted that the disposition to play the parliamentary game could only mean that official socialism had committed itself to the conservation of the constitutional, hence bourgeois, social and political structure of the peninsula.

The syndicalists reminded socialists that both Marx and Engels had characterized parliamentary politics as a form of "cretinism."[53] At critical periods during the nineteenth century Marx had indicated that the people have preemptive and revolutionary rights vis-à-vis any national parliament.[54] In effect, the syndicalists argued, parliamentary concerns might have some tactical significance in an overall revolutionary strategy, but an exclusive preoccupation with parliamentary politics could only be anti-Marxist. They could allude to the fact that in 1871 Marx had broken with one of his oldest associates, George Eccarius, in part because the latter had advocated that the conditions in England required that the English working class send representatives to parliament, and that, in order to achieve this purpose, it would be necessary for the proletariat to enter into alliances with the "advanced men of the middle classes."[55]

Even the social legislation that had been engineered through the national parliament in England—legislation which, initially, had won Marx's approval—was later characterized by Engels as serving essentially bourgeois purposes. In 1892, Engels insisted that the factory acts, which had been looked upon as the "bugbear" of the capitalists, ultimately had revealed themselves as serving the interests of the possessing classes.[56]

More than that, in their catalog of arguments against the electionist and legalitarian strategy of orthodox Italian socialism, the syndicalists could muster an impressive collection of quotations from the works of Marx and Engels that indicated that they were advocates of *violent* revolution. Arturo Labriola reminded socialists that Marx had concluded his *Poverty of Philosophy* with the quote from George Sand: "war or death, a bloody conflict or oblivion: in just such manner the question is inexorably put." In the *Communist Manifesto* both Marx and Engels had announced that communists disdained to conceal their purpose: "They openly declare that their ends can be attained only by the forcible overthrow of all existing social conditions."[57] In November 1848, the founders of Marxism maintained that "there is but one way to *shorten*, simplify and concentrate both the agonies of the old society and the birth pangs of the new— and only *one way—revolutionary terrorism*."[58] Leone concluded that Marx clearly believed capitalist society could not be reformed beyond a certain point through political maneuvering and political legislation. Beyond that point only the violent intercession on the part of the syndicates, organized labor, could inaugurate a new order.[59]

The preconditions for that new order would arise, of course, out of the economic base of society. The syndicalists recognized that no society ever perishes until it exhausts its potential for growth and development.[60] Violence is, in fact, the epilogue of social change. Throughout the process of change the contending social class undertakes persistent forays against the ensconced possessing class, but the class struggle concludes only when the infrastructure of the new society has matured within the old. The degree and nature of the violence that accompanies the transition from the old to the new will be determined by the varied and contingent circumstances that attend the final phases of the process.

By 1908 the first generation of syndicalist theoreticians had fashioned an interpretation of classical Marxism to serve as a guide to revolutionary conduct. They recognized that the impetus for their reexamination of the corpus of Marxist literature was the reformist strategy and the revisionist dispositions that had come to characterize the official Socialist party of Italy. The syndicalists sought to distinguish themselves from this opportunist and political current. They conceived of themselves as restoring the integrity of the original

27

Marxist persuasion. They insisted that only the proletariat, organized in effective economic associations, could perform the historic tasks assigned to it in the revolutionary theory left to socialism by Karl Marx. They argued that Marxism had always taught that economic factors were the most fundamental historic forces. As a consequence the working class, organized in economic, rather than political, associations, best represented the agents of historic change most frequently alluded to by the founders of scientific socialism. Not only do the syndicates, the revolutionary unions, operate at the very heart of the contemporary productive system, but the syndicates, because of their practical and explicit economic functions, recruit only true proletarians. The declassed bourgeois intellectuals, so prominent in the politically organized socialist parties, could play only a marginal role in syndicalist activities.

Revolutionary trade union associations—syndicates—occupy themselves day by day with the immediate interests of the proletariat. They are veritable schools of revolution and inure the proletariat to its responsibilities. They create a psychology of dedication, sacrifice, and commitment. The syndicates were conceived to be "associations of destiny," rather than organizations that pursue some local or temporary interests, the election of one or another deputy to parliament, or the episodic passage of some negotiated social legislation. The members of the syndicates were understood to be bound in an association that was animated by a constant concern with the day-by-day conditions of labor and the persistent struggle against the pretensions of the capitalist proprietors. More than that, the syndicates would provide the occasion for the technical and administrative training of the working class itself, a training that would be absolutely essential to the task of operating the productive system after the revolution.

The syndicalists argued that if revolution is the ultimate purpose of socialist organization, only the syndicates could meet that responsibility. Not only do the syndicates foster the consciousness of association and sacrifice which constitutes the fundamental meaning of "class consciousness," but they provide necessary training—in terms of strikes, boycotts, covert and overt resistance—for the ultimate confrontation between classes. The working class becomes effectively organized as a revolutionary army with leadership from its own class ranks, leadership which has shared its interests in the practical and daily struggle with its oppressors.

The revolution which Marx anticipated would destroy the entire apparatus of the bourgeois state. Socialists must, of needs, have an alternative social structure available to maintain the complex productive system created by the capitalist period. The syndicalists envisioned a free confederation of syndicates providing the infrastructure of a future socialist industrial system.

The first syndicalist theoreticians believed their interpretation of Marxism to be faithful to both the letter and the spirit of Marx and Engels. While they had considerable reservations concerning some of the later writings of Engels, they were convinced that the weight of evidence available in the literature left to them by the founders of scientific socialism demonstrated the revolutionary orthodoxy of their views.

In summary, the syndicalists saw special virtues in their interpretation: (1) it restored economic factors to their place at the center of the system; (2) as a consequence, it reduced the influence of political intervention, which was almost exclusively the work of bourgeois intellectuals, in the processes surrounding the liberation of the working class and thereby restored proletarian integrity to the revolutionary movement; (3) it could generate the class consciousness, the technical and administrative efficiency necessary to the governance of a postcapitalist, collectivist society; and finally, and as a consequence, (4) it provided the institu-

29

tional infrastructure of a socialist society that would satisfy the requirement that the freedom of each would be the freedom of all.

There was nothing in all this that was un-Marxian. For all the tendentious objections raised against the syndicalists, there was not only an admirable consistency in their advocacy, but there was little that could be clearly identified as a departure from the Marxism of Marx and Engels. Almost all the objections raised against the syndicalists by commentators like Plekhanov[61] could be dismissed as the product of a fundamental ignorance of syndicalist literature. The syndicalists, for example, were not anarchists. They were advocates of a libertarian socialist society, but they neither rejected political strategies nor did they imagine the future society would be without organizational discipline or institutional structure. Nor were syndicalists anti-intellectual. They were anti-intellectualist, in the sense that they deplored the influence of "classless intellectuals" in the socialist movement. They objected, in effect, to "*petit bourgeois* intellectuals" and "*petit bourgeois* intellectualism."[62] They were far from being irrationalists, although, as we shall see, they were prepared to recognize the influence of nonrational psychological factors in political, social, and economic change. They conceived of their strategy as eminently rational and scientific, and they understood it to be preeminently Marxist.

During the first decade of the twentieth century classical Marxism had resolved itself into several currents. There were those who could best be characterized as reformists, who spoke of a substantial revision of Marxism. There were the political revolutionaries, those who believed their various socialist parties to be the most effective vehicles for the violent social changes anticipated by Marx and Engels. And there were the syndicalist revolutionaries, whose revolution was predicated on the organization of the proletariat in class-conscious industrial trade unions, voluntary associations of producers that were the vital cells of the future socialist society. In France, the first generation of syndicalist theoreticians included Georges Sorel, Hubert Lagardelle, Victor Griffuelhes and Emile Pouget.[63] Syndicalism found expression in England, the United States, Russia, Holland, and Belgium; Roberto Michels, who was to be so influential among the second generation of syndicalist ideologues, attempted to foster its growth in Germany.[64]

For our purposes, it was the second generation of syndicalist thinkers who were to have incalculable impact on the shaping of Italian events. Paolo Orano, Ottavio Dinale, Sergio Panunzio, Angelo O. Olivetti, and Roberto Michels were to shape syndicalism into a belief system largely unanticipated in the writings of Arturo Labriola and Enrico Leone. They were all to contribute elements to a developing body of thought which had taken its original impetus from the ambiguous legacy of Karl Marx and Friedrich Engels. In the course of that development, they were to produce the first revolutionary socialist heresy of the twentieth century, a heresy that was to find its tribune in one of the most important Italian revolutionary socialists: Benito Mussolini.

31

TWO

THE FIRST REVOLUTIONARY SOCIALIST HERESY

In the period between 1907 and the advent of the First World War, revolutionary syndicalism transformed itself into a belief system that was clearly distinguished from the classical Marxism from which it derived. At no particular juncture in the process, however, could one identify a definitive departure. Its transformation was gradual, incremental. But at some point in time the quantitative accretions seemed to qualitatively transform the system of thought into something quite unique—an heretical socialism that was to serve as the ideological rationale for an alternative revolution.

The principal artisans of this transformation were all dedicated revolutionaries—syndicalists of distinction with considerable intellectual gifts. The most important among them, Roberto Michels, Angelo O. Olivetti, and Sergio Panunzio produced an impressive body of theoretical literature that shaped the aspirations and governed the behavior of the most dynamic and effective political revolutionaries in Italy for more than a generation.

The Evolution of Syndicalism

The syndicalism that gained currency in Italy during the first years of the twentieth century was characterized by an identifiable Marxist orthodoxy. For all its special emphases, that first syndicalism was radically antistate, antinationalist, anticlerical, and antimilitarist. The focus of its argument was the class struggle, the irrepressible conflict between the two major protagonists on the contemporary scene: the bourgeoisie and the proletariat. Its ultimate intention was the instauration of a society innocent of private property, a society in which the productive processes would be governed by collective ownership and collective control. The transition from bourgeois society to that anticipated by the syndicalists was to be attended by revolutionary violence, the handmaiden of the new order.

These convictions were given clear expression in the works of the first generation of syndicalists. They are to be found explicitly formulated in the writings of Enrico Leone and Arturo Labriola. The young intellectuals who collected around these first leaders took their point of departure from what had become a new orthodoxy of a special Marxist faction. From that point, syndicalism underwent a process of gradual change—theoretical elaboration that turned on a collection of critical issues. At the close of what was a process of transition, syndicalism revealed itself as a rationale for a nationalist, mass-mobilizing, elitist, authoritarian, and developmental movement. It was to become the first overt Marxist heresy of the twentieth century.

This transformation involved the intersection of a number of social, political, and personality variables too complex and numerous to begin to assess. For the purposes of the present narrative there were, however, a constellation of critical issues that became increasingly important in the course of discussion and lent special character to the convictions with which the syndicalists ultimately faced the crisis of the First World War.

In retrospect, the issues to which syndicalists addressed themselves can be specified with some precision. They involved (1) a searching reappraisal of what syndicalists took to be the intrinsically social nature of man, (2) an attempt to formulate some defensible generalizations concerning the psychological regularities governing life lived in association, with special emphasis on the relationships between those who lead and those who are led. These issues precipitated an

33

involved discussion concerning (3) the social and political function of a special class of ideas identified as "myths," as well as (4) the role of a select and exiguous number of men in social and political processes. Finally, the syndicalists attempted (5) to assess the implications of all these considerations in the context of a retarded economic environment.

The syndicalist treatment of these themes appears unorthodox only to those in our own time who have come to some special interpretation of Marxism. The fact is that the transformation worked by the syndicalists was licensed, at almost every step, by some Marxist insight, some Marxist analysis or injunction. In this sense, revolutionary syndicalism became a Marxist heresy, the first one of our time. Taking their departure from the given faith, the syndicalists were to draw from it conclusions that could only outrage the orthodoxy of the more traditional faithful.

Syndicalism and the Nature of Man

As early as 1908 the first generation of syndicalists had explicated a conception of man and society that, for all its special character, was understood to be fully compatible with the convictions of Karl Marx. In that year Arturo Labriola published his *Marx nell'economia e come teorico del socialismo*,[1] in which he developed what was to be the syndicalist view of the social nature of man and an analysis of the interrelationship of the individual and the social system.

Labriola, like the second generation of syndicalist theoreticians, emphasized the critical role played by the concept "society" in the lucubrations of Karl Marx. In arguments that are surprisingly contemporary, Labriola insisted that the historical materialism of Karl Marx originated in a form of anthropological materialism that was, in substantial part, borrowed from Ludwig Feuerbach.[2] Central to this materialism was the conviction that man was a quintessentially *social animal*, that sociality was the defining property of

34

humanity.[3] To support his case, Labriola could point to Marx's sixth gloss on Feuerbach, written in 1845, in which Marx wrote that the "human essence . . . is the ensemble of social relations."[4] In a manuscript unknown to the syndicalists of the period Marx had, in fact, written that "the individual is the social-being. His life . . . is . . . an expression and confirmation of social life. Man's individual and species life (*Gattungsleben*) are not different."[5]

It was evident that Marx understood man to be an essentially social or political animal.[6] This conception of man as a species being, a creature that lives by nature an associated or collective life,[7] was a conviction shared by Marxists of almost every persuasion. The conviction was understood to be part of the Hegelian heritage that survived in classical Marxism. For the syndicalists, the understanding of man as intrinsically and essentially a social animal became critical to the subsequent evolution of their thought. The earliest syndicalists addressed themselves to the issue of how that understanding might contribute to the overall comprehension of social life. If, indeed, man's essence was social, the question was, how did that sociality express itself in overt political behavior?

For all his sophistication, Marx's comments on individual or collective human psychology were almost always couched in aphorism, analogy, and metaphor.[8] In the *German Ideology*, Marx spoke, for example, of social consciousness as "directly interwoven with . . . material activity and material intercourse," as a "direct efflux of . . . material behavior," and as a "sublimate of . . . material life process."[9] None of these characterizations were particularly informative. Georges Sorel, Thomas Masaryk, Benedetto Croce, and Vilfredo Pareto all alluded to the thinness of Marx's conjectures concerning human psychology.[10] Labriola, in turn, indicated that Marx had not systematically developed a theory of social behavior, of individual or collective consciousness.[11]

The syndicalists, as a consequence, concerned themselves from the start with amplifying Marx's account. Paolo Orano, the youngest and most intellectually aggressive member of the group, undertook to write extensively on just such issues.[12] In 1902 he published his *La psicologia sociale*, and in 1903 A. O. Olivetti published his essay on collective psychology.[13] These men directed their attention to the problems entailed in any serious attempt to understand the regularities governing collective psychology.

In the half century following the publication of the *Communist Manifesto*, European thinkers, in fact, had devoted considerable intellectual energy to the problems of individual and collective human psychology. By the turn of the century, the names of Gabriel Tarde, Gustave Le Bon, Scipio Sighele, and Ludwig Gumplowicz were known to everyone who pretended to any intellectual sophistication.[14] All these men were concerned with the circumstances surrounding group life and the psychology of men living in association, and their works were employed by the syndicalists in an effort to fill in the theoretical sketch of human psychology left by Marx and Engels.

Sergio Panunzio was one of the most prominent of the syndicalist intellectuals involved in this enterprise. Born on the 20th of July in 1886 in Molfetta in southern Italy, Panunzio early identified himself with revolutionary syndicalism, and by the time of the completion of his law studies in 1908 he had already published extensively in syndicalist and socialist publications.[15]

In 1908 Panunzio wrote *Una nuova aristocrazia: I sindacati* as his dissertation for a degree at the University of Naples. He had published articles in the revolutionary socialist press as early as 1903, and in 1907 his *Il socialismo giuridico* appeared.[16] In the same year, the syndicalist *Pagine libere*, under the editorship of A. O. Olivetti, published Panunzio's "Socialismo, sindacalismo e sociologia."

Panunzio's critical preoccupations in his early works turned on the relationship between historical materialism and social psychology—the relationship between collective psychology and the economic circumstances surrounding group life.[17] Taking his point of departure from the social science of his time, Panunzio argued that revolutionary socialism, if it were to be politically effective, required a detailed assessment of the conditions governing associated life. If man was, in fact, a social animal, the regularities exemplified in social life and social psychology, hinted at by Marx, became critical not only to the theoretical integrity, but urgent to the organizational and tactical considerations, of modern revolutionaries.

Panunzio sought to identify the conditions governing generic social life. In doing so, he researched literally all the literature made available by international social science. His work was dotted with references to the books of Lester Ward, Anton Menger, Icilio Vanni, Alfred Fouillée, Roberto Ardigò, Emil Durkheim, Leon Duguit, Alfred Marshall, Herbert Spencer, Gabriel Tarde, Vilfredo Pareto, Gaetano Mosca, Ludwig Gumplowicz, Wilhelm Wundt, Carlo Cattaneo, and Sumner Maine, to mention only the most prominent. In effect, Panunzio was a revolutionary socialist intellectual of the first rank. His knowledge of classical Marxism was of an order that had few peers. By the end of the first decade of the twentieth century, Panunzio had articulated convictions about the generic social life of man that were to influence both his own subsequent intellectual evolution and that of an entire group of syndicalist theoreticians.

Syndicalism and Social Psychology

Panunzio, like Labriola and a number of other syndicalist theoreticians, attempted to formulate an account of social life that would supplement the meager suggestions to be found in the works of Marx and Engels.[18] One could say with Marx that "we must seek the anatomy of society in its economy" without coming one whit closer to understanding how social organization, or the individual and collective psychology that sustained that organization, either arose, was maintained, or underwent alteration.

In the *Communist Manifesto*, for example, Marx insisted that statute law was nothing other than the will of a specific class that had been made the law for all. The pronouncement implied that somehow or other a minority which was the ruling class—the "outgrowth of the conditions of . . . production"—imposed its will and its law on the majority. How this might be accomplished was left exceedingly obscure. How, in fact, could a minority succeed in oppressing a majority?

Marx and Engels had regularly alluded to the fact that a minority of oppressors of one kind or another had managed to impose its will and its law on a majority of the oppressed throughout history. Any explanation that pretended to account for such a pervasive phenomenon must necessarily involve complex sociopsychological variables in complex interaction. No such explanation was forthcoming in the vast literature of classical Marxism.

That a ruling class might impose its will on its subjects by simple coercion was most implausible. Coercion, pure and simple, is often inefficient, frequently provokes incalculable response, and is exceedingly expensive to maintain for any extended period of time. Since, as Marx and Engels insisted, subordination of the majority to minorities had characterized all of recorded history, it seemed obvious that the relationship between the superordinate and the subordinate must involve generic psychological traits as well as special time-specific factors. There must be some individual and collective dispositions that predisposed men to arrange themselves in an hierarchical order.

Almost all the prominent social theorists of the period were prepared to argue that collective social life was governed by generic psychological traits. Pareto spoke of the dispositional regularities that informed group behaviors—regularities later to be identified as generic "residues." Gumplowicz spoke of the "laws" of collective psychology. Tarde and Le Bon employed the "laws" of imitation and repetition to explain group behaviors. Panunzio was similarly convinced that any attempt to explain collective actions required the invocation of some discrete set of psycho-sociological regularities.

Like many of his Marxist and non-Marxist contemporaries, Panunzio began his account of social life with a recognition that men are invariably found organized in rule-governed communities. Every social system is an aggregate of social elements—families, clans, moieties, sects, castes, classes and/or occupational or professional strata. But for all the historic, economic, temporal, and social distinctiveness of such elements, they are all governed by custom, usage, traditions, and rules. Men seem to effortlessly organize themselves in rule-governed associations.

Panunzio argued that subtending all rule-governed associations was a pervasive disposition toward compliance among its members. The major factor sustaining that collective compliance is psychosocial in character. Primary and secondary socialization inures men to collective obedience and prepares them for effortless entry into social relations. Men are habituated to certain interpersonal and social relations. They conform to certain behaviors which are approved. They are socialized into a pattern of social life. "In a social group," Panunzio argued, "men are united by virtue of their unconscious adaptation to those known psychological laws, illustrated in the work of Gabriel Tarde, of sympathy . . . and suggestion, which in the last analysis, reduce themselves to imitation and repetition."[19]

The basic behavioral conformity of individuals in general, without which social life and social relationships become inexplicable, is the consequence of the social dispositions that characterize human life. An individual born to a community, Panunzio contended, is psychologically disposed to identify with those upon whom his immediate material and psychological welfare depends. In general, and as a consequence of socialization, the individual identifies with his in-group, those with whom he shares physical and cultural affinities. He is enhanced by their approval and diminished

39

by their disapproval. In the process, he becomes like them. He mimics them and adopts their attitudes and their preferences. He accepts their behavior as a norm, as the standard of appropriate conduct. When the easy socialization in custom and usage is codified and enforced by sanction, the norms of collective conduct become laws.

This was an account of social life which Panunzio shared with other syndicalists, like Paolo Orano. Orano had elaborated a similar exposition in his *Psicologia sociale*.[20] Panunzio was clearly influenced by Orano's exposition, and cited his work in his own *Socialismo giuridico*.[21] One of the principal sources for both men was the antecedent work of Ludwig Gumplowicz who devoted considerable space in his major works to an account of the development of that collective consciousness that sustains group life. Panunzio's references to Gumplowicz's work are regular and meticulous.[22]

Panunzio considered his own treatment of collective psychology and group life to be a synthesis of "historical materialism and social psychology," an application of modern social science to some of the substantive problems of Marx's historical materialism.[23] But more than an exercise in social science explanation, he believed his analysis implied much for contemporary political conduct.

Since generic collective life was bound together by rule-governed behaviors, Panunzio placed emphasis on the instrumental value of effortless and habitual behavior, concensual conduct, and behavior regulated by law. Habitual behavior was the product of the characteristic repetitive response of individuals to suggestive influence. Consensual behavior was a rational product of calculated interests. Law, finally, was not only codified custom, but was also the means society employed for controlling the behavior of those inadequately socialized, those indifferent to their own rational self-interest or to the requirements of their society and their times. Panunzio understood the existence of law to represent an acknowledgement of the imperfection of man, of the inadequacies of the socialization processes which make him a social animal, and of the changing political and economic requirements that attend social change.

Panunzio distinguished syndicalists from anarchists in so far as anarchists aspired to the creation of a society in which law would have no place, as though all social behaviors might, one day, be the consequence of simple habit or consensus. Syndicalists, Panunzio argued, recognized that man is an imperfect creature in a changing world, and that, even under the best of circumstances, man would be inadequately socialized, imperfectly habituated to time- and circumstance-conditioned public response, and often confused about his rational self-interests. In this sense, Panunzio conceived law to be constitutive of any society. He understood its existence to be perennial, although its content was variable.[24]

Having established this to his own satisfaction, Panunzio went on to analyze the unique function of statute law. Marx had clearly identified law as occupying a special place in the analysis of social behaviors and had regularly spoken of law as conforming to the prevailing "relations of production." Marx seemed to have conceived of law as reflecting the prevailing requirements of the productive system of any given society.

It is equally clear that Panunzio agreed that law was not simply sanctioned habit or customary usage. Law had a special function in the social system. Not only did it compel men to accord themselves with common custom, it satisfied, as one of the superstructural elements of society, the exigencies of the economic substructure. Somehow or other, "substructural" requirements must be made part of the "will" of the ruling class. The dominant minority must, in the pursuit of its own interests, satisfy the functional and time-specific requirements of the economic base. In effect, the ruling elite is obliged to function as the agent of historic responsibility. The ruling class must render the majority responsive to the requirements of their time by fostering a disposition toward compliance that escapes the influence

41

of social sentiment, habit, and consensual agreement. Law is the cutting edge of functionally requisite innovation, calculated to inure the majority of men to time-specific and historically necessary responses.

Marx had argued that each historic mode of production fosters rule by a select minority of men who, in turn, must establish a system of law compatible with society's productive base. The ethics and law of each particular society were understood to satisfy the requirements of that society, even if those requirements remained obscure to the majority of men. Somehow each historic population must be rendered amenable to functionally adaptive and specific rule governance.

Out of the complex web of problems Marx had left as an intellectual inheritance, Panunzio had isolated one problem that was to prove of momentous consequence. Marx had suggested that a ruling minority in any given society is obliged by historic responsibility to fashion a system of law that reflects the needs of a prevailing, or a revolutionary, productive system. Throughout history a minority of men had introduced special constraints on the majority. They had succeeded in breaking the crust of tradition and habitual behavior in order to shape human behaviors to meet the functional requirements of society's economic base. It was clear to Panunzio that general conformity to such law could not be solely the consequence of habit or the pursuit of interest. Nor could obedience be the consequence of the employment of terror or violence on the part of the ruling class. Somehow men had to be socialized "dialectically" to a complex system of social conventions and public law that satisfied the requirements of each historic period.

Panunzio was prepared to grant that the public law that served such purpose was sustained, in critical circumstances, by coercion—force sanctioned by the putative "majesty of law." But he also argued that simple force could not prevail against the opposition of the vast majority of men. Revolutionary law might be introduced through violence, but only the natural compliance of men in general could make its persistence comprehensible. After a given minority succeeds in introducing innovative law, socialization succeeds in making such law "normic." Men quickly conform to established law as long as that law satisfies the needs of the new economic system. Thus conquest can make some men slaves, but only the disposition to conform can make them compliant. Only the general disposition to adapt to social norms can render slavery "proper" for the majority of men. Revolution can make property sacrosanct, but only the disposition of the majority of men to conform to prevailing norms of conduct can secure its rights.

Marx's argument was, in substance, that each economic system requires the satisfaction of certain functional requisites and prerequisites. Some minority of men, Panunzio proceeded, must represent those requisites and prerequisites, and foster collective behaviors appropriate to their fulfillment, if society is to survive.

Syndicalism and the Social and Political Function of Myth

Given this analysis, Panunzio argued that historical materialism thus required some supplementary theses if its account of social dynamics was to be at all plausible. Only if the historic requirements of any social system translated themselves into the self-interests of a minority of men who succeeded, in turn, in eliciting conformity to the rules servicing that self-interest, could Marx's account of the relationship between the economic base and the ideological superstructure be rendered defensible.

In a slave society, the self-interests of slaveholders, a minority of men, prompted them to seek out, sustain, and employ slaves, and provide for the unequal distribution of resources and benefits—all in the service of a productive system that corresponded to the functional requirements of the available material productive forces. In a productive system characterized by productivity only marginally above

43

subsistence, slavery and differential distribution became a functional necessity. To maintain such a system the majority of men, including at least a substantial minority of slaves, must be rendered submissive and compliant.

To accomplish this demanding task, the ruling minority must have at its disposal some effective device for eliciting compliance. That device, Panunzio argued, was the "political formula" or "myth"—a complex linguistic and symbolic speech act that fostered, among the majority, attitudes, beliefs, and sentiments supportive of the social system. A successful myth was functionally adapted to the special requirements of a given socioeconomic arrangement. In a slave society, such a set of symbolic formulae rendered slavery "proper," "natural," and "moral." It tapped fundamental needs and sentiments—the disposition of all men to identify with their community, as well as their indisposition to face the consequences of radical change and to abandon the comfort attendant upon occupying a recognized place in a set of established patterns. Myths supplied the rudiments of acceptable behavior; they exploited civic virtue, in-group sentiments, and man's natural desire to seek the approval of his peers and superiors.

The men who consciously or unconsciously put together such functional myths invariably constituted a minority. They were the shamans, witch doctors, priests, and philosophers—in short, the intellectual elite. They worked their effects because men were disposed to mimic their superiors, those who occupied prestigious places in the social system. Everything Panunzio had learned from Le Bon, Tarde, and Gumplowicz suggested that men were suggestible, imitative, and eminently open to moral suasion. When the interests of a minority reflect the "historic needs" of a specific epoch, their myths can succeed in informing the sentiments and attitudes of the majority. The myth becomes the stenographic, symbolic, and refracted expression of the real needs of a given social and economic system.

Panunzio's account reflected the prevailing judgments of his time. Implicit in his rendering was the conviction that ideas in general, and political ideas in particular, were subject to selective pressures in a process that was the intellectual analogue of survival of the fittest in the biological world. Political myths prevailed because they enjoyed some survival advantage in that they were functionally adapted to the sentiments and needs of their times. Those myths that endured satisfied the historic and economic requirements of the epoch.

Once a myth had become established, socialization would assure its prevalence. The majority accommodated itself to its injunctions. Given the passivity, the suggestibility, and the disposition to social compliance of mankind, the myth would effortlessly bind the collectivity together. Only when some fundamental changes altered the economic foundations of society would the opportunity arise for significant changes in social relations. Under such circumstances, the hitherto functional myth would become increasingly dysfunctional. The route to succession would be open, and new myths would have an opportunity to replace the old. Traditional law and the political formulae that sustained easy compliance would become increasingly anachronistic, and the "relations of production," to employ Marx's phrase, would become fetters on the evolving system of production.

Within the capitalist mode of production, Panunzio proceeded, the working class had begun to detach itself from the influence of the prevailing bourgeois myths—clear evidence that the bourgeoisie were becoming increasingly superfluous as agents of the productive process. Bourgeois myths no longer elicited simple compliance on the part of increasing numbers of the subaltern classes. The working masses sought new myths to give shape to their half-felt needs and half-articulated aspirations. The working masses looked for new leadership and new symbols more consonant with the needs of their epoch. Workers had begun to organize under the leadership of a different minority, an innovative "aristocracy" that represented the demands of a new historic period.

Large minorities no longer accommodated themselves to the prevailing modes of conduct. What had been proper under the old dispensation had become, for them, improper and immoral. Men organized themselves into working-class syndicates in which they generated their own approved behaviors, social sanctions, and anticipated their own sustaining laws. The syndicates formulated group regulations, collective prescriptions, and proscriptions that governed the behavior of in-group members.

Out of the changed circumstances of modern industrial life, Panunzio identified the first stirrings of the new socialist system and anticipated the mobilizing myths that would sustain it. Like Sorel, Panunzio envisioned myths that would symbolically represent the aspirations of an ascendent social class, would more effectively address themselves to the functional requirements of a new historic period, and would insure the free compliance of men in the changed order.

The new myths were the first anticipation of a revolutionary law that would displace bourgeois law. The contest between the old and the new social systems would be violent. Bourgeois law, and the force that sustained it, would find itself opposed by proletarian violence, the first evidence of the vital energy of a revolutionary society aborning.[25]

Panunzio argued that as economic conditions alter, as one mode of production gives evidence of exhausting its potential for growth, the elements of a new system manifest themselves. The circumstances which foster such change are revealed in the growing resistance to established rule and the appearance of new myths. The cells of a different collective life begin to organize themselves under an innovative leadership. In changed economic circumstances, men group together in communities of common sentiment, common interest, and collective purpose, which evolve their own system of rule-governed behavior. Since the old social sanctions and

46

their sustaining myths no longer produce habitual conformity, tensions mount, antisocial acts become increasingly prevalent and the new associations become progressively more organized. They socialize their members to tasks and responsibilities which correspond to the new myth and its ethic. They invoke sentiment, interest, and the constraints of rule-governance to inure their members to a new collective life in the process of formation.

It was clear what this analysis implied for Panunzio. For revolution to succeed, leaders must possess a "vanguard" consciousness of the requirements of their situation, and members of revolutionary associations must obediently adhere to the discipline implicit in revolutionary organization. The leadership minority, employing myth and symbolic invocation, tapping the suggestibility and mimetic disposition of their followers, would discharge their historic responsibilities. Given this assessment of collective psychology and the responsibilities of minority leadership, Panunzio spoke of revolutionary syndicalism as essentially "authoritarian" in character.

This particular characterization, which clearly distinguished syndicalism from anarchism and reformist socialism, did not in the least embarrass Panunzio. He reminded Marxists that Engels had insisted that whoever mentions combined action speaks necessarily of organization, and whoever speaks of organization necessarily speaks of authority. But, more importantly, Panunzio reminded Marxists that Engels had spoken of the necessity of strict authority even after the socialist revolution. He spoke of the requirements of large-scale postrevolutionary industrial enterprise, the complex decisions involved in the allocation of resources, and the fixing of productive programs—all of which could only be "settled in an authoritarian way."[26]

It was clear to Panunzio that the same principles that governed generic social life would be operative in revolutionary organization, revolutionary government, and postrevolutionary society. The authority exercised by revolutionary leadership, and that anticipated in postrevolutionary rule, would exemplify the same principles of elite innovation, socialization, mimetic influence, symbolic suasion, habituation, and social conditioning that had always characterized leadership and rule in general.

Given these convictions, Panunzio did not hesitate to refer to revolutionary leadership as an authoritarian and elite "socialist vanguard" that would, through myth, help shape the consciousness of passive masses. That vanguard would be a "new social aristocracy,"[27] charged with the historic responsibilities of socializing men to new consciousness during the transition from one form of society to another. The tasks of the socialist revolutionary were the tasks required in a transitional period.

Among those tasks were those that were tutelary in character: to defend the interests of the revolutionary class even if that class had not yet developed an appreciation of its historic interests. The socialist elite was equally charged with organizational tasks: the effective organization of the loose collection of burgeoning syndical associations. Panunzio was also emphatic about the pedagogical tasks which devolved upon the socialist vanguard: the obligation of elevating the consciousness and insuring the adaptation of the revolutionary class to its historic obligations. Given his conception of socialization, the intersecting roles accorded mimetic suggestion, and the invocation of sentiment and beliefs through myth, Panunzio conceived of the propaganda and educational responsibilities of the elite to be particularly significant.[28]

The most effective instrument of political education was, for Panunzio as it was for the majority of syndicalist theoreticians, the social and political myth—a symbolic and suggestive speech act calculated to engage the most fundamental sentiments, needs, and overt interests of the potential revolutionary audience.[29] Panunzio, taking his point of departure from Sorel, understood a political myth to be symbolic and condensed speech that captured the sentiment of political actors by appealing to their feelings of community and in-group identity. An effective myth, moreover, addresses itself to felt, if only to half-articulated needs. A revolutionary myth conveys the essentials of a new and anticipated revolutionary social order.[30] The myth contains all the elements of revolutionary strategy and tactics as they were understood by the syndicalists. The working class was the class possessed of historic responsibility. That class, organized in syndicates, opposed itself to the conservative, antihistorical bourgeoisie. The myth of the general strike, the occasion when the industrially organized working class simply, and in unison, lays down its tools to bring the entire capitalist enterprise to a halt, captures all the sentiment necessary for, and addresses itself to all the needs that precipitated, revolution. When the working class is sufficiently organized, disciplined, well-led, and uniformly animated by revolutionary purpose, the general strike marks the qualitative change from the bourgeois to the socialist social system. The effectiveness of myth implies the effortless discipline, the unself-conscious exercise of authority, and the organizational integrity of the revolutionary working class. Such a myth gives expression to the sentimental solidarist disposition of men, their calculated class interests, as well as their moral aspirations. The myth was understood to be an expression of effective revolutionary will. Because revolutionary behavior requires revolutionary discipline, revolutionary sentiment, revolutionary calculation, and revolutionary will, the political and social myth, to be maximally effective, must be the seamless unity of all these elements.

The influence of the thought of Vilfredo Pareto and Gaetano Mosca was evident throughout all of Panunzio's analysis. What Pareto was to ultimately call a "derivation," and Mosca a "political formula," was, by and large, what the syndicalists, with Panunzio, called a mass-mobilizing social and political myth.[31] Given the psychological characteristics of men in general, the purveyors of such myths could only be a minority among them. Everything the syndicalists found in the writings of Pareto, Mosca, Gumplowicz, Le Bon, and Tarde confirmed them in that opinion. The innovative myth was the product of a contending elite.

Elitism

As early as 1903, Vittorio Racca, in his introduction to Sorel's *Saggi di critica del marxismo*, argued that syndicalists were convinced that the vanguard of socialist revolution could only be an exiguous minority, a political elite.[32] By 1908 and 1909 Roberto Michels, himself a revolutionary syndicalist, had drawn out of all these arguments entailments that were to provide the core of his subsequent major work on political parties.[33]

In 1903, for all the same reasons advanced by Orano, Olivetti, and Panunzio, Michels argued that the majority of men are always passive on the occasion of social change. Inured to habitual behavior by convention and suggestion, the mass remains inert unless mobilized by special needs or circumstances.[34] By 1908, Michels had developed certain arguments that carried the arguments advanced by syndicalists several steps further.

At the time of the publication of his first major work in 1908, Michels still considered himself a Marxist and more specifically a revolutionary syndicalist.[35] In that work, *Il proletariato e la borghesia nel movimento socialista italiano*, Michels accepted the notion of the generic sociality of man, as well as its corollaries: that men tend to identify with a limited community of similars, that they adapt themselves to traditional modes of behavior, and tend to be subject to the mimetic example and moral suasion of vanguard elites, or ruling classes.[36] Given these convictions, Michels spoke of the "fatality" of elite rule. Employing arguments found in the works of Gumplowicz, Pareto, and Mosca, Michels spoke of the apathy characteristic of the general population, the product of traditional and habituated response. He spoke of revolution as a "rotation of elites," in which a contending elite, a vanguard minority, mobilizes passive majorities against an ensconced, but dysfunctional elite.[37]

By 1909 Michels had advanced the notion of an "iron law of elites," the anticipation of his now classic "iron law of oligarchy." In that same year, in a presentation before the Sociological Society conference at the University of Vienna, Michels developed themes that came to characterize syndicalist thought. He spoke of the necessity of organization in the group conflicts that made up the substance of human history. Man, as an intrinsically social animal, was animated by a sense of exclusive community, in-group amity and out-group diffidence. The cooperation and mutual aid that provided the interpersonal bonds within groups fostered enmity, of varying degrees of intensity, with respect to out-groups.[38]

All of this was of particular significance for societies in the process of revolutionary change. When an old system is being displaced by one that is new, groups necessarily come into conflict. Conflict implies organization, and organization implies elitist or oligarchical tendencies. This is because, for any organization, there are certain prerequisites, the satisfactory discharge of institutional functions which necessitate actors of technical competence. That competence is possessed by only a few men. The larger and more complex an organization, the more emphatic such requirements, and the fewer candidates available for leadership responsibilities. Moreover, the tactical necessities of group struggle require, in principle, rapid executive decision and execution, which precludes the possibility of large assemblies and long deliberations on the part of the general membership. Leadership, under such conditions, would tend to become increasingly oligarchical and arrogate to itself more and more responsibilities. Moreover, Michels contended, the average man is deferential to those in leadership roles. Those who assume leadership obligations can thus exercise special influence over their constituency. Men tend to conform to what they take to be their leader's expectations.[39]

51

Both Panunzio and Michels were identifying what they held to be generic human dispositions. Both conceived of themselves as Marxist in the strictest sense. When Michels published his *Storia del marxismo in Italia* in 1909 he identified himself with all the central theses of classical Marxism.[40] As early as 1904, he had identified himself as a revolutionary syndicalist,[41] and it was as a syndicalist that he developed the central arguments that constitute the body of his major work on the sociology of political parties. It was as a syndicalist that he developed his conceptions of the relationship between the leadership and the led, between a revolutionary vanguard and a potentially revolutionary mass.

Panunzio had addressed himself to the intrinsic sociality of man, to man's disposition to identify with a community of limited membership, to the role of habit, tradition, myth, social sanction, and authority in the creation and maintenance of social systems. Michels had fleshed out the sketch with a characterization of the requirements of social organization, group struggle, the prerequisites of leadership, and the psychological properties that made the average man a passive and impressionable follower.

By the end of the first decade of the new century, all these notions had become common to the most aggressive syndicalists. Thus, Giuseppe Prezzolini, in his sympathetic account of syndicalism, published in 1909, could speak of a revolutionary aristocracy of syndicalists who would mobilize, inform, organize, and direct the proletarian masses in the imminent struggle against their class enemies.[42]

A. O. Olivetti, in turn, was even more specific. In July 1909, he published, in the pages of *Pagine libere*, an article entitled "The Syndicalists and the Elite," in which he maintained that revolution required the innovative leadership of dedicated, talented, and incorruptible men—men who were to be found only in small numbers. Once again, repeating a theme with which he had occupied himself in his essay on the psychology of groups, he spoke of the potential energy possessed by the majority of men. He insisted that the release of that elemental revolutionary energy could only be the consequence of the intervention of a minority possessed of the most advanced revolutionary consciousness: the recognition of the historic requirements of any particular time. Without such men, the mass simply lapses into somnolence, and is socialized to accommodate itself to every outrage.[43]

The syndicalists were emphatic in their judgment that sentiment and ideal purposes were the springs of political and social action. It was clear to them that, although objective conditions might well constitute the necessary ground of action, the impulse to overt collective behavior was supplied by an elite, fired by sentiment and revolutionary passion,[44] and cognizant of the requirements of the time. Michels, Olivetti, and Panunzio were all convinced that individual and collective will, informed by the sentiment and moral purpose of a select group of men, constituted the critical final link in the causal chain that produced political action.[45]

These beliefs were validated by both the spirit and the letter of classical Marxism. Karl Marx, Michels averred, was a voluntarist.[46] He had advocated socialist revolution in Germany in 1848-50, at a time when Germany languished at a primitive economic level compared to the advanced capitalist nations of Europe—at a time when only a small minority of men could have been possessed of an advanced revolutionary consciousness. Marx had advocated what he called a "revolution in permanence," under the direction of a socialist vanguard, that would drive the "bourgeois revolution" forward into socialism. In his "Address of the Central Committee to the Communist League," Marx admitted that, given the economic conditions in Germany at the time, the vast majority of men were not "urban proletarians," but "petty bourgeois revolutionaries." Nonetheless, he advocated that the minoritarian proletarian party employ every means, including secret organization, revolutionary terror, and political excesses to precipitate events.[47]

The tactics and strategy of the program advocated by the

53

young Marx were clearly predicated on a conception of political action that had little to do with any kind of simple economic determinism. The program had clear elitist and blanquist overtones. Marx envisioned a revolution brought about by the intervention of a small conspiratorial group of dedicated and impassioned revolutionaries whose will, fortitude, and mythic suasion, could inspire the masses and materially alter the shape of world events.[48]

To those Marxists who recalled that Marx had always spoken of the course of social events as a function of changes in the economic base of society, the syndicalists were quick to point out that although Marx spoke of the economic base as determining the consciousness of men, he also identified the working class, itself, as "the greatest productive power" of that economic base.[49] The relationship between the base of society, superstructural consciousness, and revolution, was not unilinear, but dialectical.

These were precisely the arguments articulated by the young Mussolini. Under the influence of the syndicalists, Mussolini spoke of vanguard minorities that could engage the sentiment, faith, and will of irresolute masses. "Syndicalism," he maintained, "did not reject 'economic necessity' " as a determinant in the complex of variables that contribute to any specific historic outcome, but "added 'ethical consciousness' " as an equally significant factor.[50] Mussolini's convictions, predicated as they were on the availability of a vanguard minority capable of mobilizing and inspiring the masses, were, as he himself characterized them, "aristocratic" and "elitist."[51]

Like Michels, Olivetti, and Panunzio, the revolutionary socialist Mussolini conceived of historical materialism as fundamentally voluntaristic, and regarded Marx, himself, as a voluntarist.[52] Without the engagement of critical political actors as leaders or as followers, the revolution would be inconceivable. At some stage in the historic process, human will must, of necessity, be engaged. That engagement required a recognition of the regularities governing collective consciousness. Revolutionary leadership would have to concern itself with the psychology of classes and with the techniques of mass mobilization. The task of the revolutionary vanguard was to raise, through myth and symbolic invocation, the consciousness of the masses to meet the requirements of a revolutionary challenge. Prezzolini had specifically referred to these moral and pedagogical obligations, and Mussolini had charged revolutionaries with the responsibility of developing the "new human character" requisite for the historic mission that faced mankind.[53]

These were all perfectly plausible conceptions of classical Marxism's revolutionary strategy. Marx's circular letter to the Communist League obviously implied some form of moral and political elitism, and clearly suggested voluntarism. The revolutionaries to whom Marx appealed were self-selected leaders of the relatively few urban proletarians in a Germany that had only begun to industrialize in the mid-nineteenth century. The leaders, possessed of "theoretical consciousness," were to effectively direct the minority of proletarians to make a revolution in an environment that was economically primitive, in which the vast majority of men were, at best, petty bourgeois. To accomplish this, they were to impose their revolutionary will on events, using every available strategem, including terror and violence.

This is not to say that the syndicalists conceived of history as merely an artifact of human will and mythic suasion. They understood that economic circumstances provided the necessary conditions for effective revolution. In point of fact, some of the critical premises in their arguments were based upon their understanding of Italian economic conditions. Olivetti, in speaking of the revolutionary elite, indicated that such an elite was a special necessity in an underdeveloped economic environment.

Because the Italian peninsula was only marginally industrialized, Olivetti argued, it was totally unrealistic to imagine that the Italian working class could either have the requisite numbers, or the requisite consciousness, to make revolution.

The retarded economic conditions of the nation left the majority of the productive population at primitive levels of social consciousness. Given the circumstances, only an intellectual and organizational elite, possessed of clear vision and impeccable theoretical consciousness, could assume the historic obligation of engineering socialist revolution.[54] Michels had regularly alluded to the marginal industrial development of Italy as a major factor in explaining the ineffectual revolutionary activity among the population of the peninsula.[55] Mussolini spoke of the retarded economic conditions that characterized the Italy of the turn of the century, and catalogued its consequences. Italy was maladministered, beset by illiteracy, its road and rail infrastructure inadequate, its system of taxation iniquitous and irregular, the administration of justice ineffectual, its agriculture retrograde, its local governments incumbered by debt, and its national government corrupt and disorganized. Italy was essentially "feudal" in character.[56] All of which had implications for the mobilization and organization of revolutionary forces on the peninsula. The socialist movement was composed of the most disparate elements—displaced intellectuals, petty-bourgeois factions, urban workingmen, agrarian landless workers, small property-holders, and declassed gentry. This situation meant that Italian socialism would have to host so many factions and so many points of view that a unified and effective social program could hardly be expected.[57]

Syndicalists clearly saw the solution in the active intercession of an effective minority, capable of guiding the elemental energies of the heterogeneous masses on the peninsula. The effectiveness of such an elite was a function of their intellectual and theoretic integrity, their moral fortitude, their personal courage, and what is now identified as their personal and situational charisma.[58] Mussolini identified the task of that elite as "preparing the consciousness" of the masses of the economically retrograde peninsula for revolution.[59] Olivetti argued that only a vanguard minority could energize through suggestion and moral suasion, the "inert body of the anonymous masses." Only they could lead in a retarded economic and social environment—an environment suffering all the disabilities of a "deficiency of capitalist development."[60]

In effect, by 1910 the outlines of a distinctive revolutionary belief system had become apparent. The syndicalists, following Panunzio, recognized that most men, of whatever class or origin, tended to be passive and compliant even in the face of the most onerous oppression. They could be mobilized to revolutionary purpose only if some minority touched their sentiments and tapped their immediate interests. That minority, cognizant of its historic responsibility, could channel collective energy through the effective use of mass-mobilizing myth, without which the majority of men would remain passively ensconced in the traditional order of society.

The syndicalists, by the end of the first decade, recognized that classical Marxism, with its anticipations of the vast "proletarianization" of the working masses, had little to say to industrially retarded Italy. As a consequence, they began to delegate more and more responsibility to revolutionary minorities. Panunzio believed that the intercession of these minorities was a necessary factor in the transition from a retrograde to a progressive social system. Michels anticipated their inevitable role in any effective organization of political change. In the event that elites failed to assume innovative historical responsibilities, their communities would be condemned to remain in the backwaters of contemporary history. Tradition, habit, custom, and general apathy would leave the masses of the peninsula passive objects of exploitation at the hands of their domestic and foreign oppressors. Only a vanguard elite, appealing to the real, rather than the immediate, interests of the masses could introduce the cutting edge of innovative and revolutionary change. The revolutionary myth would be the first expression of subsequent revolutionary law.

Because the peninsula was peopled by so disparate and

57

heterogeneous a mass—far different from the machine-me-tered uniformity of the proletariat classical Marxism had predicted—the revolutionary vanguard shouldered far more responsibility than either Marx or Engels had anticipated. The revolutionary elite would have to be far more authori-tarian, its organization far more structured by a special con-sciousness of its tasks, and far more intransigent in its tactics.

All of these conceptions were, at least in part, based on a recognition of the transitional character of the Italian econ-omy. By the end of the first decade of the present century, all of this had produced a fateful mix, central to which was a critical awareness of the state of the peninsula's economy.

Syndicalism and Industrial Development

Syndicalists had early evidenced concern for the eco-nomic development of the peninsula. They clearly recog-nized that Marx had conceived socialism to be the heir of a mature industrial system. Sorel early reminded Marxists that Marx had argued that no social system ever succumbs until it has exhausted its potential for development. In 1895, a few months before his death, Engels had indicated that so-cialist revolution could only be the consequence of the most fulsome development of capitalism. In his judgment, for ex-ample, the revolution of 1848 had been premature. The "state of economic development on the Continent at that time," he insisted, "was not . . . ripe for the elimination of capitalist production."[61]

What this suggested to the syndicalists was that part of the historic mission of revolutionaries was to stimulate the economic development of their respective nations. Labriola could insist that, as revolutionaries, syndicalists were "inter-ested in the maximum development of productivity."[62] He reiterated Marx's injunction: "The organization of revolu-tionary elements as a class supposes the existence of all the productive forces which could be engendered in the bosom of the old society."[63]

It was clear to the syndicalists that Marx believed the emancipation of the proletariat required the realization of certain material prerequisites. When Carlo Cafiero provided the first compendium of the initial volume of *Capital* for an Italian audience, Marx had admonished him not to neglect mention of the fact that the "material conditions necessary for the emancipation of the proletariat" must be "spontaneously generated by the development of capitalism (*den Gang der kapitalistischen Produktion*)."[64] The entire discussion in the *Communist Manifesto*, in fact, turned on the full maturation of capitalism as the precondition for socialist realization. Socialism, according to classical Marxism, was to be the heir of a mature industrial system.

Given this understanding, the syndicalists argued that socialists, while organizing the forces of the new society, could only advocate the fullest development of the existing industrial system of the peninsula. To this purpose, the syndicalists supported free trade policies because they believed such policies fostered the growth of industry on the Italian peninsula.[65] Olivetti appealed to Marx's essay on free trade to support the syndicalist position.[66] To make his point, he outlined what had become the Marxist interpretation of the phases of economic development, culminating in full maturation of the industrial system and the attendant production of a vast army of politically and economically sophisticated proletarians. Economic development became a central concern for the syndicalists and, thus, Italy's economic retardation became one of their principal preoccupations.

The preoccupation with production became evident early in the writings of the syndicalists. Sorel, in 1907, could argue that "Marxism is decidedly closer to Manchesterian political economy than to utopianism. . . . Marx," he went on, "considers that a revolution is made by a proletariat of producers who [have] acquired economic capacity."[67] Sorel

59

had made production critical to his conception of revolutionary politics. The syndicalists found themselves supporting the Manchesterian liberalism of "bourgeois economists" like Pareto and Pantaleoni. Georgii Plekhanov complained, as a consequence, that the syndicalists were concerned with the fabrication of a "utopia of producers."[68]

Panunzio, repeating Labriola's objections to Plekhanov, insisted that Italy had not completed the bourgeois or capitalist phase of development. Since that was the case, Panunzio argued that socialist revolutionaries were obliged to foster industrial development on the peninsula. They were not "utopian." Their historic responsibility was to "develop to its ultimate conclusion the creative elements that remain alive in capitalism."[69]

For this reason, Panunzio urged syndicalists to oppose reformism. Reformism was predicated on a policy of social amelioration—essentially a nonproductive program of distribution of welfare benefits. Industrial development, on the other hand, required a spartan husbanding of resources in the service of production. Syndicalists were productivists, rather than distributionists. However unappealing such a responsibility might be, it was clear to Panunzio that syndicalists were obliged to foster the accumulation of investment capital instrumental to the economic development of Italy. "Syndicalism," he maintained, "represents the political economy of production, while reformism represents the anti-economic policy of consumption."[70]

Panunzio considered the rapid industrialization of the peninsula the *sine qua non* of the correlative development of syndicalist potential. Syndicalism was to be the heir of a mature industrial system. "Sorel," he reminded his readers, "had written that syndicalism intended to be the heir of a capitalism that had attained its productive maximum."[71]

Everything Marx and Engels had themselves written contributed to the strength of this conviction. Marx had told his readers that the less developed economies could only see in the more developed the "image" of their own future.

And, he went on, each society is compelled to traverse the sequential stages of development. No nation can "clear by bold leaps, or remove by legal enactments" any of the obstacles involved in the "successive phases of its normal development."[72]

By 1910 the syndicalists held certain beliefs that clearly distinguished them from most of those who identified themselves, at that time, as Marxists. Syndicalists understood social change to be the consequence of a number of economic, social, and political factors, in which the innovative role of elites was critical. They anticipated that in an industrially retarded environment, such as Italy, the revolutionary vanguard would be obliged to raise the consciousness of the nation's masses in preparation for certain unanticipated historic responsibilities. The ultimate responsibility, of course, was the socialist revolution, but the path to that revolution must necessarily traverse the stage of industrial maturity, a stage Italy had not yet completed. As a consequence, syndicalists argued that the revolutionaries of the peninsula were obliged to foster the modernization and industrialization of the nation's retarded economic system.

The syndicalists conceived of themselves as operating in a transitional environment. They saw their responsibilities as turning on two critical concerns: (1) the mobilization, education, and organization of revolutionary consciousness among the developing proletarian masses; and (2) the fostering of the economic development of what was one day to be the productive base of a socialist society. To discharge these responsibilities they developed views of collective psychology that endowed creative elites with critical revolutionary functions. They also committed themselves to a productivist, rather than a distributionist, economic orientation. While reformists spoke of redistribution of welfare benefits, the syndicalists spoke of sacrifice, discipline, and rapid industrial development.

By the end of the first decade of our century, the Italian syndicalists were already unique among Marxist revolutionaries. Only some small sects among self-identified socialist revolutionaries followed anything like the same trajectory. A small group of Russian Marxists had begun to articulate arguments that bore a similarity to those of the Italian syndicalists.

In 1895, V. I. Lenin had insisted that "consciousness" played only a "subordinate part" in the history of civilization. Yet, in 1902, he was to say that "without German philosophy" there would have been no "scientific socialism"; and without "advanced theory" there would be no "vanguard fighters," without which there would be no socialist revolution, for the majority of the working class left to its own devices would remain confined to a "bourgeois" and "reformist" consciousness.[73] The statement, "without revolutionary theory there can be no revolutionary movement," clearly implies that consciousness, ideas, and commitment are important historic variables. Far from suggesting that men can or will acquire revolutionary consciousness "whether they want to or not," Lenin's convictions of 1902 suggest that leadership, organization, and theoretical consciousness are critical ingredients in the revolutionary process. Like the syndicalists, Lenin and his Bolsheviks denied that men could spontaneously develop an appropriate revolutionary consciousness. That consciousness would have to be brought to them from without by a small minority of declassed bourgeois intellectuals who would mobilize the elemental energy of the masses around a program of social revolution.[74]

Lenin argued that organization was of critical significance in such a process, and discipline a critical condition for revolutionary struggle. Lenin was to move in the direction of his own variant of heretical Marxism. At a certain stage in the process, Leninism, itself, became involved in a developmental program in which productivity was a central and increasingly critical issue. This entire process was to involve a longer period of time than had the development of Italian syndicalism; the heresy was to traverse the stages in a different sequence and was to be managed by someone other than Lenin. But for all that, by the first decade of the new century classical Marxism gave clear evidence of dissolving into heresy.

The first explicit Marxist heresy was that of Italian revolutionary syndicalism. The next decade was to close with the transformation of that heresy into the rationale of Fascism.

THREE

THE FIRST NATIONAL SOCIALISM

The initial decade of the twentieth century saw the appearance of the first revolutionary socialist heresy. On the Italian peninsula the revolutionary syndicalists had articulated a belief system that was at once authoritarian, voluntarist, elitist, mass-mobilizing, and productivist in disposition. For all that, syndicalism still remained essentially antistate, antinationalistic, antibourgeois, anticlerical, and antimilitarist. Thus, although it seemed evident to most that during the first decade of our century syndicalism had taken on some singular features, syndicalists still thought of themselves as Marxist in both spirit and letter. The orthodox seemed to identify syndicalism's heresy with its antidemocratic and productivist postures. The majoritarian socialists seemed to understand Marxism only in terms of parliamentary democracy and distributionist economic policies.

Benedetto Croce, on the other hand, understood the situation differently. He argued that Marxism had, in fact, expired, and that syndicalism was the last belated effort to breath new life into a corpse. He considered the effort a failure.[1] Whatever the case, it was clear to contemporaries that by 1910 syndicalism had worked a qualitative change in classical Marxism. In 1911 the exigencies of war produced tensions that stretched the Marxism of syndicalism still further.

Revolutionary Syndicalism: Marxism and the Problems of National Interests

When, in September 1911, Italy found itself embroiled in war with the Ottoman Turks, Italian socialists were compelled to make momentous decisions. It is true that European socialism had, for more than a decade, paid ritual obeisance to the slogans of international peace, but the outbreak of war in the Mediterranean called for more than an appeal to commonplaces.

The issues involved in the Mediterranean conflict could not have been either simple nor easily resolved among Marxists. For socialists, the threat and the reality of war necessitated the assumption of some posture or another with regard to specifically national interests and the attendant sentiments that might accompany them. But neither Marx nor Engels had left clear prescriptions concerning the position to be assumed by socialists in the event of international conflict.

On the one hand, Marx and Engels seemed to have committed themselves to a notion that only the bourgeoisie entertained national sentiment and national interests, and that, as a consequence, the proletariat no longer responded to nationalist appeals. In 1845 they imagined that "nationality [was] already dead" among the industrial working classes.[2] In the *Communist Manifesto* this was expressed in the contention that the "workingmen have no fatherland."

On the other hand, this was not all that either Marx or Engels said about national interests, national sentiment, and international conflict. On the occasion of the Franco-Prussian War, for example, Engels insisted that since that war constituted a threat to the very "national existence" of Germany, the "whole mass of the German people of every class [had] flung themselves into the fray." But more than just recognizing the fact, Engels recommended that socialists, "proletarians," join the "national movement" in the war against France. He argued that although it was true that the war would reinforce the "reactionary" Bismarck, it would none-the-less do "a bit" of "socialism's work." It would provide a secure national base for the development of the working class. It would further Germany's economic and industrial development and foster the maturation of the working class.[3]

It is clear that Engels was prepared to advocate proletarian involvement in an international conflict between two bourgeois states. He did so because he imagined that he could discern progressive implications in Bismarck's war against the second Napoleon. The war would provide the basis for the development of German industry, the prerequisite of socialist development. Since Germany had not yet modernized or industrialized, the German working class was still in its infancy. As a consequence, national sentiment still animated the masses of Germany. If Germany lost the war, that sentiment would have consumed all German energies. Since the next stage in Germany's development required modernization and industrialization—and those processes required, as an antecedent condition, the national integrity of Germany—"the struggle to restore Germany's national existence [would] absorb everything," including the dedication of the proletariat.

Thus, under certain conditions, national sentiment and national interest were legitimate grounds for proletarian involvement in international conflict. Equally evident was the fact that there was no simple guide to progressive as distinct from retrogressive national interests. For Engels, the struggle for national unification on the Italian peninsula before 1871, for instance, was "progressive."[4] On that occasion, Engels maintained that national boundaries must be "determined" by "speech and sympathies" in those nations "that are capable of an effective national existence."[5] On the other hand, small nations economically incapable of such an existence, have no claim to sovereign independence. In such cases the call to national liberation was "reactionary."[6]

These considerations allowed Marx and Engels to support movements predicated on national interests in Germany, Italy, Ireland, and Poland. To similarly progressive purpose, they were advocates of war against Russia and France.[7] All of this was clear to the first generation of syndicalists. As a consequence, the syndicalists were prepared to recognize that decisions concerning proletarian or progressive national interests were contingent on a number of historic circumstances.

First of all, if economic development, the prerequisite of socialist revolution, required national independence, the revolutionary proletariat might commit themselves to a program of nationalism.[8]

Moreover, if economic development and national integrity preconditioned each other, and both were necessary to create the material base for socialism, one might very well expect national sentiment to constitute one of the ideal and revolutionary motives animating the working classes of underdeveloped nations. In such cases, national sentiment, the preoccupation with national interests, might constitute a revolutionary proletarian concern.

In fact, as early as 1904, Michels reminded socialists that "proletarian internationalism" did not imply an abandonment on the part of the working class of its national sentiments, nor a neglect of national interests.[9] By 1908, he could point to the "socialist patriotism" of German socialism as evidence of the pervasiveness of national sentiment and of a preoccupation with national interests among working-class political organizations.[10]

In this regard, as in many others, the young Benito Mussolini shared convictions with the syndicalists. As early as 1905, Mussolini had alluded without embarrassment to his own national sentiments. In a letter to Captain Achille Simonetti, Mussolini had spoken with pride of Italian heroes who had "cemented with their blood, the unity of the fatherland." He went on to maintain that Italians must be prepared to defend their homeland against anyone who might attempt to once again reduce Italy to a "geographic expression."[11] Both Marx and Engels had been enthusiasts of Italian unification. But more than that, the fact is that the young Mussolini was early prepared to recognize that men were moved to political action not only by historically contingent economic factors, per se, but by "moral sentiments" that, at certain periods of history, arose out of a sense of community born of "blood, geography . . . and intellectual interests."[12] Thus, while serving as a socialist organizer in the economically underdeveloped Trentino in 1909,[13] the young Mussolini experienced no difficulty in committing himself, as a Marxist, to a "proletarian internationalism" that provided for a defense of the "ideal integrity of the nation," with a recognition of its "historic and moral rights."[14] He understood, in effect, that given the historic conditions of Italy and the Trentino, the political and moral significance of national sentiment and national interests were of critical importance to the revolution.

Thus, even before the outbreak of the war in the Mediterranean, the syndicalists addressed themselves to the political and revolutionary impact of national sentiment. They isolated national interests and national sentiment as significant historic variables.[15] As a case in point, the young Mussolini, in his *Giovanni Huss il veridico*, identified national sentiment as the linchpin of the revolutionary politics of the Hussites.[16]

Thus, the advent of Italy's war against the Ottoman Turks in 1911 provoked a more searching and critical assessment of national sentiment and national interest among revolutionary syndicalists. While syndicalists could, in 1908, argue that national problems should be afforded every deliberate consideration, they still felt obliged to insist that, in principle, they were opposed to any nationalistic conflict.[17] In the two or three years that followed, however, the issues became increasingly complex. So many different interests and sentiments were involved in the international politics of the period that any simple solution seemed precluded. Changing circumstances and dynamic new factors all contributed to the need for a reassessment of political postures that had become traditionally socialist.

By 1911, revolutionary syndicalists were prepared to recognize that, given the importance of national interests, two vital and antitraditional political currents had emerged: a new nationalism and revolutionary socialism. More than that, syndicalists perceived similarities in both intellectual and political movements. Both were understood to be belief systems animated by revolutionary energy and predicated on the conviction that men, in the final instance, are moved by will and sentiment. Both nationalism and syndicalism were antiparliamentarian, elitist, authoritarian, antipacifist, and, most importantly, productionist. Both understood political mobilization to be a function of strategy that invokes sentiment, commitment, and discipline through the effective employment of myth. The principal distinction that syndicalists attempted to draw between syndicalism and nationalism turned on the inability of nationalist myths to fully mobilize the requisite masses. The syndicalists insisted that only proletarian myths and proletarian symbols could accomplish this.[18] At the commencement of 1911, some syndicalists could still maintain that the proletarians had no fundamental interest in the nation, whether or not they might have contingent national sentiment. In the last analysis, the myths of nationalism, they argued, could only prove of marginal importance.

Nine months later, the outbreak of the war in Tripoli proved to be the occasion for a more thorough and thoughtful reappraisal. With the advent of war, the entire socialist movement, reformist, revolutionary, and syndicalist alike was thrown into confusion. Marxist leadership was expected to assume some posture vis-à-vis the international conflict in the Mediterranean. It was among the syndicalists that the reappraisal proved to be most significant for future revolutionary development on the peninsula.

Years later, Roberto Michels was to reflect that the outbreak of war in the Mediterranean precipitated a major intellectual crisis in his life.[19] It seemed hardly less traumatic for many other syndicalist theoreticians. In November 1911 A. O. Olivetti announced his support of the war, Arturo Labriola and Paolo Orano had preceded him; Roberto Michels was to follow. All sought to provide a vindication for that support, and all conceived of that vindication as Marxist and revolutionary in character.

Syndicalists reviewed every argument advanced by Marx and Engels to support Bismarck's war against Napoleon III. Those arguments had turned on the progressive and historic

69

implications of that particular bourgeois conflict. When Olivetti developed his arguments he alluded to what he took to be the same features in Italy's war against the Ottoman Turks.

Just as Bismarck's victory over France, in Engels' judgment, had provided the necessary conditions for the industrial maturation of marginally developed Germany,[20] Olivetti argued that an Italian victory in the Mediterranean would stimulate and augment Italy's economic development. Confined by economically developed imperialist powers and impaired by limited resources and investment capital as Italy was, only heroic efforts could move the nation out of the "limbo of precapitalism" towards its "historic bourgeois mission," the extensive industrialization of the peninsula. The war would materially assist in the creation of a "society of producers." It would provide both the material base and the psychological properties necessary for the socialist revolution.[21] The war, in effect, was "progressive."

Under such circumstances, invocations to war had the quality of effective mass-mobilizing myths. Such myths tapped real interests and dispositional sentiments and husbanded collective energies for the transition from a marginally developed to a fully mature industrial society. By that time, it had become evident to Olivetti, as it had to other syndicalists, that the life of the working class was still "involved intrinsically in the life of the nation," and that the war thus served the ultimate interest of the proletariat. By February 1912, Olivetti could applaud the war as a revolutionary necessity that carried in its train a rapid development of Italian industry, a regeneration of heroic spirit among the entire population, and a prefiguration of the revolutionary mass-mobilization of the future. Italians, Olivetti argued, long oppressed by a national sense of inferiority because of their retarded economic development, had shown themselves capable of a display of collective enthusiasm, sacrifice, dedication, and courage—all the psychological prerequisites of regenerative revolutionary action.[22]

Syndicalism and Proletarian Nationalism

One year of war produced in Olivetti, as it had among some of the most notable syndicalist theoreticians, a clear recognition that the "new nationalism"—a "revolutionary" nationalism to distinguish it from the "gouty" and "traditional" nationalism of the liberal bourgeoisie—was a force with which twentieth-century revolutionary socialism must reckon.[23] For Michels, the recognition found expression in his allusions to a "proletarian nationalism," or the nationalism of a "proletarian nation."

Michels, like other syndicalists, had early recognized the pervasiveness of national sentiment, but like other syndicalists before the crisis generated by the war in Tripoli, he conceived that sentiment to be of secondary importance. Until the Mediterranean war it was obvious that Michels saw few fundamental proletarian interests involved in the politics of nationalism. As has already been stated, however, the outbreak of war created traumatic moral and intellectual tensions for Michels. His response to that tension was research and reflection that matured into the writing of his *L'imperialismo italiano*, a defense of Italy's war against the Ottoman Turks.

In the introduction to his volume, Michels reported that he had concerned himself with the problems of the concepts fatherland, nation, and nationality for some time, but that the war, with all its evidence of popular enthusiasm and sacrifice had prompted him to attempt a comprehensive explanation of the portentious resurgence of nationalism among the masses of Italy. He believed his account outlined some of the variables that made a form of nationalism a predictable "necessity" for "proletarian Italy."[24] Michels had begun to assess national interests and national sentiment as variables of primary historic and revolutionary importance.

Michels reviewed all the factors he considered significant for his account. In the first place, Italy was an underdeveloped nation, with extremely limited resources at its disposal,

71

and with a population density that exceeded that of almost every other nation in Europe. In addition, Italian out-migrants, forced to leave their homeland, found themselves residing in foreign nations as an oppressed and frequently despised minority. Finally, Italy as a newly integrated nation, found itself opposed by the more industrially developed states who sought to maintain a status quo that would insure their continued privilege and advantage. Michels cited Arturo Labriola's characterization of the war: Italy, in its conflict in the Mediterranean, found itself opposed not only by the Turkish armed forces, but threatened by the "intrigues, the threats, the snares, the money and the arms of plutocratic Europe, which refuses to tolerate any gesture or word on the part of small nations that might compromise its iron hegemony."[25]

It is clear that in Michels' judgment, Italy's war against the Ottoman Turks was a progressive war which merited the support and participation of the revolutionary proletariat. Every argument Marx and Engels had marshalled to foster proletarian participation in the bourgeois wars of Bismarck's Germany against France and capitalist England's against Czarist Russia, could be refurbished and applied to Italy's conflict with the retrograd Turks—a people Engels had identified as having no future in the modern world.[26]

Italy's war with the Ottoman Turks would stimulate and expand the industries of the peninsula. It would undermine the stability of the advanced capitalist or plutocratic nations. It would regenerate the population of Italy, long suffering in that sense of inferiority that afflicts industrially retarded or marginally developed countries in the twentieth century.[27] Michels, like Olivetti, conceived Italy's proletarian nationalism to be revolutionary, indeed, Marxist in essence. More than that, Michels was prepared to identify national interests and national sentiments as factors of primary historical and socialist importance—a conviction that was to provide the vindication for our century's first national socialism.

Plausible as these convictions were, it is interesting to

note that not all syndicalists were prepared to accept them. Filippo Corridoni, a young syndicalist activist of whom much was subsequently to be heard, remained adamantly opposed to the war. Alceste De Ambris and Michele Bianchi, equally aggressive and later to be very important, both opposed the war. And Benito Mussolini, at that time a local leader of the Socialist party, led mass demonstrations against the war in his native Romagna.

Be that as it may, it was evident that the syndicalist heresy had taken on still more arresting features. Olivetti had begun to speak of a synthesis of nationalism and syndicalism, and, in 1913, Michels published his first extensive treatment of "patriotism" or "nationalism" as a special historic determinant.[28] At the same time, it became clear that the fabric of Michels' Marxism had loosened sufficiently to accommodate the conviction that historic events were the consequence of a complex interpenetration of factors, among which group sentiment, and in our own time, national sentiment, functioned as independent variables.[29]

The fact is that, by the commencement of the second decade of the twentieth century, revolutionary syndicalism had begun to take on features that might cleary distinguish it from the classical Marxism from which it originated. Until that time, syndicalists insisted that their Marxism was essentially that of Marx and Engels. By 1912 or 1913, however, it was more and more evident that syndicalism was undergoing a singular, creative development. While syndicalists continued to identify themselves as Marxists, a number of their beliefs were very hard to trace back to the Marx-Engels corpus. One of the most significant instances of this development can be isolated in the work of Sergio Panunzio.

Revolutionary Syndicalism, War, and Moral Philosophy

During the crisis generated by the war in Tripoli, a number of familial and personal considerations had occupied Panunzio's energies. Immediately after this interim period, however, he began to write about issues that had become critical to the syndicalists. In his *Il diritto e l'autorità*, for example, Panunzio gave clear evidence of his commitment to a form of ethical idealism, a recognition that the historical materialism of Karl Marx, if it were construed as being innocent of, or indifferent to, moral issues, was unresponsive to the problems of the twentieth century. If Marx were understood to argue that moral judgments were simple "reflexes" and "sublimates" of "determinate life conditions" and nothing more, then Marx was in error. Marx, Panunzio believed, appreciated the fact that the contemporary analysis of social problems necessarily involved moral judgments. Such moral judgments required an analysis different from those characteristic of economic history. There was, Panunzio argued, a fundamental difference between empirical assessments of any specific set of circumstances, and the moral judgment that men should labor for the realization of specific ends.[30] To supply the necessary constituents of any such argument, appeal must be made to moral principles, and for this purpose Panunzio invoked Kant and the neo-idealists, Benedetto Croce and Giovanni Gentile.

From that point on Panunzio's analysis of social dynamics included (1) an empirical assessment of concrete human needs, (2) a recognition that needs find expression in individual and collective sentiment, (3) that sentiment can be captured by appropriate symbols and political myths invoked by select elites, and finally, (4) that the competition between political appeals can only be ultimately resolved by the invocation of responsible moral argument.

This analysis very quickly matured into a set of convictions. If the proletariat had, in fact, an investment in the nation and its development—if the nation satisfied some of the real and concrete needs of the proletariat—those needs would find expression in collective sentiment. Those sentiments could be invoked by an elite exploiting appropriate symbols and myths. Those myths would allude to the cultural, historical, and social reality of the most potentially effective community in the twentieth century: the underdeveloped or marginally developed nation. By the advent of the First World War, in 1914, it had become clear to Panunzio that the principle of nationality, in such circumstances, still moved the vast majority of men to political action.

Thus, by 1912 most of the major theoreticians of syndicalism, Olivetti, Michels, and Panunzio recognized the historic significance of national interests and national sentiment. This recognition was progressively reinforced by the events that were to destabilize all of Europe.

Italy's war against the Ottoman Turks contributed to the instability already manifest in the Balkans. The Austrian attempts to control the situation directly contributed to the outbreak of the First World War. With that war, Italy found herself in particularly unhappy circumstances. On the one hand, Hapsburg interests in the Balkans directly conflicted with those of Italy. The national leadership in Rome could only view Austria's moves in the Balkans with considerable reservation. On the other hand, Italy was an ally of Germany and Austria and was treaty-bound to aid Austria in any war in which she became involved. Italy thus was in the unenviable position of being obliged to assist Austrian imperialism in the Balkans, to Italy's real and potential detriment.

The conflict which erupted in the Balkans in 1914 quickly involved the entire Continent, and Italy found herself under increasing presure to align with one or another of the combatants. Within Italy the entire left was once again embroiled in acrimonious debate concerning national foreign policy. Orthodox socialists, revolutionary socialists, and syndicalists, alike, were compelled to assume a definitive position concerning the prospect of Italy's active involvement in the conflict that by that time included every major nation on the Continent.

The socialist parties of Europe, irrespective of their frequent opposition to war in general, all supported their respective nations. The Social Democrats of Germany, almost to the man, voted war credits for the Kaiser. The Social Democratic party of Austria-Hungary, the Socialist party of France, the Social Democratic party of Russia, all in one way or another, supported their national governments at the moment of international crisis. Only some of the socialist elements in England, and the official Socialist party of Italy insisted that their governments remain neutral in the conflict.

From the very commencement of the dispute, the Italian Socialist party assumed a position of adamant neutrality. They insisted that Italy remain uninvolved in the burgeoning European conflict. Benito Mussolini, one of the most influential party leaders, and by that time editor of the party's principal newspaper, *Avanti!*, was an outspoken advocate of Italian neutrality. For reasons that need not here concern us, the young Mussolini, between 1910 and 1914, had put considerable distance between himself and the syndicalists. In the late summer and early autumn of 1914, as Europe joined in the carnage that was to become the First World War, the young Mussolini was committed to the neutralist position of his party.

As early as July 1914, Mussolini had anticipated a general conflict on the Continent. On the 23rd of July, Austria dispatched an ultimatum to Serbia. On the 28th, European hostilities broke out with a declaration of war between Austria-Hungary and Serbia. On the first of August, Italy declared its neutrality. For the moment, the Socialist party of Italy and the "bourgeois" government of the peninsula agreed on the nation's neutral position. At the same time Mussolini called for "absolute neutrality," he insisted that the Italian proletariat would know how to defend the soil of the fatherland should the nation be attacked.[31] Long familiar with the role of national interests and national sentiments in the mobilization of men, Mussolini recognized that the insistence that the "proletariat has no fatherland" was little more than a "theoretical caprice."[32] At that point, Mussolini's objections to the war were in fact tactical rather than theoretical.

On the 4th of August, in the face of the defection of the socialist parties from their commitment to international peace, Mussolini recognized that the Second International was dead and that, in reality, it may never have existed.[33] Mussolini, nonetheless, but without enthusiasm, continued to defend the party's commitment to neutrality.

From that point on, the situation developed very rapidly. The conflict on the Continent continued to expand. In France, even Gustave Hervé, the socialist who had advocated that the proletariat of France abjure all national wars and plant the flag of the fatherland on a dunghill, appealed to the French Ministry of War to be allowed to join the armed forces to defend the nation against the German invaders. The internationalism of socialism rapidly became undone. In Italy, in the first issue of *Utopia*, of which Mussolini was editor, Sergio Panunzio argued against the official socialist commitment to absolute neutrality. "The principle of nationality," Panunzio reminded socialists, was a potent force in the complex of factors that shape events in the contemporary world. Socialists, Panunzio insisted, could either recognize the fact, and influence the course of history, or neglect it and be dominated by events.[34]

On the 18th of August, one of the most influential of Italy's syndicalists, Alceste De Ambris, who had opposed the war in Tripoli, opted for Italian intervention in the war on the side of the Entente powers against the Austro-Germans. Soon afterward, Filippo Corridoni, who had also opposed the war against the Turks in 1911, abandoned his commitment to neutrality in the belief that a war against the Central Powers could be both national and revolutionary. On the 6th of September, he called upon revolutionaries to remember the "combative and patriotic spirit" of the Paris Commune and take up arms in "revolutionary and national war" against the absolutism and reaction represented by the Central Powers. In the meantime, Cesare Battisti, Mussolini's revolutionary colleague from the Trentino, having fled Austria, entered Italy and urged socialists to demand Italian intervention in the service of those conationals still under the domination of Austria-Hungary.

Sentiment in support of Italian intervention came not only from syndicalists. The national publication of socialist youth, *Avanguardia*, called for socialists to "march against the Teutonic hordes." Even Antonio Gramsci, later to found the Communist party of Italy, voiced his objections to Italian neutrality. By mid-September, the young Mussolini realized that the official party position was becoming increasingly precarious.

On the 5th of October 1914, a group of socialist theoreticians, by and large syndicalist in orientation, published a manifesto, *Manifesto del Fascio Rivoluzionario d'Azione internazionalista*, in which they called upon the working classes of Italy to demand their country's intervention in the growing conflict in the service of "civilization" and "revolution." The manifesto was signed, among others, by Michele Bianchi, Filippo Corridoni, Amilcare De Ambris, and A. O. Olivetti. On the 10th of October, Olivetti reminded his readers that the outbreak of war on the Continent had created a revolutionary situation in which men could be mobilized around an "effective and overwhelming sentiment"—that of nationality. That mobilization, he argued, under the aegis of the most compelling crisis in Europe's history, would allow the creation of a new consciousness, a dedication and commitment that would school men in the arduous responsibilities of the future. The war would create "new men" who would be both "producers" and "warriors," men who could, in servicing the developmental needs of their nation, refashion and regenerate the world. The society of tomorrow, Olivetti insisted, would be one of "producers," and the war, for all its destructiveness, would create the circumstances that would allow Italy to join the community of advanced nations. He reminded revolutionaries that the resolution of social problems could only be the consequence of the solution of national concerns. What the times demanded, and every rational calculation prefigured, was a "national socialism," an Italian developmental socialism, fashioned out of the elements of revolutionary socialist thought and national aspirations.[35]

These were convictions that were increasingly heard among revolutionaries. A group, led by Panunzio, urged the young Mussolini to reconsider his opposition to Italian intervention in the conflict. On the 18th of October, Mussolini suggested that the Socialist party review its commitment to absolute neutrality and reassess socialist strategy in view of the gravity and complexity of the situation.

Mussolini's call for a review of the official position vis-à-vis the European war precipitated a crisis among the leaders of the party. Mussolini was asked to resign his editorship of *Avanti!* It quickly became evident that he would not be able to carry either the leadership or the bulk of the membership of the official party with him. On November 10th, the young Mussolini, still attempting to salvage support within the party, called upon socialists to recognize that recent events had revealed, with crystal clarity, the ineffectiveness of the socialist international. Addressing himself to the Milanese section of the Socialist party, Mussolini argued that Italy as an historic reality remained a focus of "proletarian" interest, and an object of sentiment, for much of the population of the peninsula. "The sentiment of nationality exists," he maintained, "and cannot be denied. The old antipatriotism has run its course."[36]

Mussolini, at that critical point in his political life, was voicing convictions which had become commonplace among the revolutionary syndicalists with whom he shared so many affinities. As early as September, Roberto Michels had alluded to the same considerations Mussolini had invoked to justify his call for a modification of the official socialist position on the war.[37] Michels reviewed what he took to be the orthodox interpretation of historical materialism—an interpretation which made only immediate economic factors the ultimate determinant in any historical situation. He exposed the implausibilities involved in such an interpretation.

79

Once again, he insisted that any historic event is a function of the interaction of many variables, among which national sentiment, a specific political culture, and general political interests exercise significant influence.

It is abundantly clear that Mussolini's decision to object to the official socialist policy of neutrality was predicated upon what had come to be accepted syndicalist convictions. Every argument he marshalled to his purpose was an argument already implicit in the syndicalist beliefs he had entertained since 1904. When Mussolini, expelled from the official Socialist party, and editor of his own daily, explicitly advocated Italy's intervention in the "revolutionary war," the syndicalists rapidly collected around him.[38] His daily, *Il popolo d'Italia*, became the unofficial propaganda vehicle for the interventionist *Fascio*.

The major intellectual and political crisis which involved Italian Marxism in 1914 moved the syndicalists to develop their belief system with impressive dedication. By 1917, Sergio Panunzio, for example, had published two monographs, *Il concetto della guerra giusta* and *Il principio e diritto di nazionalità* in support of Italian intervention in the war. The first was devoted to the concept of a "just war" and the second to the principle of nationality. Roberto Michels, for his part, published a number of short pieces and several articles specifically concerned with intellectual and theoretical issues that the war had provoked. Throughout the period, the young Mussolini attempted to articulate a belief system that would give a "social content" to the "revolutionary war."

As we have suggested, Panunzio was among those revolutionary socialists who early opted for Italy's intervention in the First World War. In the fall of 1914, he had alluded to the war as revolutionary in character and he took up the same theme in the pages of *Avanti!*[39] The war, he insisted, would not only be revolutionary, it would be a "just war," one that serviced the ultimate interests of mankind. That latter judgment, as far as our exposition is concerned, is more interesting and more important, for it turns on Panunzio's conviction that nationality was critical to the self-actualization of men.

Panunzio wrote his *Principio e diritto di nazionalità* in the fall of 1917. It was written without specific political intention, but clearly contained the elements of an argument that was to become central to Panunzio's social and political philosophy and to the belief system of Fascism. In his *Principio* Panunzio recognized the social and political significance of the sentiment of nationality.[40] Such a recognition clearly implied, given Panunzio's analysis of individual and collective psychology, that the origins of national sentiment lay in fundamental human needs. Panunzio argued that the nation is a contemporary, if time-conditioned, form of human association, and natural human associations service human needs. A nation is an organic association of men sharing common territory, origin, customs, language, and culture.[41] National identity provides the human agent with roots, a cultural patrimony rich in language, the arts, symbols of association, religious beliefs, the sciences, and every attribute that distinguishes man from beast. Far more than any other association of our time, natural or contrived, the nation supplies the essentials of man's humanity. The nation is, in a critical sense, an "ethical entity," the very foundation of human personality. As a consequence, to defend and foster the nation's development is to defend the essentials of one's self. To foster the interests of the nation is to foster one's self-actualization.

Panunzio resolved the intellectual and moral crisis that the First World War had produced for him by attempting to understand the implications of individual and collective behavior he had witnessed. He had seen large numbers of men respond to the symbols and slogans of national identity. They had made the "selfless," "heroic," and "warrior" response expected of the working class by syndicalists, who conceived the syndicates to be the critical association in the life of modern man.

With the actual response to national appeal, many syndicalists recognized the historic reality of national interests. Engels had clearly indicated that the response of the German proletariat to Bismarck's invocations evidenced the reality of Germany's developmental needs. And the development of the nation inevitably enhanced the life circumstances of the working class. Men responded to the appeals of national identity because the nation represented an inevitable stage in the historic fulfillment of mankind. Men characteristically identified with restricted communities: tribes, clans, city-states, and nations. Such associations allowed them to recognize a place, a culture, a population, a history, and a language as truly their own. The selection of such associations was determined by the necessities of each historic period. In the contemporary world, the nation was that privileged and charismatic association.

In effect, during this period Panunzio was putting together the principal elements of the rationale of Fascism. He gave himself over, explicitly, to a form of neo-idealist and developmental nationalism. What this meant was that Panunzio was to entertain an interpretation of revolutionary politics that made human self-fulfillment the categorical imperative governing men's moral priorities,[42] and national development its functional requirement. The ideals which animated political actions were essentially moral, and as a consequence, fundamentally different from simple factual considerations.[43] This was not to say, for Panunzio, that facts were irrelevant to moral concerns,[44] for he insisted that national development was an historically contingent requirement to contemporary moral fulfillment.

Given this analysis, Panunzio was not content simply to rely on the fact that many Italians had responded to the myth of the nation as a justification of political nationalism. What he attempted was both a moral vindication and an empirical interpretation. As early as his *Sindacalismo e medio evo*, Panunzio recognized that any interpretation of facts was governed by a point of view, a moral perspective.[45]

His early arguments were not well-formulated, but the first germs of the distinction between moral and factual concerns were evident. In developing his exposition, Panunzio articulated special arguments that were to later reappear in the rationale of Fascism. One of those arguments is particularly interesting because commentators have so frequently caricatured its intention and substance. One of the most significant differences between moral and factual concerns in Panunzio's analysis arose from the recognition that no simple recitation of facts could move men to political action. Action arises only out of moral impulse.[46] Every action is sparked by sentiment and sustained by will. The necessary condition for the generation of that sentiment and that will is moral concern. Moral concern was thus central to Panunzio's "activism" and "voluntarism." The will is engaged when men see moral purpose in action—and action must follow when the will is truly engaged.

This moral concern is itself governed by what Panunzio called "rational natural law."[47] What this meant for Panunzio was that men are moved, and their will is informed, by rational moral purpose. Panunzio identified self-actualization as the goal to which all means are instrumental. Only such a goal can awaken the sentiment and the will to act necessary for its fulfillment. Self-realization, once chosen requires, in turn, a careful assessment of facts instrumental to its realization.[48]

Syndicalism, Nationalism, and Economic Development

These conceptions, taken together, allow us to reconstruct Panunzio's thought with considerable accuracy. Sentiments reflect needs. The sentiment of sociality is an expression of the need to self-actualize. Man is a social animal because he can find fulfillment only in community. In both a factual and a moral sense, man is an intrinsically social animal.[49] Sociality articulates itself, and finds manifest expression, in spontaneous and natural associations: the family, the eco-

83

nomic syndicate, and the nation. These associations arise out of felt need. In his youth, Panunzio was convinced that economic associations—the syndicates that had grown up spontaneously throughout Europe—constituted the primary and exclusive community for modern man. Men could find fulfillment only in total commitment to their economic and productive communities. In the face of the tragic and ineluctable facts of the First World War this conviction was significantly amended. It became evident to Panunzio that the economic syndicate, under contemporary historic conditions, could not satisfy all the complex needs of human beings. There was a wider and still more complex association that constituted the material base of man's self-actualization: the nation.

In Panunzio's judgment, the war had revealed the nation rather than the syndicate, to be the primary object of human loyalty—the foundation of man's collective life-interests, the material and spiritual vehicle for his self-actualization. Without the language, art, music, science, technology, philosophy, history, and economic potential of which the nation is the bearer, the individual would be without human substance. It became evident to Panunzio during this period of transition, that he had misconceived the syndicates as being too rich, too complex, too all-encompassing. He had charged the syndicates with obligations that Marx himself had recognized could only be fulfilled when the nation had completed its bourgeois development. The years before the First World War had dramatically revealed that the Italian nation had not yet completed that process. Unified late in the nineteenth century, the nation still suffered grievous political and economic retardation. As a consequence, the proletariat remained immature. It could only respond to historically appropriate invocations: the call to the nation's defense and its development. The nation, and the nation alone, could discharge the functions Panunzio had assigned, but a few years before, to the proletarian syndicates.

By 1918 Panunzio had reorganized his system of beliefs.

He was to identify that modified belief system as "national syndicalism" to distinguish it from that syndicalism that had been transformed with the advent of the First World War. At about the same time, Benito Mussolini identified himself with similar beliefs which he, too, characterized as "national syndicalism."[50] The transitions in Panunzio's thought were far from idiosyncratic. Similar transitions could be identified in the thought of a number of revolutionaries. Only his death, early in the war, cut short such changes in the syndicalist convictions of Filippo Corridoni.[51] The elements of a "national syndicalism" are prefigured in his political testament.[52] The work of Roberto Michels, as well, reveals the same features.

As early as the war in Tripoli, Michels had begun a careful reformulation of his convictions. He had early argued that the analysis of any complex social event required an account of an indeterminate number of interacting variables. By the time the First World War occupied the theoreticians of social change, Michels, as we have suggested, had clearly identified national sentiment as one of the most important of those variables. In his discussion of the sociological conceptions of Vilfredo Pareto, Michels indicated that men are moved to social action only when possessed of a faith, a conviction, that can engage their sentiments. Pareto had identified national sentiment as one of the most effective mass-mobilizing sentiments available to revolutionaries. Pareto spoke of constants that governed the behavior of men. One of those constants, a group-building and group-sustaining disposition, found expression in nationalist sentiments.[53]

Like Panunzio, Michels clearly distinguished between factual and moral appraisal.[54] Unlike Panunzio, he was not immediately concerned with providing a moral vindication for Italy's international political strategies. But it is clear that Michels was prepared to offer such a vindication. He spoke of Italy as a nation that had achieved nationhood late, as a nation afflicted with a lack of natural resources and subject to population pressures unique on the European

85

Continent. He recognized that there were "privileged," "plutocratic" nations that enjoyed special advantages in the modern world denied to "proletarian Italy."[55] Italy, in opposing those nations, could appeal to a moral right to its place in the sun.

All of these considerations, those of Olivetti, Panunzio, and Michels resonated in the articles published by the young Mussolini during the war years. Mussolini articulated arguments that either paraphrased those to be found in the works of the major syndicalist theoreticians or assumed those arguments as premises. He was prepared to recognize the pervasiveness of national sentiment, and, like the syndicalists, he recognized that sentiment arises out of felt needs. He reflected upon the needs which subtended, in his judgment, the sense of nationality that had moved men of all classes to action in the "Great War." He spoke of the moral dimensions of the conflict.

Mussolini alluded to the diminished welfare that attends an underdeveloped nation. He spoke of the oppression and exploitation suffered by every member of a community that has no international status.[56] The proletariat of Italy suffered humiliation and diminished fulfillment not only because they were proletarian, but because they were Italians. The proletariat was an intrinsic part of the nation and as the nation suffered so suffered the proletariat; the nation unfulfilled left the proletariat unfulfilled. Thus, the realization of the nation's potential was the precondition for the self-actualization of the proletariat.[57] The proletariat, as a consequence, could not "deny the fatherland."[58] The proletariat could no longer distinguish its cause from that of the nation in its entirety, for the ultimate interests of the working classes were "intimately and fatally linked" with that of the fatherland.[59] Any socialism that failed to understand the fundamental reality of national interests was a socialism devoid of political future.

For the young Mussolini the only viable socialism of the twentieth century would be a national socialism, in which the nation would constitute the *prima facie* object of loyalty. All population elements would be fused in the "idea of the nation," the mythic and symbolic expression of the real and fundamental interests, both material and ideal, that unite men in the contemporary world.[60] In the service of national regeneration men would adapt themselves to the ethic of sacrifice and heroism that was the analogue of the "warrior ethics" early espoused and advocated by revolutionary syndicalism.[61] The postwar world would see men organized in a union of national solidarity, unanticipated by prewar revolutionaries. They would be led by "saints or warriors" and would be animated by grand purpose.[62]

The myth, the "ideal representation of a possible future,"[63] that would animate the masses would be a symbolic representation of the vital needs of the national community and would resound in the sentiments of all men.[64] Appealing to those interests and that sentiment, a "vanguard elite," an "audacious minority," would detonate the elemental but latent energies of the "numberless" masses.[65] By moral suasion, and mimetic example, resolute leaders of the masses might turn collective energies to collective purpose.

By 1918, Mussolini had synthesized every insight provided by the Italian syndicalists. Mussolini conceived of Italy as an old/new nation commencing its modern development. He argued that Italy, for centuries an oppressed and humiliated nation, had only recently begun to challenge the advanced nations of the earth for equitable status and place. Necessary to that challenge was a development of the peninsula's industrial potential. The obligation that would fall on any revolutionary government would be the "salvaging, protecting and assisting [of the nation's] magnificent industrial development"—the very precondition of the "new and greater Italy."[66] The demand that Italy expand its productive capabilities became central and critical to Mussolini's ideological program.[67] "We have become, and will remain," he maintained, "a people of producers."[68] With rapid industrialization, Italy would reveal herself as a modern nation, the equal of any on the globe. No longer a tourist stop on the odious itinerary of a Baedeker guide book, Italy would cease to be peopled by dealers of dusty art objects or be a refuge for the idle. Italy would no longer be afflicted with an economy characterized by agriculture and home industries alone, or one in which ownership remained largely in foreign hands.[69]

It was during this period that Mussolini changed the subtitle of his newspaper from "A Socialist Daily," to "A Daily of Combatants and Producers."[70] The subtitle prefigured the "society of producers" anticipated by Sorel, Olivetti, Corridoni, and Panunzio. "Proletarian" Italy, under the aegis of a "vanguard elite," was to marshall her energies and compete with the "plutocratic" nations of the world. Her mobilizing myth was to be the myth of a regenerate nation, no longer humbled by "capitalist" powers—a nation secure in her destiny. What the future required was a disciplined drive toward rapid national development under the direction of an informed and competent political hierarchy.[71]

The logic of Mussolini's position was transparently clear. The tasks that faced proletarian Italy were tasks that were essentially bourgeois. Italy required the completion of national integration, unification having been achieved less than half a century before. Italy needed to mobilize its entire population—a population that had remained largely passive during the process of unification—to the tasks of nation-building. Italy required economic and industrial development, technical efficiency, and a modern system of production. All these tasks were part of the historic "bourgeois mission" that Marx had imagined would have been completed prior to the socialist revolution. The issue, as Mussolini identified it, was not whether Italy had bourgeois tasks before it, but rather whether Italy had a bourgeoisie capable of discharging its historic obligations.[72] Should the bourgeoisie prove inadequate to its responsibilities, the historic tasks would fall upon the popular masses and a "vanguard elite" equipped to meet the challenge of the twentieth century.[73] Under the aegis of that elite, Italians would reconstitute themselves a "new people"—the population of a Greater Italy—an Italy that was to be the creation of a "new race of producers."[74]

Mussolini argued that, for as long as Marxism had been a vital intellectual and political force, socialists had been called upon to involve themselves in bourgeois tasks. They had been called upon to assist their several nations in the processes of liberation and unification, the necessary preconditions for industrial development. Both Marx and Engels had understood economic modernization and industrial maturation as the prerequisites of socialism. To these ends, both Marx and Engels had supported Bismarck's war against France, and Engels had applauded the expansion of the "bourgeois" United States into the continental southwest at the expense of the "lazy Mexicans."[75] Similarly, Engels justified Germany's annexation of Schleswig from Denmark as "the right of civilisation against barbarism, progress against quiescence"—in effect, the right of a developing "bourgeois" society as opposed to that of a more traditional and "static" agrarian society.[76] For the same reasons, Engels supported the "imperialist" and "bourgeois" French against the native Algerians. He argued that "bourgeois" virtues were preferable to traditional "barbarism."[77]

Both Marx and Engels had taught that underdeveloped nations see in developed nations their own future. It was the task of the bourgeoisie to fabricate an economic system that satisfied all the prerequisites for socialism. But it was equally evident that other classes or fragments of classes might be charged by history with bourgeois responsibilities. The syndicalists had early argued that case. Marx and Engels had advocated social revolution in economically retrograde Germany in 1850. They could have only understood that, under such circumstances, successful revolutionaries would have had to face the historic bourgeois task of developing the economic system of nonindustrial Germany.

By the close of the first world conflict, in the fall of 1918, the thirty-five year old Mussolini had drawn together a number of syndicalist arguments, and had articulated a coherent revolutionary belief system that he chose to call "national syndicalism" or "national socialism." National syndicalism would guide Italy from the stage of economic inferiority, dominated by foreign investment capital, to the status of an independent, sovereign, and industrially mature community. The axiom, the essential commitment of this belief system, was production. Italy must be compelled to "produce, produce with efficiency, with diligence, with patience, with passion." "Producers," Mussolini insisted, "represent the new Italy, as opposed to the old Italy of balladiers and tourguides. . . . The reality of tomorrow will be marvelous. There are those capitalists possessed of a sense of their historic function and are prepared to throw themselves into the effort; there are proletarians who comprehend the ineluctability of this capitalist process and can appreciate the mediate and immediate benefits this process can deliver. . . . To confine the productive forces of Italy is to condemn Italy to remain a secondary power."[78]

For more than a decade syndicalist theoreticians had gradually woven together the threads of these arguments. Roberto Michels had reinvoked the name of Carlo Pisacane to remind Italian revolutionaries that socialism had long been associated with national aspirations.[79] When, immediately after the Fascist March on Rome, Curzio Malaparte rehearsed the intellectual antecedents of Fascism, he marshalled to his purpose all the syndicalist arguments of Labriola, Olivetti, and Panunzio. The social and economic content of nascent Fascism was the product of syndicalist lucubrations, syndicalist sentiment, and syndicalist convictions. The pure syndicalism of the turn of the century had become the transformed national syndicalism that carried syndicalists into the First World War. With the termination of hostilities, syndicalism had become a Marxist heresy that advocated mass-mobilization in the service of the completion of bourgeois historic tasks. It was an elitist, antiparliamentarian, mythic, and heroic doctrine that drew out of a Marxist postindustrial revolutionary creed a revolutionary program adapted to a traditional and retarded industrial environment.[80] The failure of orthodox socialism in Italy was a consequence of its unsuitability, its irrelevance. Italy, at the time of the first world conflict, was not an advanced capitalist nation, it was still largely agrarian and artisan. Innocent of a modern bourgeoisie, beset by regionalism and provincialism, malintegrated and maladministered, the class struggle as conceived by the orthodox succeeded only in retarding the necessary development of the peninsula and impairing Italy's capacity to withstand the impostures of the plutocratic nations of the North. The syndicalists argued that any enterprise that impaired Italy's developmental process was counter-revolutionary and antihistorical.[81] Syndicalism conceived of the Italian proletariat as the heirs of bourgeois historic responsibilities.[82] The revolutionaries of the twentieth century, the syndicalists argued, when they find themselves denizens of undeveloped economic communities, are charged with bourgeois tasks.

National Syndicalism and Lenin's Bolshevism

Only time and the pervasive ignorance of Italian syndicalist literature had succeeded in dimming the Marxist credentials of these first Fascist commitments. More than that, time and ignorance have conspired to dull our appreciation of the affinities shared by the first Fascism and that Marxist heresy which came to power in defeated Russia at about the same time. Those affinities, however, were not lost upon contemporaries. In 1920, Max Hirschberg very carefully documented the theoretical and tactical similarities shared by revolutionary syndicalism and Lenin's Bolshevism. He emphasized, for instance, their shared commitment to action-oriented strategies, to mass-mobilization by revolutionary elites employing mythic invocations. He recognized their mutual antiparliamentarianism and their espousal of

91

the politics of violence and confrontation.[83] Similarly, and at the same time, Torquato Nanni, himself a revolutionary socialist and an early acquaintance of Mussolini, provided an analysis of Fascism and Bolshevism that attempted to assess the common economic foundations that produced the related strategic, tactical, and institutional features of the first two mass-mobilizing, developmental revolutions of the twentieth century.

Torquato Nanni argued that Marxism had taught modern man that the history of the contemporary world is a function of stages of economic maturation, and that socialism was predicated on the maturation of the economic potential implicit in the capitalist organization of society. As a Marxist, Nanni argued that contemporary revolutions could only serve either to fulfill Marxist revolutionary predictions or to create the preconditions for their fulfillment. Either revolution occurs in an advanced economy—and then a socialist society becomes a real possibility—or revolution occurs in a primitive economy, and revolutionaries inherit the bourgeois responsibility of developing the economic base requisite to socialism.

Nanni reminded socialists that Engels had warned that when a revolutionary captures an economic environment inadequate to his social aspirations, such a revolutionary is compelled to service the historic and economic needs of his time, rather than the putative needs of a class whose time has not yet matured. "The worst thing that can befall a leader of an extreme party," Engels insisted

> is to be compelled to take over a government in an epoch when the movement is not yet ripe for the domination of the class which he represents and for the realization of the measures which that domination would imply. What he can do depends not upon his will but upon . . . the degree of development of the material means of existence, the relations of production and means of communication upon which the clash of interests of the classes is based

every time. . . . In a word, he is compelled to represent not his party or his class, but the class for whom conditions are ripe for domination.[84]

In effect, what Nanni argued was that, since both the Fascist and Bolshevik revolutions had captured economically underdeveloped communities, both would be obliged to develop the industrial and economic potential of each if they were to discharge their historical responsibilities. The development of such potential was a bourgeois responsibility and as a consequence, both Fascism and Bolshevism were obliged to devote themselves to the historic mission of the bourgeoisie.

In 1873, when Engels voiced his judgments about revolution in economically primitive environments, he argued that "the revolution sought by modern socialism is, briefly, the victory of the proletariat over the bourgeoisie and the reorganization of society by the abolition of all class distinctions. To accomplish this," he went on, "we need not only the proletariat, which carries out the revolution, but also a bourgeoisie in whose hands the productive forces of society have developed to such a stage that they permit the final elimination of all class distinctions." He insisted that socialism could only be possible in an economy which had attained a "very high stage of the development of the productive forces." He went on to add that "this stage of development is only reached in bourgeois production. The bourgeois," he concluded, "is consequently equally as necessary a precondition of the socialist revolution as the proletariat itself."[85]

Like the syndicalists, Nanni maintained that the first responsibility of contemporary revolutionaries in societies suffering retarded industrial development was to foster capital accumulation, technological sophistication, and economic growth. He reminded Marxists that Lenin, himself, seemed clearly aware of these historic responsibilities. As early as 1905—at about the same time the Italian syndicalists were developing their productivist arguments—Lenin insisted that the forthcoming revolution in Russia would be faced with the obligation of clearing "the ground for a wide and rapid . . . development of capitalism." The revolution, "far from destroying the foundations of capitalism . . . broadens and deepens them." Lenin went on to add that "the idea of seeking salvation for the working class in anything save the further development of capitalism is reactionary. In countries like Russia the working class suffers not so much from capitalism as from the insufficient development of capitalism. The working class is, therefore, most certainly interested in the broadest, freest, and most rapid development of capitalism."[86]

Nanni argued that revolutionaries in both Italy and Russia, irrespective of the differences in historic, cultural, and political circumstances, faced the same historic bourgeois tasks. Those tasks could be discharged only within the political and geographic confines of historic nation states. As a consequence, the socialism that must assume bourgeois responsibilities could not alienate itself from the bourgeois sentiment of nationality. The socialism of underdeveloped nations, as national syndicalism early recognized, and Bolshevism was ultimately to recognize, must be, in some significant sense, national in orientation and class collaborationist in character. It must be capable of mobilizing and organizing the energies of all productive elements of the national community, and it must somehow accomplish the effective collaboration of all functionally necessary population components in the development program. Whether collaboration is purchased by the protection of special privilege, or the payment of differential wages, by the inequitable distribution of welfare benefits, or through the liberal use of terror and compulsion, revolutions in underdeveloped economic environments are charged with common historic tasks that create pervasive similarities in political form and institutional structure.[87]

The political form and the institutional structure assumed

by the heretical socialism of the first quarter of the twentieth century was initially, or was ultimately to reveal itself as, national socialism. Its clearest prefiguration is to be found in the writings of Italian syndicalists. It was syndicalism that provided the Marxist vindication of the first Fascism. And it was Fascism that identified the central responsibilities of revolutionaries in the twentieth century.

FOUR

THE PROGRAM OF FASCISM

By the time Fascism constituted itself a political movement with the meeting at San Sepolcro in March 1919, the belief system of its leadership had already taken on not only the style, but the content, that would characterize the revolution. Of all the folk wisdom surrounding Fascism, the conviction that it was no more than opportunistic, anti-ideological, antirational, and consequently devoid of programmatic and strategic content, is both significantly untrue and most difficult to dispell. For half a century, authors have insisted that such was the case, and the objections raised during the last decade have had only marginal impact. Born of an intransigent anti-Fascism that articulated itself between the two world wars, and of the animosities generated by the war against Fascism, the insistence that the movement founded by Benito Mussolini in 1919 was innocent of any intellectual or moral substance found ready acceptance among Anglo-Americans and ultimately among Europeans on the Continent. That Fascism had no ideological substance was a notion that offered so many pragmatic, mobilizational, and propaganda advantages, that any effort to resist the claim was almost certain to be dismissed as either special pleading or apologetics. Circumstances in our own time have altered the intellectual environment somewhat, but traditional wisdom dies hard.

All of which is very unfortunate. Not only have we lost much of the substance of a particular period of European political and intellectual history, but such convictions lead us to overlook a great many similarities that, in a substantial sense, suggest that the left and right-wing mass-mobilizing movements of our time are members of the same political genus. For the fact is that Italian Fascism was the natural child of revolutionary Marxism, and revolutionary syndicalism was its midwife. The intellectual substance that made up Fascism derived from the revolutionary national syndicalism that had gradually articulated itself on the Italian peninsula during the prewar decade.[1] Years later, in 1932, when Mussolini sought to trace the ideological pedigree of Fascism for the audience of the *Enciclopedia italiana*, he alluded to that current of revolutionary syndicalist thought that had fed substance into the movement. He spoke of the French syndicalists, Sorel, Péguy, Lagardelle, and then of Enrico Leone, A. O. Olivetti, and Paolo Orano.[2] He spoke of Fascism as that "national syndicalism" that had grown out of the revolutionary Marxism of the prewar period. Whatever qualifications scholarship may append to his schematization, Mussolini's characterization was, in fact, substantially correct. Fascism was the direct and documented heir of revolutionary syndicalism, and as such forever bore the inexpungable species traits of that heretical Marxism in which it found its point of origin.[3]

Recently, Adrian Lyttelton maintained that Fascism, at its official founding after the termination of the First World War, was possessed of neither a body of doctrine, a particular social philosophy, nor determinate economic interests.[4] This judgment is, at best, only partially true. How much doctrine, philosophy, or economic interests is understood to animate a political movement is, at least in part, a function of how rigorous, emphatic, and elaborate the philosophy, or how explicit the economic interests, are expected to be. The fact is that Fascism, as most commentators are now prepared to recognize, was the intellectual heir of revolutionary syndicalism, and revolutionary syndicalism had elaborated a doctrine and a social philosophy, and had identified its economic interests, with impressive emphasis and specificity.

97

It was a doctrine, a social philosophy, and a collection of interests the young Mussolini had made substantially his own.[5]

Even prior to the advent of the world conflict in 1914-1918, Mussolini—like the syndicalists, fully cognizant of the retarded state of the peninsula's economy—had argued that Italian capitalism had not yet completed its historic function. As early as January 1914, Mussolini had maintained that the "orthodox" socialists had made a "grave error" in imagining that capitalism had "concluded its historic cycle." Capitalism remained, in his judgment—a judgment, as we have seen, he shared with Lenin—capable of "further development." There were even intimations that the "industrial bourgeoisie," the "youthful and bold" agents of economic progress would be essential to that development. Such arguments, as we have seen, had become commonplace among revolutionary syndicalists, who as "productivists," had lamented that Italy had lodged herself in the "limbo of precapitalist development."[6]

Before the First World War, in one of the first issues of his theoretical journal, *Utopia*, Mussolini had prominently reproduced Marx's familiar judgment that no society ever perishes until it has fully developed all its productive potential.[7] The necessary antecedent to any future socialist society was clearly the full maturation of the industrial and economic potential of the peninsula.

For Mussolini, as we have seen, the conviction that any revolution in Italy involved a vast program of social change, economic modernization, and development, was conjoined with the equally firm judgment that such a process required the intercession of a vanguard elite capable of mobilizing the latent energies of the masses.[8] Like the syndicalists, Mussolini argued that the revolution he anticipated and the mobilization it required, could take place only under the stimulation of an animating sentiment and an articulated "faith."[9] The process could only be characterized as "heroic" and "idealistic."[10]

These convictions, in turn, rested on a general social philosophy. Mussolini, like all the socialists of his time, was a convinced "collectivist," that is, he believed man could realize himself only within the confines of a rule-governed community.[11] Irrespective of the expansive role afforded the individual leader and the exiguous elite in the affairs of men, Mussolini was convinced that "the instinct of association . . . is inherent in human nature. An individual who lives outside of the chain of association is inconceivable."[12] The moral imperative that man fulfill himself as man[13] can only be discharged when the individual, moved by fundamental needs and animated by sentiment, lives out his existence in a historically determined community, an in-group of similars infused by "laws of solidarity."[14]

All of this was Marxist in inspiration, socialist in general character, and syndicalist in immediate origin. Before the advent of the First World War, Mussolini's political activities were inspired by a general social and political philosophy, which constituted the intellectual basis of a strategy and corresponding tactical postures, almost all of which Mussolini shared with the revolutionary syndicalists of his time. When the First World War precipitated his expulsion from the official Socialist party, Mussolini found himself leagued most intimately with the syndicalists, who, by that time, had made their transition to national syndicalism.

Mussolini's disposition had always been essentially pragmatic in character. He had early identified himself with the pragmatism of Sorel, Olivetti, and Panunzio. He shared the programmatic orientation of the *Vociani*, the thinkers that had grouped around Giuseppe Prezzolini. By 1914 Mussolini, like the syndicalists, was convinced that the sentiment of nationality was a variable of pragmatic, historic, and consequently, revolutionary mass-mobilizing importance. At the time he advocated Italy's intervention in the First World War, Mussolini recognized that the nation constituted the charismatic object of loyalty for the vast majority of men, bourgeois and proletarian alike. Every historic, economic, political, and moral significance he had invested in social

99

class was transposed, as a consequence, to the nation. Like the revolutionary syndicalists before him, Mussolini had discovered the focal community of the contemporary world: the historic nation.

Throughout the war years, Mussolini remained a collectivist, convinced that individuals could find fulfillment only in a community of men with whom they shared loyalty, discipline, sacrifice, commitment, and ideal aspirations. By 1915, that community was the historic nation, the "proletarian nation" that had so much inspired the syndicalists in 1911.

For the interventionist Mussolini, the nation was bearer of that patrimony of spiritual values, economic satisfactions, and psychological identity without which men remain morally and materially unfulfilled. To effectively serve as such a vehicle, the nation must develop its full potential. It must learn to move, Mussolini was wont to say, "with the rhythm of machines," heir to the historic patrimony of the developmental bourgeoisie.[15] By the close of the First World War, Mussolini, like the syndicalists, identified the industrial and economic development of the peninsula as one of the central commitments of the interventionist *Fasci*.

By that time, he had also decided that the vanguard for his nationalist, productivist, and mass-mobilizing revolution would be the entire class of veterans returning from the trenches. In his judgment, the "aristocracy of the trenches" would return to staff the revolutionary movement.[16] Recruitment could take place among all population elements as long as they committed themselves to the creation of a new and greater Italy.

By the end of the war, Mussolini's political convictions were held together by two critical commitments: a commitment to the functional and political myth of the nation, and a commitment to industrial and economic modernization and development. In an impoverished, humiliated, and retrograde nation, the individual, no matter what his immediate circumstances, attains only the semblance of humanity. In a world in which proletarian nations must compete for space and resources with plutocratic nations, only the rapid development and modernization of one's nation can provide for meaningful self-realization. The life circumstances of each individual, of whatever class, are inextricably interwoven with the fate of his nation.[17]

The Fascism of San Sepolcro

By the time Mussolini was preparing the meeting that would count as the official founding of the Fascist movement in 1919, he possessed a social philosophy, a doctrine, and the strategy that doctrine implied. The first Fascists were almost exclusively war veterans, the elite of the trenches. Understandably, their primary concern was a moral and political defense of Italy's involvement in the war. Their opposition to socialism turned almost exclusively on the official socialist resistance to that war. They, like Mussolini, insisted that the war had been the harbinger of vast social changes. Like Mussolini, they anticipated a new and regenerate Italy, and they advocated a vast program of economic and political modernization and development to that end. The Futurists among them, for example, envisioned a modern and mechanized Italy that would take its place among the advanced nations of the world. The Futurists were the lyricists, the poets, of modernization and development.[18] The fact is that the formal social philosophy and political doctrine of the first Fascism was the product of antecedent revolutionary socialist and syndicalist thought. The violent opposition to organized socialism was dictated not by Fascism's philosophical or programmatic commitments, per se, but by Fascism's defense of Italy's intervention in the First World War. Mussolini, and the revolutionary syndicalists, regularly reiterated that their objections to organized socialism arose almost exclusively from its antinationalism and its inflexible opposition to Italy's participation in the conflict of 1914-18.

By the end of 1918, revolutionary national syndicalists

101

like Agostino Lanzillo, A. O. Olivetti, and Sergio Panunzio had formulated the ideology of Fascism. At the time most syndicalists still identified themselves as revolutionary Marxists, adamantly opposed to the doctrinaire antinationalism of organized socialism. When Mussolini rose to speak at the founding meeting of the Fascist movement in March 1919, he thus gave voice to the heretical Marxism of revolutionary national syndicalism.

Mussolini gave expression to all the aspirations and fears, the rancor, and bitterness of returning war veterans. He spoke of those who had fallen in the war. He spoke of the "petty souls" that had opposed the war and denigrated the memory of the heroic dead. He spoke of making the war itself an issue. He emphasized the rights of those who had fought for the nation. All of these themes were contingent and tactical, calculated to correspond to the immediate interests of his constituency. But more than that, Mussolini addressed himself to a broad program that would animate the strategy and constitute the critical ideological core of nascent Fascism.

The parts of Mussolini's delivery that were not devoted to the immediate concerns of the first Fascists were necessarily stenographic and schematic. He spoke of a world in which proletarian nations found themselves disadvantaged in the competition with "imperialist" and "plutocratic" nations. He argued that the orthodox socialism of the peninsula was incapable of affording Italy, as a proletarian nation, the possibility of survival in such an environment. Given such preoccupations, Fascists entertained but two critical programmatic commitments: a commitment to the nation and a devotion to the maintenance and furtherance of production.

To serve those ends, Mussolini insisted that the revolution must be directed by an active and aggressive minority, animated by national syndicalist persuasion. He anticipated a "dictatorship" of "will and intelligence" that would "educate" the working classes to their responsibilities, that would insure technical development and the effective representation of all the "corporative" interests involved in the processes of production. He insisted that capitalists would have to innovate and renovate the industrial system of the peninsula.[19]

Mussolini recognized that such suggestions were transparently nonspecific. He maintained that more precise political tactics would have to be a function of unforeseeable contingencies. But the fact of the matter was that, however programmatic and schematic Mussolini's suggestions might have been, the first statement of Fascist policy was the product of a long and sophisticated ideological development. Fascist ideology was the direct heir of national syndicalist thought, and whatever else it was, national syndicalist thought was as complicated, sophisticated, and competent as any in the revolutionary tradition. Every ideological theme that Fascists ultimately developed was prefigured in the literature of revolutionary syndicalism. Whatever differences of emphasis and modifications of tactics characterized the trajectory of Fascism, the core program was either anticipated or articulated by the principal theoreticians of revolutionary syndicalism by the beginning of 1919.

Irrespective of these facts, it is sometimes argued that Fascism was devoid of ideological content until the theoreticians of Italian nationalism had contributed their stock of political and social convictions to the doctrinal emptiness of Fascism.[20] Actually, a more defensible characterization of what transpired was captured by Herbert Schneider, when he spoke not of Fascism taking on the ideological commitments of nationalism, but rather of an increasing rapprochement, an increasing fusion, of nationalism and national syndicalism.[21]

Syndicalism, Nationalism, and Fascism

There was, in historic fact, a gradual reduction of the ideological distance between the most radical of the syndicalists and the most antitraditional nationalists during the years before the First World War. As has already been suggested, both nationalists and syndicalists early became aware of their increasing affinities. At about the same time that A. O. Olivetti was identifying the ideological elements shared by revolutionary syndicalism and nascent nationalism, Enrico Corradini, one of the founders of Italian nationalism, was cataloging many of the same similarities for his nationalist audiences. Corradini identified, for example, the shared opposition to parliamentarianism, the common belief that men are moved by myths that tap pervasive sentiments, and the shared conviction that human will and ideal aspirations influence the movement of society and history. Corradini recognized that both political movements encouraged discipline, advocated a readiness to sacrifice, and aspired to the inculcation of a new consciousness, a new commitment, and a new sense of mission among Italians long afflicted with a sense of inferiority, long denizens of a nation without status and without contemporary significance. "We can conceive," Corradini remarked in 1909, "of a syndicalism that confines itself to the political boundaries of the nation and does not extend beyond—that ceases, that is to say, to have international pretensions and is active nationally. Under such circumstances, workers would unite, but not with the workers of the world, but with their conationals."[22]

By 1911, syndicalists were prepared, in turn, to recognize the political and historic significance of national concerns, and the first intimations of a national syndicalism surfaced in the political prose of Olivetti, Orano, and Panunzio. As both belief systems matured, the distance between them diminished. Shared themes became substantive programmatic similarities. Thus, as early as 1914, Alfredo Rocco, one of the principal ideologues of the new nationalism, could address himself to Italy's major problems with arguments that would be appreciated only by the most advanced national syndicalists.

Rocco spoke, as a case in point, in terms of a vision of

man and society that saw the individual as a "function" of his community. Here was the same explicit rejection of liberal individualism that characterized the syndicalist persuasion. Rocco proceeded to identify the fulfillment of the individual with the realization of the full potential of the community of which he is an inextricable part. Given this conviction, the fact that Italy was an underdeveloped or marginally developed nation in a world of advanced capitalist states became a central concern in his argument. Because Italy was a proletarian nation in competition with capitalist states, Italians were impoverished, humiliated, and oppressed. What Italy required was a rapid and effective expansion of its economic potential. Italy should be immediately concerned with the enhancement and effective expansion of production, rather than the socialist preoccupation with distribution. Nationalism, Rocco argued, proceeded from "two premises" that he identified as "opposed to those of socialism," but fully compatible with national syndicalism: (1) the economic problem of Italy is one of production and not distribution; and (2) the national economy must be conceived of in an international context, in a world in which advanced industrial nations enjoy resource, capital, and political advantages denied the proletarian nations. Rocco argued that if the masses of Italy were ever to enjoy a standard of living comparable to the advanced countries of Europe, the gross national product of the peninsula would have to be tripled and quadrupled in the shortest possible time.[23]

As a nationalist, Rocco advocated a far-reaching program of industrial development and economic modernization: the technological modernization of agriculture, the expansion of irrigation systems, reforestation of lands, the development of hydro-electric power as a substitute for imported fossil fuels, and the expansion of industrial plants. He spoke of a vast program of renewal, an orchestration of collective energies behind the rationalization of production, and an increase in technical and technological efficiency. The productive elements of the national community would be organized in pro-

105

fessional associations that would negotiate whatever differences might arise between them. The unity of the nation would be preserved in its competition with the "sated" plutocratic powers. As the productive capabilities of the system expanded, the upward mobility of status-deprived and economically underprivileged members of the population would dissipate the disruptive "class war." What would result would be a "national syndicalism"—an orchestrated union of producers working towards a maximization of industrial productivity and economic development.[24]

By 1919 Italian nationalists had organized themselves into a political association animated by a belief system remarkably similar to that of the revolutionary national syndicalists. The nationalists recognized that organized interest groups constituted the ligaments of the emerging Italian industrial society. Corradini and Rocco identified "syndicates," "corporations," organized professional, economic, and special interest associations, as the "vital" and "organic" constituents of modern society. For Corradini and Rocco, the notion that modern society is composed of individual "citizens" who periodically select a general representative to service their needs in a national legislative body, did not correspond in any way with the political realities of the time. Like the syndicalists, the nationalists argued that men were not simply "citizens," but economically active "producers," who organized themselves in rule-governed associations to protect their vital interests. As a consequence, the parliamentary governments of the time were, by and large, elaborate facades that managed to obscure the reality of the largest and most effective interest groups locked in a struggle over the welfare benefits modern society might afford.[25] Nationalists argued that elections which pretend to afford "citizens" the right to select a "representative" to serve their "general" interests were elaborate charades designed to conceal the real battle that took place between effective interest groups.

By 1918 the nationalists were arguing that the phenomena of individuals organizing into aggregates in defense of their specific collective interests were common and predictable features of modern society. What political realism required was an organization that allowed effective control over the several interest groups, "syndicates," or "corporations," in the service of national development. Liberal parliamentary systems could never serve in such a capacity.

Like the syndicalists, the nationalists were productivists in that they identified expansion, rationalization, and improved technical efficiency of industry and agriculture as the most immediate priority for retrograde Italy.[26] As early as 1916, Corradini had published his *La marcia dei produttori*, in which he argued that Italy's foremost goal should be a husbanding of natural and human resources in the service of expansion and modernization of production.[27] To accomplish this, the nation required a new political infrastructure.

For both nationalists and national syndicalists, Italy was an underdeveloped nation. Illiteracy was pandemic; the means of communication were inadequate; the road system fragmentary and insufficient; the personal life of each citizen insecure; banditry was rampant; regionalism abounded; poverty weighed heavily on the vast majority of the population and overpopulation drove hundreds of thousands of Italians out of their homeland.[28] Both nationalists and revolutionary syndicalists recognized that the economic base of the peninsula required development if Italy were to effectively meet the challenges of the modern world. The nation in its entirety was proletarian, subsisting marginally in the contemporary world on the sufferance of capitalist powers.

The historic mission with which the nationalists wished to inspire the population of the peninsula was the bourgeois obligation of national industrial and economic development. Because they believed the parliamentary system maladapted to that historic charge, they looked to an elite of activists, a dynamic, authoritarian, and determined leadership that would move Italy out of its somnolence into the twentieth century. Only the myth of such a mission could dispel the

107

effects of centuries of servility, humiliation, oppression, and foreign occupation.[29] Once again, the "myth" was understood to be a symbolic formulation calculated to give expression to real needs and pervasive sentiments. It was a political formula capable of energizing men to the arduous requirements of vast social, economic, and political change.[30]

Thus, by 1919, Italian nationalism and revolutionary national syndicalism shared substantial similarities. The general social philosophy that subtended both—that men were, in essence, social creatures finding fulfillment only in an organic community of similars—provided the moral and ideal basis for their doctrinal emphases on mass mobilization, mimetic example, elite rule, mythic suasion, and collective development and modernization. Both rejected the traditional world of prewar Italian politics; they rejected the "little Italy" of the past—oppressed, impoverished, illiterate, humiliated, and scorned. They anticipated a "Greater Italy" that, as a respected and modern nation, might provide the necessary preconditions for the fulfillment of individual lives. To these ends, both nationalism and revolutionary national syndicalism advocated an ethic of discipline, sacrifice, and labor for a nation still caught up in the psychology of underdevelopment. They conceived of a modern Italy moving at the pace of modern machinery.

What this implied, minimally, was that the historic, political, cultural, and economic nation constituted that community in which the individual had primary and fundamental interest. Whatever regional, local, or immediate economic interest influenced his behavior, was derivative of his interest in the historically constituted nation. For revolutionary syndicalists this was so because Italy had not yet traversed the bourgeois phase of industrial and economic development. As Marxists—and most syndicalists still considered themselves in 1919 to be Marxists—they recognized that internationalism could only be a function of the full maturation of the international economic base. As long as there remained proletarian and plutocratic nations, functional internationalism was a vain aspiration. The vitality of national sentiment among the populations of economically retrograde and retarded nations was sufficient evidence of the vanity of socialist internationalism.[31] The First World War had seen nations commit themselves to international carnage in the service of national goals and aspirations. The oldest socialist organizations of Europe had committed themselves to the service of national interest.

In May 1918, Olivetti could speak of the nation as a "fundamental contemporary historical fact" with respect to which class interests were contingent and derivative.[32] By that time, Olivetti could address himself to the "two historic realities" of the twentieth century: the nation as the necessary existential base for the working classes, and production as the source of the material prerequisites for life fulfillment. Virtue, discipline, and energy would be sustained by the irrepressible sentiment of nationality and the rational calculation of individual and collective interest.[33] "Class," Olivetti insisted, "cannot deny the nation . . . the entire working class movement must be orchestrated to the overarching ends of the nation."[34] "The nation," he went on to say, "is an all-embracing syndicate: the common interest of all those who suffer, labor and produce within a territory defined by historic, linguistic and cultural boundaries."[35]

These convictions, shared by the revolutionary national syndicalists and the nationalists, abound in the writings Mussolini published about the time of the founding of the Fascist movement. In April 1918, Mussolini spoke of the proletariat as a constituent part of the "people," the population of a sovereign nation-state.[36] He spoke of the proletariat as part of a collective enterprise committed to maximizing production under the auspices of a state that would promote, protect, and expand the productivity of the nation.[37] He spoke of a revolutionary institutional infrastructure that would house and represent all the vital productive interests of the nation in a form of corporative national socialism.[38] He spoke of a new ethic of discipline, sacrifice, and dedication, founded upon the pervasive sentiment of nationality and the appeal to immediate and mediate interests.[39] He characterized all this as a "Latinization," or an "Italianization" of Marxism—a Marxism transformed to meet the special needs of a special social, political, historic, and national environment.[40] If any form of socialism was to survive in the twentieth century, it would have to be tailored to the national exigencies of the respective peoples of the earth. It would have to be national, and in cases of underdeveloped communities, productionist. This national socialism would have to be emphatically "pragmatic." It would integrate the working classes into the organic totality of the historic nation. The working classes, taken as aggregates and in terms of the individuals that compose those aggregates, would attain the full stature of manhood only when the nation was accorded a place in the modern community of nations.[41] The Italian population was characterized by a "precapitalist" and traditional mentality. What was required was the inculcation of a modern mentality, methodical, diligent, patient, and dedicated.[42] Such a program could only be effectively undertaken by a responsible, committed, and enterprising elite.[43]

The rationale for these doctrinal developments was provided by the young Mussolini in a review of what passed as orthodox Marxist analysis. The orthodox socialists, Mussolini maintained, insisted that socialist revolution could only come about after the full maturation of the economic base of modern society. Only a society that enjoyed a surfeit of productive capabilities could produce a class-conscious, technically efficient, and revolutionary proletariat. The preconditions for socialism could only manifest themselves in advanced capitalist countries. Unhappily, Mussolini went on to argue, revolution had invested essentially underdeveloped communities. As a consequence, the orthodox analysis becomes largely irrelevant.[44] Underdeveloped nations like Russia and Italy were possessed of but meager proletarian elements, often characterized by ineptitude, traditional prejudices, and inefficient organization. The tasks that face such nations were bourgeois tasks. Underdeveloped communities must negotiate these tasks with a weak, often ineffectual, and dispirited, bourgeoisie and an equally weak and dispirited proletariat. To husband such elements through the trajectory from underdevelopment to economic maturity required the intercession of dedicated revolutionary elites.[45]

All these common arguments surfaced and resurfaced with almost tedious regularity throughout the months before, during, and after the official founding of the Fascist movement. Panunzio, about a week before San Sepolcro, spoke of a "Marxism" adapted to the realities of Italy's conditions. He spoke of the economic retardation of the peninsula, of a technically and politically immature proletariat, and of a state compelled to inculcate a new consciousness among the masses of the nation. He spoke of a revolutionary conception of property rights which would make ownership contingent upon national concerns—primarily the requirements of increased national production. He spoke of the integration of productive categories into the "integral nation" through a national syndicalism or corporativism.[46] All of this would be accomplished with discipline, sacrifice, and dedication under the auspices of an authoritarian and hierarchical political system that would force-draught the nation through the process of capital accumulation, industrial expansion, and economic rationalization.[47]

The core of the Fascist program during the early twenties was thus the consequence of the internal evolution of the doctrine of revolutionary syndicalism.[48] Years later, Sergio Panunzio was to write an introduction to a volume by Romolo Ronzio that traced that evolution and identified its affinities with the ideological postures of Italian nationalism.[49] It is not true that nationalism provided the ideological, doctrinal, and programmatic content of Mussolini's Fascism. However programmatic the Fascist movement might have been at its inception, Fascism's commitments distinguished it from any other competitor for political power at that time. Moreover, those commitments were the consequence of an internal process of theoretical development reflected in the works of the principal syndicalist thinkers before Fascism's fusion with nationalism. The authors of those developments, particularly Olivetti, Orano, Michels, and Panunzio, were to subsequently staff the Fascist Center for Political Studies at Perugia.[50]

Fascism and Ideology

Italian Fascism faced the first years of revolutionary challenge possessing as coherent an ideological posture as any on the Italian scene. Part of that posture was to advertise the "pragmatism," the "actionism," and the "voluntarism" of the movement. Activism and voluntarism took on the form of objections to intellectualism, sustained criticism of the "abstract ruminations" that proved sterile in the face of practical challenge. One week before the meeting at San Sepolcro, for example, Panunzio wrote, "Today is a time not for thought but action." He then went on to clarify his position:

> Let me explain myself. Today what is required is that thought that is so precise and mature that it finds expression in action. We reject the counterfeit of thought, abstract thought that has left facts and circumstances behind it, the thought of the weak and those forever formulating projects. . . . To really think means to interpret reality and act within that reality. . . . Today we need political realism and not doctrinaire thought. [One must] act, that is to say, think before acting and then to act, and not allow oneself to be overtaken by . . . events.[51]

Fascists, Mussolini in particular, prided themselves on being political realists, prepared to act within and upon the reality of their times. But to argue that as realists they entertained no theoretical, ideological, or doctrinal preconceptions is simply untrue. Lenin, Castro, and Mao were no less realistic than Mussolini. Few would argue that Lenin's thought, or Mao's thought, or Castro's thought was, or has

112

been, any less theoretical for its realism. All mass-mobilizing revolutionary leaders have insisted on some doctrine as the guide to their political conduct, but more often than not their immediate tactics have all the surface features of political realism, behaviors governed at least as much by circumstances and political contingencies as by theoretical conviction.

For our purposes, it is enough to show that the principal spokesmen of revolutionary syndicalism early expressed all the themes that were to characterize Fascism throughout its tenure. Those revolutionary syndicalists who, like Arturo Labriola, did not follow the trajectory into Fascism, early dropped away. Others who remained, in some critical sense, libertarian, were either gradually alienated or expelled from the movement. All modern, mass-mobilizing movements have endured such periodic purges. No one has seriously suggested that such purges and defections constitute evidence of a lack of ideological commitment on the part of the movement.

It is often suggested that Fascism's purported lack of ideological commitment is evidenced in its opportunistic shift from the left to the right during its struggle for political power. Mussolini, the argument proceeds, used any theme he believed attractive to his audience. As Mussolini's audience changed, so did his themes. In 1919, so the story goes, Fascism was oriented to the left, while in 1921, Fascism had made a transit to the right.

As a matter of fact, all the themes that commentators usually cite as evidence of this so-called opportunism were already present in the thought of syndicalists when they first formulated the rationale of Fascism in 1919. At a time when most syndicalists still considered themselves Marxists, they were articulating beliefs that later analysts were to identify as anti-Marxist and rightist. As a case in point, Fascism's emphasis on the role of the state, frequently alluded to as its cardinal right-wing commitment, found expression in the writings of the revolutionary syndicalists some considerable

113

time before the founding of the Fascist movement. As soon as revolutionary syndicalism conceived of the nation as the vehicle of collective interest, the notion of an agency that might represent that interest independent of the several class and category interest groups that make up the organic community, suggested itself. Once syndicalism recognized the fact of nationality as "immanent, fundamental and supreme," and the nation as a "great productive syndicate,"[52] the necessity of some political agency that might express that immanent, fundamental, and supreme interest became apparent. As early as 1918, Panunzio spoke of the construction of a "syndicalist state"—the dissolution of the "bourgeois" and "parliamentary" state and its reconstruction and reorganization into a state that might truly represent the integral interests of the nation. By August 1919, he could affirm that "statism and syndicalism are in the process of fusion."[53]

For Panunzio, the issue had clarified itself as early as 1914 when he had begun work on a volume devoted to the theory of the state. The intellectual development antecedent to that work can be traced with considerable specificity. In his earliest work, Panunzio had recognized that the development of syndicalism implied, on the one hand, the persistence of law-governed relations between organized producers, and on the other, a hierarchical and authoritarian confederation in which these law-governed relations would effectively culminate. By the time of Italy's involvement in the First World War, Panunzio recognized the historic viability of the nation. As a consequence, the organized productive syndicates that made up the fabric of the nation were conceived of as "one great confederation," and the agency that expressed the authoritative and integral will of that confederation was the state. The state was the juridical, authoritative, and ethical embodiment of society organized in productive syndicates.[54] By early 1920, Panunzio identified the relationship between the state and the syndicates as one of the most portentious problems of our time.[55]

114

The conviction of many specialists that Fascism at its initiation was leftist, and subsequently became reactionary, or rightist, is thus only qualifiedly true. Mass-mobilizing movements attempt to mobilize masses. As a consequence, they are sensitive to the immediate and historically contingent interests of their potential recruits. Leninists, when they were trying to recruit urban working-class masses, promised "all-power" to working-class organizations. They subsequently created a control system that was hierarchical and dominated by a minoritarian and authoritarian party. When peasant support was sought, Leninists spoke of "land to the peasants," only to ultimately deliver forced collectivization. The first Fascists advocated the confiscation of church property, the abolition of the Senate, and proportional representation when their appeal was to left-wing subversives. They abandoned these themes when they recruited elsewhere. Such postures are generally explicable on the grounds of immediate recruitment interests. There is no reason to insist that Fascism made a transit from left to right between 1919 and 1922 merely because of these recruitment tactics.

On the other hand, Lenin's programmatic *State and Revolution* of 1917 was clearly anarcho-syndicalist in character, advocating and anticipating the all-but-immediate "withering away of the state," with Lenin's advocacy of universal suffrage, referendum and recall, representatives confined by restricted mandates, and elected officials paid workingmens' wages. The "state capitalism" with its authoritarian and hierarchical command structure that Lenin advocated early in 1919 and again in 1922 was a far cry from the left-wing commitments of 1917.

The fact is that Bolshevism had its ultraleftists in 1917 who were quickly suppressed, just as Fascism had its early libertarians and antiauthoritarians. But Fascism, unlike Leninism, harbored all the right-wing tenets it was to display in 1921-22 as early as 1919. It is not the case (1) that Fascists put together rightist convictions after 1921, or (2) that their rightism derived from nationalist sources. Unlike Len-

115

inism, whatever rightism was to be found in Fascism was already present at the origins of the movement.

It is not the case that Fascism was proletarian in orientation at its founding and subsequently became bourgeois. Fascism was never simply proletarian or bourgeois. Fascism, from its inception, sought to recruit from all classes, among proletarians as well as among the productive and technical bourgeoisie. As early as 1909, in fact, the young Mussolini had alluded to the elements of the productive bourgeoisie that might serve as allies in the regeneration of Italy.[56] By 1918, he could speak of members of the "so-called bourgeoisie" as potential recruits of a renovating revolutionary movement.[57] By 1919 the major syndicalist theoreticians, like Mussolini, were addressing themselves to all the productive classes of the peninsula. The distinction they chose to draw was between productive and nonproductive elements of the population rather than the studied distinction between the bourgeoisie and the proletariat. It was not a question of class origins, the syndicalists insisted, but a question of what individuals or groups of individuals would be necessary to the productive program of integral national syndicalism.[58] Fascism, thus, never sought an exclusively proletarian base. The veterans who constituted the first recruits of nascent Fascism derived, in fact, from all classes. Since national syndicalists were prepared to grant that the nation represented the most fundamental interests of all Italians, it would be unlikely that they would seek to recruit exclusively among proletarians. As early as 1911, Olivetti was prepared to grant that national interests encompassed the interests of the proletariat, and by 1915 he recognized that those same interests involved the concerns of the productive bourgeoisie as well.[59]

Thus, by the time the Fascist movement was founded in March of 1919, all the ideological and doctrinal elements that were to characterize it were already well articulated. If Fascism was to be right-wing because of its multi-class recruitment, its emphasis on production, as well as the integralist and authoritarian functions it accorded the state, then Fascism was rightist from its inception. That some themes received more explicit restatement as the movement recruited masses of different class provenience is not particularly significant. No more so than the fact that Bolshevism was clearly more libertarian and anarcho-syndicalist when it recruited among displaced peasants and organized labor than when it had to attract the technical and enterprisory bourgeoisie. If one sees some merit in making a distinction between a democratic or libertarian phase in mass-mobilizing revolutionary movements, and a subsequent rightist or "Thermidorian" phase, then such a characterization would seem to apply equally well to the first phases of Bolshevism as to the first phases of Fascism. All of which would tell us very little about the ideological intentions of the movement. In each case there were relatively constant ideological and doctrinal commitments subtending the different phases.

Long before Fascism became a successful mass-mobilizing movement, it entertained ideological, doctrinal, and programmatic commitments which it acted out once in power. Those commitments were largely, if not exclusively, the product of the intellectual enterprise of the most aggressive and youthful revolutionary syndicalists. While the first generation of syndicalists, like Arturo Labriola, early fell away from Fascism, those like Agostino Lanzillo, Massimo Rocca, Michele Bianchi, Edmondo Rossoni, Michels, Olivetti, and Panunzio became immediately or in the course of time, the ideologues of the new movement, most of them remaining with the movement until their deaths or until the destruction of Italian Fascism at the close of the Second World War.

The tactical maneuvers of the first Fascism—specific responses to immediate issues—hardly determined the core content of its ideological and doctrinal commitments. Advocacy of the confiscation of church property, abolition of the Senate, or proportional representation, was hardly more influential in determining the ultimate character of the movement than was Lenin's advocacy, in 1917, of a constituent assembly to determine the will of the Russian people. Bol-

117

sheviks were as quick to abjure their commitment to a democratically-elected constituent assembly as were Fascists to abandon the demand for a confiscation of war profits or church property. In neither case should ideological or doctrinal commitments be confused with the tactical postures assumed at any specific juncture in the revolutionary process.

Four months before the Fascist seizure of power, Edmondo Rossoni could address the first congress of Fascist syndicalists and outline a program that was, in all its essentials, the program of the revolutionary national syndicalists of 1919. He spoke of the requirements of increased and rationalized production. He spoke of the nation as the historic foundation of contemporary revolutionary politics. To the five hundred labor delegates who represented half a million Italian workers, Rossoni insisted that the proletariat of Italy did not have the technical skills nor the institutional disciplines necessary for the maintenance and furtherance of the nation's productive system. What was required, he maintained, was a collaborative enterprise involving all the productive categories of the nation, the new and dynamic entrepreneurial bourgeoisie, the displaced, revolutionary intellectuals, the agrarian small-property holders, the agricultural workers, and the national proletariat. He characterized such a program as that of Fascist nationalism, a program that had little to do with the gouty and traditional "old nationalism" of the decadent bourgeoisie.[60]

Like the revolutionary national syndicalists of 1919, Rossoni, in 1922, recognized that the Fascist program was designed to shepherd the population of the peninsula through the stages of economic modernization and large-scale industrial enterprise. Only by bringing to a conclusion the "bourgeois tasks" of national integration, economic modernization and development could the population of Italy escape the centuries old humiliation and oppression at the hands of more advanced states.[61]

Rossoni, in 1922 and 1923, simply provided a synoptic and stenographic rendering of arguments that had become commonplace among the revolutionary syndicalists by the end of the First World War. Rossoni argued that Italy had not completed the prerequisite bourgeois cycle necessary for the birth of socialism, and as a consequence faced tasks for which Marx had left no formulae. Italy required not the post-industrial revolution anticipated by Marx, but an organization of production calculated to create a modern economic base for a retarded social system. In order to accomplish so demanding a task, Rossoni insisted, Fascist syndicalists must invoke sentiment and interest. The nation must be understood to be the repository of collective sentiment on the one hand and conceived of as one great economic syndicate on the other. The union of sentiment and interest would provide the energy, the dedication, and the collective discipline that would carry Italy to a higher stage of associated life.[62]

Thus before its merger with Italian nationalism in 1923 —in fact even before Fascism began to attract the displaced middle-class intellectuals, the small and large-scale property holders of the Po valley, and the support of individual businessmen in early 1922—Fascism had as well defined an ideological and doctrinal personality as any revolutionary mass-mobilizing movement in the twentieth century. Every element of Fascist doctrine can be traced to the belief system of revolutionary national syndicalism as that syndicalism emerged from the First World War.

At the base of Fascist ideology was the commitment to a solidarist or integral community. Only in association could individual men achieve their full potential. Between 1914 and 1921, Sergio Panunzio developed the ethical and philosophical rationale for the "Stato Etico," the Hegelian "totalitarian" state. By the time Panunzio published *Lo stato di diritto* in 1922, there was, on the part of revolutionary syndicalism, a recognition that the state was not only the juridical incarnation of the nation, but it was an "ethico-pedagogical organism" obliged to raise the consciousness of all citizens to the level of associated, hence "non-alienated"

119

life. Statute law, Panunzio argued, provided the partial integration of the individual into a law-governed community, but moral education provided for the full integration of the empirical self into the universality of national life. The anti-statism of the first syndicalism had evolved into the "ethical" and "totalitarian state" of Hegel and Giovanni Gentile.[63] In this new context, Panunzio reinvoked themes he had employed as a revolutionary syndicalist theoretician years before. The syndicates were understood to be those interest groups animated by immediate material concerns. They provided the consensual behaviors that characterized material activities. The state, in turn, was the originator and repository of statute law potentially capable of inuring men to their ultimate, if not yet fully conscious, interests. The sentiment of nationality, which animated the union, was the product of peer group pressure, the result of man's dispositional need to identify with a limited number of his species. In the years that followed, Panunzio was to expand upon these constant themes.

If Italians were to actualize their full potential, the nation had to break the fetters of economic retardation. In order to accomplish this, the energies of men must be invoked by effective political myth, the tapping of pervasive sentiment and abiding interest. The consciousness of the masses must be elevated to the responsibilities of modern obligations. The masses must be organized, educated, trained to effective and serviceable skills, integrated into the productive and life processes of the community. The state must take on supervisory, pedagogical, and tutelary obligations. The nation must be united behind the leadership of a politically dynamic and goal-directed elite.[64]

Under this revolutionary dispensation, the structure of the state would be composed of worker and entrepreneurial syndicates. All the productive and vital elements of social life would be concentrated in specific communities of interest, each animated and synthesized by the sentiment of national identity.[65] By 1929 all these ideas found expression in Panunzio's *Il sentimento dello stato*.[66] By 1939 his *Teoria generale dello stato fascista* became a standard work of Fascist ideological apologetics.[67]

A similar process can be traced in the work of Olivetti. By 1924 he could synthesize all the convictions of revolutionary national syndicalism into a social, philosophical, and doctrinal rationale for the Fascist revolution.[68] By 1930 Olivetti could provide a rationale for the Fascist state by reinvoking all the themes we have traced in the evolution of revolutionary syndicalism.[69]

We shall have occasion to reconstruct a similar process in the works of Michels, who after his official adherence to Fascism, was selected by Mussolini to become one of the principal ideologues of the regime.

Thus, whatever else it was, Fascism was the heir of a long intellectual tradition that found its origins in the ambiguous legacy left to revolutionaries in the work of Karl Marx and Friedrich Engels. Fascism was, in a clear and significant sense, a Marxist heresy. It was a Marxism creatively developed to respond to the particular and specific needs of an economically retarded national community condemned, as a proletarian nation, to compete with the more advanced plutocracies of its time for space, resources, and international stature.

Fascism and Bolshevism

Fascists early recognized their affinities with Lenin's Bolshevism. As early as 1914, Dino Grandi, who was to loom large during the years of the regime, and who had taken at least some of his intellectual inspiration from revolutionary syndicalism,[70] insisted that the First World War was a "class struggle between nations," the "proletarian nations" against those that enjoyed every "plutocratic" advantage.[71] In 1920 Grandi could argue that Italian socialists had failed to understand the simple reality of what was transpiring in revolutionary Russia. Grandi maintained that the Bolshevik revolution was nothing less than the struggle of an underdeveloped and proletarian nation against the more advanced capitalist states.[72]

In mid-1921 Olivetti reminded socialists that Marxism had always conceived the revolution to be a function of the maturity of society's economic base. As a consequence, whatever was transpiring in Russia could not be a socialist revolution understood in any comprehensible theoretical sense. Russia, Olivetti argued, clearly faced bourgeois developmental, and not distributionist socialist, tasks.[73] Because the Bolsheviks failed to early perceive the nature of their historic responsibilities, the process of development, begun under the Czars, had begun to flag. A socialist program of distribution was totally inappropriate in an economy of declining productivity.[74] The Bolsheviks failed to acknowledge that where the industrial and economic base of society was not mature, the proletariat could only be devoid of all the technical and psychological prerequisites of the socialism Marx had anticipated.[75]

Mussolini's judgments concerning the Bolshevik revolution are similarly instructive in this regard. For our purposes, the Fascist characterization of Lenin's Bolsheviks as "traitors" during the conflict against the Germans is of little consequence.[76] More interesting is the fact that by 1919, Mussolini could refer to the absolute decline in economic productivity in Soviet Russia as evidence of its failure to recognize its historic obligations.[77] Mussolini argued that the ground of revolutionary politics in the twentieth century must necessarily be the historic nation in which the sentiment and the interests of contemporary populations are anchored. As a consequence, he insisted that whatever Bolsheviks might say, they must ultimately commit themselves to national reconstruction and national defense.[78] In effect, whatever his immediate postures, Lenin must inevitably give himself over to some form of national socialism. Because the exigencies of national politics in the twentieth century required the expansion and modernization of retarded or underdeveloped economies, Lenin would necessarily have to appeal to bourgeois expertise in the effort to restore and expand Russia's impaired economic potential. A retarded or underdeveloped economic system required, of necessity, the talents of the bourgeoisie. As early as 1919, Mussolini referred to Lenin's inability to address all these issues as evidence of Bolshevism's failure to comprehend the revolutionary necessities of the times.[79]

Because the maintenance and development of industry required a disciplined and technically efficient labor force, Mussolini argued that Bolshevism must necessarily "domesticate" labor to the task of intensive development.[80] Mussolini maintained that all of this could well have been anticipated since Marxism had made quite clear that society required the fullest maturation of the economic base before any form of socialism was possible.[81] What Russia required, in effect, was a form of developmental national socialism.

By 1921 the Bolsheviks found themselves possessed of a nation in ruins. The national income of Russia had been reduced to one third of that of 1913. Industrial output had declined to one fifth during the same period. The economic infrastructure of the nation had disintegrated under the pressures of international conflict, revolution, and civil war. By 1922, threatened with total collapse, anarchy, and famine, the Bolsheviks took stock of their revolutionary illusions and the economic and political realities of their time. A monetary economy was reintroduced. Peasant land tenure was (at least temporarily) assured in the effort to promote agricultural production. The profit motive was reintroduced in industry. Orthodox fiscal policies were reestablished with the stabilization of the ruble in 1923. At the same time that capitalism resurfaced in much of the economy, the Bolsheviks "commanded the heights" with increasingly authoritarian, bureaucratic, and oligarchic decision-making procedures.

Throughout the period between 1917 and 1923, the Bolsheviks had no real, coherent domestic policy. Their tactical

123

activities were governed by a conviction that the European revolution would erupt and provide the advanced economic base that all Marxists understood was prerequisite to international socialism. In 1918 Lenin publicly lamented that "at all events, under all conceivable circumstances, if the German revolution does not come, we are doomed."[82] Thus, while the first Fascists were organizing for a national revolution, the Bolsheviks were still absorbed in the dream of international insurrection. It was an illusion that was to fitfully persist until Stalin announced the advent of a "creative development" of Marxism: a national socialism.

Fascists watched the devolution of Leninism with considerable satisfaction. What had begun with the anarcho-syndicalist promises of Lenin's *The State and Revolution* had rapidly developed into a hierarchical and authoritarian governance of a weak and faltering economy. Lenin began to speak of discipline and obedience. Where the first phases of the Bolshevik revolution were characterized by spontaneous movements "from below"—the seizure of property and plants by workers and peasants—it soon became evident that the economic system could not be stabilized, much less developed and rendered more productive, without increasingly hierarchical controls. In early 1919 Lenin spoke of the introduction of the "most energetic, ruthlessly determined and Draconian measures to improve the self-discipline and discipline of the workers and peasants of Russia." In terms more than reminiscent of Fascist authoritarianism, he spoke of holding the entire fabric of society together with "a single iron will."[83] Where he could speak of the state "withering away" immediately after the revolution in February 1917, by March 1918 Lenin admitted that any such withering away of the state was "still a long way off."[84] Lenin began to speak of "one man managerial authority" which he frankly admitted could be conceived of as "dictatorial." He spoke of the maintenance of the "strictest order created by the single will" of managerial and state control and of the necessity of fostering "large scale machine industry" through a

124

control apparatus that would restore "discipline" to the working class. Like Fascism's national syndicalists, he conceived of labor unions as state agencies responsible for carrying out the policies of the central government. "It is quite impossible," he went on, "to fulfill this task without coercion. We need the state, we need coercion."[85]

Thus, while the first Fascists were formulating the rationale for a mass-mobilizing, developmental, authoritarian, hierarchical, and statist program, the Bolsheviks were forced to assume similar postures by the course of events. For the revolutionary national syndicalists of Italy, the devolution of Bolshevism confirmed their analysis. In an underdeveloped economy, the proletariat has neither the technical competence nor the consciousness requisite to the fulfillment of bourgeois developmental tasks. Lenin's long essay on "The Immediate Tasks of the Soviet Government," written in March-April 1918, was a candid recognition of the fundamental backwardness of Russia and of the Russian proletariat. Since the proletariat was technically and organizationally unsuited for the management of a developmental system, it could only be driven to the tasks of development through what Lenin termed "the sharp forms of dictatorship." More than that, Lenin went on to admit, the technical and entrepreneurial bourgeoisie would have to be attracted to the service of the state through the payment of differential wages. The bourgeoisie would have to be cajoled, coerced, or bribed into collaboration with the Soviet state in an obvious analogue to Fascist "class collaboration."[86]

During this stage of devolution, Lenin spoke of the system he had introduced as "state capitalism"—a form of forced industrialization that would bring to Russia all the benefits of capitalism. In effect, Lenin, in arguing against the "Left Communists," insisted that capitalism had not completed its cycle in Russia. The Bolshevik government was committed to a program of state-controlled capitalism, complete with a monetary economy, private incentive, and the payment of differential wages that would insure the collaboration of the productive elements of the bourgeoisie, a domestication of labor, and a hierarchical, elite control of the entire process in the service of national economic development. Lenin's talk, which until 1917 had been characteristically distributionist, became, after 1918, increasingly productionist. The libertarian, anarcho-syndicalist pronouncements of *The State and Revolution* were lost in the authoritarian and etatist organizational principles of state capitalism.[87] Lenin advocated the typically capitalist expedients of piece work and the rationalization of productive practices embodied in the American "Taylor system."[88]

Between the period of Lenin's advocacy of state capitalism and the renewed effort at economic development undertaken with the New Economic Policy of 1922, the Bolsheviks slid into the horrors of what was to be called "war communism." But it is clear that as early as 1918 Lenin had begun to recognize the requirements of his time. What "proletarian Russia" required was not "left-wing childishness," but rapid industrial development under state auspices and unitary party control.[89] This historic judgment, already arrived at by the revolutionary national syndicalists in the case of proletarian Italy, was reflected in the Fascism to which Italian syndicalists committed themselves.

FIVE

THE POLITICAL ECONOMY OF FASCISM

While it has become traditional to deny Fascism any ideological substance, it is specifically Fascist economic policy that is most frequently deemed innocent of any programmatic commitment or consistency whatsoever. Fascism, so conventional wisdom would have it, acceded to power without any immediate or general economic program.[1] Alternatively, it is held that Fascism's economic policies were those of industrial, financial, or agrarian captalists, or, in turn, all the elements of the "big bourgeoisie" in collusion.[2]

Actually, most modern scholarship agrees that such facile judgments are, in a substantial sense, false. First of all, it can easily be established that Fascism, prior to its advent to power, advertised a specific program addressed to immediate problems that afflicted the national economy. Moreover, Fascism entertained a long-range economic program that was reasonably well articulated in the doctrinal literature of 1921 and 1922. Furthermore, while it is true that Fascism's immediate, and some considerable part of its more comprehensive programs, were not incompatible with the interests of important segments of Italy's economic elite, those programs were autonomous, originating among its principal ideologues before allies previously unattached to the movement joined forces with Fascism. Whatever accommodation there might have been with the established economic interests of the peninsula, this accommodation was a contingent, rather than a constituent, characteristic of Fascist economic policy.

127

As we have seen, by 1918, the national syndicalists were prepared to commit themselves to the economic development of the peninsula under the auspices of a revolutionary vanguard inspired by a national ideal. Their critical attention was, as we shall see, largely devoted to the problems of how labor might be organized under such circumstances. And, as in all revolutionary movements, the judgments of how the entire process might be conducted varied with each spokesman. Nonetheless, a common core of implications—easily inferred from the recognition that Italy suffered the special disabilities that attend underdevelopment—lent shape to shared economic commitments.

The national syndicalists opposed the impostures of international, plutocratic capitalism. The "Greater Italy" that they anticipated emerging from the trial of the First World War would require the expansion and technical modernization of its industrial potential if it were to survive. As a consequence, national syndicalists were opposed to any political experiments that might impair Italy's economic potential. They rejected, as we have seen, the "radicalism" of Lenin's Bolshevism on the grounds that it was "ahistoric" in its attempt to introduce, in a totally unsuited economic environment, a socialism predicated on the availability of a mature industrial base. They understood the collapse of Russia's economy after the Bolshevik Revolution to have been largely the consequence of Bolshevism's failure to recognize its historic obligations. At least in part because of the Bolshevik experience, the national syndicalists rejected class warfare as an element of their revolutionary strategy. Instead, they understood their historic responsibilities to be those that would foster, refurbish, expand, and modernize Italy's nascent industrial system. To that end, they advocated a careful marshalling and orchestration of the energies of all productive classes on the peninsula. Italy remained, in their judgment, at the bourgeois phase of economic development and, as a consequence, would require bourgeois talents, energy, and participation. Capitalism had not, in effect, completed its historic cycle.

If national syndicalists were prepared to recognize the potential vitality of Italian industrial capitalism, they were equally prepared to recognize the deficiencies of the Italian proletariat. The national syndicalists early argued that the working classes of Italy displayed clear evidence of an incapacity to control, govern, and expand the industrial and economic potential of the nation.[3] As we have seen, everything they had learned from Marx and Sorel had taught them that the proletariat is equipped to govern an advanced industrial system only through long exposure to, and experience with, such a system. Advanced industrial systems train the proletariat to its historic tasks. Where such industrial systems have not yet developed, the proletariat could only remain immature, innocent of the technical, planning, and administrative skills necessary for the superintendence of a complex economy.

All of this had evident implications for economic policy. Thus, while Fascism adopted a variety of tactical postures during the first two years of its development, by 1921 the movement had put together a program that prefigured the economic policy to be immediately implemented by the subsequent regime.[4] Given the recognition that Italy had only begun its industrial development, and that its development would be capitalist in character, the Fascist program of 1921 advocated immediate tax reforms that would stimulate savings as a source of investment capital for the expansion of the productive base of the nation. The program also advocated a reorganization of the financial structure of government and a reform of the administrative apparatus of the state on the grounds that both contributed to the nonproductive employment of scarce capital at a time when the nation required all its financial resources to expand and modernize.

The program of 1921 also supported a return of the tele-

129

phonic, telegraphic, and postal systems to private enterprise, in the belief that the state, as it was then constituted, had demonstrated its incapacity to effectively and economically direct and administer them, and, as a consequence, wasted scarce investment resources. In point of fact, the first Fascism directed a great deal of attention to the nonproductive employment of capital. Fascist objections to the state support of cooperatives, for example, turned on the contention that the capital employed in such subventions could be more efficiently employed in the expansion and modernization of existing plants, rather than in experiments with collective ownership, management, and control.[5]

In summary, the immediate economic policy of the Fascists in 1921 entailed: (1) the generation of investment capital in economic circumstances of capital scarcity; which implied (2) a reform of tax and financial legislation and (3) a reduction of state expenditures and a balancing of the budget to that end; all (4) in the service of expanding and rationalizing the economic capabilities of the nation.

Ancillary to these commitments was the advocacy of the expansion of the communications and transportation infrastructure of the developing nation. Thus, the Fascist program of 1921 supported an expansion of the peninsula's rail, maritime, and road systems. Tariff protection was to be offered to noncompetitive industries in the face of pressure by foreign producers. In an effort to reduce trade imbalances, a promise of public works was extended with emphasis on the development of hydroelectric power as a substitute for imported fossil fuels in resource-impoverished Italy. All of this was to be conducted in an environment of disciplined class collaboration, which would allow for the expansion of educational facilities and the inculcation of a new public morality.

Thus, by 1921, Italians had every reason to believe that Fascism offered a reasonably specific and immediate economic program for the nation. Fascism promised protection for private property as long as that property served the developmental needs of the nation. Small property holdings would be insured as long as the economic needs of the peninsula could be met. State fiscal responsibilities would be discharged, savings accelerated, investments fostered, inflation controlled, unemployment reduced, public works instituted, private enterprise protected, and organized labor integrated into a program of national development.

In such guise, Fascism's economic program was one that could be attractive to economic liberals as well as national syndicalists. Economic liberals conceived the program as productivist and national syndicalists understood it as harbinger of a "New Italy," a revolutionary policy that would provide the economic and industrial modernization that Italian syndicalists had long advocated. It allowed, for example, ample room for "market mechanisms" to influence the course of events. Both Italian liberals and national syndicalists had long advocated such policies. As we have seen, the syndicalists, no less than the liberals, had early identified with the "Manchestrianism" and the free trade policies of economists like Maffeo Pantaleoni. Pantaleoni, on his own account, supported Fascist economic policy largely because of its liberal and free market character.[6]

But for all its real and seemingly Manchestrian character —its advocacy of the immediate reduction of the parliamentary state functions to those of finance, police, and defense— Fascist economic policy was far from liberal. Fascists early anticipated a corporative and revolutionary state that would displace the ineffectual parliamentary regime. That new state would undertake extensive intervention in labor relations; it would institute tariff protection (and, by implication, subventions) for selected industries. Moreover, Fascists expected that their strong state would provide the impetus for the expansion and modernization of the entire economic infrastructure of the nation—the development of hydroelectric power, irrigation systems, land redevelopment, and

131

reforestation. The revolutionary state was expected to institute a system of education charged with creating citizens capable of guaranteeing the economic progress of the nation. That state would inculcate the new national consciousness neglected by the "agnostic" state.

Nevertheless, in the first years of Fascist rule, there were many reasons, both political and economic, that rendered Fascists well disposed toward relatively liberal economic policies. Most of Fascism's nonmovement allies were liberal by persuasion, and Mussolini's control over the peninsula was far from secure between 1922 and 1925. To have alienated liberal support would have been politically ill-advised. Moreover, there was good reason to believe that the Italian economy had inherent strengths and that the creation of a stable political order and the enactment of legislation favoring savings and capital accumulation would stimulate economic and industrial expansion. But for all that, Fascists made equally evident their intention to intervene anywhere whenever they saw a threat to their overall program.

This should have been evident to everyone. As has already been indicated, by the beginning of 1922 Sergio Panunzio had published his *Lo stato di diritto* in which he committed himself, as a Fascist ideologue, to the conception of the "total state," the state as an "ethico-pedagogic" organism charged with the tutelary obligation of protecting the collective interests of those generations of Italians as yet unborn.[7] Such a state could hardly be the individualistic Manchestrian state so dear to economic liberals. In fact, Panunzio's conception of the total state is clearly the ideological rationale for the dirigentist and interventionist state.

Fascist intentions were implicit in much of the propaganda during the first years of Fascist rule. When Panunzio spoke of the liberalism of Fascism, it was clearly a very singular liberalism. He spoke of it as a liberalism of groups rather than a liberalism of individuals, that is, an "ordering and disciplining" individuals and groups under the aegis of a "hierarchical" and "revolutionary" "New State."[8] In retrospect, Panunzio's liberalism of 1922 appears to have all the descriptive characteristics of the totalitarianism of 1935.

Panunzio articulated these convictions while he was the principal intellectual spokesman of Ferrarese Fascism. And Ferrara was one of the two main centers from which Fascism radiated outward during its mass-mobilizing phase.[9] In effect, Panunzio was a Fascist spokesman of authority, and it is clear that he conceived of Fascism's general, as distinct from its immediate, economic program as far from liberal in any traditional sense of the term. More than that, Panunzio's judgments reflected Fascist opinion as it was expressed in official party documents.

By 1921, Fascism had a relatively specific economic program that was to govern its immediate enterprise. As the time drew closer for the Fascist seizure of power, that economic program became increasingly specific, and by the end of 1922 Fascism's immediate economic program had been all but fully articulated.

There was little that was unorthodox about that program. Beneath the surface of orthodox intentions, however, were all the implications of a much more portentious long-range economic policy. The outlines of that policy are best expressed in the works of Alfredo Rocco, who came to Fascism as one of the principal theoreticians of Italian nationalism.

Alfredo Rocco, Nationalism, and the Economic Policy of Fascism

The national syndicalists who had articulated Fascism's ideological commitments had, as we have seen, early advocated a policy of national development. By the termination of the First World War, they had identified themselves as productivists, advocates of the rapid industrialization of the peninsula. By 1918, they recognized that the international class struggle against the plutocratic nations required that Italy solve the problems of economic retardation, overpopulation, and political ineffectiveness, by undergoing the arduous process of economic development and modernization.

It was in this context that the work of Alfredo Rocco began to take on more and more significance for Fascists. The national syndicalists had developed a program for the syndical and corporative organization of the economic activities of the peninsula, but their commitments to a general economic program remained generic and unspecific. On the other hand, as early as 1914, Italian nationalists had articulated a long-range economic program for the peninsula. And it was Rocco who was, at that time, nationalism's principal architect and spokesman.[10]

Alfredo Rocco, born in Naples on the 9th of September, 1875, had come to Italian nationalism out of a rigorously academic background. In his youth, he had identified himself with the political left, the socialists and the radicals,[11] but by the time he returned actively to politics in 1913, he had committed himself to a specifically antisocialist and antiliberal national and developmental program.

Given these commitments, Rocco opposed both orthodox socialism and economic liberalism on the grounds that both ill-served the nation's economic and industrial development. He argued that both, predicated as they were on hedonism and individualism respectively, were calculated to foster consumption and dissipate energies rather than stimulate development. Like the national syndicalists, with whom he early sympathized, Rocco maintained that Italy was an economically retarded nation forced to compete in the international arena with far more powerful nations for resources, capital, markets, and space. Liberalism, failing to understand the Italian predicament, would reduce Italy to a dependent "client state," while orthodox socialism, because of its preoccupation with "equitable distribution" would dissipate the nation's scant capital on "demagogic" programs. Italy's only recourse, Rocco argued, was a program of rapid economic and industrial development, productive rationalization and industrial expansion under the aegis of a strong state.

To serve these ends, Rocco advocated a program of intensive capital accumulation to offset the general capital scarcity that had characterized the economic takeoff of the peninsula a scant generation before. He insisted on a state-supported policy of technological innovation and an orchestration of citizen support in a political program he identified as "national syndicalism."[12]

With the passage of time, he elaborated these themes. He rejected traditional economic liberalism and socialism as politico-economic strategies that would merely redistribute the scarce welfare benefits available to Italians at a time when Italy's population had already exceeded the carrying capacity of the nation. Rocco characterized Italy as a country hurt by the proliferation of self-serving capitalists, artisans, intellectuals, civil servants, and workers, each pursuing immediate interests to the detriment of any overall policy of collective development and modernization. He insisted that such special interest groups could only generate centrifugal tensions in a nation faced by the competition of more resource and capital-favored nations. As a consequence, he advocated the creation of a strong state capable of articulating a nationalist policy that would coordinate all the parochial, regional, and special interests of the nation in a collective undertaking calculated to foster economic expansion and rationalization.[13] He believed the ultimate goal to be some sort of effective economic self-sufficiency for the peninsula, a capacity to use the nation's own resources to support its growing population, provide for its collective defense, and meet the needs of a modern industrial and economic system. To reach this goal, Italy—which had arrived late at the first phase of industrialization, afflicted as she was with resource and capital shortfall, burdened by a population density

135

unmatched almost anywhere on the Continent—required discipline, sacrifice, careful political calculation, and a rigorous policy of economic stimulation.[14]

By 1919, the Central Committee of the Nationalist Association published a "Political Program," written by Rocco, in which all these themes were restated. The specific economic planks of this program turned on financial and tax reform that would stimulate the capital accumulation necessary for the immediate expansion of national production. There was a demand, moreover, for a reduction in the economic activities of the state as it was then constituted. In his reply to queries, Rocco made quite clear that the advocacy of the reduction of state involvement in the economy was not based on an opposition to state intervention in principal, but was the consequence of the ineptitude of the existing parliamentary system. Only a "corporativist" or "national syndicalist" state, orchestrating the multiplicity of organized interest groups that constituted the productive and functional organs of the nation, could effectively intervene in the national economy. As long as such a state remained only an aspiration, the parliamentary and political state should be reduced to those functions absolutely necessary for the immediate survival of the national community.

The Nationalist Association program of 1919, like that of the first Fascism, called for a reform of the state bureaucracy in the effort to reduce expenses, inefficiency, and redundancy. It called for fiscal reform calculated to balance the state budget, tax reform which would insure an adequate financial base for state activities and stimulate savings that could be employed in capital investment. The program called for an expansion of Italy's merchant marine, increased technical efficiency in agriculture, and an expansion of industrial plants, if necessary with the support of tariff protection.[15]

In the effort to reduce the dependency on the importation of fossil fuels, Rocco, like the first Fascists, called for the rapid expansion of the facilities for hydroelectric power, the subsequent electrification of Italy's network of railways, and a more efficient and serviceable national road system.[16] The central theme throughout remained the urgent necessity to increase the productive potential of the national community, which would not only require the mobilization of collective energies, but the massive accumulation of investment capital.[17] The urgency surrounding capital formation found regular expression in Rocco's demand that Italy's tax system be reorganized to favor capital accumulation. The first problem Italy faced if it were to become a "great industrial state" was the problem of capital accumulation.

In substance, the Association's program contained the economic policy proposed by the Fascists in 1921, two years before the merger of the two movements. Both movements had begun the process of ideological rapprochement. But more than that, Rocco's economic program for the nation explicitly formulated a number of long-range goals that were present, but often only implicitly, in Fasoist literature, or appeared there in fragmentary form. The long-range economic program revealed in Rocco's earliest publications anticipated several developmental phases for the nation: the first involved intensive capital accumulation and investment, the development of both the economic infrastructure and the basic heavy industries necessary for rapid industrialization. The subsequent phase would involve the development of national self-sufficiency at least in terms of those critical industries necessary to national defense and political independence. The final phase would be territorial and market expansion—predicated on the antecedent industrial growth and economic modernization—that would permit Italy the economic self-sufficiency prerequisite to its assumption of the responsibilities of a "great power."[18]

In 1921 Rocco focused on the immediate problems that faced the Italian economy. His programmatic recommendations became increasingly specific and were fully consonant with those advertised by the first Fascists. As a case in point, Rocco, like the Fascists, opposed the demand that stockholdings in Italy be registered in the name of the individual stockholder on the grounds that such legislation, given the real threat of punitive taxation, would precipitate the flight of capital and reduce the disposition among those with funds to invest in Italian industry. On the same grounds, both Rocco and the first Fascists opposed the heavy tax on property and inheritance. Rocco, like the national syndicalists, similarly opposed the surtax on putative "war profits" as being "demagogic" in character, lacking in specificity, and inhibiting capital formation at a time when capital investment was critical to Italy's industrial and economic future.[19]

As we have seen, by the time of its advent to power, Fascism had an immediate economic program that distinguished it from its political competitors on the peninsula. It was a program that shared many affinities with that of Alfredo Rocco. This immediate program represented the first phase of a general developmental plan, and, while it had features that rendered it reasonably attractive to economic liberals, it was not a liberal economic program. Not only did it harbor an explicit interventionist and dirigentist disposition, it was also committed, in the final analysis, to an antiliberal program of national self-sufficiency. The goals of Fascism's long-range economic policies, were in fact and in effect, not liberal goals. When the national syndicalists identified the nation as the primary object of loyalty in the modern world, they committed themselves, by implication, to an antiliberal economic policy designed to advance Italy to the rank of a modern, industrialized state, a policy which involved, ultimately, the creation of an "autarchic" community, resting on an adequate resource and territorial base that would enable Italy to become a great power.[20]

While liberals conceived of an interdependent world market, characterized by an international division of labor, Fascists committed themselves to a world view characterized by international class struggle, in which plutocratic nations opposed the aspirations of proletarian nations. The inspiration for this was not Adam Smith, but Friedrich List.[21]

Like List, Rocco and the Fascists were to argue that as long as the nation was at all dependent upon foreign imports of raw materials, specifically fossil fuels and iron ore, to sustain its industrial activities, and upon foodstuffs to support its population, the range of its political options would be dictated by foreign plutocracies, sated and conservative capitalist powers.[22] Only with the creation of a modern industrial sector and a viable agricultural economy could Italy ultimately aspire to the conquest of foreign markets, secure sources of requisite raw materials, and gain access to territories where it might settle its excess population.[23]

Both the national syndicalists and Rocco's nationalists conceived the nation to be the single most important social community of the modern world, and, as a consequence, both framed economic problems in singularly national terms. The nation was understood to be the foundation of each man's personal identity as well as the principal historic agent in the modern world. And it was "economic space," resource availability, and support capacity, that determined how far, and to what effect, that development would proceed. The first theoreticians of Fascism recognized that continental powers—nations like the United States, Russia, and ultimately China, all possessed of singular resource and territorial advantages—possessed all the prerequisites for future survival and international power. Nations like England, France, and Japan had won similar advantages, and would exercise international power only by expanding into the resource and territorial space that remained available. Italy, with few resources and a growing but confined population, was singularly disadvantaged. Without rapid industrialization and subsequent commercial and territorial expansion, Italy must resign herself to economic and political dependency upon more favored nations.[24]

While all these themes found expression in the prose of Alfredo Rocco, they were both implicit and explicit in Fascist thought as early as the founding meeting at the Piazza San Sepolcro, and in the thought of national syndicalists at least from the time of the war in Tripoli. These same themes had animated the interventionists in their defense of the victory at the conclusion of the First World War. Although, in spite of this confluence, a considerable number of nationalists continued to entertain reservations, men like Rocco had recognized that by the beginning of 1922 there was little that could distinguish the long-range economic program of the Nationalist Association from that of Fascism.[25]

Fascism's commitment to production, its appeal to the rapid industrialization and modernization of the nation, was clearly compatible with nationalist economic goals. As early as 1918, before the formal founding of the Fascist movement, the nationalists recognized that Fascism's national syndicalist appeal to industrial development was fully compatible with the program advanced by Rocco in 1914.[26] With Fascism's abandonment of the tactical demand for an extraordinary tax on war profits, to which nationalists had objected as an unnecessary and demagogic restriction on capital formation,[27] the economic policies of Fascist national syndicalism increasingly approximated those of the nationalists. By December 1922, less than two months after the March on Rome, Rocco could insist that Fascism had acceded to power possessed of an economic policy that was specific in terms of long-range goals as well as immediate tactical programs.[28] Under the auspices of the coalition government that characterized the first years of Mussolini's rule, legislation was implemented that inaugurated the first phase of Fascism's economic program.

Economic Policy from 1922 until the Great Depression

In retrospect, it is quite clear that Fascist economic policy was predicated on the judgment that a revolutionary breakthrough was unnecessary to accomplish the first phase of economic modernization and development of the peninsula. Italy had begun its industrial takeoff during the Giolittian period before the first world conflict. The postwar economic dislocations had impeded the process irregularly, but auspiciously, launched a decade or so before. The rapid industrial expansion that took place during the war,[29] which had so much impressed the young Mussolini, had been obstructed by political policy failures and not by institutional or intrinsic economic constraints. Fascists were convinced that Italy's immediate industrialization and economic modernization did not require "surgical intervention," but an application of "homeopathic" measures: the creation of an auspicious investment climate, the restoration of a stable political order, the provision of a disciplined labor force and a technically efficient managerial and entrepreneurial leadership.[30] Fascists conceived of such a policy as the alternative to the egregiously mistaken policies implemented by Lenin's Bolshevism, and as appropriate to the problems of immediate modernization and development.

Because their goal was clearly industrial and economic modernization and development rather than utopian universal equality and human liberation, Fascists supported specific remedies for specific economic problems. They sought to impose industrial peace, reduce the loss of man-hours in labor time as a consequence of strikes and lockouts, restore the efficiency of public services, renew confidence in the nation's economy, provide for a more rapid accumulation of investment capital, institute a rationalization and modernization of government bureaucracy, maintain, foster, and expand productive plants, communications, and agricultural potential.

While the dislocations that followed the war created grievous tensions for Italy's economy, the resolution of some international economic difficulties assisted Fascism's immediate rehabilitative and developmental efforts.[31] In effect, it early became clear that Fascist judgments had been correct. Italy's economy required homeopathic therapy rather than radical surgery. Italy's immediate postwar problems turned on labor unrest, a dearth of fresh investment capital,

141

the snarl of complex, sometimes conflicting, tax laws, the financial failure of some of the largest industrial and banking establishments on the peninsula, and a crisis in agricultural production.[32] The most urgent problem, in the judgment of almost all commentators of that period, turned on state finances and the tax system that subtended it. A week before the March on Rome, Giolitti insisted that the state's financial difficulties—a state deficit of six billion lire, encumbered by an annual interest payment of 400 million lire—constituted the gravest peril to the economy of the peninsula.[33]

Almost immediately after the March on Rome, Mussolini appointed Alberto De' Stefani Minister of Finance. De' Stefani, armed with special decree powers, proceeded to reform the nation's fiscal system, abolish the extraordinary tax on war profits and property, and rescind the requirement that stocks and bonds be registered in the name of the owner, all in an effort to stimulate savings and capital investment. De' Stefani further undertook to reduce the state's expenditures and balance the national budget. He introduced reforms in the national bureaucracy, reducing both the number of state employees and administrative costs.

At almost the same time, the Fascist government returned the telephone system to private management and opened the insurance industry to private capital, thus abolishing the state monopoly that had been in force since 1912. Ansaldo, one of Italy's largest mechanical and conglomerate industries, and the Banco di Roma, one of the nation's largest financial institutions, were salvaged from liquidation by government intervention. In March of 1923 a parastate consortium was established by decree law to provide low-interest capital loans to industry.

All of this, as has been indicated, had been prefigured in Fascist policy statements before the March on Rome.[34] It was a coherent and relatively well integrated program of fiscal responsibility, capital accumulation, and industrial and economic development.[35] What it produced was a balanced state budget by 1925, a rate of savings and capital accumulation unsurpassed until Italy's "economic miracle" of the 1950s, and a rate of industrial growth that doubled the peninsula's total output by 1929.[36] Iron and steel production was doubled between 1922 and 1926; electrical power generation doubled between 1922 and 1929; the total net tonnage of the Italian merchant marine increased from 835 thousand tons in 1920 to 1,877 thousand tons in 1926.[37] In 1922 Italian industrial production was 81 percent, and by 1929 it was 142 percent, of that of 1913. Italy had sustained a rate of industrial productivity that exceeded the rate of any of its major European competitors. In 1929 the index for total output of French production stood at 139 (1913=100), while the index for Germany, that same year, languished at 111, and the productivity of the United Kingdom failed to reach the levels it had attained in 1913.[38]

These were the years that saw the introduction of "Fordism"—the rationalization and acceleration of production per man-hour—into Italian industrial plants.[39] By 1929 Fascist Italy's output index per man-hour (using 1913 as 100) was 143.7, exceeding that of all its major European competitors save France. In that year Germany's output per man-hour was 113.2, and that of Britain 140.3. Only the output per man-hour of French industry exceeded that of Fascist Italy at 154.6.[40]

What was transpiring in Fascist Italy was evident to most analysts. Even among the most cautious observers, there was a recognition that Italy was undergoing extensive and intensive economic and industrial development and modernization. Franz Borkenau, writing in 1933, could maintain that "Fascism has discharged its historic function. It has multiplied industrial production. Electrification was undertaken, resolving, in part, some of the peninsula's raw materials deficiencies. The automobile and rayon industries have developed into enterprises of world rank. The plodding ways of the past, the pervasive lack of punctuality, have been overcome. The banking system has been centralized, and the independence of the banking institutions in the south has been broken. Agriculture has been modernized. . . . Accumulation of capital has been accelerated and assured."[41]

For Borkenau, Fascism's "historic function" was that of developing the industrial and economic potential of the retarded Italian peninsula. It is, in fact, clear that during the period between 1922 and the international economic crisis of 1929, Italy had experienced a rate of industrial and economic development matched only one time previously in its history, and surpassed only in the 1950s.

By the time of the depression, on the other hand, Italy had already begun to experience difficulty. An inauspicious trade balance, aggravated by large grain, coal, and scrap metal imports, began to create structural tensions throughout the economy. The trade deficit of the beginning of 1926 was one and a third billion lire greater than the deficit of 1922. The consequence was a fairly precipitate decline in the international exchange value of the lire. Between January 1925 and June 1925, the lire fell from an exchange rate of 117.50, to a level of 144.92 lire, to the pound sterling. By the summer of 1926, the lire had fallen to an exchange rate of 153.68 to the English pound.

In the face of the international situation the Fascist government increased its legislative controls over the financial institutions of the peninsula. The centralization of banking to which Borkenau later alluded was begun during 1926. By the fall of 1926 a government *Istituto di Emissione* became the central agency for the issuance of national currency. Although full control was only to be effected with the legislation of 1936, the first substantial moves in state intervention were undertaken during this period.[42]

There were two immediate and important consequences of the international exchange crisis of 1925. The first involved the decision on the part of the Fascist government to undertake a "Battle for Grain" that would make Italy independent of foreign grain imports; the second was a decision to stabilize the lire (the "Battle for the Lire") at an international exchange rate of approximately 90 lire to the pound sterling.

During the years immediately preceding its advent to power, Fascism regularly alluded to Italy's dependency on foreign grain imports as a critical drain on the nation's foreign exchange capabilities. While little could be done to expand the fossil fuel and metal resources of the nation, it was argued, the nation's ability to feed itself might be enhanced by intensive technological and scientific innovations in agriculture. As early as 1923 the Fascist government introduced prizes for increased grain yields in all the provinces of the nation. But in June 1925, as Italy's foreign exchange deficits became increasingly onerous, Mussolini announced the beginning of a systematic program to increase the cereal and grain yield of the peninsula.[43] In 1925 Italy had imported almost twenty-two and a half million quintals of grain at a cost of almost four billion lire, approximately half the outstanding foreign exchange deficit. The clear intention of the Fascist government was to reduce Italy's dependency on foreign bread, the first effort to fulfill the Fascist programmatic goal of making the nation as self-sufficient as possible.

Beginning with 1926 the entire propaganda machinery of the Fascist state was invoked to increase the productivity of Italian agriculture. Conjointly, a vast program of modernization was introduced. The *Cattedre ambulanti d'agricoltura*, traveling agrobiological teams, were dispatched throughout the country to introduce the latest scientific methods of field husbandry. In 1928 an extensive program of land reclamation and improvement was introduced, ultimately involving public expenditures more than three times the total amount spent by all previous governments since the unification of Italy in 1870. The comprehensive program of land reclamation and the technological and scientific modernization of agriculture were to be numbered among the most successful efforts of the regime.[44] Even those postwar commentators who could have little reason to approve any aspect

145

of the Fascist regime, found merit in the programs both in terms of performance and social significance.[45] Production of grain per hectare was increased from 10.5 quintals, which was the annual average for the five years preceding the First World War, to 13.9 quintals per hectare in 1931, to reach 15.2 quintals per hectare in 1932.[46] Irrespective of whether the program benefited the larger rather than the small proprietors, or whether the overall costs were excessive and impaired the production of more commercial agricultural products for export,[47] by 1935 Italy was no longer compelled to expend fifteen percent of its total foreign exchange for the importation of cereals, an expenditure exceeded only by the costs involved in the necessary import of coal.

At the same time the "Battle for Grain" was undertaken, Mussolini decided to stabilize the exchange rate of the lire at a ratio of about 90 lire to the pound sterling, a rate that required the devaluation of the lire within the internal market. The reasons for settling on such a program of stabilization and for selecting that particular rate were many and varied. At the time the Fascists maintained that the reasons included (1) a defense of savings and investment capital; (2) protection for those living on fixed incomes and pensions; (3) the necessity of maintaining a "strong" national currency; and (4) a reduction of foreign imports to those levels absolutely necessary for the maintenance of the developmental program.[48]

The stabilization of the lire at "quota novanta" was undertaken at Mussolini's insistence[49] against the emphatic objections of some of the strongest representatives of Italy's industrial and financial elite. The most convincing evidence available indicates that Mussolini insisted on stabilizing the lire at this rate for political reasons of his own, against the objections of almost the entire leadership of the financial and industrial community.[50] In fact, it was predictable, even then, that stabilization of the lire at that level would be, at best, difficult and would require enormous sacrifice.

While it seems reasonably clear, from an orthodox and

traditional point of view, that Mussolini's decision to peg the lire at "quota novanta" was of doubtful economic value, it seems equally obvious that the Fascist government had a great deal of political capital invested in the "strength" of the "symbol of the nation's wealth."[51] But more important than that, the "Battle for the Lire" seems to have afforded Mussolini the occasion for an extension of Fascist political control over the economy.

In retrospect, it appears that Mussolini had begun to prepare for such an eventuality in 1925. In October of that year he had articulated the formula that constituted the core of Fascist totalitarianism: "Everything within the state, nothing outside the state, and nothing against the state." After the resolution of the political crisis precipitated by the murder of Giacomo Matteotti in 1924, Mussolini had begun to extend his control over the peninsula. In January 1925, he announced the intended "fascistization" of the state. Throughout the period beginning with 1925, Mussolini's brother, Arnaldo, in authoritative articles in *Il popolo d'Italia*, indicated that Fascism, after its political victory, was prepared to "command the economic heights" of the nation.[52] At this time Mussolini himself characterized the processes through which the nation was passing as those which had seen the conclusion of Fascist political victory, and which were now exemplified in Fascism's struggle to domesticate the "existing economic elites."

By 1926 Mussolini gave every indication that he was prepared to extend his controls over the entire economy of the peninsula. In effect, the first phase of Fascist economic policy had been concluded. Fascism was prepared to embark upon the second phase: the construction of an insulated economy, an economy capable of sustaining itself against the impostures of the plutocratic and capitalist powers.

It seems reasonably clear that at this time Mussolini was preparing to extend his controls over the activities of his nonmovement allies. The issue of the international value of the lire afforded Fascism the opportunity of establishing its

147

authority in the face of the organized opposition or passivity of the traditional economic elites. As soon became evident, it was also the occasion for the elaboration, expansion, and enforcement of Fascist controls over almost all sectors of the economy.

It appears that the policy of radical monetary deflation was calculated to draw Italy out of the international market in anticipation of the extension of state controls. Almost immediately, because of the relatively high labor costs generated by deflation of the national currency, Italian exports became too costly to compete on the world market. Exports declined by sixteen percent. At the same time, because of the increased controls over foreign imports inaugurated to protect Italy's reserves, imports declined by twenty-one percent. An elaborate system of tariff protection was erected around home industries.[53] With that protection, the major sectors of the national economy—the chemical, textile, metallurgical, and mechanical industries—began to expand and modernize after the economy had begun to restabilize subsequent to the dislocations imposed by devaluation. Industries that had devoted their energies to the export market were forced to reorient.

By 1929 Italian industry had begun to overcome the difficulties inherent in the new policies. ENIOS, the *Ente nazionale italiano per l'organizzazione scientifica del lavoro*, was organized to introduce the business methods of "Tayloristic" industrial work management and scientific rationalization into Italian plants. The *Ente nazionale per l'unificazione dell'industria* was charged with reorganizing enterprise in accordance with large-scale, standardized production. An *Istituto per il credito navale* was instituted to subsidize and reorganize shipbuilding and the merchant marine.

Before the depression of 1929, Fascists had already begun to put together the first instruments of economic control. Italy had commenced its withdrawal from the world market and the Fascists had extended controls over the internal market that were to create an autarchic economic system. Mussolini's speech at Pesaro in 1926, stabilizing the lire at a rate of 90 to the pound sterling, was, in fact, a signal that the first phase of the long-range Fascist economic program had drawn to its close. Using the occasion of the international deterioration of the value of the lire as a pretext, Mussolini was prepared to launch Italy on the second phase of Fascism's developmental program. That program was designed to enhance the defensive, aggressive, and self-sufficiency capabilities of the nation in anticipation of expansion against the plutocratic and capitalist nations. What this would ultimately entail would be the autarchic development of the key industries of the peninsula: the hydroelectric, mechanical, metallurgical, chemical, and shipbuilding facilities, as well as the expansion of the telecommunications and transportation infrastructure. This, conjoined with the modernization of agriculture in order to afford as much self-sufficiency in food production as circumstances allowed, would permit Italy the international political independence to which the Fascists aspired.

All of this had been implicit with the fusion of nationalism and national syndicalism. When national sydicalism identified itself with national and developmental aspirations, the economic nationalism of the Nationalist Association became its long-term strategy. As a consequence, Fascism was to mobilize the nation behind a developmental program that would foster the growth and defend the viability of critical industries and provide the minimum self-sufficiency required by a "great power" foreign policy in the twentieth century.

By the end of 1926, the chemical, metallurgical, mechanical, and shipbuilding industries, as well as the hydroelectric industry, had been significantly expanded and modernized. The communications network on the peninsula had been expanded and, in large part, electrified. Fascist Italy had more than doubled its industrial and productive capacity.

It was then that Fascist Italy was prepared for the creation of a modern industrial base that could support a "great power" foreign policy. That economy was expected to be as self-sufficient as the peninsula's limitations would allow. It had been abundantly clear to Fascist theoreticians as early as 1922 that if Italy were to be a great power it must assure itself access to resources adequate to the demands of a modern economy and economic space sufficient to support its growing population. Such a program would require considerable time, astute diplomacy, and almost unrestricted independence of action. As was his wont, Mussolini used the crisis precipitated by the question of international parity of the lire to launch the new phase of the Fascist program by increasing controls over the economy of the peninsula. It was during the "Battle for the Lire" that the outlines of the controlled autarchic state, prefigured in the Fascist program of 1922, began to make its appearance.

Among the conservative non-Fascist allies in the industrial and financial community there was little support for such a program. The business community had chosen to believe that Mussolini and the Fascists were disposed to restore order and normalize postwar Italy. Actually, Fascism had never intended to serve as a conservative movement. Fascism sought the creation of a "Greater Italy," an Italy that would divest itself of all the traits of international inferiority and submissiveness that characterized, and in large part still characterize, the industrially retarded nations in the modern world. By the end of 1926 Mussolini was prepared to drive his nonmovement allies into a specifically Fascist economic program.[54] Fascist Italy sought secure access to its necessary raw materials and an effective outlet for its overpopulation.

The rapid industrialization that had followed the Fascist advent to power on the peninsula had required a twofold increase in the import of raw materials.[55] Fascist economists calculated that Italy was the most resource-impoverished nation of the modern industrial world. The United States had access to ten times the amount of raw materials available to Italy; Great Britain enjoyed almost eight times the access;

France had a two hundred and fifty percent greater availability.[56]

To offset this disability, Fascists envisioned several alternatives: (1) the intensive exploitation of whatever national resources were available; (2) aggressive commercial penetration into areas where raw materials might be obtained; and (3) colonial penetration into land areas that were not as yet preempted by the plutocratic and privileged powers. To the orthodox business community, the first alternative appeared to be singularly uneconomical in terms of liberal, free-trade economics. They understood the second alternative, at best, in terms of bilateral trade arrangements. The third was dismissed as far too risky.

Fascists, on the other hand, conceived of the development of marginal national resources as a necessary element in their program. Such an enterprise would have to be conducted under the auspices of a strong, interventionist, and fundamentally antiliberal state. Economic penetration, in turn, was understood in far more aggressive terms than any entertained by the traditional business community. Mussolini's efforts to establish an Italian presence in the Balkans with special access to Rumanian oil, his disposition to afford military guarantees to Rumania, his visit to Libya, and his preparations for moves against Turkey, are all to be read in the context of Fascism's efforts at economic penetration in a search for resource availability. All these moves were undertaken on Mussolini's initiative without the prior support or advice of his conservative nonmovement allies. Business interests were prepared to accommodate to Fascism's policies, and often profitted as a consequence, but the policies undertaken by Mussolini, already prefigured in his public speeches as early as 1920[57] were autonomous.

That Fascism was equally prepared to embark upon colonial expansion as early as 1928 is evidenced not only by Mussolini's political maneuvers and the concern for raw materials during this period, but by the increased attention devoted to the "demographic problem" at that time. Granted

151

that the decision on the part of the United States to restrict Italian immigration served as a pretext for Mussolini's reaction, it is clear from his response that he once again was using the prevailing circumstances as the basis for reinvoking the demand, made as early as 1919, for adequate living space for the growing population of the peninsula.[58] The call for a colonial solution to Italy's population problem was a constant theme in the earliest Fascist literature, and the second phase of Fascist policy opened with its reiteration.

Thus, before the world economic crisis of 1929, Fascist economic policy had begun to take on the outlines of what later commentators saw as the result of the crisis itself. Autarchy was already one of the motives behind the "Battle for Grain." At the same time similar motives could be divined in the first moves to create industrial and agricultural consortia. During 1928-1929, more than 200 combinations involving 500 firms had taken place, facilitated by favorable decree legislation. The internal market, moreover, was insulated by tariff protection from foreign competition. Producers' consortia were fostered in both the agricultural and the industrial sectors. Cartels were organized in the metallurgical and shipbuilding industries. Economies of large scale were introduced, production increasingly rationalized, and administrative and technical reorganizations of industrial plants were undertaken.[59]

Thus, it is not true that Fascist economic policy during the 'thirties was simply an *ad hoc* response to the crisis conditions that afflicted the world economy. Before the advent of that crisis and its attendant dislocations, Fascism had already begun to articulate the policies of the "closed industrial state," the substance of which was the developmental economic nationalism that characterized Fascism's ideological origins. The crisis of the 'thirties accelerated and exacerbated the process, but that process had been initiated at least two years before the depression. Fascism was, in fact, implementing an economic program it had carried with it to power in 1922.

Fascist Economic Policy after the Great Depression

Fascist Italy was no less vulnerable to the impact of the worldwide depression of 1929 than were other, more favorably circumstanced, nations. All the major nations of Europe, better provided with raw materials and enjoying the advantage of internal markets of more ample dimensions, suffered grievous economic damage. Like them, Italy fell heir to all the consequences of severe economic dislocation. Stock market values collapsed. Foreign trade, already disrupted by the effort to stabilize the international value of the lire, declined by almost two-thirds. Italian unemployment increased until it involved over a million workers. By 1932 industrial production had contracted by almost 35 percent.

Most of the policies pursued by the Fascist government in response to the crisis were, in many ways, similar to those undertaken by non-Fascist governments on the Continent and in the United States. Protectionist trade policies, business salvaging, extensive public works, and social welfare legislation became the order of the day throughout most of the industrialized world.

But Fascist economic legislation had, in significant measure, anticipated these developments, and were as much the overt expression of a policy that had been prefigured in the earliest doctrinal literature as they were a response to economic crisis. Before the onset of the international depression, standard Fascist accounts had outlined a policy of maximal "national economic independence" that Fascists conceived to be prerequisite to Italy's international political independence.[60] If Italy were to assume the responsibilities of a great power, it must enjoy a military and economic capability sufficiently insulated from foreign interdiction to allow national leadership the freedom of action necessary to any major nation in crisis circumstances. It was recognized that Italy's dearth of raw materials necessary for industrial production created special problems, but the commitment to a form of autarchic self-sufficiency, at least in terms of key industries,

153

was already a cardinal feature of Fascist economic policy before the economic collapse of the 'thirties imparted special urgency to the process.[61]

As early as 1924, as a case in point, Mussolini had called for the creation of special parastate agencies that would undertake the research, discovery, and exploitation of the economically marginal natural resources of the Italian peninsula. In 1926 the *Azienda generale italiana petroli* (AGIP) was organized both to supplement the efforts of private capital in the exploitation of possible oil resources in the peninsula or the Italian colonies and to directly undertake geological exploration for new national oil sources and industrial research that might facilitate the processing of petrochemicals. Italy's lack of petroleum resources constituted one of the most significant constraints on its self-sustaining industrial growth.

A similar parastate agency, *S. A. fertilizzanti naturali Italia* (SAFNI), was organized in 1927, with joint public and private capital, to promote the growth and technical rationalization of the critically important chemical industries. At about the same time, the *Istituto per il credito navale*, was organized to coordinate and foster the development of the Italian merchant marine. As early as 1924 the Fascist government created the *Istituto di credito per le imprese di pubblica utilità* to further the elaboration of the telephonic and radiophonic telecommunications infrastructure of the peninsula.

In effect, the first years of the Fascist regime saw the creation of a special class of parastate agencies, independent of the regular administrative structure of the state and responsible by and large only to the immediate Fascist leadership,[62] that were clearly designed to further the control and development of critical key industries. When the Fascists were faced with the problems of the great depression, they responded with the further creation of similar parastate agencies. In 1931 the *Istituto mobiliare italiano* (IMI) was founded to provide funding for companies threatened with immediate failure. In January 1933, in the depth of the depression, the *Istituto per la ricostruzione industriale* (IRI) was organized to provide systematic, coordinated, and long-term funding for the private sectors of the national economy.

These latter agencies were similar in role and function to analogous agencies that made their appearance in non-Fascist industrial environments. In retrospect, however, it is clear that the Fascist regime was employing these agencies not as temporary and episodic expedients to resolve specific and contingent problems, but as the most immediate and effective way of politically controlling the economy. As long as economic circumstances had allowed the Italian business community to operate at attractive profit levels before 1929, the Italian economic elites were ill-disposed toward extensive government intervention in the economy. Although the Fascist Labor Charter of 1926 clearly anticipated government intervention whenever it was conceived to be in the "national interest," or whenever private enterprise proved to be deficient, the Italian business community had employed every strategem and every influence to restrict Fascist moves in that direction. With the crisis of the early 'thirties, however, the Fascists found themselves in a position of strength. Very rapidly a plethora of parastate agencies appeared that, together with the syndical, intersyndical, and corporative institutions already in various stages of development, extended government controls over imports, exports, services, wages, prices, conditions of labor, the allocation of materials, the licensing of new plant construction, and the rationalization and modernization of existing establishments.[63]

The pace of this process was governed by a variety of contingencies, international affairs being among the most important. By 1935 Italian industrial production had once again reached the level attained before the crisis. By that time controls had been extended throughout the economic system of the peninsula. After February 1935, for example, all import activities had to be licensed and were under strict marketing controls of the several consortia and corporations.

Export activities were similarly controlled. At the same time, extensive price controls were instituted and initially administered by agencies of the *Partito nazionale fascista* itself. In 1936 the party created a central committee, the *Comitato centrale di vigilanza sui prezzi*, to discharge price control responsibilities. Finally, the fact that the IRI and the IMI owned large blocks of stocks in the industries of the nation insured effective government intercession whenever it was politically expedient.

The Ethiopian War, with the League of Nations effort to control Italian foreign policy through punitive sanctions, and the military involvement in the Spanish Civil War, reinforced all these tendencies. Industrial concentration and cartellization, undertaken presumably to reduce redundancy and to effect economies of large scale, proceeded throughout this period. What resulted was an industrial complex composed of large-scale producers all linked through a variety of parastate entities to the government itself. Within this mixed economy, about two hundred parastate agencies—some autonomous, supported by direct public funding, and others supported in part by private capital, but all under state control—were to assume an increasing variety of productive and regulative functions.

Mussolini had used the economic crisis of the 'thirties, and the attempt on the part of the "sated plutocratic powers" to constrain Italy's aggressive foreign policy through economic sanctions, as the occasion to declare the end of "liberal capitalism" as an economic system, and to institute an official policy of national self-sufficiency in critical economic sectors.[64] Mussolini spoke of attaining, in the shortest possible time, "the maximum degree of economic independence for the nation." Once again he rehearsed the list of industries that were critical for such an enterprise. The list was the same as that to be found in the essays published by Alfredo Rocco as early as 1914. Italy was to reduce its dependency on the importation of fossil fuels. Research was to be conducted to enhance the production of liquid fuels, the hydrogenation of lignite, the distillation of alcohol from plants and asphaltic schist. Marginal coal resources were to be maximally exploited, and hydroelectric generating facilities modernized and expanded. Increased investments were to be made in the metallurgical, textile, mechanical, and chemical industries. The development of synthetic fibers was stressed and the production of chemical fertilizers enhanced; synthetic rubber was to be produced. To these ends, controls would be exercised over the entire credit system. Finally, the transportation and telecommunications network of the peninsula was to be further articulated. Mussolini spoke of these developments, and the controls, priorities, and regulation they assumed, as realizing "in full the fundamental postulates acclaimed by the Fascist revolution seventeen years ago at the meeting in the Piazza San Sepolcro."[65] He clearly understood the announced program as an integral part of that long-range developmental and autarchic goal that was intrinsic to the first Fascist commitments.

The economic program that found expression in public policy after the crisis of the 'thirties was implemented jointly by syndical, intersyndical, and corporative agencies, by the ministries and the administration, as well as by the parastate agencies that had begun to appear during the first years of the regime. In fact, when the League of Nations imposed its sanctions against Italy in November 1935, Fascist Italy already possessed an elaborate control infrastructure capable of completely monitoring foreign trade, and had already begun a program addressed to a maximum self-sufficiency. It was not, in effect, the sanctions that had inaugurated Fascist Italy's new economic program. Whatever disclaimers Fascist apologists attempted,[66] it is reasonably clear that Fascism had long anticipated just such a policy. The sanctions had provided an appropriate climate for its more effective implementation.

As the world economy emerged from the depression, Fascist Italy was compelled to choose between reestablishing itself in the liberal international market or constructing a relatively closed economic system characterized by self-sufficiency in critical industrial and agricultural sectors. The selection of Thaon di Revel as Minister of Finance in January 1935 signalled Fascism's choice of the second alternative.[67]

As Fascists themselves had long anticipated, even minimum self-sufficiency could be purchased only with a great deal of collective sacrifice. But the program once undertaken was not without considerable success and considerable significance for the development of a modern economy on the peninsula. As we shall see, the principal costs involved the maintenance of a relatively low standard of living, considerable neglect of the nonindustrial portions of the peninsula, and the massive public subvention of noneconomic enterprises. The long-term positive results of the program included the creation of a modern industrial sector fully capable, after the Second World War, of effectively insinuating itself in the economic boom of the 'fifties and 'sixties.

In the course of its developmental and autarchic program, in 1937, the Fascist government declared the IRI a permanent parastate agency. By that time the *Istituto* controlled over forty-four percent of all Italian capital stock, and almost eighteen percent of the total capital of the nation. For all intents and purposes, the credit system of the nation was under the control of state and parastate agencies. By the end of the 'thirties, approximately eighty percent of the credit available in the Italian economy was controlled directly or indirectly by the state.[68] The Fascist government had developed more elaborate controls over the economic enterprise of the nation than any other state of the period save the Soviet Union.[69]

On the peninsula the nation's energies were employed in satisfying Fascism's minimum demands for national self-sufficiency. Efforts to develop the hydroelectric capabilities were intensified. Between 1934 and 1938, for instance, the generation of electric power increased by twenty-seven percent, the bulk of it hydroelectric and destined, by and large, for industrial and transport employments. By 1935 the *Azienda carboni italiana* (ACAI) was organized as a parastate agency with the responsibility of administering the total coal resources of the nation. In 1936 the *Azienda minerali metallici italiani* (AMMI) undertook geologic exploration, direct development, and exploitation of the mineral resources of the peninsula. Given the scant resources, the improvement in mineral extraction that characterized these years was impressive.[70] In the chemical industries, under the leadership of Montecatini and parastate agencies, programs were undertaken to reduce national dependency upon foreign sources for chemical fertilizers, cellulose, rubber, benzine, and other critical defense materials. By the end of the 'thirties vast programs of rationalization and modernization had been completed which made the Italian chemical industries the peers of any in the world. By that time Italian industry was providing the nation with seventy-five percent of its necessary chemical fertilizers and had considerably improved its ability to produce petrochemical surrogates for imported raw materials, and to deliver liquid combustibles for industrial and transport use.[71] At the same time, shipbuilding and the management of the Italian merchant marine came almost completely under the control of the *Società finanziaria marittima* (Finmare).

By 1938 the Fascist government had identified those establishments critical to the survival of a politically independent Italy as the extractive, telecommunication, steel and iron, mechanical, electric, textile, naval, and chemical industries. In recognition of these considerations, the IRI was reorganized into five large stockholding subagencies: *Finsider*, the iron and steel industries; *Finmeccanica*, the mechanical industries; *Finmare*, the shipping and naval industries; *Finelettrica*, the electricity generating industries and STET, the telecommunications industries. The chemical industry developed under the joint aegis of the privately held Montecatini and

159

various parastate agencies such as the *Azienda nazionale idrogenerazione combustibili* (ANIC) and the *Istituto per lo studio della gomma sintetica.*

By 1938 the IRI, through the various agencies of control it had generated, governed seventy-seven percent of the iron and forty-five percent of the steel production of Italy. Eighty percent of all shipbuilding was controlled by the IRI. In effect, the direct and indirect involvement of the Fascist government in the economy of the nation was extensive, and, in key sectors, predominant. Whatever real or fancied benefits Italian capitalists may have enjoyed under Fascist rule, they were purchased at the cost of their political and, in a real sense, entrepreneurial independence. There is little doubt that the economic elites of the peninsula were, in general, opposed to the autarchic and interventionist program of Fascism.[72] The clear consequences of Fascism's economic policy were an increased state dominance in the economic activities of the peninsula, and the loss of ownership prerogatives. In the judgment of a recent Soviet commentator, the result was that Italian capitalists were forced to subordinate themselves to the Fascist regime.[73]

By the advent of the Second World War, Fascism had achieved all that could have been achieved of its national economic program. It had developed the economic base of the peninsula to the fullest extent possible given the dearth of raw materials and its commitment to maximum self-sufficiency. The requirement that Italy develop an industrial base sufficiently insulated from the world market to allow a great power political independence created tremendous burdens. The enterprise in Ethiopia had been undertaken at least in part in anticipation of the exploitation of raw materials necessary for the effective self-sufficiency of Italy.[74] But the investment in the 4,000 kilometers of roads, in electric plants, in irrigation and water supplies, in the 4,000 small and medium sized industrial plants created in the new territories, all taxed the limited resources of the nation. Similarly, the program devoted to the development of surrogates for imported materials was extremely expensive. All of this was sustained, as we have suggested, by strict control over consumption and the maintenance of a standard of living that remained among the lowest in the Europe of the time.

For all that, by 1937 Italy had become a modern industrial nation. For the first time in its history, industrial production outstripped that of agriculture. Italy had recovered from the depression with an overall volume of output (1913 = 100) that achieved a level of 153.8 by 1938, compared with the 132.9 attained in 1929—a performance at least comparable to that of Germany, whose index was 149.9 and the United Kingdom whose index was 158.3, and considerably better than the performance of France which languished at 109.4.[75] In point of fact, Fascist Italy maintained a level of industrial development at least equal to that of its more resource-favored neighbors while it was attempting to create a measure of self-sufficiency that required enormous commitments in terms of resources and investment capital. While the extensive cartellization of Italian industry and the abundance of relatively cheap labor afforded little intrinsic incentive for technological innovation and industrial modernization, output per man in Fascist Italy rose from the index 126.3 (1913=100) in 1929 to 145.2 in 1938, an output performance that surpassed that of any other industrial or industrializing nation save Norway and Switzerland. Similarly, during the same period, output per man-hour in Fascist Italy was superior to the performance in almost every other European nation with the exception of Norway.[76]

By 1938 all of this had placed an almost intolerable strain on the nation's economy. In recognition of that fact, Felice Guarneri, a spokesman of the *Confederazione generale dell'industria italiana* (*Confindustria*), the principal organization of major industries in Italy, advocated an immediate cessation of the development of Ethiopia, and a massive reduction in military expenditures. These recommendations would have, in effect, compelled an abandonment of Fascist policy. But by that time the possibility of a military solution to

161

Italy's resource problems had begun to mature. For the Fascists, the advent of a major war in Europe carried with it the promise of a redivision of available resources, a major Fascist preoccupation since the end of the First World War. At the outbreak of the Second World War, Fascists were clearly convinced that only a peace settlement that followed the successful conclusion of a major conflict would finally resolve Italy's raw materials and natural resource problems with the creation of viable living spaces for the resource-poor proletarian nations. The war would finally break the hold of the "plutocratic and hegemonic powers" over the "proletarian" nations.[77] Those proletarian nations—Germany, Japan, and Italy—delayed in their industrialization and confined to restricted economic space, would finally attain their merited status as economically and politically sovereign major powers.

The Political Economy of Fascism and the Revolutionary Socialist Tradition

As we have suggested, once the revolutionary syndicalists of Italy recognized that the political and economic environment in which they found themselves was substantially innocent of all the objective preconditions for Marxist revolution, they sought an alternative to the strategies and tactics associated with classical Marxism. If economic development was to be the historic responsibility of the period, the distributionist preoccupations of orthodox socialism were seen as singularly inappropriate. If industrial expansion was on the historic agenda, what was required was an accumulation and effective employment of productive capital, increased labor discipline, the inculcation of a suitable work ethic, the application of technical and administrative skills to the modern sectors of the economy, and the maintenance of a high level of emotional salience to sustain the community through the tensions that could be expected to attend vast social and economic changes.

162

All of these bourgeois responsibilities could be under-taken only within the appropriate historic vehicle, the nation-state. Classical Marxism, in fact, had insisted that such historic tasks were bourgeois in character and had, in the past, been discharged within the historic and political confines of the nation-state. By 1912 the revolutionary syndicalists of Italy had made all this part of their political belief-system. They had but little distance to traverse to find themselves making common cause with the economic nationalism of Alfredo Rocco.

The recognition that "uneven development" characterized industrialization and modernization, compelled the protofascist syndicalists to distinguish between capitalist and proletarian nations. The competition implicit in the distinction led the syndicalists to become advocates of rapid national development to unite Italy against the impostures of the privileged plutocratic powers. By the mid 'twenties, most of the prominent theoreticians of national syndicalism identified themselves with the developmental and modernizing program of economic nationalism. The names of Sergio Panunzio, A. O. Olivetti, and Roberto Michels appear and reappear in the Fascist doctrinal literature of the period. Revolutionary national syndicalism and nationalism had fused to produce the economic program of Fascism.

Years later, when Mussolini spoke of Alfredo Rocco having brought the "light of his doctrine" to Fascism,[78] it was testimony to the distance traversed by Italian revolutionary syndicalists between 1912 and 1922. They had transformed classical Marxism into a doctrine of rapid industrialization and modernization.

That just this process of "involution," or "creative development" was not peculiar to the national syndicalists of the Italian peninsula is evidenced, as has been argued, by an analogous development that characterized the Marxism of the Soviet Union. It is, of course, not at all clear what the Bolsheviks expected on the eve of their revolution, but it seems reasonably certain that Lenin expected a revolution

163

that would involve at least the most advanced industrial states of the western world. When Lenin wrote *The State and Revolution* in 1917, it is obvious that he imagined that socialist revolutionaries would have only to solve the problem of distribution, the problem of production having been effectively resolved by capitalism. Marx had led his followers to believe that the revolution would involve all the advanced industrial nations. As a consequence, Lenin expected backward Russia to be heir to that capitalist patrimony.

When revolution failed in the West, the Bolsheviks faced the problem of what they were to do with the relatively primitive industrial and economic system they had captured. For some considerable length of time there was literally no economic policy. The conditions that prevailed were so different from anything anticipated in theory, that there was little guidance to be found in the abundance of classical Marxist literature.

As we have seen, in March 1918, Lenin could still argue that an "all-Europe revolution" would be Bolshevism's "salvation" from the difficulties that attended the Marxist capture of an economically underdeveloped nation.[79] He went on to insist, "I have said . . . outright several times already, [that] . . . the workers of the most backward country will not be able to hold the [revolutionary] banner unless the workers of all advanced countries come to their aid."[80]

When it became evident that there was a real possibility that the workers of the industrially advanced West might not salvage the Russian Revolution, Lenin began to formulate the first outlines of a singularly Leninist economic program. As we have seen, he began, at that juncture, to talk about "disciplining" workers to the tasks of "raising labor productivity." He spoke of recruiting "bourgeois experts," and of stimulating "competition" between producers in the effort to improve efficiency and increase production. He began to talk of "one-man management" in productive plants to foster that "order" which could only be the product of the "will" of a single person.[81] What Bolshevik Russia needed,

Lenin affirmed, were the "achievements of capitalism." In order to accomplish the steady and regular increments in production backward Russia required, the Bolsheviks were advised to recognize that the Russian proletariat, "compared with people in advanced [industrial] countries," was "a bad worker." Lenin informed his followers that it would be necessary to involve all the coercive machinery of the state to inculcate discipline and increase productivity among the workers. "The task," Lenin insisted, "is to ensure the strictest discipline and self-discipline of the working people. . . . It is quite impossible to fulfill this task without coercion. We need the state, we need coercion."[82] Lenin did not hesitate to refer to the system he was recommending as "state capitalism." "If in a small space of time," Lenin argued, "we could achieve state capitalism in Russia, that would be a victory."[83]

Thus, as early as 1918, Lenin, like the Fascist syndicalists before him, recognized that classical Marxism would be a poor guide to revolution in an economically retarded environment. He admonished his closest collaborators to "forget their booklearning" and recognize that what Russia required for survival was an effective and expanding productive system. As long as the anticipated period of survival involved only the interim between the Russian Revolution and the saving revolution in the West, it was possible to distinguish Lenin's economic policy from that articulated by Itay's national syndicalists. But when, after Lenin's death, Joseph Stalin advocated "socialism in one country," and that advocacy involved the industrialization and modernization of backward Russia, the distinctions between the economic nationalism of Italian national syndicalism and the developmental program of Stalinism became increasingly diaphanous.

Stalin committed Russia to a vast program of industrialization and modernization, a program which made little sense in the context of classical Marxism. Classical Marxism had anticipated a revolution in an advanced industrial environment beset by the burdens of overproduction, a super-abun-

165

dance of heavy industry, and a vast industrial army that involved nine-tenths of the population. Classical Marxism conceived of its revolution as taking place in all the advanced industrial nations at once, nations in which a small class of capitalists owned the means of production, but in which the proletariat possessed all the skills requisite to industrial activity. For their part, the revolutionary syndicalists of Italy had anticipated a revolution in individual backward countries, and, as a consequence, they committed themselves to a developmental program that recognized the lack of technical and administrative skills among the working classes, the necessary function of the entrepreneurial bourgeoisie, and the massive intervention of the state. Only with the death of Lenin did the Bolsheviks come to grips with just these considerations. The Italian syndicalists had argued that if Italy were to compete in the twentieth century it would have to industrialize very rapidly and largely with its own resources. By the time Stalin committed the Bolsheviks to the first five-year plan, he was similarly prepared to argue that Russia was "fifty or a hundred years behind the advanced countries," and that, "we must make good this lag in ten years. Either we do it or we go under."[84]

All the questions that had occupied the national syndicalists and Fascists haunted the Bolsheviks throughout the first decade of the Russian Revolution. There was the question of domesticating labor, eliminating labor strife, attracting bourgeois talents through the payment of differential wages, and accumulating investment capital in sufficient quantities to fuel rapid industrialization and modernization. Strikes were made punishable offenses; differential wages were paid for necessary skills; piece work and efficiency techniques borrowed from advanced capitalist systems were introduced. Long and tortured discussions were conducted to decide how the necessary capital for industrial development might be effectively accumulated. As early as 1924, Eugenii Preobrazhenskii could address himself to the problems of "primitive socialist accumulation," the necessity of generating and accumulating sufficient capital to industrialize the backward economy of Bolshevik Russia.[85] Since, theoretically, the Bolsheviks operated in a system that would eliminate interest, rent, and profit, the issue of capital accumulation involved special considerations.

During the period immediately following the revolution, the Bolsheviks were concerned with reactivating and restoring dormant or damaged productive facilities. After 1924, the issue was no longer one of simply setting existing plants in operation, a process which involved little capital investment in the form of inventory and repairs, but one which anticipated a high capital-output ratio with far more capital required to produce the same increase in industrial yield. The Bolshevik solution to the problem of investment capital was simply to divert income into forced saving, reflected in a gross fixed capital formation as a percent of gross domestic product of about 24 percent.[86] The Bolsheviks met the problem of capital accumulation by directly transferring "surplus value" from consumption to the state industrial sector. The result was that wages were kept very close to subsistence minimums throughout the entire period of industrialization. As late as 1952 the real wage of the urban consumer was still below that enjoyed in 1928 and the standard of living of the peasants was probably lower.[87]

Like Fascism, Bolshevism paid the capital investment costs of industrialization by controlling consumption. Fascism channeled savings through high profit rates into investment in capital intensive industrial expansion; the Bolsheviks simply transferred surplus value from the workers and peasants into the developing sectors. In both cases, an elaborate state apparatus was necessary to accomplish the tasks. Very early in this period, Trotsky recognized that the Soviet state would do everything other than wither away. While he granted that it was expected, in theory, to wither away one day, during the period of industrialization, Russia would experience "a period of the highest possible intensification of the principle of the state." Trotsky went on to insist that,

167

"before disappearing," the Bolshevik state would take on the form of the "dictatorship of the proletariat, i.e., the most ruthless form of state, which embraces the life of the citizens authoritatively in every direction."[88] Stalin was to similarly insist on the expanded role of the Soviet state in the long and indeterminate period of transition between capitalism and communism. In fact, Stalin warned that if "capitalist encirclement" should extend into the period of communism, the state would remain as the focal institution of the Soviet system.[89]

What had transpired by 1925 was an all but total transformation of Bolshevism as an ideology. Bolshevism had become the rationale for a modernizing and developmental dictatorship under unitary party auspices. It conceived of the state apparatus as necessary to the enterprise, and sought to fund the entire process by controlling consumption and accumulating investment capital by forced savings. Like Fascism, it disciplined labor in the service of maximizing production, distributed differential wages, provided welfare benefits to attract the bourgeois experts necessary to the enterprise, and extended state control over the entire economic system of the nation.

More than that, the entire program was national in inspiration and autarchic in intention. In his report to the Fourteenth Congress of the Communist Party (Bolshevik) of the Soviet Union in December 1925, Stalin announced that it would be necessary to industrialize Russia outside of the "world capitalist system." The development of the Soviet Union would have to be accomplished as an "independent enterprise involving only the internal market," rather than as an appendage of the international economic system.[90] What Russia required was "a massive development of the nation's industries," particularly the key industries, the extractive, hydroelectric, chemical, steel and iron, and mechanical industries, with critical emphasis on the armaments plants.[91]

All of this necessitated a regimen of scarcity in an insulated economic environment, state control over enterprise, imports and exports, finances, and the allocation of resources. Russia, as a proletarian power, was required to defend herself against the encircling capitalist nations. More and more frequently the appeal was to the "socialist motherland," and the invocation of "socialist patriotism" became more and more indistinguishable from the stoking of nationalist enthusiasm.[92]

Alexander Gerschenkron was neither the first nor the last economic historian to recognize that Stalin's program had only "very remote, if any, relation . . . [to] Marxian ideology, or any socialist ideology for that matter."[93] The fact is that the political economy of Stalinist Russia had no more, nor any less, affinity with classical Marxism than that shared by Italian national syndicalism. When Stalin opted to create socialism in one country—to industrialize backward and isolated Russia—he was assuming the historic tasks that Italian national syndicalists had identified as revolutionary in economically retarded environments. At that point, there was little to distinguish the aspirations of Russian nationalists from those of Russian Marxists. Russia was to become a great nation, never again to be defeated in the field, capable of defending itself against a conspiracy of capitalist powers. Bolshevism exemplified the same fusion of developmental and nationalist aspirations that characterized Fascism.

Leon Trotsky was to recognize the involution. During the interwar years he insisted that "Stalinism and Fascism, in spite of a deep difference in social foundations, are symmetrical phenomena. In many of their features they show a deadly similarity."[94] The effort to construct a modern industrial economy on what Trotsky called a "pauper technical basis," in a nation by and large isolated from the world market, generated an economic strategy, an institutional infrastructure, and political tactics that shared remarkable similarities with those of Fascist Italy. Years later, reviewing the entire experience, Bruno Rizzi, a convinced and knowledgeable Marxist, could argue that the assumption of similar de-

169

velopmental and autarchic responsibilities could only generate social and ideological similarities as its consequence. Stalinism was to be understood as one expression of the "same historical forces" of which Fascism was another.[95] As we have seen, Torquato Nanni, himself a Marxist, had anticipated these developments as early as 1922. He conceived of both Fascism and Lenin's Bolshevism as attempts to fulfill "bourgeois historic responsibilities": the industrialization of backward economies and the defense of the nation-state that would serve as the necessary vehicle for that process.

None of this was lost on Fascist theoreticians. In 1937, in one of the principal theoretical journals of Fascism, Agostino Nasti identified the "cardinal features" of Stalinism with the non-Marxist effort to "galvanize the Russian people in the service of a nationalist program of rapid industrial and economic development."[96] As early as 1933 Fascists recognized what had transpired. Stalinist Marxism had followed the trajectory traced by revolutionary syndicalism in the years immediatedly before the First World War.[97]

Fascists insisted that because Russia faced developmental tasks, the Marxists would have to take on more and more of the institutional and political species traits of Fascism.[98] With the abolition of property the bourgeoisie, as such, ceased to exist in the Soviet Union, but the requirements of development necessitated the recreation of their functional analogue: the entrepreneurial, tutelary, and technical bureaucracy, which may not have owned, but certainly controlled, the means of production. Contemporary Marxists have learned to allude to these elements as the "new bourgeoisie" produced under the developmental dictatorship of Stalin.[99] This new bourgeoisie provided the directive and skilled talent requisite to industrial development and economic modernization. They enjoyed all the differential benefits enjoyed by any superordinate class.[100]

All of this was anticipated by the more astute Fascists. They saw our century as a century of contending nation-states and geopolitical blocs, with survival, effective sovereignty, and political victory a function of abundant and politically disciplined populations, available raw materials, and technically efficient, self-sufficient, and productive industrial systems. Economically and industrially retrograde nations have no other option but to modernize and industrialize if they are not to remain satellite dependencies of those more advanced. This requires an arduous and controlled program of collective self-sacrifice under the auspices of an authoritarian state in an insulated environment. Little has transpired in the last half-century to suggest that the Fascists were very far wrong.

SIX

THE LABOR POLICY OF FASCISM

The labor policy of Fascism evolved out of the interaction between Fascist commitments and the contingencies that characterized the social, economic, and political circumstances of the years between 1919 and 1925. In retrospect, the broad outlines of what was to become Fascist labor policy were discernible as early as the founding of the movement, but the particulars were a function of circumstances that could hardly have been anticipated in 1919.

We have briefly reviewed the general policy commitments that animated the first *Fasci*. They implied certain orientations vis-à-vis organized labor and labor in general. But it was only with the close of 1920 that Fascism directly concerned itself with the organization of labor per se, the mobilization of the working masses, and the inauguration of a specifically Fascist syndicalism.

The Origins of Fascist Syndicalism

As we have seen, the principal ideologues of nascent Fascism were almost all revolutionary syndicalists of prewar provenance. Sergio Panunzio, A. O. Olivetti, Michele Bianchi, Alceste De Ambris, Paolo Orano, Massimo Rocca, Edmondo Rossoni, and Guido Pighetti had all been proletarian and Sorelian syndicalists. All entered into the leadership ranks of Fascism, and almost all were to remain there as ideologues of the regime throughout its tenure.

Mussolini's concern with syndicalism remained constant,

from his first commitment to the formulations of national syndicalism in 1918 until mass mobilization in 1921 and 1922 provided the membership for the Fascist syndicates. In the interim, Fascism—as an essentially political movement—gradually articulated an explicit policy for dealing with organized and unorganized labor within the confines of its overall economic program. For two years, Fascism had little occasion to invoke that policy because there were few workers to organize.

At the termination of the First World War, Fascism was a small political movement of revolutionary dissidents without membership and with only marginal potential for recruitment success among the masses of the peninsula. The nonproletariat of the nation seemed wedded to the political formulae and the political parties of the prewar period. The proletariat, in its turn, remained similarly and by and large, locked into the orthodox socialist organizations of prewar vintage. The difference between the bourgeois and the proletarian circumstances was that the working-class organizations gave every evidence of expanding membership, while bourgeois parties languished. The *Confederazione generale del lavoro* (CGL), the trade union arm of official socialism, expanded its membership from approximately 250,000 members in 1918 to 2,200,000 members by 1920. The socialists polled about one-third of the total popular vote in the electoral campaign of 1919, and secured 156 seats out of a total of 508 in parliament, compared to the 52 they had obtained before the war. By the end of 1920, the Socialist party had enrolled about 200,000 members, about ten times the number it had had at the conclusion of the war. The socialists controlled 2,162 of the 8,059 communes and 25 of the 69 provinces of the peninsula.

Given this situation, the first Fascism had very little room to maneuver. The bourgeoisie could see little merit in a political organization composed largely of left-wing dissidents. The working classes of the peninsula could divine small profit in joining a political movement, no matter how

173

attractive, that had no trade union organization, and afforded no promise of immediate satisfaction for any particular material need.

Unlike the national syndicalists, the traditional working-class organizations had retained their institutional integrity throughout the war that they, unlike the interventionists, had resisted. The Socialist party and the CGL emerged from the war with an intact organization capable of satisfying the immediate interests of the Italian working class. The syndicalists who had opted to support Italian intervention in the First World War, on the other hand, had not only not been successful in bringing much of the organized labor movement with them at the time of intervention, they had been forced to neglect critical organizational tasks throughout the conflict. Even the most aggressive syndicalists, those organized by Filippo Corridoni and Alceste De Ambris, had failed to follow their leadership in their advocacy of intervention without massive defection.

The commitment to the war implied the departure of many of the national syndicalists into military service, which meant, in turn, that the interventionist syndicates could hardly maintain any substantial institutional continuity throughout the war years. During this time, most of the national syndicalist leadership was serving at the front. While they remained politically active as individuals, it was difficult for their organizations to continue effective day-to-day existence. As a consequence, the end of the war found the interventionist syndicalists at a considerable disadvantage with the socialists and socialist-affiliated organizations dominating organized labor. The members of the working classes who did not feel comfortable in the "red" ranks chose an alternative in the progressive and moderate *Confederazione italiana dei lavoratori* (CIL), a confederation of Christian, that is to say, Roman Catholic, trade unions.

When Fascism constituted itself a political movement in 1919, it operated in an environment with severely restricted recruitment possibilities. It enjoyed only the loosest contacts with organized labor. Mussolini's general syndicalist affinities, as well as his overt commitment to national syndicalism, recommended collaboration with the *Unione italiana del lavoro* (UIL) of De Ambris, Bianchi, and Rossoni, a recently reorganized national syndicalist labor organization. In fact, the official publication of this organization, *Il rinnovamento* —to which Panunzio and other syndicalist theoreticians were to regularly contribute—became a major source of many of Mussolini's ideas during this period.[1] More than that, the UIL could boast a membership of more than one hundred thousand, a support base that Mussolini could only welcome.

For all that, the affiliation between political Fascism and the national syndicalist UIL and cognate organizations, remained informal. Many syndicalists, true to their antipolitical prewar postures, insisted on maintaining the apolitical and autonomous character of their syndicates.[2] This was particularly true of syndicalist organizations like the *Comitato nazionale di azione sindacale dannunziana* and the later *Confederazione italiana sindacati economici* (CISE). Nonetheless, irrespective of their autonomy, the syndicalists of the UIL, CISE and related groups, were animated by the national syndicalism of Fascism, and De Ambris characterized the intimacy of the relationship between Fascism and the national syndicalist workers' associations when he wrote in *Il rinnovamento* that the *Fasci* represented the only political force in Italy capable of effectively opposing the "incapacity of the existing dirigent class as well as the demagoguery of the socialists."[3]

Between 1919 and the end of 1920, Fascist syndicalism remained in this parlous condition. There is very little evidence of recruitment successes, and while syndicalist intellectuals and organizers remained active, they could record little in the way of penetration among the working masses of the peninsula. During the same period, the orthodox socialist organizations enjoyed their greatest organizational, recruitment, and electoral successes. The myth of the Bolshevik Revolution radiated throughout the peninsula, and the lead-

175

ership of both the orthodox Socialist party and the CGL paid constant lip service to the "inevitability" of the "soviet revolution" in Italy. The organized working masses were charged with revolutionary emotion, and the socialist revolution was heralded as on the immediate agenda. In 1919 there were 1,663 industrial, and 197 recorded agricultural, strikes. They involved almost two million workers, costing approximately 12 million days of lost labor time. In 1920 there were 1,881 industrial and 180 agricultural strikes, involving a million and a quarter industrial, and over one million agricultural, workers, costing almost 30 million days of lost labor time.[4] In January 1920 the state employees of the postal, telegraphic, and railroad services embarked on a series of strikes. In February and March strike activity extended to the agricultural regions of the north in Ferrara, Mantova, Novara, Pavia, Padua, Verona, Arezzo, and Parma. Even the Catholic unions, the *Conferazione italiana dei lavoratori* (CIL), became involved.

Most of the strikes had immediate economic motives and they followed no preestablished program. They succeeded in seriously dislocating economic activities in the agricultural regions for weeks and months at a time, often at the cost of enormous losses in farm products and agricultural livestock. Workers who refused to participate in strike activities, for whatever reason, were subject to punitive sanction, often involving onerous boycotts that denied them every survival necessity and social convenience.[5] The strikes of state employees, in turn, created almost intolerable tensions in the urban areas with the interruption of public services that frequently left city dwellers without essential services, and, more frequently, seriously discomfitted. Rail transit was often halted in order to force members of the constabulary, or the military, or simple clerics, to remove themselves from railway cars. Shipments of munitions were halted at the will of railway workers. Mail was often not delivered at all, and, if delivered, only after long delays. On occasion, strikes were called for little or no reason in what even the most well disposed commentators have called a "strike mania."[6]

In the summer of 1920 the leadership of the CGL signed a statement drawn up in Moscow that advertised the advent of the "triumph of the social revolution and the universal republic of the soviets." It was anticipated that "all power" would soon devolve upon the working classes of the peninsula. But for all the revolutionary talk, neither the Socialist party nor the CGL prepared the necessary institutional infrastructure, nor the revolutionary program, to accomplish such a purpose. In August 1920, out of a series of apparently negotiable and relatively inconsequential grievances, a threat of a strike among metallurgical workers mounted in the north. The *Federazione degli operai metallurgici* (FIOM) prepared to embark on strike activities in the Alfa Romeo plant in Milan; the proprietors prepared to respond with a lockout. In reaction, on the 31st of August, workers occupied 280 metallurgical plants in Milan. During the following days the movement to occupy industrial plants spread throughout Italy until hundreds of thousands of workers were involved. In Turin alone, over one hundred thousand workers were mobilized.

The occupation of the establishments in the north required the subsequent occupation of those plants providing raw and partially worked materials to sustain production. Ultimately, the seizures extended as far as Sicily in the south. In many establishments, the red flag was flown over the walls of occupied buildings and "soviet power" was proclaimed. In many places arms were stacked or concealed against the possibility of any effort to dislodge the workers from the buildings occupied. Armed units of "red guards" were assembled to perform services of security and defense. There was talk of the direct intervention of "Russia of the Soviets" to provide "the means for the consolidation of the workers' victory."

Actually, what looked like the prologue to revolution was

177

a spontaneous, disorganized, and ill-conceived explosion of collective frustration. Neither the official Socialist party nor the CGL was disposed to take responsibility or leadership of the movement. In the occupied factories difficulties began to mount almost immediately. In some places technical personnel and engineers balked at working under the direction of "workers' councils." Money for wages was soon in short supply. In many factories the complicated network of supplies and services necessary for production was interrupted, and productivity levels could not be maintained. There was little or no preparation for the distribution of whatever production was accomplished. Gradually workers began to abandon the factories. The "red guards," originally organized to defend the newly acquired "workers' properties," were employed, in many places, to keep workers at their posts. Defections were severely punished. In some instances, technical personnel were forced to continue work under threat of violence.[7]

During the three weeks of workers' insurrection, the government of Giovanni Giolitti refused to directly confront the workers in the occupied factories. The authorities reasoned that any effort to dislodge the workers by force would require massive military intervention. The proprietors could expect catastrophic losses in plant, machinery, and inventory. Giolitti argued that the movement should be allowed to run its course. He expected the workers to lose their enthusiasm, exhaust their limited funds, and ultimately recognize that they could not maintain production or distribution. That was, essentially, what transpired. By the end of September, the factories had been restored to their owners and elaborate negotiations were begun to formulate some kind of compromise that might satisfy everyone involved.

In retrospect, it is clear that the occupation of the factories in September 1920 marked the flood tide of the socialist efforts at revolution. Although the socialists continued to attract mass support in the elections of November of that year, there were any number of signs that resistance against the socialists was beginning to crystallize on the peninsula.

For the nascent Fascist movement, and for its allied syndicalists, the last half of 1920 was extremely critical. During the disturbances of September, Mussolini made quite clear that he was prepared to support the workers' occupation of the factories only under certain conditions. As early as 1919 Mussolini had, in fact, supported the UIL's "occupation" of the metallurgical plant *Franchi e Gregorini* at Dalmine in a strike that he characterized as not "interrupting production." Workers, Mussolini went on to insist, have a right to "parity" with employers, and to strike to obtain it, but only if the working class could show clear evidence of both a will to participate as equals in the productive process, and a capacity to discharge the obligations which necessarily attend that participation.[8] On the occasion of the events of September 1920, Mussolini assumed a similar stance. He insisted that in occupying the factories the workers had undertaken truly "revolutionary" action. On the other hand, he made it clear that his support was contingent on clear evidence that the workers who had seized the factories possessed the "collective capacity" to maintain production. He insisted that Fascists entertained no *a priori* commitment to the special sanctity of property, but that they "considered the problem solely from the point of view of production."[9] Any commitment to "private property" and "private initiative" made by the Fascists was contingent upon the conviction that the nation's economy was so complex[10] that it required technical, managerial, and administrative competence that the proletariat, alone, could hardly be expected to possess.[11] At the conclusion of the workers' occupation, Mussolini once again reiterated the conditions under which Fascism and Fascist syndicalism would countenance workers' control: "We demand," Mussolini insisted, "that control be exercised with seriousness, by persons both competent and above suspicion."[12]

In the final analysis, it became clear that Fascists were con-

179

vinced that the occupation of the factories had established both the technical and administrative incompetence of the working class, and the revolutionary velleity of the Socialist party and the CGL. By October 1920, Mussolini recognized that the revolutionary working-class movement had begun to decompose.[13] By the end of the year Mussolini could read signs of a "profound change in the mood of the proletariat." The "working masses," he went on, were by that time convinced that the "fundamental problem" which beset the nation was the "problem of production"[14] rather than the "expropriation" of capitalists. He anticipated a move away from the orthodox socialist organizations and new recruitment opportunities for Fascist syndicalism. He reminded the working class of Fascism's support of the occupation of the factories, but reiterated that any such action would have to prove itself compatible with the ultimate interests of the nation.[15]

Mussolini spoke of Italy's disadvantaged position in the modern world and restated the Fascist economic program: economic development under the collaborative auspices of private enterprise and national syndicalist organization in the pursuit of national self-sufficiency and the ultimate "grandeur" of the nation.[16] Italy, he went on, remained "enslaved" by its industrial retardation, by its dependence on the importation of coal and grain. Only accelerated national production, collaborative enterprise, disciplined labor, rationalization and modernization of all sectors of the economy could liberate the nation from its subordination to others.[17] Rather than the "dogmas" of traditional socialism, Italy required the programs of national syndicalism.

As early as August 1920, Mussolini foresaw a broad expansion of Fascist syndicalism based upon a recognized need for increased national production which implied the collaboration between efficient and supportive private ownership and syndicalist discipline. Fascism would soon commence its mass mobilization.[18]

In the last six months of 1920 the number of sections of the *Fasci* increased from 150 to over 800. In December 1920,

Ferrara had been a "red" region. By January 1921, the *Fasci* of Ferrara submitted a request to the Central Committee of the party for 2,000 membership cards, all of those available having been exhausted in the preceding months as a consequence of rapid recruitment. By mid-February the Fascists of Ferrara announced a party membership of 6,000. In the beginning of April 1921, Mussolini was greeted in that city by a crowd of 20,000. Forty thousand Ferrarese workers had been organized in the Fascists' autonomous syndicates, and the party polled 50,000 votes in Ferrara during the elections of May.[19] Throughout the length of the "red" Po Valley, the *Fasci* began to enjoy unparalleled recruitment successes. Bologna and Ferrara could soon boast more members in the party than could Milan, the center of the movement. In November 1920, the first *Fasci* had been organized by students in Reggio Emilia. By May 1921, the autonomous Fascist syndicates in the area were attracting sufficient members to compete with the established socialist, and Catholic, labor organizations.[20] In the early months of 1921 the Fascists moved into Tuscany, Umbria, and Puglia. By May, they had enrolled almost 200,000 members and could effectively compete, politically, with the Socialists and the Popolari. In Modena, Reggio Emilia, Parma, Cremona, Pavia, Veneto, Rovigo, Padua, Verona, and Vicenza the situation matured very rapidly.

Under these auspicious circumstances, the autonomous syndicalist organizations that had sympathized with Fascism from its inception, began to look with increasing favor on a formal alliance with the expanding political movement. In February 1921, the first specifically Fascist syndicates were organized in San Bartolomeo in Bosco in Ferrara. In April of that year, at the regional congress in Bologna, Fascism organized its first official confederation of Fascist syndicates. In October 1921, Edmondo Rossoni, secretary of the *Camera sindacale* of Ferrara, argued that national syndicalism would have to move beyond the position assumed by the UIL, and the autonomous syndicates, and organize a specifically Fas-

181

cist confederation of syndicalist associations. In November 1921, the problem of the organization of Fascist syndicates was placed on the agenda of the congress of the *Partito nazionale fascista* held in Rome. By that time, there were 64,000 members of the specifically Fascist syndicates. Guido Pighetti and Michele Bianchi called for an organized confederation of Fascist syndicates whose members would commit themselves to the national syndicalist political priorities of dedication to the nation and the maximum development of production[21]—priorities that had been central to the Fascist program since its first articulation in 1919. The days of the autonomy of Fascist syndicalism were numbered.

In January 1922, the Fascist syndical organizations participated in the Congress of Bologna. At that congress, a decision was made to integrate all Fascist syndicalist organizations into *Corporazioni nazionali* under the leadership of Rossoni. Michele Bianchi, Secretary General of the party, provided the first institutional rationale for an official Fascist syndicalism. The Fascist "union of corporations" would include all those syndicates "whose programs and activities [were] in substantial conformity to the program and statutes of the *Partito nazionale fascista*." The Order of the Day that concluded the meeting established that the leadership and the organizers of the syndicates would be nominated and controlled by the political leadership of the party. In effect, by the beginning of 1922, Fascist syndicalist organizations committed themselves to political subordination to the Fascist party. The Fascists had accomplished something that had forever escaped the Socialist party. The socialists had had to remain content with an "economic arm," the CGL, that was only prepared to enter into conditional alliance with the party.

In June 1922, at the second congress of the Fascist syndicalist organizations, with Mussolini in attendance, Rossoni welcomed 427 delegates representing 458,000 members. More than half of them (277,000) were members of the agricultural syndicates. Seventy-two thousand members were industrial workers, and 43,000 were workers in the transport industries. Thirty-one thousand were white-collar employees, and 8,200 were technicians or technically skilled workers. The remainder were workers in the local public service industries.[22] Fascist syndicalism had become a major recruitment competitor for the socialist and Catholic workers' organizations. By this time the Fascist syndicates identified themselves specifically as the *Confederazione nazionale delle corporazioni fasciste*. Fascist syndicalism had become the economic extension of the political movement.

Throughout the remainder of the summer of 1922 there was a rapidly accelerating expansion of membership in the Fascist syndicates. At the same time there was a correlative collapse of the traditional working-class organizations. The *Federazione nazionale dei lavoratori della terra (Federterra)*, which enjoyed a membership of 800,000 in 1920, found itself with a reduced membership of 300,000 in the summer of 1922. The CGL, of which *Federterra* was a component part, was reduced to a membership of 400,000 in mid-1922, after having had a peak membership of over 2,000,000 in 1920. Even the Catholic syndicates of the *Popolari* suffered the same rapid loss of members. In 1920 the Catholic syndicates had a membership of about 1,250,000; in 1921 membership had declined to about 1,000,000, and in 1922 to about 540,000.[23] By the time of the Fascist seizure of power in October 1922, the traditional socialist organizations had been substantially defeated. Entire organizations of workers and peasants that had functioned for years as part of the CGL passed under the guidons of the Fascist syndicates. Without the passive support of Fascist syndicalism, and the neutralization of socialist working-class organizations, the political victory of Fascism in October 1922 would have been far more difficult if not impossible.

The Rise of Fascist Syndicalism

The victory of Fascist syndicalism was correlative to and causally associated with the political victories of the Fascist movement. Like all complex social events, the triumph of

183

Fascist syndicalism was a function of the intersection of an indeterminate number of factors. It seems reasonably clear that pervasive public attitudes, conditioned by the long, bitter, and enervating economic strife that had ravaged the peninsula, played a significant part in subsequent events. The patience of a broad segment of the population of the peninsula had been exhausted by a continuous series of strikes—sometimes provoked by the most minor grievances—which had unsettled social relations, discomfitted many, and threatened the national economy with collapse. Members of the constabulary and the military had been grievously offended by socialist and "bolshevik" postures that characterized them as suborned agents of the capitalists. Large segments of the petty-bourgeoisie had been incensed by their characterization as "parasitic." A large minority of students were outraged by the socialist objections to a war just recently won at great sacrifice and war veterans were alienated by a socialist public policy of defamation and renunciation concerning that war.

After the occupation of the factories in September 1920, many, if not most, Italians conceived of the revolutionary appeals of the socialists and "bolsheviks" as irresponsible if not criminal. More than that, proprietors felt immediately threatened by the possibility of "revolutionary socialist expropriation." Almost immediately upon the conclusion of the occupation, local *Fasci* began to resurface, after a long period of dormancy, throughout the peninsula. Very often, around a nucleus of student and veteran groups, these *Fasci* rapidly became the catalysts of antisocialist and antibolshevik reaction. Interestingly enough, this reaction developed most momentum in the Po Valley in the rural areas. Frequently initiated by urban *Fasci*, reaction against the rural socialist organizations very quickly took root in the farming communities. Fascist squads, often originating in the urban areas, ranged widely into the rural zones and in some cases, particularly around Ferrara and Bologna, very rapidly won local support. Systematic "punitive raids" were conducted against the "league" and "chamber" headquarters of socialist and *Federterra* organizations. The *Fascio ferrarese*, for example, was founded only in October 1920, a scant few weeks after the collapse of the movement to occupy the factories. There were at that point about 40 members. A month later there were 300 members. By the end of December there were between two and three thousand.[24]

All the factors that have been alluded to contributed to the rapid expansion of the Fascist movement. For our purposes, there are several considerations that are central to any discussion of the specific success of Fascist syndicalism. First of all, it is clear that Fascist success cannot be construed as solely the consequence of the systematic employment of violence on the part of the "punitive squads." Certainly Fascist violence was critically important, but as Gaetano Salvemini was to persuasively argue, no political movement can succeed exclusively by virtue of its employment of violence. The opponents of Fascism were defeated, at least in substantial part, because of their own intrinsic weaknesses and political ineptitude,[25] a judgment later reaffirmed by Communist critics. In 1923 Clara Zetkin insisted that "before Fascism defeated the proletariat with violence, it had won an ideological and political victory over the working class movement."[26]

The evidence indicates that by the end of 1920 there was, in fact, a large reservoir of free-floating hostility against the socialists which the Fascists adroitly exploited. Already prior to the political takeoff of Fascism late in 1920, there were many signs that the mood on the peninsula had changed. As we have suggested, Mussolini had read those signs as early as August. In some of the major cities of Italy citizen groups had spontaneously resisted the strikers on public conveyances. In November 1920, on the second anniversary of the armistice that ended World War I, the national flag was unfurled throughout the nation for the first time since 1918, and the socialists could do little to dampen the nationalist enthusiasm that that display signalled.[27] More specifically,

185

and especially in the vast agricultural areas of the Po Valley, socialist organizations had come to dominate the local economy after the war. In the two years that followed the close of hostilities, those organizations obtained a virtual monopoly over the disposition of labor in many of the rural locales. Their leaders more and more frequently insisted upon "assigning" workers to farmers during critical periods of production under conditions established by the socialist leagues. Those who resisted were boycotted, boycotts that often involved the interdiction of feed for livestock and medical assistance to farmers in need. There were times when draconian measures were employed against agricultural workers who sought work without the approval of the league leadership. Agricultural laborers who did not operate through the socialist organizations were identified as "strikebreakers" and "scabs," and their lives made more than difficult. There were also land seizures, at times of well-tended and prosperous lands which then were subsequently neglected.[28] Individual league leaders, like Giuseppe Massaraenti, came to wield tyrannical power not only over proprietors, but over workers as well.[29] There were provocations that incensed national sensitivities: the national flag was defaced; soldiers were abused and insulted, and churchmen outraged.

Perhaps most important was the fact that in the rural areas the war had brought significant social change. The high prices paid for agricultural produce during the war years permitted many sharecroppers and renters to purchase, for the first time, their own small bit of property. The unstable conditions that followed the war had induced many proprietors to sell land. Thus, a new class of small landholders had grown up in the agricultural areas of the north. When the socialists began to insist on "collectivization of the land," they threw themselves athwart the immediate and salient interests of this new, aggressive class of small landholding agrarian proprietors. Men who had labored for years to own property of their own suddenly found themselves threatened by what appeared to be a monolithic and intransigent political movement committed to the abolition of private property.[30]

In retrospect, it appears that the socialism in the rural areas was no more monolithic nor political than it was in the urban centers. Socialist organization was fragile and its political control was episodic and inconsistent. There was a great deal of talk about "revolution," "soviets" and "collectivization," but precious little serious organizational and preparatory work. Nonetheless, at the time, the threat appeared real enough, and with the occupation of the factories in September 1920, the crisis seemed to reach its ominous peak.

Almost immediately there were many who saw in the small bands of Fascists the only remaining defence against the socialist threat. For almost two years small groups of Fascists had struggled against the socialist organizations. In the closing month of 1920 there were many who felt abandoned by the government's inability to protect them against socialist "expropriation," and the Fascists appeared to be the last recourse. Money began to cascade into Fascist coffers and new membership collected around the revived *Fasci*. The process, as we have seen, was most rapid in the rural areas. Not only the large, but the small landholders began to assist the Fascist movement with money, support, and membership. Support came not only from the agrarian associations, but from sharecroppers, and not infrequently from agricultural day laborers, who, faced with growing unemployment in 1920 and 1921, felt constrained by the employment monopolies enjoyed by the socialist leagues. By 1921 the Fascists of Reggio Emilia, for example, could announce that the majority of the movement's membership was of working-class origin, that is to say, composed of agricultural day laborers.[31] All these elements constituted the mass base with which Fascism operated in 1921 and 1922 in the agricultural areas of the north.[32] And these were the elements that would pass into the ranks of the Fascist syndicates. Often entire sections of the socialist *Federterra* would aban-

187

don the CGL and identify themselves as Fascist labor organizations.

Similar movements, if on a much more restricted scale, took place among industrial workers. Many workers felt that the occupation of the factories had revealed the ineptitude of socialist strategies. Even in the judgment of Salvemini, the socialists had seized the factories only to discover that the working class could not maintain production without the active collaboration of the petty-bourgeois technicians, administrators, and merchants[33]—something the national syndicalists had long insisted upon. Roberto Michels, himself a proletarian syndicalist for years before his commitment to national syndicalism, pointed out just such circumstances in his assessment of the occupation of the factories.[34]

The events of September 1920 had disillusioned many workers.[35] How many of them defected to the ranks of Fascism is difficult to determine. There are few reliable statistics available for the period in question. But that there were a significant number of such defections is acknowledged by almost all commentators.[36] In fact, the first *Fasci* in Liguria had been organized by industrial workers, and the Fascists increased working-class recruitment after 1920 if for no other reason than the fact that the industrialists throughout the industrial triangle in the north provided Fascist syndicates privileged access to scarce employment opportunities. The increasing unemployment in 1921 afforded the Fascist syndicates special advantage. Employers would more readily hire members of the Fascist syndicates, and as a consequence, more and more industrial workers were alienated from socialist organizations. By the summer of 1922 the *Fasci* in many industrial centers were composed almost entirely of working-class members, even though the leadership may have been petty bourgeois intellectuals, young war veterans, technicians, and professionals.

It would have been surprising if much of the working class had not been disenchanted by traditional socialism by 1921. By the end of 1920 the socialists and the affiliated

CGL had almost completely isolated themselves. They had succeeded in antagonizing nearly the entire nonproletarian population, the forces of public security, and the military. In a series of ill-conceived and ineptly undertaken enterprises, they had discredited both themselves as serious revolutionaries and the government as a credible agency of law and order. Fascism and Fascist syndicalism could only profit from the circumstances.

The occupation of the factories in September 1920 marked the beginning of the rapid disintegration of the socialist alternative to Italy's postwar crisis. The CGL soon disassociated itself from organized political socialism and the coalition of forces that had towered over the events of the "revolutionary biennial" collapsed. Of the two million members of the CGL of 1920, only little more than 200,000 remained by the end of 1922. In the meantime, the membership in the Fascist syndicates had grown from the 458,000 of June 1922, to over 500,000 by the time of the March on Rome in October. For a variety of reasons, a considerable part of the working class of Italy had abandoned socialism before the Fascist seizure of power in October 1922. Many workers simply moved into the Fascist syndicates as a viable and effective alternative. The Fascist syndicates were frequently more successful in obtaining employment for their members in the reduced employment opportunities of 1921 and 1922. The Fascist syndicates were protected by well-equipped and mobile "action squads" of former war veterans and students. Often the military actively participated in Fascist squads. The Fascist organizations were often subventioned by bourgeois funds as insurance against socialist expropriation. The constabulary clearly favored Fascists in any conflict with the antinational and "bolshevik" socialists. The Fascist syndicates thus enjoyed every advantage, and gave every evidence of servicing the immediate needs of large segments of the working class. That Fascist syndicalism expanded rapidly during this period was no mystery. The mystery is that its growth was not more rapid.

189

In its turn, Fascist syndicalism served the Fascist political movement by neutralizing the socialist and non-Fascist working-class organizations and by providing many of the foot soldiers for the armed squads that ultimately secured for Fascism vast territories and many major cities on the peninsula before the actual March on Rome. National syndicalism provided not only the critical ideological elements for the Fascist victory, it mobilized a good part of its necessary mass.

The Evolution of Fascist Syndicalism

By 1919 the core elements of the ideology of Fascism had already been put together so that the broad outlines of Fascist labor policy could be anticipated. When Agostino Lanzillo published his *La disfatta del socialismo* in January 1918 —a book which had significant impact on Mussolini[37]—he simply restated many of the themes that had already been developed in the antecedent work of Panunzio and Olivetti. It was clear that the current of authoritarianism and elitism was strong among the national syndicalists. Panunzio had made the necessity of authority central to his discussion as early as 1909. Panunzio, Michels, and Olivetti had all insisted upon the revolutionary and social function of elites, a revolutionary aristocracy, and a vanguard leadership. A new consciousness was to be generated among the working masses of Italy—long humbled by the effects of economic retardation and foreign occupation—by the mimetic example, pedagogical influence, and tutelary control exercised by a heroic and revolutionary elite who had won the right to rule in battle. All of this had been articulated in considerable detail in the many works of Panunzio, Michels, and Olivetti.

Those national syndicalists in the Fascist ranks who resisted, for whatever reason, these interpretations of social life and revolutionary strategy very soon found themselves isolated in the developments that followed the organizational victory of Fascist syndicalism. Those, like De Ambris, who

190

continued to conceive of the syndicalist struggle in terms of a kind of economic democracy, in which voluntary associations of producers would govern the industrial and agricultural processes of the nation, became increasingly alienated. By the end of World War I, those theoreticians who were to lend intellectual substance to Fascist policy had already begun to think of syndicalist organizations as hierarchical and authoritarian structures which would facilitate political control by the state.

Of all the syndicalist theoreticians, Sergio Panunzio is clearly the most representative of specifically Fascist thought during this period. More than that, it was Panunzio who exercised documented influence on the development of Mussolini's thought during the critical period between 1914 and 1922. It was during that transitional period that Panunzio moved from a position of "pure" or "proletarian" syndicalism to the "state syndicalism" found in his "Stato e sindacati," written immediately prior to the Fascist accession to power in October 1922, and published immediately after in January 1923.[38]

The distance traversed by Panunzio from 1914 to 1922 can be reconstructed in impressive detail. In an essay written in 1914, "Il socialismo, la filosofia del diritto e lo stato,"[39] Panunzio entertained an antiorganicist, libertarian, and tendentially antistate position. At that time Panunzio argued that true socialism, that is to say "proletarian syndicalism," traced its origins to Kant and not Hegel. For Panunzio, Kant was the philosopher who defended libertarian rights, the rule of law in the service of individual freedom, while Hegel was the philosopher of the integral and universal state into which the individual was absorbed without remainder. It was clear that Panunzio then identified with Kant, the philosopher of individualism, rather than Hegel, the advocate of universalism.

In 1914 Panunzio was a libertarian by philosophic disposition. By 1922 he had become the advocate of the state as

191

the principle of organic unity, supreme authority—a juridical force having "absolute preponderance" over any constituent association.[40]

Panunzio indicated that the theoretical position entertained by syndicalism had undergone pervasive and substantive changes between 1914 and 1922. By 1921 syndicalism had discovered the historic significance of the nation, and the state as its informing principle. Given the convictions entertained by the more aggressive syndicalists—the recognition of the economic retardation of the peninsula, the technical and political backwardness of the working masses, the role of energizing vanguard elites—the state began to assume increasing pedagogical, enterprisory, and tutelary, obligations. By 1922 Panunzio believed the syndicates to be the functional components of society, for which the state provided necessary juridical form and general superintendance. The syndicalism that, at one time, had been vehemently antagonistic to the state, had begun to recognize its special function in circumstances of economic backwardness.

Panunzio argued that during intervals of vast social and economic change—"revolutionary periods"—society attempts a restructuring of social relations. The old society disaggregates and the state enters into eclipse. But with the conclusion of the transition, a period of "reconstruction" commences in which new social relations are codified in law and the state is refashioned and restored. After any period of centrifugal disaggregation, an "organic" period of restoration must be begun. Panunzio argued that Italy was at the threshold of such a period in which the state would husband all the subsidiary social aggregates through a period of rapid reorganization and development—a period of "revolutionary conservatism," in which the "eternal" state would be charged with its new historical responsibilities. The "revolutionary, negative, partial and proletarian syndicalism" would emerge as the "constructive, organic, constitutional, general and integral syndicalism" that had attained its theoretical integrity by 1922.[41]

What this meant for Fascist syndicalism became apparent almost immediately. More significant for our purposes is the fact that national syndicalism, by the time of Fascism's advent to political power, had already acceded to a theoretical position very similar to that advanced by most antitraditional Italian nationalists. Panunzio's synthesis of statism and syndicalism reproduced in faithful outline the position taken by Alfredo Rocco some considerable time before the merger of the two movements. In effect, it was not the case that Fascism simply adopted nationalist postures vis-à-vis the organization of labor. There was a parallel evolution exemplified in the assessments of both the most aggressive national syndicalists and the most antitraditional nationalists. Those elements of Fascist state syndicalism to be found in the works of Alfredo Rocco, for example, are similarly found developed in the works of Sergio Panunzio between 1914 and 1922.[42] In 1926 A. O. Olivetti, as a consequence, could remind Italians that Fascism had been the product of syndicalist lucubrations and that syndicalism and nationalism had been parallel and mutually interactive currents of thought for more than a decade before Fascism's advent.[43]

By 1929 Olivetti, in language very similar to that employed by Rocco or Panunzio, could speak of the "new national syndicalist state," the state which exercised "command" and "control." He spoke of a state possessed of tutelary, solidarist, pedagogical, and entrepreneurial responsibilities, a state that infused its citizens with a "new consciousness," that "coordinated" private and associational interests in the service of the collectivity. The "new state" was the "society of producers" in action, and its purpose was the "maximization of production" in the service of the nation's historic greatness.[44]

For the syndicalism that adopted the standards of Fascism this meant, in effect, the subordination of specifically economic interests to the political purposes of the movement. When the more conservative allies of the movement became disquieted by the vast expansion of the organization of labor

193

under Fascist leadership, that disquiet was dispelled by the frank appraisal, offered by Fascist leadership, of the relationship understood to obtain between organized labor and political control.

Michele Bianchi, himself a longtime syndicalist, insisted that Fascist syndicalism could not, under any circumstances, pose a threat to the integrity of the state. The organizational procedures that gave shape to Fascist syndicates, Bianchi reminded the Grand Council of Fascism in 1923, were "absolutely dictatorial." Edmondo Rossini, the general secretary of the syndical organizations, was a party functionary, and it was he, who, in the final analysis, selected the leaders of working-class organizations.[45] Fascist syndicalism was subordinate to the political control of the movement, and as a consequence, would never constitute a threat either to the integrity or purposes of the Fascist state. The function of the Fascist syndicates was the creation of a new national consciousness, rather than the simple self-defense of the working classes. The first statutes of the Fascist syndicates had expressly stated that their purpose was the furtherance of "progressive and more intense national production" rather than "class struggle." The problems of production had explicit priority, in accordance with the governing strategy of national syndicalism. In conformity with the general economic program of Fascism, Fascist syndicalism committed itself to assisting in the generation of investment capital, in the rationalization and intensification of production through collaboration with management, rather than the provision of agencies for the defense of working-class interests. While this need not be understood to necessarily imply a neglect of the immediate interests of their members, it was clear that the Fascist syndicates had a set of priorities that made the sacrifice of immediate interests of the working classes in the service of long-range collective interests a real, and perhaps recurrent, possibility.[46]

What was unmistakably clear was that Fascist syndicalism

194

would be subordinate to the overall political priorities of Fascism. Syndicalists like Bianchi, Rossoni, and Pighetti specified those priorities with considerable candor. Rossoni reminded the working-class members of the Fascist syndicates that a nation could not be governed well without "disciplined labor." As long as the "capitalist mode of production" gave evidence of superior productive capability, workers must responsibly collaborate in the interests of the "proletarian nation." Labor must be disciplined to increased production not only to assure workers employment and a living wage, but also to create the material preconditions for the elevation of Italy to the rank of an equal and sovereign power among modern nations. That could not be accomplished without frugality, application, and self-discipline. If Italy was to create large-scale industry in circumstances of limited capital and limited resources, labor must commit itself to "loyal cooperation" in the service of a "Free and Greater Italy."[47]

Guido Pighetti, in his turn, was equally explicit. He repeated all the admonitions to be found in the prose of Rossoni. Both had put disciplined labor in the service of the modernization and development of the nation's economy. Both rejected strikes and work stoppages as standard means of class or category defense.[48] Because of Italy's limited productivity, labor would have to work for its increase before it could expect increments in the collective and individual standard of living. To these purposes, Pighetti charged the syndicates with the pedagogical responsibility of reeducating the working classes, so long subject to the antinational and antieconomic influence of traditional socialism. Out of the sentiments and the real, rather than the immediate, needs of the workers of Italy, the syndicates would foster an animating myth that would inspire the greater productive efforts that time, circumstance, and the nation required. The syndicates would function as moral agencies for the Fascist state, a strong state that constituted the unitary and integral

195

will of the nation. "Syndicalist organization," Pighetti told the members of the syndicates, "is one of the instruments with which the Party seeks to accomplish its exalted tasks."[49]

The "majority of Fascist syndicalist theoreticians" Pighetti concluded, recognize the "logical connection" between the historic tasks of the moment and the necessity of a "strong" or "absolute" state, a "dictatorship," that would discipline all the factors of production. Pighetti conceived of that discipline as effected through political means and essentially political agencies.[50]

The Functions of Fascist Syndicalism

These were the general precepts that governed the functions and the ultimate institutionalization of the Fascist syndicates. Even before the March on Rome that brought Fascism to power, the Fascist syndicates had subordinated themselves to the political purposes of the movement. In 1931 Oddone Fantini could insist that "the syndical and corporative movement is . . . controlled by the political movement —the *Partito nazionale fascista*—which exercises an educational and selective control over it, and by the government through the *Consiglio nazionale delle corporazioni* and the Minister of Corporations created by the Regime to organize and discipline all the forces of the nation to the ideal ends of the Revolution."[51]

Even before the Fascist advent to power, the Fascist syndicates, which were to function as organs of the state's political policies, had expanded rapidly. The traditional organizations of labor had disintegrated before Fascist violence, Fascist blandishments, the privileges enjoyed by Fascist organizations, and the lure of the Fascist program. Once Fascism acceded to power there was a literal flood of defections from the socialist and Catholic organizations. By early 1923, the more than two million members of the CGL had dwindled to a mere 212,000. In the same year, the membership of the Catholic CIL was reduced to 450,000 from the

1,250,000 enrolled in 1920. At the same time, Fascist syndicates increased their membership. By 1923 there were more than a million members in the Fascist ranks, and by 1924 that number was over 1,775,000. There were almost two and a half million workers enrolled in the Fascist syndicates by 1926.

How Fascism was to orchestrate this mass became evident almost immediately. In his first address to the assembled parliament, Mussolini maintained that Fascism sought to create the conditions that would make Italy a major world power. To that end, "all interests would be harmonized with those of production. . . . The increase of a nation's prestige is proportional to the discipline it displays internally. . . . The state is [now] strong and it will demonstrate that force against any and everyone. . . . The state does not intend to abdicate before anyone. Whoever opposes the state will be punished. . . . [Fascism] fought and has won in order to create a state that imposes its will on all, on everyone, with necessary and inexorable energy."[52]

The Fascist program of 1921 had explicitly stated that syndicalism was to be understood as serving two fundamental objectives, the same objectives Mussolini had identified in the meeting at San Sepolcro that founded the Fascist movement: national solidarity and the development of the nation's production.[53] The political and economic priorities could hardly have been made more transparent. In June 1923, Rossoni characterized the disposition of Fascist syndicalism as one of "loyalty and collaboration" in the service of Fascism's political ends.[54]

The influence of this disposition among Fascist syndicalists, conjoined with the disintegration of the traditional working-class organizations resulted in a rapid decline in strike activity on the peninsula. In 1921 there had been a total of 1,134 strikes in industry and agriculture. By 1922, with the rapid expansion of Fascist syndicalism, that number had declined to 575 to recede still further in 1923 to 201.

The result of the decline in aggressive working-class defense of wages and living conditions was a correlative diminution of real salaries. The Italian working classes enjoyed a wage level index of 127.01 (computed at 1913=100) in 1921, the last year of activity by the then formidable traditional working-class organizations. In 1922 the index declined to 123.61, and in 1923 it fell to 116.05, to be further reduced in 1924 to 112.62, and finally to reach its lowest point, before the great depression, at 111.48 in 1926.[55] It was during this period that savings and capital accumulation in Italy reached levels not to be attained again until the boom of the 'fifties and 'sixties. In effect, collaboration meant significant constraints on the wage demands of the Italian working classes in order to foster capital accumulation necessary for rapid industrial growth and maintenance. Fascist syndicalism was clearly an instrument of Fascist economic policy.

While Italy was undergoing one of its most impressive periods of economic growth between 1922 and 1929, Italian labor was remunerated at levels only marginally above that of 1913. While industrial production more than doubled on the peninsula, the standard of living of Italian workers remained at about the level attained in 1923.

For the first three years of Fascist rule, the traditional working-class organizations continued to compete with the Fascist syndicates, although their room to maneuver was increasingly restricted. In January 1924, political authorities were given the legal right to oversee "any association or corporation of whatever nature sustained by contributions from workers," in order to assure their "integrity." Authorities could dissolve any offending organization and its property could be transfered to other organizations. Instances of violence were not uncommon. In October 1925, in an agreement signed at the Palazzo Vidoni, representatives of the *Confederazione generale dell'industria*, the chief representative institution of Italian business, agreed, in principle, to recognize the Fascist *Confederazione delle corporazioni* as the sole bargaining agent for the entire Italian working classes. The two confederations, one representing industry and the other the Fascist syndical associations, monopolized the negotiation of labor contracts, thereby excluding from any participation in the nation's economic life both the traditional working-class organizations as well as the locally elected factory committees that had grown up after the end of the First World War.

In November the pact was made law. Labor contracts for entire categories of workers and industries could be entered into only by the Fascist syndicates. In effect, the non-Fascist organizations no longer had any significant economic function. Soon after, the CGL was dissolved and the Catholic CIL was absorbed into the Fascist confederation. By 1925 Fascism had obtained a monopoly of working-class representation.

This monopolization of labor representation was by no means welcomed in industrial circles. While the projected elimination of factory committees restored entrepreneurial control in the individual factories, the threat of massive Fascist control over labor prefigured formidable state intervention in labor negotiations. A Fascist monopoly threatened to severely limit management's freedom of action. Fascist legislation was seen as a serious political threat to capital's freedom to negotiate. Fascists had insisted on the creation of compulsory Labor Courts that would arbitrate labor disputes, an action which industrialists strenuously resisted. The industrialists would have much rather negotiated with competing working-class organizations, each representing only a fractional part of their workers, than face a monolithic Fascist organization and compulsory Labor Courts. In substance, organized industry preferred a liberal arrangement in their disputes with labor at a time when Mussolini and Fascism had made abundantly clear their disposition to abandon economic liberalism.[56]

All this became increasingly apparent as Fascism prepared legislation that would make the pact of the Vidoni Palace the law of the land. From November 1925 until April 1926, the Fascist government prepared legislation formalizing the

199

institutionalization of syndicalism. Both Alfredo Rocco and Mussolini, himself, provided the formal rationale for that legislation in a series of discourses to the Italian parliament. In those speeches, the functions of syndicalism were specifically characterized. For Mussolini, Fascist syndicalism had drawn together the agricultural and industrial working masses of the peninsula and housed them in organizations that "Fascism and the government fully control: they constitute," Mussolini went on, "a mass which obeys."[57]

Mussolini identified the tasks that Fascism had assumed. Its purpose was to husband all the resources available on the peninsula to augment the productive power of the nation. A nation without discipline and without power would be a nation humiliated and oppressed. To enhance the nation's competitive potential all the inherent vitality of capitalism was to be recognized, and the responsibilities of the "captains of industry," the "organizers" of production, must be protected. The working masses must recognize that the enhancement of production and the development of the peninsula required disciplined collaboration under the aegis of the state. But this was not understood to mean that only labor would be subject to Fascist control. The state, Mussolini went on, must assume "imposing tasks." Ultimately, it must "control all the forces of industry, all the forces of finance, and all the forces of labor."[58] Fascist intention, and the intention of the legislation on the syndicates, was totalitarian and hegemonic in purpose.

This was made abundantly clear in the speeches of Alfredo Rocco. Fascism, Rocco told his audiences, had prepared a definitive break with liberalism in all its forms. In a nation such as Italy, without natural resources and afflicted with limited capital and abundant labor, the state must assume the responsibility of resolving the problems of industrial and agricultural labor relations in the interest of "ever increasing intensification and ever increasing rationalization of production." In order to accomplish this, it would be necessary to provide "juridical recognition of the syndicates under the rigorous control of the state," which in turn, would afford "a complete guarantee of discipline and of devotion to the overarching purposes of the nation."[59] All of which implied that both capital and labor would have to subordinate their immediate interests to the long-range interests of Fascism's economic program.

The entire rationale of national syndicalism was, once again, rehearsed. The principal challenge in the modern world was understood to arise out of the conflict between proletarian and plutocratic nations. If Italy would prevail in such a contest, intensive collaboration of all the productive energies on the peninsula must be assured. At this point in history, it was the collective energy of the working classes that required "integration." "The syndicate," Rocco stated, "must necessarily be subject to the control of the state. The syndicate [must become] an organ of the state."[60]

Rocco, like Mussolini and the major theoreticians of national syndicalism, believed the reconstruction of the working-class movement to be the issue of immediate priority because he understood the traditional working-class movement of Italy to be antinational, antistate, and antidevelopmental, and, consequently, a threat to the developmental potential of the nation. By 1926 the domestication of socialism had been accomplished, the traditional working-class organization dismantled, and the agricultural and industrial labor force marshalled into institutions rigorously controlled by the party and the state.

But, as we have seen, in speaking of the new legislation, Mussolini had alluded to control over all the productive forces of the nation. Rocco, in his official defense of the new laws concerning the organization of industry, reminded his audience that Fascism sought not only to control the organization of labor, but "all the forces of the nation," all of which "must be dominated by the state."[61] In fact, it would seem that the legislation devoted to the integration of the syndicates as state organs marked the end of one phase of Fascist policy and the commencement of another. In August

1926, a few short months after the promulgation of the law on the juridical recognition of the Fascist syndicates, Mussolini made his speech at Pesaro in defense of the lire. As we have suggested, the defense of the lire at "quota novanta" signalled Fascism's intention to control its nonmovement allies in the industrial and financial community. In fact, less than a year later, Mussolini's undersecretary, Giacomo Suardo, spoke of the processes involved in the creation of the Fascist state: the first devoted to the defeat of its antinational political enemies, and the second a struggle against "the old economic elites."[62] After the institutionalization of Fascist syndicalism, the effort to extend controls over the industrial and financial elites of the peninsula began with the articulation of an elaborate infrastructure of parastate agencies that would eventually exercise virtual control over the entire productive enterprise of the peninsula. That control was effected through agencies that grew up parallel to the syndical and corporative institutions.[63] The principal function of these latter institutions seems to have been the domestication of labor. The function of the former, the control of capital.

After 1926 strikes were proscribed. The conditions of labor, wage rates, and mobility were determined by state functionaries. In a system of representation that was essentially appointive, the syndicates remained throughout the Fascist period under the dominance of the party and the state.[64] In law, the entire system of syndical organizations was directly, or indirectly (through the minister of corporations), "supervised and controlled" by Mussolini, himself, as head of the government, to "insure the competence, the morality and the secure national faith of its leadership."[65]

By 1930 Sergio Panunzio could provide a rational reconstruction of the historic process that had resulted in the institutionalization of the syndical organizations within the Fascist state structure. He reminded Fascists that the syndicalism of the first Fascists had been one that had recognized the social and historic function of hierarchical and authoritarian organization. It had been a syndicalism that had recognized the necessity of leadership in an environment like that of politically and economically retrograde Italy. The earliest syndicalists had clearly identified the role of elites in periods of vast social and economic change. They had anticipated that men would be mobilized by an appeal to sentiment and to mediate and immediate needs through the agency of myth. Moreover, they had been unalterably opposed to the parliamentarianism that characterized prewar Italian political life.

What had been missing, by and large, before the occasion of the First World War, was a focus for syndicalist mobilization. The war had provided that focus and had transformed the movement into the irresistible political machine it was to become. That focus was the nation. Once the nation was recognized as the center of the belief system of the revolutionary syndicalists, the remaining elements of the system fell effortlessly into place. Every constituent association within the nation state could be bent to the purpose of the state which was the necessary incarnation of the historic community.[66] Like every other constituent association, the syndicates were to be coordinated and subordinated to the absolutely sovereign state.[67] The entire system was animated by myth, ideal aspirations (what Panunzio called its *jus condendum*), and structured by legislation and positive law (*jus conditum*) calculated to service its realization.

The myth of the Greater Italy was understood to serve the most fundamental sentiments and ultimate needs of Italians, and the structure of law created by the revolutionary mass movement was understood to further its realization. Italy had too long remained subject to foreign dominance. If the nation was to free itself from that dominance, what was required was an integral, disciplined, and infrangible unity. The state, through the subsidiary agencies of associated life, would inculcate a new consciousness of dedication, sacrifice, frugality, and enterprise among the masses of the peninsula. Workers' syndicates, business associations, women's groups, student organizations, would all become "schools" for the creation of the "new Fascist man." The

203

state would then discharge an ethical or pedagogical function that would distinguish it from the "neutral" or liberal state. It would become sovereign, not only politically and economically, but ethically as well.

Other than its political and pedagogical functions, the state would assume entrepreneurial functions. It would adjust all sectors of the national community to fulfill the "superior interests of production" in a developmental and modernizing program that would create the necessary conditions for the survival of the nation in a world of competing national units.[68] The state would control the syndicates by its superintendence of the productive processes through price and resource allocation control, exercised either via syndical and intersyndical collective agreement, legislative enactment, or the creation of special parastate agencies which would directly enter into enterprise.[69]

Thus, by 1930 much of the character of the subsequent development of Fascist syndicalism was already explicit. With the crisis of the great depression, the centralization and bureaucratization of the system proceeded apace.[70] These developments did not advance without misgivings on the part of many Fascist syndicalists themselves, but economic problems and Fascist priorities by and large dictated their course.

The immediate effect on the masses organized in the syndicates was a continued policy of controlled consumption to fuel the arduous program of economic restabilization after the depression, and further development under the rigors of autarchy. The wage rates for industrial workers remained fairly constant through 1935 oscillating around 120 (with 1913 = 100). By 1939 the wage rate index had fallen to 105.7, marginally above the wage rate level of 1913.

The evolution of Fascist syndicalism and the consequent creation of an elaborate corporative infrastructure for the peninsula merits treatment in its own right. For our purposes, the principal function of Fascist syndicalism seems reasonably clear: to provide a disciplined and obedient work force that, under the requirements of controlled collective consumption, would provide the energy and the wherewithall for the rapid modernization and industrialization of a retarded economy. It seems equally clear that no matter how much the capitalist classes of Italy were compensated by Fascism, the developmental program was one that was neither of their own choosing, nor one to which they submitted without resistance. That notwithstanding, the entrepreneurial class always operated from a position of strength throughout the life span of the regime. Mussolini, himself, and the Fascist hierarchy in general, recognized the critical functions discharged by a class of reasonably efficient and competent directors in their program of industrial development. Towards the end of his life, Mussolini candidly recognized the privileged position such men occupied in the system.[71]

Given the configuration of forces extant at the time of Fascism's advent, its policies were comprehensible. To some, they even seemed inevitable. Recently, Mihaly Vajda, a Hungarian Marxist attempting an interpretation of Fascism, argued that given Italy's industrial retardation, its singular lack of financial and natural resources, and the technical and organizational "immaturity" of the working classes, "Italian Fascism remained the only progressive solution" to the peninsula's backwardness. Any socialist government of the time would have "justly distributed" Italy's limited resources at the cost of necessary capital accumulation.

> The alliance with Mussolini, on the other hand, meant that the *haute bourgeoisie* renounced political power, but would become able to vigorously increase its economic power: a path to capital accumulation . . . Under Fascist rule, Italy underwent rapid capitalist development with the electrification of the whole country, the blossoming of automobile and silk industries, the creation of an up-to-date banking system, the prospering of agriculture, the reclaiming of substantial agricultural areas through the draining of marshlands, the construction of a considerable network of highways, etc. Italy's rapid progress after WWII

205

and the fact that today it is already moving toward intensive capitalist development would have been unimaginable without the social process begun during the Fascist period.[72]

In effect, however else one chooses to interpret the Fascist experiment in Italy, it is clear that Fascism undertook to modernize and industrialize a retarded industrial and economic system in the effort to create the necessary material foundation to effectively compete with those nations more privileged by nature, history, and circumstance itself. To effect that purpose, Fascism domesticated the forces of labor, and through a concerted policy of controlled consumption, generated the investment capital necessary to sustain the entire enterprise. Fascism conceived of the organizations of labor as "schools of Fascism," "transmission belts" for Fascist purposes. The syndicates, whatever other services they performed, were charged with the obligation of inculcating frugality and a will to service and sacrifice among the working masses of the peninsula. In this, they were by and large successful. By 1935 the working masses of the peninsula, irrespective of the sacrifices they were obliged to bear, were supportive of the regime.[73] By the mid-'thirties, even the most exacerbated anti-Fascist critics were compelled to grant that Fascism had made substantial inroads among the workers of the peninsula to the extent of enrolling them in the party itself.[74]

The Labor Policy of Fascism and Revolutionary Marxism

By the time of its accession to power, Fascism had provided unmistakable signals concerning its subsequent labor policies. Some of the most prominent revolutionary national syndicalists had outlined the relationship they anticipated would obtain between organized labor and state control. The same could hardly be said for Bolshevik theoreticians. Fascism, at its very commencement, provided the rationale for a policy that it would, in substance, effectuate. Bolshevism, on the other hand, was to temporize, vacillate, and obfuscate for more than a decade before its labor policy became reasonably apparent. This is not to say that there was no confusion surrounding Fascist syndicalism. There were those syndicalists in the Fascist ranks who clearly sought an autonomous and libertarian labor policy, but the main current of Fascist thought, exemplified in the works and public statements of Mussolini, Rocco, Pighetti, Panunzio, and Rossoni made abundantly clear the principal features of Fascism's anticipated relationships with labor. In contrast, it was not until the end of the 'twenties, with the inauguration of the first of the five-year plans that the principal function of the trade union organizations of Soviet Russia became evident.

In retrospect, it is reasonably clear that by 1918 Lenin had already begun to significantly modify his conception of the role of workers' organizations in the Soviet Union. His anarcho-syndicalist views of 1917 were very rapidly transformed into those that conceived of the organizations of labor in Russia as agencies of Bolshevik political and economic policy rather than voluntary associations governing industry. As we have suggested, Lenin very soon began to insist on a disciplined labor force that would serve the purposes of increased national production. As early as 1918, Lenin warned labor organizations that the Soviet state could not always meet labor's demands for increased wages, and that the principal function of labor organizations could not be exclusively a defense of the living conditions of the working class.[75] Workers were to serve the general interests of the socialist community rather than their own immediate economic needs. Their function was not that of a "bourgeois trade union." With the advent of socialism, their responsibilities had been transformed.

It was in this context, in the first years of Bolshevik power, that Emma Goldman could lament that "nowhere in the world are labor organizations as subservient to the will and the dictates of the state as they are in Bolshevik Russia."[76] In this regard, Leon Trotsky was characteristically candid. "Socialist theory had no answers," Trotsky informed his audience, with regard to the "quite new questions and new difficulties in the sphere of the organization of labor." He went on to indicate that economic requirements had created unanticipated fundamental problems for Marxists. Marxism had apparently failed to recognize that "man is a fairly lazy animal" and, as a consequence, it would be necessary to discipline labor to its obligations through the liberal use of "state compulsion." "State compulsion," Trotsky insisted, "not only does not disappear from the historical arena, but on the contrary will still play, for a considerable period, an extremely prominent part. . . . The problem before the social organization is just to bring 'laziness' within a definite framework, to discipline it."[77]

In Trotsky's view, the purpose of working-class organizations in Bolshevik Russia was

> not for a struggle for better conditions of labor—that is the task of the social and state organizations as a whole —but to organize the working class for the ends of production, to educate, discipline, distribute, group, retain certain categories and certain workers at their post for fixed periods. . . . For we cannot build socialism on decreased production. . . . The creation of socialist society means the organization of the workers on new foundations, their adaptation to those foundations, and their labor reeducation, with one unchanging end of the increase in the productivity of labor. . . . We say directly and openly to the masses that they can save, rebuild, and bring to a flourishing condition a socialist country only by means of hard work, unquestioning discipline and exactness in execution on the part of every worker.[78]

It was during this first period that labor union leaders were more frequently appointed than elected, and labor organizations were charged with the responsibility of enforcing discipline. They were not to interfere with the one-man management advocated by Lenin as early as 1920. Party groups in the unions and the power of the party to control the appointment of union officials insured political control over the economic organization of the working masses.[79] The state established "wage funds" within which collective contracts were negotiated between management and the monopolized trade union groups. It was within this context that the working-class organizations of the Soviet Union displayed that singular disposition to demand systematic reductions in wage rates even when management was prepared to increase wages. Like the Fascist syndicalists, their principal concern seems to have been the maximization of production at minimal cost.[80]

For a substantial period of time, there were long and acrimonious debates within the Bolshevik ranks concerning the role and function of the labor organizations. Lenin had attempted to compromise the various tendencies within the party, but by the Twelfth Congress of the party most of the "defensive" functions of the unions had been supplanted by a directive that charged them with the obligation of superintending production, reducing absenteeism and labor turnover, and increasing per capita output. By the time Stalin had embarked upon the rapid industrialization and modernization of an autarchic national economy, the labor unions constituted, in fact if not in law, agencies of the state, required to "work out higher production norms; to accept compulsory arbitration—with management in a strong position; to tolerate state regulation of hours and state control over recruitment, the over-all wage bill and contract making."[81] In July 1933, G. D. Veinberg, secretary of the Soviet trade union council, insisted that

> no one but management shall be primarily responsible for technical standardization, for wage scale, quotas, piece rates, etc. Today quite a few comrades in the plants share the idea that the union should have as much to say about

209

wages as management. That is a fundamental error. It would imply that the union takes the place of management. It is a 'leftist' opportunistic distortion, undermining of one-man management, interference with the operational functions of management. This must be stopped.[82]

After 1929, under the direct pressure of the party, the unions were assigned essentially one task, that of increasing output at minimal costs. "The unions, considering themselves guardians of 'financial discipline,' strongly objected to payrolls in excess of plan estimates. They went so far as to bring charges against plant executives for 'exceeding payroll limits.' "[83] Like their Fascist counterparts, the Soviet trade union officials committed themselves to a concerted policy of controlled consumption in the service of the nation's arduous developmental program. The result was, of course, a significant reduction in wage rates. Victor Serge estimates that workers' wages declined as much as sixty percent as an immediate result.[84] By the end of the 'thirties there is some considerable evidence that workers looked upon their unions as nothing more than agencies of management, the party and the state being unable or unwilling to service the immediate economic interests of their members. After 1932 the Congress of Trade Unions, in fact, ceased to meet and no further sessions were called until 1949.[85]

Soviet industrialization during the 'thirties was paid for in substantial part by the workers through a sharp decline in their real earnings. The real earning power of the Soviet worker remained below the level attained by 1928 until long after the termination of the Second World War.[86] Systematic control of consumption through a draconian wage policy provided the compulsory savings necessary to sustain Russia's economic growth. The official text of Stalin's first five-year plan characterized what was to transpire in the following fashion: "Our country makes the unprecedented experiment of tremendous capital construction carried out at the expense of current consumption, at the price of a harsh regime of economy and by sacrificing the satisfactions of today's needs in the name of great historical aims."[87] Soviet Russia had created the mobilizing myth of national greatness and, like Fascist Italy, had conceived of the hierarchical and authoritarian organization of labor as instrumental to the realization of its goals.

Although the Soviet Union has never declared trade union organizations to be official state organs, and although strikes have not been officially proscribed, it is reasonably clear that the controls exercised by the party and the state have effectively orchestrated the work force of the nation to the service of the nation's economic programs. During the 'thirties, the trade union organizations in socialist Russia were transformed from agencies of workers' defense, to schools of communism, the training institutions for dedicated, disciplined, and efficient workers. As such, trade union organizations renounced the bourgeois concern with wage levels, and devoted their energies to the long-range concerns of the Soviet people.

The results obtained were purchased through the exercise of compulsion, violence and the threat of violence, moral suasion, and the invocation of national sentiment. However accomplished, it seems clear that one of the principal functions of the trade union organization in the Soviet Union was control of labor in order to reduce nonproductive consumption. Once Stalin embarked upon a program of rapid industrial development in an isolated economy, his system took on some of the cardinal features of Mussolini's Fascism.

In 1934 Mirko Ardemagni, as a Fascist theoretician, could argue that

> in the course of the Russian Revolution . . . there has been a surreptitious adoption of some of the fundamental political principles that characterize Fascism. . . . Fascism, however one chooses to name it, has made its appearance in Russia . . . [The Bolsheviks] have lit the fires of a patriotism that was unknown in the time of the Czars. . . . They have embraced a conception of nationalism that has more affinities with the political thought of Mussolini than

211

anything imagined by Lenin. . . . Aping the Fascist example, the Bolsheviks no longer address themselves to the "class struggle," but discipline the working-masses to the purpose of the community.[88]

These themes became fairly commonplace among syndicalist theoreticians. Panunzio regularly alluded to Soviet Russia's gradual approximation of Fascist political and economic instrumentalities.[89] Fascists generally recognized the political, economic, and institutional affinities shared by their regime and that created by Stalin during the years of Russia's rapid industrialization and modernization.[90]

The devolution or creative development of revolutionary Marxism into something all but totally unanticipated by traditional socialism has left many socialists more than a little perplexed and dismayed. René Dumont has simply dismissed Stalin's "neo-despotic state" as a "real counter-revolution" which flouted "almost every socialist principle."[91] Bruno Rizzi, on the other hand, maintained that a centralized, bureaucratized and productivist economy, engineered to foster rapid industrialization and modernization, requires the domestication of labor in the service of rapid capital accumulation. The consequence can only be the "involuntary construction of that which Fascism consciously undertook."[92]

As early as 1933 Paul Einzig, as a traditional economist, had called attention to these phenomena. At that juncture he stated:

There is one particular feature of the Fascist economic system which could not escape the attention of the careful reader, that is, the striking similarity between Fascism and Socialism. . . . In the Communist state, where the government is practically the only large employer, relations between employer and employed are governed by substantially the same principles as in the Fascist state. Under both systems strikes are outlawed and production is treated as a public service. . . . It is . . . evident that the aims of Fascism and Socialism are to a very great extent identical.

212

In fact, it may be said without exaggeration that what is happening in Italy today, in the economic sphere, is substantially what would happen under a Socialist government. . . . To a very great extent Fascism is Socialism.[93]

As early as 1920 many revolutionary national syndicalists in Italy, and some traditional Marxists, anticipated just such an involution of revolutionary Marxism in the Soviet Union. They had recognized that the requirements of intensive economic development, totally unanticipated by classical Marxism, would create intolerable tensions in any political system born of revolution in a backward economic environment. They anticipated that the economic functions discharged by the entrepreneurial bourgeoisie would have to be undertaken by their functional surrogates in any developing system, and they recognized the necessity of domesticating and reeducating the working masses. They argued that any program of development must presuppose the geographically defined political nation as its base. And they believed in the necessity of a directive, tutelary, and entrepreneurial elite unitary party in such circumstances. They recognized that competing political parties, organized associations of special interest groups, and regional provincialism, could only dissipate collective energies necessary for the arduous transition from a retarded to a developed industrial and economic system.

Whether the devolution of revolutionary Marxist systems into the analogue of Fascism was an historic necessity, or simply one alternative of a number of alternatives, is a question that can only be addressed by those disposed to write counter-factual history. The fact is that the Soviet Union generated a system sufficiently similar to that of Mussolini's Fascism to be recognized as such by Fascists, Marxists, and bourgeois commentators alike. More than that, the affinities shared constitute evidence that Italy's revolutionary national syndicalists had not been wrong in interpreting Fascism as a modern, if heretical, variant of Marxism.

213

SEVEN

THE ORCHESTRATION OF CONSENSUS

By the time of Fascism's advent to power, its relationship to the masses was already governed by a number of programmatic convictions. Immediately before the seizure of power, for example, in a book heralded by Dino Grandi, one of the hierarchs of the movement, Nello Lazzeroni announced that Fascism, upon acceding to power, would have to assume the responsibility of "educating the masses to a sense of national discipline." Moreover, he characterized the masses as composed of those who "have always allowed themselves to be guided by a minority. . . . The crowd," he further maintained, "must always be led."[1]

Such an assessment of the relationship between Fascist leadership and the masses had become commonplace in the doctrinal literature of the movement. In July 1922, for example, months before the March on Rome, Augusto Turati, subsequently to serve as general secretary of the party, spoke without hesitation of the relatively marginal significance the masses, lacking effective leadership, had had in the events that had transformed the times.[2] Mussolini, himself, long before his accession to power, consistently maintained that Fascism was a movement of a "vanguard minority" committed to mobilizing "inert masses" to collective enterprise.[3]

We have already seen that the most aggressive revolutionary syndicalists had long since argued that revolution required the intercession of a vanguard minority that would serve as a catalyst precipitating revolutionary mobilization. As early as 1903, when they were still orthodox Marxists,

214

A. O. Olivetti, Paolo Orano, and Roberto Michels had explicitly addressed themselves to these issues and given themselves over to these convictions.[4]

Here, again, is a summary of the argument: Men are characteristically and essentially social animals disposed to react to social stimuli. They are subject to mimetic influence; they are preeminently suggestible. They mimic each other and consequently behave in a standard and predictable manner until crisis conditions and special circumstances destabilize established patterns of behavior. At those times, specially gifted individuals, and/or specially gifted minorities, can act as agents of innovative and substantial changes in collective response. Under some indeterminate set of circumstances a small group of men can become spokesmen for a "revolutionary idea" that succeeds in engaging the masses, reorients their behavior, and elevates their sentiments to collective purpose.

Such energizing ideas, as we have seen, were identified by the revolutionary syndicalists as myths, representations of a potential future that would satisfy both the real and immediate needs, as well as the normative sentiments, of potential recruits. For several years the syndicalists conceived of the effective myth in terms of the proletarian general strike. By the end of the first decade of the twentieth century the mobilizing myth, the grand moral idea of the mass-mobilizing minority, had begun to transform itself into the alternative myths that would animate the postwar Fascist movement. At the same time, a select group of younger syndicalist intellectuals were putting together a collection of interrelated propositions about the psychology of collective life, propositions that were to augment the theoretical sketch developed by Marxist heretics as early as 1903.

Syndicalism, Fascism, and the Psychology of the Masses

By the end of the first decade of the present century, syndicalist intellectuals like Roberto Michels and Sergio Pa-

215

nunzio were to provide an account of the factors influencing collective life which was to remain central to Fascist political strategies.

As we have seen, Panunzio understood the interpersonal behaviors of men in social groups to be a function of man's generic suggestibility. He argued that hierarchies, exercising authority and providing mimetic example, organized social life around that suggestibility. By 1908, in a series of articles, Michels took it upon himself to develop just these themes.

In his volume, *Il proletariato e la borghesia nel movimento socialista italiano*, published in 1908, Michels already advanced themes that were to remain critical to the public rationale for Fascism's mobilizational and organizational strategies. In that work, Michels reviewed some of the characteristics of organized socialism in Italy. One of its most salient traits was the leadership of the proletarian masses by declassed bourgeois intellectuals. Wherever the working classes enjoyed an option, Michels argued, they invariably chose intellectuals, journalists, lawyers, professors, and other academicians, as their leaders. But more important than the fact of bourgeois intellectual leadership, were the reasons Michels advanced as its explanation.

Michels argued that the development of organization for the pursuance of collective ends necessarily implies leadership roles for those few men possessed of technical and administrative capabilities. The leadership roles of any organization tend to be occupied by a relatively small number of the membership. Most members are so organizationally and technically incompetent that they could not be expected to exercise any decisive functions. But more than that, Michels went on, most people have an "atavistic need to be led by someone."[5] The masses have a generic disposition to search out leaders.

By the time Michels' volume appeared in print, it was obvious that his generalizations concerning the nature of organizations, leadership, and the relationship of leaders to those led, were not to be restricted to socialist parties in general, or to Italy in particular. In the *Riforma sociale* of 1908 Michels could bring himself to speak of the universal "fatality of the 'political class' "—the historic "necessity" of elite rule. The inevitability of minority rule is a consequence of the fact that "the majority of humanity is, and will always remain, unable and perhaps incapable of governing itself. . . . [The] majority of men are constrained, by an historic fatality, to submit to the dominion of a minority and to serve as a pedestal to its glory."[6]

To support these general claims, Michels listed the factors that contributed to their historic manifestation. He spoke of the "apathy" characteristic of the vast majority of men. Only under critical conditions could the "inert masses" be moved by the invocations of a mobilizing minority. Michels alluded to the antecedent and contemporary work of Victor Considerant, Ludwig Gumplowicz, Gaetano Mosca, and Vilfredo Pareto, men whose work had become increasingly influential among the revolutionary syndicalists.

In another piece published a scant two years later, Michels maintained that the contemporary world was characterized by the nominal involvement of the masses in public events. For a variety of reasons, he argued, the pursuit of contemporary goals requires, more than ever, some kind of organization that could accommodate available masses. Organization, in turn, requires the allocation of authority. The effective exercise of authority implies leaders possessed of the skills requisite to its discharge—once again, a minority. "Whoever speaks of organization," Michels concluded, "necessarily speaks of a tendency toward oligarchy."[7]

All the necessary features of organization—rapid executive decision, technical and administrative skills, the continuity required by bureaucratic structures—demand a controlling hierarchy of restricted and essentially self-perpetuating members. But, once again, more than these institutional and technical requirements, Michels spoke of "psychological properties" "common to humankind" that made minority rule a predictable eventuality: "The natural thirst for com-

217

mand that characterizes leaders corresponds to the natural need on the part of the crowd to be led as well as by the apathy of the masses. Moreover among the masses there is a profound impulse to venerate those who are their superiors. In their primitive idealism, they have a need for a secular 'divinity,' to whom they become attached with blind affection."[8] Moreover, the masses display an overwhelming gratitude toward those who lead them, a display that is continually reinforced by the very suggestibility of crowds.

In the course of his discussion, Michels spoke of "every human aggregate" and "every organization" as characterized by these endemic features, but he addressed himself specifically to "revolutionary parties" at critical points in his exposition. If revolutionary movements entertain the prospect of success, they require a leadership capable of making rapid and decisive judgments and implementing their decisions. In parties where leadership does not enjoy the effective power to undertake such judgments and pursue such decisions, opportunities are lost. The movement bogs down in complicated and tortuous deliberation, ideas and principles are compromised, and theories are diluted by qualifications that make them ineffectual. The suggestibility of masses, which renders organization powerful and combat effective, dissipates itself in factional and sectarian strife. Under the conditions of intraorganizational strife, individual leaders collect their respective following around themselves, and the organization disaggregates. All the strengths that attend the suggestibility and the "religiosity" of crowds are turned inward and the revolutionary party disintegrates under centrifugal pressures, each factional leader carrying his followers with him.[9]

All these arguments found their most explicit expression in Michels' *Zur Soziologie des Parteiwesens in der modernen Demokratie* published in 1911. That volume has now become a classic in Anglo-American political sociology under its English title, *Political Parties*. In fact, the book was addressed to those critical syndicalist concerns with the relationship between the leaders and the followers in political and revolutionary organizations. In it Michels restated the conviction, largely shared by revolutionary syndicalists like A. O. Olivetti, Paolo Orano, and Sergio Panunzio, that "in the mass . . . there is an immense need for direction and guidance. This need is accompanied by a genuine cult for the leaders, who are regarded as heroes." The mass needs leadership because "the principle of organization is an absolutely essential condition for the political struggle of the masses," and organization requires all those technical, administrative, and leadership talents distributed so parsimoniously among men. The consequence is elite or oligarchical rule: "organization implies the tendency to oligarchy."[10]

In his *Zur Soziologie* Michels repeated the convictions underlying the arguments of three or four years earlier. The masses were apathetic, characterized by a need for guidance and possessed of sincere gratitude "for those who speak and write on their behalf." As a consequence, political leadership finds itself with the opportunity of employing a "bad means to a good end." The apathetic and incompetent masses can be mobilized, activated, and directed to serve collective purpose —ends they would never serve as individuals or without leadership. Political leaders, during "periods of lively excitement," can orchestrate the sentiment of masses, their dependency, their disposition to venerate "heroic" leaders, and their suggestibility, to great revolutionary and historic enterprise.[11]

Those leaders who succeed in mobilizing masses generally display a number of charismatic attributes. They are effective speakers, prideful, determined, and knowledgeable. They frequently display "a catonian strength of conviction, a force of ideas often verging on fanaticism, and which arouses the respect of the masses by its very intensity, [and a] self sufficiency, [often] accompanied by arrogant pride."[12]

In effect, technical, administrative, and institutional requirements, conjoined with the generic psychological dispositions of the majority of men, and enhanced by the personal attributes of the leadership itself, make minority dominance

219

an operational necessity and a predictable eventuality in political life.

More frequently than not, of course, political life displays a stability and continuity that bespeaks the tolerance and the passivity of the masses. Only a crisis of objective social, economic, and political contingencies sets the stage for the mobilization of collective energies. Furthermore, those energies are fired only if a "recognition of those crisis conditions" is inspired by an aggressive and gifted leadership that more often than not originates among the "privileged" classes. "It would seem to be a psychologico-historical law," Michels argued, "that any class which has been enervated and led to despair in itself through prolonged lack of education and through deprivation of political rights, cannot attain to the possibility of energetic action until it has received instruction concerning its ethical rights and politico-economical powers, not alone from members of its own class, but also from those who belong to what in vulgar parlance are termed a 'higher' class." Such leaders are the principal precipitating causes of vast social change. Armed with the "preponderant energy of a comprehensive theory" they can marshall mass sentiment and emotion to a grand historic mission.[13]

It seems obvious that for Michels, in circumstances where objective crisis does not exist, and historic missions are precluded, some form of competitive democratic pluralism—with each political faction competing with others—is the rule. Such pluralistic systems are the least hazardous form of political polity.[14] But equally obvious is the fact that during "revolutionary epochs" a self-possessed, authoritarian, and voluntaristic elite recommends itself to the service of vast social change. Revolutionary parties require the single-mindedness of "theory," and centralized direction and control, if the suggestibility and obedience of masses are to be orchestrated to revolutionary purpose.[15]

These were the convictions shared by those revolutionary syndicalists who passed effortlessly into the Fascist ranks in 1919. And these were the convictions, however fragmentary and elliptically expressed, to be found in Mussolini's prose and discourses produced between 1910 and 1919 during the incubation period of Fascism.

For the purposes of our account, the most important development that took place between 1910 and 1919 was the syndicalist discovery of the myth of the nation. As we have seen, the syndicalists had already discovered the functional utility of nationalist appeals with the War in Tripoli. Michels himself, who could still speak of the "unreality" of the nation as late as 1908,[16] published a tightly constructed defense of Italy's national aspirations in its war against the Turks three years later. By 1911 the "sentiment of nationality" began to figure prominently in his analysis of complex social and political events.[17] By 1914 he could allude to the influence of national sentiment in the evolution of contemporary and historic events as evidence of a failure on the part of "historical materialism" to adequately assess the impact of noneconomic variables upon social life.[18] In 1917, in his discussion of the sociological views of Vilfredo Pareto, Michels spoke of the role of sentiment in the mobilization of otherwise inert masses, and specifically alluded to the importance of national "ideals" and national "faith" as just such animating sentiments.[19]

The logic of Michels' argument is quite transparent. Men, to be mobilized to a collective mission, must be infused with some grand ideal that harnesses their energy, prompts them to self-sacrifice and obedience, and disciplines their enterprise. Collective purpose requires a sentiment of solidarity, and solidarity is born of sustained common interest, common suffering, and shared aspirations. Such a sustained common experience requires organization to achieve its resolution, and organization necessarily entails oligarchy.[20]

As long as Michels believed the interests, suffering, and aspirations central to the twentieth century to be those of the proletariat alone, the mobilizing revolutionary myth was understood to be that of the general strike or the working-class revolution. When he discovered the reality of the

221

"proletarian nation," a reality that involved substantially all Italians, Michels identified national ideals as the central mobilizing myth of our time.[21]

All that is necessary to provide the outlines of Fascism's mobilization strategy at this point is to reflect for a moment on Michels' analysis of collective psychology. If the nation is the critical institution of our time, if organization is necessary to further the interests of the nation, and if oligarchy is necessary for effective organization, one needs but one further element to complete the rationale for Fascist politics. That element is the decisive function of the "Leader." And Michels early provided for just that function.

In his discussion of the role of leaders in organization, Michels indicated that in circumstances where revolutionary organizations are effective, and conditions are critical, the masses will often understand the leader to be the very "incarnation" of the revolutionary party.[22] Since the party acts in the ultimate interests of the nation, the leader becomes the incarnation of the nation. The consequence is a politically convenient series of substitutions: the leader is identified with the party and the party is identified with the nation. Whatever the leader chooses to do constitutes a choice made by both the party and the nation. Mobilization takes place around the leader as the living embodiment of revolutionary and national purpose.

In 1926, when Michels addressed an academic audience at the University of Rome, his rationale for Fascism's "charismatic dictatorship" was simply a reiteration of the arguments he had put together as a syndicalist long before the founding of the movement.[23] Mussolini acknowledged his debt to Michels by charging him with the responsibilities of teaching the party cadre of the "new Fascist generation," and from 1928 until his death in 1936, Michels served on the Fascist Faculty of Political Science at the University of Perugia as a colleague of A. O. Olivetti, Paolo Orano, and Sergio Panunzio.[24]

It is quite clear that the revolutionary syndicalists provided Fascism with its conceptions of mass-mobilization and the orchestration of consensus. At the same time that Michels was publishing his work on the psychology of masses, Sergio Panunzio was publishing his rationale for revolutionary violence, its place in the mobilization of masses, and the role of the revolutionary party in the political struggles of postwar Italy.

The Rationale of Orchestrated Consensus

By the end of the first world conflict, Panunzio had made the transit to a form of revolutionary national syndicalism. As we have seen, he had already recognized the mobilizational function of national myths—political formula—in which the nation was the primary object of collective loyalty. In Panunzio's judgment, each man's most fundamental interests were invested in the nation.[25] He was to argue, with Michels,[26] that those interests, under the conditions which prevailed in the twentieth century, were best served by the rapid industrial and economic development of the nation.

As we have seen, Panunzio saw the First World War as the occasion of Italy's liberation from the constraints imposed on its development by the advanced capitalist nations. The central argument in his *Il concetto della guerra giusta*, a defense of Italy's involvement in the First World War, was predicated on just such a conviction. Italy's war as a "revolutionary war" because it augured the destruction of the established international *status quo* in which Italy was assigned a subordinate place among nations. The "liberating" war would free the forces of national development and end the subservience that had weighed heavily on Italians for three centuries.

Panunzio understood the commitment to intervention in the war of 1914-1918 to have been the consequence of the confluence of pervasive and natural national sentiment and the evident and felt needs of economic development. Mass mobilization was possible because of just such a confluence

223

of "ideal" and "material" interests. A new social system was contending for a place in the international arena.

Panunzio maintained that at critical junctures in history violence attends the advent of a new social system. Such is the case when the "new order" is compelled to struggle against the force that sustains the traditional establishment. Under such circumstances, violence is necessary to break through the crust of conventional behaviors, locked fast in habit and conformity, and sustained by establishment force. At such times, a small vanguard leadership energizes revolutionary resistance by mobilizing those elements of the community most directly caught up in revolutionary sentiment, and most characterized by antiestablishment interests.

It was clear that in Panunzio's judgment the revolutionary interventionists, the radical syndicalists, constituted the leavening for the popular insistence upon Italian involvement in in the First World War. The interventionists saw the war as a revolutionary occasion for the completion of Italy's unification as well as for its industrial and economic development.

After the successful conclusion of the war, Panunzio wrote his *Diritto, forza e violenza*, the rationale for "internal war," the revolutionary advent of Fascism.[27] The *Diritto* was published in 1921, coinciding as it happened, with the mobilizational phase of the movement. It was obviously written much earlier. And, in fact, the logic of his argument was the same as that which sustained his rationale for Italy's involvement, in 1915, in the "revolutionary war." That war having been concluded, Panunzio turned his attention to the internal war, the struggle against the old political dispensation that seemed to inextricably hobble the peninsula's developmental potential.

The crisis that had invested the peninsula after the termination of international hostilities provided the occasion for a revolutionary advent of a "new state" as opposed to that which was "old" and "traditional."[28] In Panunzio's judgment, there were new and dynamic interests that could not be accommodated within the structure of the liberal parliamentary

224

state. Those interests, fired by the new sense of nationality, provided the energy for vast social and political change. Alienated from the network of established political institutions, there were masses to be mobilized through the agencies of the Fascist party and the Fascist syndicates. Against the traditional mimetic behaviors of a population schooled in the old system and constrained by established law, the Fascist mobilization would precipitate changed behaviors, mimetic responses to Fascist invocation and inspired by Fascist example. Such a tempered and disciplined mass would exercise the right of violence in the service of the revolutionary potential state against the moribund traditional system sustained by conventional legal, and counter-revolutionary, force.[29]

In Panunzio's judgment, that violence which is the handmaiden of a new state aborning is a "licit," even a "moral" violence, rationally calculated to foster the advent of a system more responsive to the imperative needs of a new epoch. Moreover, the manifestation of that violence, Panunzio took to be a sign heralding the new system of laws opposed to the established "positive law" of the system in decline. In the sense that the violence of revolution is the preamble to a new system of laws and a new state order, that violence is "dialectically" "conservative." In principle, the state, and the laws that constitute the rule governance of the state, is perpetual, eternal.[30] Revolution employs violence in the service of the *idea* of the state and of the law, but it is a moral violence in the service of a new state.

As we have seen, Panunzio identified the period of insurrectionary violence as the transitional phase between two concrete and historically determinate state systems. Once a revolutionary phase is closed, it is necessary to codify and formalize the new laws implicit in the revolution. This latter period he identified as that of *revolutionary dictatorship*, a period in which collective behaviors have not yet been fixed and the new legal and institutional forms have not yet been firmly established.[31]

Revolutionary dictatorship is the product of successful

225

revolutionary violence, and that violence is a rational, organized, moral, and progressive necessity in a given set of international, social, historic, political, and economic circumstances. The agency that moblizes popular energy behind the revolutionary violence and incorporates the directive will of the emergent new state system is the minoritarian revolutionary party. The forces mobilized to revolution are animated and disciplined by mimetic example and authoritarian leadership under the aegis of the party. Control under such circumstances is often irregular and episodic. The suggestibility of masses, collective behaviors sustained by social sanction and shaped by peer pressures, are all effective for revolutionary purpose, but not sufficient to insure the instauration and perpetuity of the new dispensation. What is required at the close of the insurrectionary period is the systematic inculcation of a new morality, a new system of interpersonal behaviors, a new mentality, an effortless discipline, and organized commitment among the passive majority. As a consequence, the revolutionary party and the revolutionary dictatorship must assume pedagogical and moral responsibilities that distinguish them from liberal and parliamentary movements and pluralistic rule.[32] The revolutionary dictatorship is obliged to create a new consciousness among the majority of citizens.

The minoritarian revolutionary party and the revolutionary dictatorship are phenomena peculiar to the modern world. They are products of the availability of mobilizable masses prevalent only in our own times. Because of such an availability, coupled with an effective communications media which make the masses specially responsive to political suggestion, mythic language and symbolic speech have become the necessary instruments of contemporary revolutionary politics.[33]

Successful revolution that fully mobilizes the elemental energy of the masses, and marshalls it in effective organization ultimately produces revolutionary dictatorship, which, as the state, monopolizes all the agencies of formal sanction and public education in the totalitarian defense of emergent revolutionary law and its ancillary institutions. More than that, Panunzio continued, the psychological characteristics of masses, the demands of revolutionary activity, and the requirements of rapid industrial and economic development, produce an atmosphere of intense emotion. The masses need reassurance, a sense of collective confidence, an instrumental purposefulness. What results is an atmosphere that is "religious" in character. Masses must be inspired by the revolutionary vanguard minority with faith in order to negotiate the difficulties that attend all these processes. The revolutionary party and its dictatorship become "ecclesiastical" and "missionary" in character. The nation embarks on a grand "historic mission."[34]

The masses search out a symbol that incarnates collective aspirations, that embodies collective ideals, that affords assurance of success. The dictatorship becomes "heroic," and the leader of the revolution becomes the focus of collective faith. What emerges is the *heroic dictatorship*, a special instance of revolutionary dictatorship in which the single leader becomes the embodiment of the ideals of the masses. At that point, Panunzio closed his argument with a reference to Michels' conception of "charismatic rule," and the rationale for government by orchestrated consensus was complete.[35]

The Apparatus of Orchestration

By the time Fascism came to power, it possessed a fully articulated set of convictions about the governance of masses. Among these was a conviction that several critical myths would provide the rationale for its mobilizational and governing strategies: the myth of the "Greater Italy" and the myth of the "Duce." In some ultimate sense, given the series of substitutions implied in Fascism's commitments, the Greater Italy was the Duce and the Duce was the incarnation of the hopes and potential of the Greater Italy. "Productivism," in turn, was an ancillary myth, a programmatic commitment

227

necessary to the grandeur of the nation. All of Fascist propaganda, throughout the years of Fascist rule, turned on these mutually interpenetrative and supportive myths. Fascists were convinced that the invocation of these myths would create a unified and disciplined consensus out of a divergent and heterogeneous population.

Some considerable time before the March on Rome, Michels had reminded revolutionaries that as early as the mid-nineteenth century Carlo Pisacane, the revolutionary socialist, had recognized that only national sentiment could bind the heterogeneous population of the peninsula into a disciplined and effective unity.[36] Fascist mobilization, propaganda, and institutional arrangements, were predicated on just that conviction. A new national consciousness would assume priority over class, regional, sectarian and organizational interest. To this end, almost immediately upon the seizure of power, the Fascists attempted to impose the new "national perspective" on the principal newspapers of the peninsula. They used party funds or funds subventioned from nonmovement allies, to purchase control over some of the major newspapers of Italy.[37] Where this was impossible, they used violence and threats of violence to suppress the public expression of antinational sentiment. Legislation promulgated in July 1923, less than a year after the seizure of power, placed newspapers and periodic publications under the control of the provincial prefects who were charged with insuring that no "articles, comments, notes, titles, vignettes" might be published that would "impair the nation's interests . . . provoke alarm among the people or disturb public order." Anything that conduced to "crime, inspired class hatred, provoked disobedience, or compromised discipline" was to be suppressed.[38]

Mussolini had early expressed the conviction that daily newspapers, the principal mass medium available at the time of Fascism's advent to power, were of critical importance in the orchestration of public sentiment. He was quick to place the press office directly under his ministrations and charged Cesare Rossi, in whom he had complete confidence, with control over the issuance of official information. With the legislation of 1923, the Fascist party gave clear evidence of its intention to significantly shape public belief and public attitude. Through that legislation, and with his control over the press office, Mussolini effectively dominated some of the most significant avenues of public communication.[39]

Furthermore, although radio communication had not yet developed to the point where it could be considered a mass medium, Mussolini insured government control over the installation of radio communications facilities with decree legislation in February 1923, about four months after the seizure of power.[40] The new legislation anticipated control of radio communication to preclude the possibility that any transmissions "offensive to the regime" might be effected.[41] In August 1924, the state assumed monopoly control over radio communication with the creation of the parastate agency *Unione radiofonica italiana* (URI).

In effect, from the very commencement of the regime, Fascists concerned themselves with the control of information and the mass media of communication. In November 1925, the government created *l'Unione cinematografica educative* (LUCE), charged with the preparation of films for the general public.

By 1925 the regime had largely succeeded in controlling the press. In that year, an official governmental syndicate for journalists was instituted, a state organization which would include, in principle, all practicing newspapermen. The syndicate of newsmen would be recognized, in law, by the state. Governing the state syndicate would be a regulative body equivalent to the licensing and control agency familiar to practicing attorneys and physicians in the United States. The difference, of course, turns on the criteria of competence employed in their respective licensing procedures. Physicians and lawyers, presumably, must meet some objective tests of

229

competence. In Fascist Italy, journalists had to meet some moral, that is to say political, criteria before their competence could be certified.[42]

As early as 1925 the radio programming from Milan was under the direction of Ettore Romagnoli, a Fascist intellectual, who considered the medium serviceable for education of the listening masses. The number of receivers in Italy was, of course, very small, but as early as Mussolini's announcement of the "Battle for Grain" in 1925, the radio was employed to generate collective enthusiasm for the enterprise. In the rural areas, where receivers were not available, the radio communications were tied into public address systems and the agricultural population collected in town squares to receive the Duce's admonitions. Radio time was allotted to the information bulletins of the agrobiological teams who were encouraging large-scale utilization of contemporary, scientific animal husbandry and farming methods. In effect, as early as 1926, a systematic effort was made to create a radio communications infrastructure that would reach a mass audience. At the same time, children's broadcasts were initiated to influence the "new generation."[43]

For the first two or three years of Fascist rule, political circumstances rendered it all but impossible to systematically implement Fascist strategies of moral education for the inert masses. Mussolini found himself confined by the quasi-liberal convictions of his nonmovement allies. Nonetheless, the first moves in the direction of political control of the media of information were undertaken. After the successful resolution of the Matteotti crisis, which had threatened the regime in 1924, the implementation was undertaken with considerably less reservation. By 1926, the control of the press had been all but entirely accomplished in principle. The Fascist government had already begun to lay heavy hands on the radio and film industries. It was clear that Fascism was prepared to control the mass media in the effort to remake Italians in the Fascist image.

In March 1925, two months after the resolution of the

Matteotti crisis, Fascist intellectuals met in Bologna to inaugurate a massive "reeducation" of the Italian citizenry through control over the principal agencies of Italian intellectual life. The talk was of "disciplining" the nation's culture. In June of that year, less than six months after Mussolini's speech announcing the end of the "liberal" period of coalition and marking the end of the Matteoti crisis, the party founded the *Istituto nazionale fascista di cultura*. At the inaugural meeting of the Institute, Giovanni Gentile, who was to serve as the "philosopher of Fascism," announced that the function of the *Istituto* would be the "creation of a new consciousness" for the Italy that Fascism sought to engender. Italy, he argued, must become Fascism, all one and seamless. The identification would be governed by the guidance of a "hero," the "incarnation" of the idea which would make nation and party a comprehensive unity. Masses would be animated by a "faith," by "myths" which generate a consensus of the majority. Intellectuals would foster a consensus that would feed on the "force of sentiment and will" and would enable vast social and historic change. All of this would be inspired by the "thought" of a "few guiding spirits"—in fact, by the thought of a single man, the Duce.[44]

The *Istituto* attracted many of the luminaries of Fascism. The administrative council included men of unquestioned ability such as Balbino Giuliano, Francesco Ercole, Arnaldo Volpicelli, and the internationally famous Gioacchino Volpe. The functions of the *Istituto* were clearly prefigured in the strategies suggested by the revolutionary national syndicalists some considerable time before Fascism's accession to power. Even Gentile's characterization of the Institute's tasks were fully compatible with the goals envisioned by the revolutionary national syndicalists.

Given this orientation, it is clear that the Fascist concern with culture did not necessarily involve commitment to any specific content. One might be a cultural traditionalist or a Futurist, a classicist in artistic or literary representation, or an impressionist, and still represent Fascist culture. Refer-

231

ences to a specifically Fascist culture alluded to the inculcation, among the general citizenry, of a few politically significant convictions: an identification of Fascism with the nation, and a recognition that the Duce was the incarnation of both the party and the nation.

One need only peruse the literature produced by Fascists devoted to Fascist culture to establish this fact. Balbino Giuliano published a little book on Fascist culture in 1929 which made this quite evident. For Giuliano, Fascist culture implied no less and no more than inspiring, among the masses of the peninsula, a disposition to see the nation as the subtending reality of all their most fundamental needs. To instill, in the consciousness of Italians, the elements of Fascist culture meant to make them aware that Italy's poverty, its retarded economic development, and its international inferiority, could only be offset by collective enterprise, dedication, sacrifice, discipline, and collaboration. To animate Italians with Fascist culture meant, for Giuliano, to compel them to recognize that what the new Italy required was accelerated capital accumulation, industrial production, economic modernization, effective access to raw materials, colonial expansion, and the creation of enhanced defense capabilities.[45]

To accomplish this, all citizens must be inspired with a sense of duty, discipline, and sacrifice. Each must be moved by a "religious faith" which would sustain enterprise and justify, if necessary, even "supreme sacrifice."[46] In substance, Fascist culture throughout the tenure of the regime referred to the elements of what is identified, in our own time, as "political culture"—the inculcation of certain "functional virtues" among citizens. The institutions of Fascist culture were charged with the responsibility of awakening among the masses the recognition of civil responsibility.[47]

Throughout the Fascist period, Fascists remained reasonably discrete about what the specific aesthetic orientation of a Fascist culture might be. They insisted that Fascism "operated with maximum prudence, refusing to impose precon-

ceived and obligatory schemata for artistic expressions."[48]
Mussolini and the Fascist hierarchy remained circumspect
about the particular artistic content of Fascist cultural enterprise. While there was a tendency to favor a kind of heroic
realism, there was an indisposition to insist on artistic or
literary conformity.[49] Gentile, in one of the more sophisticated expressions of this commitment, insisted that Fascist
culture did not possess a specific content, but was characterized by a certain "style." It was "national, disciplined, religious, serious" and preeminently political. It was "antiag-
nostic," "antineutral." It was calculated to fashion the "new
man" and the "new consciousness" suitable to the "new
Italy."[50] Gentile recognized that there were "instrumental
elements" in the national culture that were utilitarian and
governed by nonpolitical criteria (the technical and applied
sciences). He also recognized that the norms of competence
for disciplines such as history were essentially nonpolitical.
But he maintained that there must be a "Fascist science" and
a "Fascist historiography," a study of science and history that
satisfied the independent and intrinsic norms of research,
scholarly and archival study, but which could be put to the
service of furthering Fascist purpose.[51]

For Fascists, then, Fascist culture implied, in substance,
effect, and intention, a commitment to a relatively specific
party political culture. Its specific immediate purpose was to
"unite all the Italians in the new faith."[52] As long as scientists and artists of whatever sort, and the cultural agencies
of the peninsula of whatever character, displayed a "proper
sense of political responsibility,"[53] the particular scientific,
aesthetic, or artistic form of expression undertaken was of
relatively little concern to the party. Those who have sought
to identify Fascism with a specific form of scientific or artistic
expression, empiricism, romanticism, classicism, Futurism, or
what have you, have missed the central instrumental and
politically functional character of Fascist cultural concerns.[54]
Neither Mussolini nor the party ever anointed a particular
form of scientific or artistic expression as official. Whatever

233

inured men to collective purpose, collective enthusiasm, and political conformity, became a constituent part of the Fascist cultural apparatus. The entire enterprise was an acting out of those strategies put together long before the March on Rome.

The Fascist Institute of Culture was only one among the first of several similar intellectual organizations that served as vehicles for Fascist political culture. In 1923 the theoretical journal *Critica fascista* had been founded along with *Educazione fascista*. During the first years of the regime the *Consiglio nazionale delle richerche*, devoted to the organization and control of scientific research, was inaugurated. This was followed by the *Istituto di studi Romani* for the study of Roman history, the *Istituto internazionale del cinema educativo* for the film industry, the *Commissione nazionale italiana per la cooperazione intellettuale* and the *Accademia d'Italia* which brought together some of the most important intellectual elites of the peninsula. With the incorporation of scientists, professionals, artists, and writers in state-controlled syndicates after 1926, much of Italian intellectual life thus fell under the direct or indirect influence of Fascist political culture. Alongside the control of the mass media, Fascists anticipated a centralized and bureaucratic control over the critical elements of intellectual life that would domesticate it to political purpose. The process, if it were to be effective, could not rest there. Fascism, from its very inception, concerned itself with the youth of the nation and its political integration. That preoccupation found expression in the program of Fascist education.

By 1926 Fascism had organized the principal instruments to orchestrate the public life of Italy. By that time the youth formations that had accompanied the rise of Fascism in 1921 were reorganized into the *Opera nazionale Balilla* (ONB) which enrolled into its ranks all the youth of the peninsula from six to eighteen years of age. Children from six to eight were organized in the *Figli della lupa*; those from eight to fourteen were marshalled into the columns of the *Balilla*; and those from fourteen to eighteen constituted the membership of the *Avanguardisti*. At eighteen, the young men passed into the *Fasci giovanili di combattimento* or the *Milizia volontaria per la sicurezza nazionale* (the institutionalized "squads" of the insurrectionary period). The women, in turn, were enrolled in the *Fasci femminili*. At twenty-one, both men and women were incorporated into the party.

The *Opera nazionale Balilla* served as a docile conductor for political propaganda. Members swore an oath of fealty and obedience to the Revolution and the Duce. Political indoctrination turned on the standard themes of national integrity, development, and prospective glory.[55] The figure of the "Dux" loomed large over all the activities of the ONB.

University students, in their turn, were mobilized into *Gruppi universitari fascisti* (GUF). Their activities were supported by direct state subvention. Their function was to devote themselves to the "betterment" of their members, to "nurture, under the austere discipline of the Party, a political consciousness and passionate patriotism that would foster a will to spontaneous and joyous obedience."[56] However complex, conflicting, and acerbic the debate among Fascist educators concerning the particulars of their undertaking, the intention of Fascist education was transparent. The central and critical pedagogical concern was political.[57] Pedagogues were charged with the responsibility of creating a unified community that would serve as a support base for a regime of national unity and economic development. That base would have the tensile strength to sustain the pressures generated by a program of development that would lift the nation out of its long-standing international inferiority to a level of international power.[58] The educational system, as early as 1924, was assigned the task of fostering a "profound and unitary national sentiment" that would satisfy the precondition for the economic and industrial expansion of the national community.[59]

The new consciousness exemplified in that pervasive, unitary, and developmental sentiment would be animated by the

235

"myth of the nation . . . the myth of the greatness of the nation" and a dedication to the man who incarnated that myth, the "genius Mussolini."[60] Anything else would dissipate collective energies and impair collective effort.

For all intents and purposes, Fascist education, like Fascist culture, simply implied the indoctrination of Fascist principles. It was Fascism's political and developmental program that provided the content of both culture and pedagogy.[61] For Fascists there could be no art for art's sake, nor science for science's sake, nor education for the sake of education. Educational effort, like every cultural expression, was a political statement. As a consequence, every artist, scientist, and pedagogue had to deliver evidence of political orthodoxy. The more intransigent Fascists demanded, in fact, not only orthodoxy but political enthusiasm. Teachers were enrolled in Fascist syndicates controlled by the party and the state, and ultimately, in 1931, university professors were obliged to take an oath of allegiance to the regime (an oath they all took with rare exceptions).

All Italians were to be trained to a "devoted subordination" to the national regime. They would learn to sacrifice and obey; they would learn to submit to rigorous discipline and suffer privation, all in the service of the advancement of the national community.[62]

The justificatory rationale for such postures was as transparent as its purposes. In 1926 A. C. Puchetti provided an account of the sociological bases of Fascist cultural and educational policies in which he rehearsed all the arguments that had been broadcast by Michels, Panunzio, Olivetti, and Orano. What the nation required, according to Puchetti, was a dedicated elite, capable of providing mimetic models for the masses, masses that were "technically and psychologically incapable of directly governing themselves." Employing imagery made familiar by Pareto, he spoke of society as a "pyramid," at the base of which "indifferent and inert masses" were to be found. Shaping that potential and elemental energy was the party, itself dominated at the apex, by an exiguous minority.[63]

These, of course, were convictions Fascism had carried with it to power in October 1922. Its control of the press, radio, and film production[64] constituted an acting out of just those convictions. Its control of education constituted but one further instance of their application. By 1926 much of the foundation for the orchestration of public opinion had been excavated. However incomplete the edifice, and however incompetent the individual or collective effort, the intentions of Fascist policy were clear.

During those same years, Fascist policy extended its control over the population through intrusions into leisure time. In May 1925, the *Opera nazionale dopolavoro* (OND) was founded, an after-work organization that gathered the working masses together for state-sponsored activities. Illiteracy was still high, particularly among the older workers, the availability of radio receivers minimal, and regular access to films unlikely. Through the agencies of the *Dopolavoro*, Fascism could cultivate the elements of Fascist political culture among those who might otherwise remain outside the intersecting circles of the press, the radio, and the cinema.

The *Dopolavoro* organization was under the direct control of the secretary of the party, and, through him, under the tutelage of Mussolini himself. The organization provided a wide range of cultural and leisure-time activities for the industrial and agrarian working class. It sponsored music recitals, excursions, sporting events, films, radio, theatrical and folkloric presentations, educational courses, and national ceremonial displays. Its immediate purpose, in the words of Achille Starace, was to "elevate" the working masses, to "make them love their nation," to generate in them the enthusiasm that sustains collective enterprise, to provide them with the realization of the historic significance of the Fascist revolution.[65]

The *Dopolavoro* was further conceived as a means of en-

237

hancing the productivity of the masses.[66] It thus served at least two critical functions for the regime: it provided a channel for inculcating a new Fascist consciousness among the working classes and it provided technical and vocational training designed to augment the efficiency and productivity of Italian workers.[67]

Between 1926 and 1932, the *Dopolavoro* succeeded in attracting almost 600,000 industrial workers that might otherwise have remained partially insulated from the regime. Passively organized by Fascist syndicalism in their capacity as workers, the same mass was actively organized by voluntary involvement with the *Dopolavoro* during their leisure time. The *Dopolavoro* was to become one of the most effective instruments of the regime. A substantial number of workers were attracted to the party through the offices of the *Dopolavoro*, and as we shall see, its social impact was significant. Herman Finer, certainly no apologist for the regime, characterized the undertakings of the *Dopolavoro* as "splendid work, grandly conceived and enthusiastically executed, with great benefits to those who [took] part."[68]

By the time of the Great Depression the basic framework for the control of public information, intellectual life, and formal and informal education, had been constructed. During the 'thirties the process continued at an accelerated pace. By 1934 the relatively modest *Ufficio stampa*, Mussolini's press office, was transformed into the Undersecretariat for the Press and Propaganda, a transitional characterization of what was to become, in 1937, the Ministry of Popular Culture. During the same period there was a proliferation of control agencies for every aspect of public cultural life. There were "inspectorates" and "committees of vigilance" superintending radio communications, the theater, the various arts, sports, and tourist information. The entire apparatus became more centralized and technically efficient, but the subtending principles remained the same. Fascism conceived of its tasks as quintessentially political. Its manuals of instruction characterized Fascist culture not as concerned with imposing a specific scientific or aesthetic form on intellectual and cultural activity, but rather as devoted to the cultivation of a "style" or a "mood"—an express commitment to the regime. Artists and intellectuals, whatever their artistic or cultural persuasion, were expected to be role models for the general citizenry. An entire special literature developed which provided heroes for public emulation.[69] Handbooks of Fascist style were prepared for the instruction of party members and the general citizenry.[70]

During this entire period, the cult of the Duce was assiduously fostered. Mussolini became the object of unrestrained adulation. He was "always right." His thought was impeccable, his reasoning irresistible, his aesthetic sense perfect, his political acumen incomparable, his physical stamina supernormal, his health exemplary, his virtues unparalleled, his instincts sure, his charity bountiful, his mercy unrestrained, his love of Italy boundless, his concern for his people depthless, and his programs invincible.[71] As early as 1927 Enrico Ferri, the onetime revolutionary socialist[72] and internationally celebrated penologist, could maintain that Mussolini, as a

political writer, politician and man of government, [had] reached the pinnacle of statesmanship, which is the superior expression of political thought and action. . . . He . . . rescued Italy from chaos and . . . has given her order and discipline . . . [In] four years of government . . . he has done and realized more than . . . in forty years by the governments that preceded him . . . Where Mussolini appears really great as a modern statesman and leaves an indelible imprint in is the judicial, political and social organization which he created. . . . [Mussolini enjoys] the approval of every class of citizen. . . . He has a double superiority over Cromwell and Napoleon when they are considered as statesmen . . . [He] has ruled the country without giving anybody the possibility of thinking that he does it for personal gain or egotistic ambition. He has of-

239

fered himself entirely and religiously to his goddess, which is called Italy. [He exemplifies] a disinterestedness which is absolute and which makes [of him] . . . an admirable puritan . . . One cannot miss seeing in this man, a leader of souls, the mystic depth of his own soul. He lays on the altar of his country all that he can give her: his work, his youth, his life.[73]

In 1934 Ottavio Dinale could insist that

The Fascist Revolution . . . was the expression of a Genius, a Hero. . . . [The] entire battle of the intervention was fought under the guidance and command of that Man prepared to face destiny. . . . His outstanding form, monolithic, eminently real, both in history and as a projection into the future, dominating men and things, as a prince of statesmen, as a Genius of the race, as the Savior of Italy, as a Roman, in myth and reality . . . is the personification and synthesis of the Idea. . . . It is the figure of a giant, who with his mysterious divinations controls not only the destiny of Italy, but that of Europe and the world.[74]

Hundreds of instances of this kind of apotheosis could be collected from the literature of the period. There were literally thousands of articles, speeches, tracts, and volumes dedicated to the myth of the Duce. Antonio Canepa could write three volumes devoted to what was essentially an exegesis of the thought of Mussolini.[75] Armando Carlini could write a monograph on philosophy and religion in the thought of Mussolini.[76] There were any number of collections devoted to selections from the thought of Mussolini.[77] There were even celebrations of Mussolini's special talents. Adolf Dresler devoted two hundred pages to Mussolini's special gifts as a journalist.[78] There were books concerned with Mussolini as artist, those which expounded on Mussolini as musician, and Mussolini as educator, and so on and so forth. There was, in substance, a veritable industry devoted to the cult of the Leader.

At the outbreak of the Second World War, Italy possessed a fairly effective and well-articulated network of controls over the communications media and intellectual life that we now recognize as characteristic of those regimes that orchestrate public sentiment and collective commitment. The regime had put into practice the convictions that first found expression in the literaure produced by the revolutionary national syndicalists long before the foundation of the Fascist movement.

The Fascist Rationale

By the mid-'thirties, the regime had created the consensus of which De Felice writes so persuasively.[79] Among the many factors that contributed to that result was the theoretical literature produced by those syndicalists who now numbered among the most prominent ideologues of the movement. In 1926 Michels published his *Psychologie der antikapitalistischen Massenbewegungen* which proved to be a veritable handbook of mass-mobilizational and consensus-generating techniques. Ostensibly written about socialist mass movements, the monograph was a sophisticated sociological study of the psychology of politically organized masses.[80]

Michels had always been convinced that collective life was governed by unrestricted empirical generalizations, lawlike regularities.[81] The "laws" of oligarchic rule, mass incompetence, mass susceptibility to suggestive influence, the disposition to organize into in-groups animated by ethnocentrism, and the special political and social functions of elites and the charismatic leader, were among the most prominent. With the advent of Fascism, Michels devoted more and more of his research time to the analysis of these regularities, but more particularly to the impact of national sentiment on the mobilization, domestication, and orchestration of masses.

241

In 1929 Michels published a major treatise in political sociology devoted to an analysis of patriotism. In that work, he attempted to articulate a collection of logically related and empirically confirmed generalizations about the nature, genesis, and contemporary function of patriotic sentiment. With Pareto, Michels tended to conceive of national invocations as "derivatives" of more fundamental and generic sociopsychological "residues." Such invocations were "political formulae" or "myths" employed to produce solidarity among masses—formulae that proved most effective among populations that had long suffered collective humiliation and which labored under the onus of an insistent sense of inferiority. Michels spoke of the character of effective mobilizational myths, the myth of special origins, that of a special history, and a special destiny, all generative of a sense of collective worth and integrity. Because of their emotive, teleological, and prescriptive character, such functional myths take on "religious" and "charismatic" properties.[82]

These mass-mobilizing myths were the propaganda of an exiguous minority. Such an elite, exploiting every natural disposition that characterizes mass psychology, could orchestrate consensus to serve the missionary and developmental purpose of the modern mass-mobilizing revolutionary party.[83] By the early thirties, Michels had elaborated a persuasive doctrine of the functional significance of national myth and the historic role of mass-mobilizing elites.[84] To complete the rationale, Michels envisioned such an elite—employing mass-mobilizing myths and utilizing all the appurtenances of the strong state—driving the modern nation into a developmental sequence that would fulfill the obligations that history and modern economic necessities have visited upon contemporary collective life.[85] In the Fascist case, what this meant was the construction of a corporative and hierarchical political and social social system, dominated by the will of the charismatic leader and operating under the aegis of the revolutionary party.[86]

In effect, the orchestration of consensus in Fascist Italy,

irrespective of how puerile some of its efforts may have seemed, and however ineffective some of its particular applications may have been, was the consequence of some very sophisticated social science thinking. Of all the contemporary regimes that have employed mass-mobilizational strategies, Fascism seems to have been among the most theoretically sophisticated and articulate. And Roberto Michels, Sergio Panunzio, and Paolo Orano, clearly occupy undisputed place among the most sophisticated theoreticians of mass mobilization. They were the intellectual architects of the Fascist policy of consensus politics, and they suggested the significance of mimetism, the role of uniforms, songs, ritual, symbol, and the control of information, in the orchestration of public sentiment and the integration of immediate interests in a program of collective development.

When Michels published his *Italien von Heute*[87] in 1930, he rehearsed all the convictions that had animated syndicalists. Michels celebrated the economic achievements of the regime, and argued that these achievements could only have been the consequence of an orchestration of public sentiment, a mobilization of will, commitment, and sacrifice.[88] This could have been accomplished only through the intercession of the "charismatic party," capable of orchestrating the "ineluctable tendencies of human psychology" to great historic purpose.[89]

These were convictions shared by the best of the Fascist ideologues, and more specifically by those revolutionary syndicalists who had assumed responsibilities with the *Facoltà fascista di scienze politiche* at the University of Perugia— Sergio Panunzio, A. O. Olivetti, Paolo Orano, Roberto Michels, and Oddone Fantini, the most prominent among them. Panunzio, in what was his major work, undertook a detailed account of the Fascist experiment, and spoke, without hesitation, of the "spiritual, ethical and pedagogical" functions of the regime in the creation, fostering and maintenance of "new, revolutionary consciousness." This would require control over every "cultural, sporting, military, communications

243

. . . social, economic and syndical association."[90] Similar characterizations can be found in the major works of Olivetti and Orano.[91]

More important for our purposes is the fact that not only did Fascists provide a rationale for the orchestration of consensus that found its origins in the heretical Marxism of the revolutionary syndicalists, but they recognized that the developmental regime in the Soviet Union shared with Fascism not only the same dispositions vis-à-vis the masses, but that the Bolsheviks, like the Fascists, were Marxist heretics. The legitimacy of both regimes inextricably involved an appeal to some "ultimate interests" that could only become manifest through the systematic orchestration of public sentiment. Fascism, like Bolshevism, was a unitary party regime, a regime predicated on the mobilization and domestication of masses. Such a regime legitimizes itself via consensual and plebiscitary approval—an approval that is one by-product of orchestrated public life.[92]

Revolutionary Socialism and Charismatic, Consensual Regimes

That Leninism, and subsequently Stalinism, evolved (or devolved) into a form of developmental, etatist, orchestrated, and charismatic system hardly requires extensive argument. That the arduous requirements of rapid industrial and economic development fostered the correlative development of extensive, if not omnicomprehensive, controls over all the media of communication, education, and national culture suggests itself. It seems reasonably clear that as long as Leninists believed that the proletarian revolution would make socialism the fortunate heir of a developed capitalist industrial base for its experiment in utopianism, government was conceived as nothing more than the effortless interaction of voluntary productive communes, peopled by class-conscious workers in much the manner anticipated by Marx and Engels in their speculations on the Paris Commune. It is true that

244

Lenin's notions about the special role of vanguard elites in the revolutionary process cast a shadow across these notions, but as long as Leninists were convinced that the future society would be one blessed by abundance, and by the international collaboration of the universal working class, they anticipated a classless, stateless, coercion-free, and egalitarian social order. Animated by these convictions, the Leninists, even after the seizure of power, could continue to allow the publication not only of Menshevik and opposition socialist publications until 1920, but could even permit the occasional appearance of the bourgeois opposition as well.

But there were misgivings early in the history of Bolshevism. Immediately after the revolution, Rosa Luxemburg recognized that the "most intensive political training of the masses" had become essential to the continuity of the Bolshevik system. But she warned that

> freedom only for the supporters of the government—only for the members of one party—however numerous they may be—is no freedom at all. Freedom is always and exclusively freedom for the one who thinks differently. . . . The only way to a rebirth is the school of public life itself, the most unlimited, the broadest democracy and public opinion. . . . [Without] unrestricted freedom of press and assembly, without a free struggle of opinion, life dies out in every public institution, becomes a mere semblance of life, in which only the bureaucracy remains as the active element. Public life gradually falls asleep, a few dozen party leaders of inexhausible energy and boundless experience direct the rule. Among them, in reality only a dozen outstanding heads do the leading and an elite of the working class is invited from time to time to meetings where they are to applaud the speeches of the leaders.[93]

Not only was it intuitively clear that the masses of Russia needed political education to insure the continuity of the regime, but it had become evident to Rosa Luxemburg that the Bolsheviks were little disposed to entertain notions about freedom of the press or the apolitical character of culture and education. Intimations of this sort, in fact, were already heralded in a book by Nikolai Bukharin and Eugene Preobrazhenskii, published in 1919, that was to serve as the most important handbook of Bolshevik political strategies until its authors were purged and executed in the 'thirties. In that early volume we are told that a minority (albeit a proletarian minority) must assume the responsibilities of leadership and organization in the Soviet Union. Such a minority must "raise all the backward strata of the working population to the requisite level of communist consciousness." That minority must "use the schools . . . to sweep away the last traces of spiritual slavery from the consciousness of the workers." Just as Fascist education was charged with the obligation of offsetting the effects of centuries of oppression at the hands of "plutocratic imperialists" and the "decadent bourgeoisie," Bolsheviks insisted on the Leninist obligation of "imposing" a "proletarian mentality" on the majority of citizens in the Soviet Union. Bukharin and Preobrazhenskii insisted that the function of education was to "make ready" the minds of men for "new social relationships." To these ends the minority party must educate both the majority of adults, and particularly the new generation, to the tasks of the new society. "Communist propaganda," they maintained, "has become a necessity for the whole society now undergoing regeneration. . . . It is therefore necessary that not merely the proletarian school but in addition the whole mechanism of the proletarian state should contribute to the work of communist propaganda. . . . This propaganda must be . . . carried on in and by all the instruments of the Soviet power."[94]

As early as 1919, the Bolsheviks anticipated monopoly control by a minority over all the principal communications, information, and cultural media in Russia in order to generate a "new consciousness" among the Russian masses.

In 1920 A. V. Lunarcharskii, who would subsequently serve as commissar of education, could write:

Art must become the tongue of the revolution. . . . The Communist Party must arm itself with all the weapons of art. . . . Not only posters, but paintings and sculpture . . . can become the means for conveying communist truth. . . . Music has played an important role in mass-movements. . . . We anticipate the wide use of architecture for propaganda purposes. . . . The most contemporary art forms, like the films, and dancing as well, can be employed to good effect. . . . We can expect to produce dynamic masses, thousands and ten thousands of men, and not simply crowds, but a veritable army of freedom animated by one single thought.[95]

For Lunarcharskii, it was not so much that the state would dictate specific aesthetic expression. The state was concerned with political content.[96] The distinction between aesthetics and political content has always been obscure, no less in the Soviet Union than in Fascist Italy, and in 1934 Andrei Zhdanov made that distinction still more diaphanous.

Zhdanov conceived of the task of education and art to be essentially functional: the "radical alteration" of "the consciousness of [the Soviet] people." Under "the guiding genius of [the] great leader and teacher, Comrade Stalin," the USSR was to become an advanced industrial country. To that end, education and all cultural expressions must be employed to destroy all the "relics of bourgeois influence." Every effort must be made to destroy any dispositions toward "laxity, frivolity, and idling, against petty-bourgeois individualism and lack of discipline, against an attitude of greed and dishonesty toward public property." Education and culture must be "impregnated with enthusiasm and the spirit of heroic deeds"; it must be "optimistic in essence."[97] Just as the Fascist press, Fascist literature, and Fascist art were forbidden to broadcast accounts of crimes, scandals, natural catastrophy, and public failure[98]—and counselled to celebrate the successes of the regime with fulsome optimism[99]—every public expression in the Soviet Union was orchestrated to serve the political goals of the system.

247

As early as 1926 René Fueloep-Miller could write that "the whole of education in Soviet Russia does not aim, as in Western Europe, at the training of free individuals for a lofty human culture, but at creating as quickly as possible useful fighting troops for communism."[100] Like Fascist pedagogues, Soviet educators and writers were expected to provide "positive models of militant initiative and enthusiasm" as stimuli for the imitative and suggestible millions.[101]

Every possible means from mass education to the use of communications media and art was marshalled to the purpose of "engineering human souls." "Socialist realism" was a general characterization that referred to the ability of education and culture to deliver the political "socialist message." Neither educators nor artists could be apolitical, agnostic, in the struggle for socialism. The demand for *partiinost* (partisan loyalty) carried "all the overtones of enthusiastic, intelligent, loyal and yet essentially uncritical acceptance of the Communist belief system."[102]

The engineering of majority consensus by infusing the millions with a single set of ideas required a focus, a central apparatus for decision making that would insure consistency and the suppression of factional and sectarian strife in the party. In 1931, when Emil Ludwig interviewed Stalin and asked the question, "Who decides?" with respect to the general plan and the general political orientation of the nation, Stalin replied that such decisions involved no more than seventy men.[103] For all practical purposes this was perhaps a generous estimate.

Very soon during the Stalin period it became evident that Stalin, whom Lenin had advised the party to "remove," had undergone a transformation. Stalin had become "the genius, the leader and teacher of the Party, the great strategist of Socialist Revolution, helmsman of the Soviet State and captain of armies." The Russian masses were told that Stalin exemplified

   . . . an implacable attitude towards the enemies of socialism, profound fidelity to principle, a combination of clear revolutionary perspective and clarity of purpose with extraordinary firmness and persistence in the pursuit of aims, wise and practical leadership, and constant contact with the masses. . . . Stalin guides the destinies of a multinational Socialist State. . . . His advice is a guide to action in all fields of Socialist construction . . . his energy truly amazing. The range of questions which engage his attention is immense, embracing the most complex problems of Marxist-Leninist theory and school textbooks. . . . Everyone is familiar with the cogent and invincible force of Stalin's logic, the crystal clarity of his mind, his iron will, his devotion to the Party, his ardent faith in the people, and love for the people. Everybody is familiar with his modesty, his simplicity of manner, his consideration for people. . . . Everybody is familiar with his intolerance of ostentation. . . . Stalin is wise and deliberate in solving complex political questions. . . . In the eyes of the peoples of the USSR, Stalin is the incarnation of their heroism, their love of country, their patriotism. . . . Stalin's name is a symbol of the courage and glory of the Soviet people, a call to heroic deeds for the welfare of their great Motherland. . . . The name of Stalin is a symbol of the moral and political unity of Soviet society.[104]

By the time Stalinism had matured into a system of orchestrated consensus, the entire population had been mobilized into state organizations, ranging from the youth in the Young Pioneers and adolescents in the Young Communist Leagues, to peasants and workers in a variety of state associations. The "entire machinery by which public opinion is formed [was] controlled by the state and thus by the Communist Party which controls the state." Any organization, any expression of political opinion that was not "tendentious," party political, was deemed a "ridiculous, absurd, scandalous, and harmful thing."[105] Every energy was marshalled to the "construction of great industrial plants" in the service

249

of "Soviet patriotism" and motivated by "love for the Socialist Motherland," all under the sure guidance of the "world historical genius and teacher" Joseph Stalin, *Vohzd*, "duce" of the minority party and the nation.

Throughout this process there was a clear and progressive involution of Marxism from the majoritarianism and the determinism of classical Marxism to the elitism, voluntarism, and activism of Stalinism. As early as Nikolai Bukharin's *Historical Materialism*, it was evident that Bolshevism was preparing to systematically revise classical Marxism.[106] Where classical Marxism had been generally conceived of as deterministic—both the early Lenin and Plekhanov had so construed its intention—Bukharin argued, with some support from the later Engels, that while the economic base of society determined the superstructural elements of society (social psychology, the social-political order, and "such phenomena as language and thought"), that superstructure, under certain conditions, can interact with the economic base, thereby "reversing the order of influence."[107]

Bukharin attempted to accommodate modern theories of social psychology within the general theoretical structure of classical Marxism. In effect, he attempted to fill out the nineteenth-century theoretical sketch of historical materialism with the twentieth-century discoveries concerning collective psychology. The turn of the century had produced a great deal of work on the nature of primary and secondary socialization, the development of social attitudes, and the communication of moral and political sentiments. As a consequence, Bukharin was compelled to consider the impact of psychosocial influences on the political orientation of the masses. In fact, Bukharin argued that the ideational elements of the superstructure, so long conceived by Marxists as "echoes" or "reflexes" of more fundamental economic determinants, were functionally capable of influencing collective action and thereby sustaining or compromising the integrity of any social system. When a society is in crisis, a political and social revolution is the consequence of an energizing "mental revolution." And when a social system attempts to stabilize itself, psychological factors can exercise decisive and effective influence over collective behaviors.

What Bukharin attempted was a synthesis of those elements of classical Marxism that had survived into the twentieth century with the insights of his contemporaries, men like Vilfredo Pareto, Max Weber, and Roberto Michels.[108] This process of evolution was to continue throughout Bukharin's active intellectual life. By 1921 he fully recognized the anomaly of the Bolshevik revolution. The revolution had captured a primitive economic base. As a consequence, Russia was preoccupied, not with the construction of the anarchosyndicalist and stateless voluntary community of Lenin's *The State and Revolution*, but, rather, with the construction of an economic base capable of carrying Russia into the twentieth century. Under such circumstances, the role of the "superstructural elements" began to loom large in Bukharin's account of historical change. What Russia required was the creation of the "prerequisites of civilization" through diligent and systematic economizing, the disciplining and technical preparation of labor, and the collboration of an entire heterogeneous population in an exacting program of massive development. Bukharin spoke of the abandonment of "illusions" and a recognition of the demands of "reality."

What all this precipitated was a frank recognition that the dictatorship of the proletariat was, in fact, a dictatorship of the minority party over the primitive proletariat and peasantry—a dictatorship serviced by an elitist technical intelligentsia of nonproletarian origins. Bukharin apparently recognized all the hazards implicit in such a conception of "modern Marxism." He acknowledged the possible creation of a new minority class of bureaucrats that might come to dominate the system. But the requirements of Russia's developmental program prompted the mobilization of human and material resources under the guidance of an exiguous and "theoretically integrated" leadership. Bukharin fully understood the significance of Roberto Michels *Zur Soziologie des Parteiwesens*, with its emphasis on the oligarchic tendencies of contemporary political life, but he hoped that one day the "incompetence of the masses" would give way to their technical and political efficiency to avoid any "tragic outcome" for the revolution.[109]

Bukharin, of course, was to perish in Stalin's purge, but the elements of his analysis were to survive in Stalin's increasing emphasis on the political orchestration of mass consensus. Stalin was to increasingly emphasize ideological inculcation in the effort to create the support base for massive industrial development. By 1934 Stalin could insist that "the part played by objective conditions" in the historical changes wrought in the Soviet Union "had been reduced to a minimum; whereas the part played by our organizations and their leaders has become decisive, exceptional."[110] "Subjective factors" and "exceptional leaders" began to function in the system as critical variables. Men were to be trained by a political elite to function in the Soviet system as disciplined, dedicated, frugal, hard-working, and competent agents of social change. Education was mobilized to this purpose. Art, literature, the films, and the theater, were to provide mimetic heroes who were capable of inculcating civic virtue among "Soviet patriots."[111]

The "new Soviet man" was to be an activist, an enthusiast, and a voluntarist—the engineered product of a vast network of educational and cultural institutions assiduously controlled and directed by the minoritarian party leadership. Dedication, sacrifice, obedience, and discipline were to be fostered by the provision of a model incarnation of collective enterprise: the infallible leader. More and more insistenly, orchestration made appeal to the myth of the leader, to the requirements of the "Socialist Motherland," and to the necessities of intensive industrialization.

With this perspective we can identify the stages traversed by Bolshevism. They are, in substance, the same stages traversed by Italian revolutionary syndicalism long before the advent of Fascism. The recognition that revolution in underdeveloped economic circumstances requires the mobilization and orchestration of masses to collective purposes divined by select elites and incarnated in the person of a single charismatic leader are themes that became common to Fascism and Bolshevism. That they should have created analogous strategies for the orchestration of consensus hardly seems remarkable. However different they were in their respective efficiencies or inefficiencies, brutalities or paternalisms, successes or failures, the fact remains that the Bolshevik commitment to the "engineering of souls" is the analogue of Fascism's efforts to create the "new Fascist man."

EIGHT

THE SOCIAL POLICIES OF FASCISM

The actual policies of the Fascist regime were a function of the complex interaction between ideological commitments, the informal logic of political deliberation, and the specific contingencies of the times. This was true, at least in part, because Fascists were convinced that politics required principled responses to particular problems. Moreover, Fascist ideologues believed successful governance to be a product of the calculated manipulation of collective sentiment and the resolution of urgent concerns. The revolutionary syndicalists of the period before the First World War had all been schooled in the traditions of classical Marxism in which immediate material interests were emphasized as factors influencing historic and social events. As the syndicalists matured in the prewar period, they came to recognize that historic events were the consequence of a number of complex variables of which material interests were but one.[1] Nonetheless, material interests constituted a major political preoccupation, and both revolution and successful governance required that those interests be serviced. Panunzio, Olivetti, and Orano, for example, all spoke of political and social action as the consequence of the confluence of material and ideal interests. They did not deny the impact of economic considerations, but they supplemented their analysis with an assessment of the influence of collective sentiments, symbolic invocation, and group suggestibility on mass behaviors.

The revolutionary syndicalists had learned much of this from Pareto. In those works that had a special influence upon the syndicalists, Pareto had argued that there were two influ-

254

ences shaping overt collective behavior: one was "ideational" or "sentimental," the other "economic."[2] Michels, like the syndicalists in general, regularly acknowledged his indebtedness to Pareto, and in 1926, after the Fascist regime had been well established on the peninsula, he could characterize the "history of mankind" (as Pareto might) as "determined" by the intersection of individual and collective "feelings, instincts, desires and interests."[3] In his lectures at the University of Rome, published in 1927 after his assumption of obligations as a Fascist ideologue, Michels reiterated just such an analysis. Human behavior, both individual and collective, was the product of the conjunction of both economic interests and the "stimulus of pure idea," the interactive influence of both material and ideological factors.[4] In point of fact, an effective mobilizing myth was just such a synthesis, the union of pervasive collective sentiment and the appeal to immediate and mediate material interest.[5]

Mussolini, for his part, regularly spoke of mass-mobilization and governance in essentially the same manner. In 1919 he alluded to mass-mobilizing nationalist myths as addressing themselves to both "sentiment" and calculable "interests."[6] In 1932, in his conversations with Emil Ludwig, he reiterated that the governance of men required the employment of two human elements: "enthusiasm" and "material interests."[7]

In effect, Fascist ideologues maintained that both mass-mobilization and political governance involved the implementation of strategies that appealed to both the sentiments, ideals, and faith of men, as well as to their urgent concrete interests. As a consequence, there would be every reason to expect that Fascist policies would reflect just such convictions. In fact, a considerable part of Fascist legislation was calculated to deliver at least the impression of systematic concern for the immediate and mediate material interests of the masses. The propagandists of the regime were to allude to that body of legislation as evidence of Fascism's concern with social justice.

Much of the legislation passed by the regime during the

more than two decades of Fascist rule could best be identified as "social welfare legislation," dealing with conditions of labor, sanitation, housing, insurance, education, unemployment, and medical benefits. Such legislation was always heralded as peculiarly Fascist accomplishments in the obvious effort to satisfy one of the principal requirements of what Fascists understood to be effective governance. If Fascists were masters of the use of symbolic and evocative language, they were equally disposed to at least appear concerned with the real interests of their subjects in order to create the "consensual, charismatic regime" invoked by Michels, Panunzio, and Olivetti.

Another substantial part of this social legislation was the derivative consequence of Fascist ideological commitment. The programmatic commitments of the first Fascists translated themselves into specific pieces of legislation in spite of the rapid changes of a complex, political, social, and economic environment. Thus, it was not the case that Fascism's demographic policies, its efforts at "ruralization," and its treatment of women, were simply *ad hoc* and arbitrary acts of an unthinking and whimsical dictatorship as is sometimes suggested.

Fascist social policies were the result, by and large, of ideological commitments which recommended social welfare programs calculated to render the masses of the peninsula governable, and programmatic commitments which implied certain policy enactments given specific circumstances. In substance, Fascism was as consistent in practice as any revolutionary ideology in the twentieth century. In fact, a case can be made that Fascism was one of the most consistent ideologies of our time.

The Social Welfare Legislation of Fascism

A week after the seizure of power in 1922, Mussolini addressed the workers of Milan and announced the "three fundamental considerations" that would govern the legislative enactments of the Fascist government: a preoccupation with the "irrepressible reality of the nation"; a concern with the maximization of production; and a tutelary dedication to the "just interests of the working class"—all in the service of the progressive development of what had been a "retarded" nation.[8] With respect to the third consideration, Fascism proposed a series of legislative enactments that would provide for the essential material interests of the working class in the candid effort to wed them to the new political dispensation. While Fascist propagandists heralded Fascist legislation as motivated by the "moral" concern with abstract "social justice," the more serious ideologues spoke frankly of the need to dissipate the "discontent of the working classes" in order to avoid any threat to the "well-being, the internal security, the power and the existence of the state." More than that, Fascist ideologues insisted that a minimal concern for the well-being of the labor force would enhance the nation's productive potential.[9] It is reasonably clear that Fascists had both ideological and prudential reasons for pursuing at least the semblance of progressive social legislation. Their convictions concerning the governance of men, the instrumental necessity of deflecting social discontent, as well as the maintenance of requisite levels of health and labor effectiveness, recommended some such course.

Almost immediately after the March on Rome, the Fascist government ratified the Washington Convention of 1919 which recommended the universal adoption of the eight-hour working day. Prior to that time, the Italian government had authorized the eight-hour day only for special categories of the labor force. With the advent to power of the Fascists, the eight-hour day was established throughout industry, with some significant exceptions and some subsequent modifications. Irrespective of the exceptions and modifications, however, the principle of the eight-hour day, forty-eight-hour week, had been established. From that point on a series of legislative enactments governing child labor, the employment of women, and the conditions of labor were passed.

257

Fascists argued that such legislation not only enhanced the productive capabilities of the working class and thereby served the ultimate interests of the national community, they also insisted that such programs proved that Fascism had transcended "bourgeois parliamentarianism," enacted as these programs were by a government that operated independently of any and all special pressure groups.[10] Oddone Fantini, one of the more important ideologues of the regime and a member of the Fascist Political Science Faculty at Perugia, argued that one could expect the Fascist government to continue to evince concern with such legislation because of its ideological, instrumental, and prudential preoccupations. Such legislation, he maintained, served the national interests, and provided evidence that Fascism had no need for the complex machinery of democratic parliamentary arrangements.

With the promulgation of the Labor Charter in 1927, Fascism explicitly committed itself to a complex social welfare and assistance program that Werner Sombart characterized as the "most audacious" in Europe.[11] The twenty-fifth, twenty-sixth, twenty-seventh, and twenty-eighth paragraphs of the charter committed Fascism to an extensive program of state-supported accident, unemployment, maternity, and occupational disease insurance. The twenty-fourth, twenty-ninth, and thirtieth paragraphs addressed themselves to the provisions for vocational and technical training for the working classes.[12]

The Fascist program of 1921, before Mussolini's accession to power, had prefigured, in fact, the commitments of the charter. That program anticipated the establishment of the eight-hour day—always with due regard for the exigencies of production. It advocated a modern insurance, provident, and social welfare system that would include accident, sickness, unemployment, and old-age provisions.[13] It was clear, even at that time, that such provisions would be made for a disciplined (*inquadrate*) working class, rather than as concessions to an organized, independent, and aggressive labor movement. This was regularly reiterated in the Fascist dictum: "the rights of labor depend upon labor's discharge of its obligations."[14]

Irrespective of the ideological climate in which such legislation was passed, the regime did embark upon an elaborate program of social welfare. In December 1925, even before the publication of the Labor Charter, the *Opera nazionale per la protezione della maternità e dell'infanzia* (ONMI), a national maternity and child welfare foundation, was established. Between 1925 and 1939, as a consequence, approximately eight million mothers and infants were given financial, obstetrical, and pediatric aid, nursery school, and food supplementary assistance through ten thousand agencies, 1,500 dispensaries, and 260 "Homes for Mothers" (to assist the indigent and the illegitimate). Like many of the institutions that serviced the population of Italy during the period, ONMI was a parastate agency under the direct control of the government, with party functionaries very much in evidence. The maternity and infant care program was supplemented by private efforts like those of Gerolamo Gaslini who, in the spirit of "Fascist class collaboration," founded an elaborate "Children's City" to service the needs of working-class children.[15] One of the immediate consequences of these programs was a decline of over 20 percent in the mortality rate of infants between 1922 and 1936. In the triennial period between 1922 and 1925, 4.3 percent of all births were stillborn. In the three years between 1932 and 1935, irrespective of the arduous conditions that attended the international economic crisis, this had declined to 3.4 percent. In 1925 the number of stillborn infants was 48,117 while in 1935, the overall increase in population notwithstanding, the number was 33,800.[16] By 1936 maternity insurance, which had previously covered only female workers in trade and industry, was extended to approximately 600,000 female agricultural workers from 15 to 50 years of age.

At about the same time that the provisions for maternity and child welfare were being instituted, the regime undertook a concerted campaign against tuberculosis, which had claimed 280,000 lives every five years from 1901 through 1925. Tuberculosis was a major factor in Italian national mortality figures. Pre-Fascist governments had made efforts to combat the scourge, but only with the legislation of May 1928 was insurance against tuberculosis made compulsory in order to provide the funds for a correlative expansion of preventive and therapeutic interventions. As a consequence, the 50,169 deaths from tuberculosis registered in 1929 were to decline, within four years, to 35,420. Between 1924 and 1935, the death rate from tuberculosis fell from 1.56 per 1,000 to .65 per 1,000 inhabitants. Between 1929 and 1935, 240,000 tubercular patients were afforded treatment in 42 sanatoria at a cost of seven hundred and fifty million lire. By 1941 almost two and a half billion lire had been spent in the effort to control and treat the disease.[17] Similar efforts were made to combat malarial infection. Prevention was linked to the development and reforestation of rural areas, particularly the reclamation of swamps that served as breeding grounds for the anopheles mosquito.

Associated with maternity assistance, infant care, public hygiene, and disease control, was a substantial investment in public education. Between 1862 and 1922, the Italian government had disbursed sixty million lire for school construction; between 1922 and 1942, the Fascist government devoted 400 million lire of public monies to the enterprise. The total expenditure on education rose from 922.4 million lire in the financial year 1922-23 to 1,636 million lire for 1936-37. In 1930 there were 110,200 public elementary schools while the number, by 1935, had risen to 126,934. Attendance in public elementary schools increased by twenty-five percent between 1922 and 1935. In 1935, Herman Finer, a principled opponent of Fascism, could write:

> [It] is undeniable that in the last twelve years a great service has been rendered by the Fascist government to Italian education, regarded from the angle of organisa-

tion, method and opportunity. . . . Attendance at school, which formerly had been compulsory to the age of twelve, was raised to fourteen, and the enforcement of attendance was made more efficient. New schools have been built and old ones improved. In 1932, the elementary schools and all the teachers were brought under the direct dependence of the central authority. All this is an exceedingly important step forward, and the Government has increased the expenditure on all forms of education (including libraries) by 50 percent over that of 1922-25, and this is a currency worth much more.[18]

In this same period, the disease control, insurance, and provident efforts of the regime were organized in the *Istituto nazionale per l'assicurazione contro le malattie* (INAM), the *Istituto nazionale per l'assicurazione contro gli infortuni laborativi* (INAIL), and the *Istituto nazionale per la previdenza sociale* (INPS). These parastate agencies, the first dedicated to the prevention and control of contagious and occupational diseases, the second for the prevention and treatment of occupational accidents, and the third for general social insurance, were, by 1939, charged with providing assistance and support for maternal and infant care, disease and accident, unemployment, old-age, and general disability.[19] Between 1922 and 1935, 515,000 old-age and disability pensions were paid at a cost of approximately two billion lire. By 1941 785,000 pensions were being paid at an annual cost of 700 million lire. By 1939 twenty million Italians were covered by old-age and disability insurance. By 1938 over one billion fifty million lire were being paid in indemnities for occupational accidents. Between 1922 and 1941, two billion 225 million lire were paid in unemployment benefits. In 1937 a general family assistance program was introduced under the auspices of INPS which provided wage-supplementary family allowances per child. During the first year of implementation, 500 million lire were disbursed. By 1940 1,710 million lire were being paid out to working-class families employed in industrial, agricultural, commercial, credit, and insurance enterprises.

The specifically Fascist institutions, the *Opera nazionale Balilla* (ONB) and the *Opera nazionale dopolavoro* (OND), provided further welfare supplements for Italian families. Between 1922 and 1942, over eight million children were provided trips to camps by the *Balilla* and the *Dopolavoro*. As was earlier suggested, the *Dopolavoro* developed into one of the most effective agencies of the regime. In 1926, when the OND began its operations, there were 280,000 members, with 200 factory groups, 300 communal groups, and 500 other local groups of various kinds participating. By 1942 there were almost five million members in thousands of local, regional, and factory groups. By 1932 67 percent of the membership was composed of manual workers. For the annual cost of four lire, members in the OND had access to an array of cultural, vacational, sporting, and recreational facilities. By 1941 600,000 members of the OND enjoyed operatic and theatrical performances *in situ*, and the 75 travelling companies of the "Cars of Thespis" performed 4,308 times for two million seven hundred thousand spectators. By 1941 the OND operated 1,016 cinemas and provided 160,000 showings for an audience of millions. In the same year, 20,800 technical and cultural courses were conducted by the OND with several hundred thousand workers participating. As early as 1932, the OND had organized 2,130 orchestras, 3,787 bands, 994 choral societies, 10,302 professional and cultural associations, 6,427 libraries, and 11,159 sporting groups (with a million and a half active members). With a working population of approximately twelve million, the effectiveness of the OND was impressive.

Long after the war, Claudio Schwarzenberg could write:

In the years between 1934 and 1939 there was a progressive centralization of insurance and provident undertakings in several parastate institutions, accompanied by a notable extension of coverage. The working classes received undeniable concrete benefits: paid vacations, indemnities in the event of job loss, protection of employment on the occasion of illness, family support, the expansion of mutual assistance agencies, and the various forms of assistance provided by the *Opera nazionale dopolavoro* (group trips at minimal cost, theatrical performances, recreational centers), and so on.[20]

These were general judgments similarly advanced by Herman Finer and William Welk forty years before. At that time, Welk wrote that "it must be recognized that under Fascism social welfare has been in the forefront of public attention and that institutions of considerable benefit to the mass of the Italian people have been perfected or created *de novo*."[21]

Given the capital scarcity that characterized the Italian economy, the relatively modest industrial development of the peninsula, as well as the high population density, Fascist social welfare legislation compared favorably with the more advanced European nations and in some respects was more progressive.[22] As Gaetano Salvemini has clearly indicated, many of the Fascist programs were continuations of those already begun under the parliamentary system that the regime displaced, and many had their functional analogues in the sometimes more generous legislation enacted by parliamentary governments on the Continent and in North America. Some, however, like the *Opera nazionale dopolavoro* were clearly unique, more comprehensive and popular than any generated in the non-Fascist systems.

What seems to have distinguished Fascist social welfare programs from others was the fact that Fascist programs were clearly instrumental in purpose. Irrespective of the undeniable benefits that they afforded, they all served to generate, in the first instance, political support for the regime. Every benefit and assist provided by such legislation was advertised as originating with the regime. Every program was characterized a Fascist program inspired, more frequently than not, by the Duce himself. All of which was perfectly compati-

263

ble with the ideological convictions concerning population management entertained by Fascists before their advent to power.[23]

The centralized organization of the insurance and provident system succeeded in concentrating an impressive amount of scarce investment capital in the hands of the Fascist state. Fascist ideologues called attention to the fact that, by 1940, INPS made more than four billion lire available to the government for public works and public housing construction, and more than three and a half billion lire for the comprehensive development of rural areas and for reforestation.[24] Thus, the approximately 4.5 percent of their salaries paid by workers into insurance and provident plans was a means of forced savings that, while benefitting participants, also provided investment capital to fuel, in some substantial part, the public works and developmental plans of Fascism.

Fascism's electrification of 4,722 kilometers of railway track between 1922 and 1942 (compared to the 702 kilometers electrified between 1862 and 1922), its allocation of 1 billion 655 million lire for aqueduct construction during the same period (compared with the 310 million lire spent during the sixty years preceding the Fascist period), its reforestation of 130,000 hectares (compared with the 51,000 undertaken during the antecedent six decades), its expenditure of 14 billion lire for comprehensive development of the agricultural regions (compared with the 702 million lire disbursed during the sixty years before its accession to power), its 1 billion 540 million lire employed in building construction (compared with the 60 million spent between 1862 and 1922), all attest to Fascism's developmental program, as well as its maintenance of controlled consumption and the exploitation of forced savings.

The control of consumption was made tolerable not only by the orchestration of consensus—the displays, the sloganeering, the mass demonstrations, the systematic inculcation of civic virtue, the appeal to the myth of the Greater Italy, and the inspiration of the providential Duce—but by the provision of welfare benefits calculated to provide security for the average Italian. The insurance and welfare benefits returned to the individual citizen were celebrated as special accomplishments of the regime. In turn, the forced savings that collected in the parastate insurance and provident agencies supplemented the investment capital necessary to Fascism's overall economic and political program.

Fascist Demographic Policies

If Fascism's social welfare legislation illustrates something of the relationship between ideological commitment, prudential concerns, and the influence of contingencies in the formulation of policy, Fascism's concern with demographic problems reveals not only some of the same features, but reveals as well entailments involved in the informal logic of doctrinal commitment.

Mussolini's preoccupation with Italy's birthrate became critical during the late twenties and thirties. With the speech of May 26, 1927,[25] the regime committed itself to an explicit population policy and thereby involved itself in complex legislative enactments to arrest the nation's declining birthrate. Mussolini's speech, identified as "Il discorso dell'Ascensione," was delivered at a time when the Fascist government was well ensconced. The rate of industrial development was impressive, opposition had been neutralized, electoral reforms and Fascist legislation firmly anchored the regime. Mussolini was soon to face the issue of the international parity of the lire, and had already begun the "Battle for Grain" calculated to enhance the self-supportive capacity of the economy. As we have seen, as early as 1919 Mussolini had occupied himself with the peninsula's ability to provide minimum agricultural self-sufficiency for the population. That self-sufficiency was intimately connected with the absolute size of the population. Italy's population density had always been a consideration for the peninsula's political leaders, and it was no less a concern for Mussolini and the intellectuals who

265

were to function as ideologues of the regime. With "Il discorso dell'Ascensione," Mussolini brought together a number of critical themes that could be traced back to the founding of the Fascist movement and beyond.

Some contemporary commentators have treated Mussolini's speech, and the legislative program that followed it, in a singularly curious fashion. Recently, Riccardo Maniani has maintained that the program outlined in the speech of May 1927 constituted nothing more than another instance of Mussolini's disposition to "improvise." Bereft of any ideological consistency, we are told, Mussolini simply put together the demographic policies of Fascism out of his episodic reading of some of the writings of Oswald Spengler. We are led to believe that Fascism's demographic policies were simply a product of Mussolini's inconstancy, his perennial search for "theoretical" legitimacy for what was little more than whimsy.[26] Renzo De Felice, for his part, is much more cautious and circumspect. The speech of 1927 is referred to as the "first explicit theoretical expression" of Mussolini's position.[27] De Felice speaks guardedly of the influence of Spengler on Mussolini, but does not maintain that Mussolini's demographic policies originated in his familiarity with Spengler's publications.[28]

In this regard, De Felice is certainly more correct than Maniani. Mussolini's concern with the growth rate of the peninsula's population certainly antedates his reading of Spengler. Long before his alienation from orthodox socialism Mussolini, in fact, was concerned with the nation's inability to support its own abundant population.[29] The first Fascists regularly alluded to the problem of Italian outmigration as a "bleeding" of the nation's precious human resources. Mussolini's *Il popolo d'Italia* regularly published articles on just such themes.[30] Early in 1921, Mussolini spoke of the "force of numbers" in his anticipation of a specifically Fascist foreign policy.[31]

Some considerable time before their advent to power Fascists had formulated a demographic policy for the nation.

266

They welcomed the exuberance of Italian reproductive rates as a force that would affect the future of international politics. Italy as a young and vital nation required resources and space for its abundant population. Italians, hitherto compelled to emigrate to find employment that would provide an income adequate to their simplest needs, must be accommodated within the political confines of the nation in order to preserve the demographic force necessary for subsequent change.

Agostino Lanzillo had voiced all these themes as early as 1918 in a book well known to Mussolini. As a national syndicalist, Lanzillo argued that hedonism, individualism, and a diminishing sense of civic virtue, had produced a declining birthrate throughout Europe, a decline that heralded the cultural and political eclipse of the Continent. In 1921 Mussolini expressed the same preoccupations. The "axis of world history," he suggested, was "shifting." The United States, with its abundant population—Mussolini specifically mentioned the seven million inhabitants of New York City as one of the "greatest agglomerations of humans on earth"— and Japan, with its incredible population density, seemed to him to constitute alternative "world focal points." There was also the "revived pan-slavism" of the hundreds of millions of Slavs. A greater Russia, Asia, and North America seemed to loom large, in the near future, as contenders for the position of hegemonic powers. Europe appeared on the defensive. One of the factors contributing to that decline was Europe's relative decline in numbers.[32]

The logic of Mussolini's convictions seems clear and the elements of his arguments can be identified in the writings of some of the more important revolutionary syndicalists before the First World War. The syndicalist defense of Italy's proletarian war against the Turks in 1911 was based, in substantial part, on the argument that critical population pressures necessitated an expansion outside the immediate limits of the peninsula and justified territorial acquisition. "Old nations," those with stable or declining populations, pos-

267

sessed of vast and underpopulated territories throughout the world, had no moral right to deny "young nations" their place in the sun.[33] It was the war in Tripoli that led Michels to devote considerable intellectual energy to the relationship of population to the problems of emigration, national economy, and national aspirations. Michels considered these issues long before the advent of Fascism and at least a decade before his entry into the ranks of the movement.[34]

In his defense of Italy's involvement in the war in the Mediterranean, Michels maintained that Italy's abundant population required some outlet that did not work to the disadvantage of the national community. The peninsula suffered one of the highest population densities of Europe. Outmigration, which had been considered for some time as a happy solution to the problem, had revealed itself to be, at best, a temporary palliative which ultimately proved a considerable disadvantage to the mother country. Not only were five million Italians lost to the national community through outmigration, but overseas Italians almost invariably established industries and agriculture that worked in direct competition with the industries and agriculture of the motherland. More than that, outmigrant Italians were disproportionately of military age. As a consequence, their loss impaired the nation's military capabilities.[35]

Michels argued that emigration as a solution to Italy's population problem was to be deplored for a number of other reasons. Italian outmigrants invariably found themselves thrust into established communities where they were, at best, tolerated, and at worst systematically reviled and discriminated against. Without a powerful national government to defend their collective interests, Italian immigrants in Europe, North and South America, found themselves prey to every oppressor.[36]

Michels, like many of the revolutionary syndicalists, recommended the rapid industrialization of the peninsula and the modernization of agriculture as the most immediate remedy to offset the pressures which caused outmigration.[37]

He recognized Italy's singular disabilities in that regard: its all but total deficiency in fossil fuels and natural resources that were prerequisite to industrial development. A partial solution to that particular problem, he suggested, might be sought in the rapid development of hydroelectric power. Michels recognized that these recommendations constituted but partial and temporary remedies, and that, ultimately, Italy must obtain access to adequate space and resources.

Recognition of these difficulties suggested the possibility of a "sane neomalthusian policy" for the nation. Michels recognized the economic and moral reasons for some kind of voluntary limitation on procreation.[38] On the other hand, he recognized that the expansion of peoples, and the subsequent advance of civilization, had always been a function of an "exuberant" birthrate. Had England, France, or Spain voluntarily restricted their respective reproductive rates during the sixteenth, seventeenth, and the first half of the eighteenth century, there would hardly have been the diffusion of European technology, science, and culture that now characterizes the modern world. Michels argued, that a "deliberate restriction of births may be disastrous. . . . [It] may be a crime not simply against nationality, but even against civilization."[39] It is clear that, at that point, Michels was prepared to recognize the right of every individual to limit the number of his offspring. It is equally clear that Michels recognized that such decisions might have profound political, international, and broadly historical significance. Furthermore, he insisted that his advocacy of birth control was contingent upon industrial, support capability, political, and international circumstances.[40]

By 1914 Michels had traversed much of the distance that had separated him, as a revolutionary syndicalist, from the Italian nationalists. In his *Imperialismo italiano* he quoted, with evident approval, passages from some of the most important works written by Enrico Corradini, a prominent nationalist theoretician of the period.[41] In effect, by this time, most of the revolutionary syndicalists had assumed positions that brought them close to the "anti-Malthusianism" of the most antitraditional nationalists. Once the nation became the charismatic object of loyalty for the syndicalists, the logic of a revolutionary nationalist position became increasingly compelling. And by the advent of World War I, the nationalist position with regard to the demographic problems of the nation was clearly defined.

Once again, it was in the writings of Alfredo Rocco that the nationalist position was delineated. The work of Corrado Gini was to influence both Rocco and Michels. Gini, a demographer, statistician, and sociologist, was later to serve on the committee for constitutional reform called by Mussolini shortly after the Fascist advent to power. Gini was to become a Fascist intellectual of considerable importance. More than that, he was to exercise influence on both nationalists and syndicalists during the preparatory pre-Fascist period.[42] With regard to specifically demographic issues, Gini's volume, *I fattori demografici dell'evoluzione delle nazioni*, published in 1912, was to influence both Michels and Rocco, and clearly contained the unmistakable outlines of subsequent Fascist policies.

Gini argued that the history of civilized nations is characterized by cyclical phenomena, one of the most important of which is that exemplified by reproductive rates. He spoke of a "parabola" of population growth, commencing with surprisingly low rates of reproduction, a subsequent "J curve" of increment which ultimately peaked, to be followed by a descending phase almost as sharp as the antecedent ascending phase, to close with an all but literal biological extinction of a people. Each phase was accompanied by political phenomena. The period of low reproduction was characterized by static political forms and stable cultural expressions. The period of exuberant reproduction was accompanied by colonial expansion and territorial conquest, political change, and rapid cultural development. The period of declining reproduction was one of increasing egotism and individualism, a preoccupation with material and consumer comforts, an indisposition to face challenge, and a general decay of institutions. The final period was one of "decadence" and "decline" when the "dying civilization" was more frequently than not submerged under the weight of "young populations" entering the ascending period of population growth.[43]

For our purposes, there are several elements in Gini's schematization that are instructive. He associated the peaking and subsequent decline of populations with increasing urbanization, the "agglomeration" of masses in urban centers and the depopulation of the countryside.[44] The decline in births is first localized in the urban areas, and as rural peoples are drawn into the cities, the decrements in births become general. Gini cited the instructive case of France. During its period of reproductive exuberance, France expanded both its influence, and its political and military control throughout Europe and the New World. As the process of declining births set in, its political and cultural influence correspondingly diminished. Per capita wealth had increased and the adventurous explorer, soldier, and colonist had given way to the shopkeeper and the "good urban bourgeoisie."[45]

In the effort to arrest such a process a variety of strategies was recommended, one such strategy being the inculcation of a sense of responsibility toward the nation's future among the general citizenry. Larger families were to be systematically recommended by all the agencies of the state, and might even be given awards. Institutions were to be established for the care and succoring of mothers and children; a cult of the family might be instituted, and births and childhood celebrated.[46]

Gini was not sanguine concerning the prospects of success for such efforts. Only if the process of "senesence" had not progressed too far might it be significantly arrested. It was obvious that Gini felt the process had reached the point of irreversibility with respect to France. He went on to indicate that almost all the nations of Europe gave symptoms of a similar decline. Thus he anticipated, in the relatively near future, a similar decline in the population of the United

Kingdom, and a subsequent and associated decline in its imperial, international, and economic fortunes. As evidence, he cited the rapid growth of urban centers in England, the depopulation of the countryside, and the contingent increase in per capita wealth that was the harbinger of subsequent decline.[47]

As far as Italy was concerned, irrespective of its seeming overpopulation, there was every evidence that the nation had already peaked in terms of effective population growth. Italy, by Gini's estimates, already suffered a stationary population growth. For a nation such as Italy the prospects were dire. Thirty-five to forty percent of its effective population growth was lost through outmigration, a loss which impaired its military effectiveness. In circumstances which found Italy without resources and without sufficient agricultural land to support its current population, the future held only political and cultural subjugation. Italy was on the margin of a continental area of demographic decay. It had begun its development only after the other European powers had preempted resources and territory. It was now so confined by established powers that natural expansion was impossible and intensive internal development precluded. Its population had already peaked and whatever demographic resources it might have used for expansion into resource or support areas were being dissipated in outmigration.[48]

By 1914 Gini's convictions were given political expression in the prose of Alfredo Rocco. Gini and Rocco worked closely on the preparation of Rocco's analyses,[49] and Gini's influence is clearly evident throughout Rocco's exposition. In the course of his discussion, Rocco identified population as a critical component in the constellation of forces available for the potential development of Italy. "Numbers," he insisted, "constitute the ultimate strength of the race."[50] The relationship between potential military strength and population size was too obvious to labor.[51] Rocco advocated not only an effort to restrict the outmigration of Italians, but he urged Italians to attempt to maintain a high reproductive rate.[52] Although the immediate effect was to increase the pressures on the support capabilities of the peninsula, Rocco argued that population growth was the prerequisite to the ultimate solution of Italy's servile and subservient position with respect to its more privileged potential adversaries. The alternative was to allow the nation to remain a secondary and satellite power, subordinate to those nations that had industrialized earlier and who had preempted vast regions of the globe.

Rocco advocated a policy of intensive propaganda and legislation in support of a high birthrate. One of the more immediate consequences of such a policy was resistance to the individualism and liberalism of parliamentary democracy. Any program of hedonistic calculation could only recommend a restriction of family size to allow contemporary individuals a more convenient and comfortable existence— to the detriment of the nation's long-range future.[53] In the effort to mitigate the sacrifice that the policy of large families would necessarily involve, Rocco, like Michels and Gini, recommended rapid industrial development and economic modernization of the peninsula to service the needs of its population and render individuals more disposed to maintain high reproductive rates.

The ultimate solution to Italy's problems was expansion: effective access to available raw materials, autonomy from foreign sources of supply, economic expansion in terms of market supplements for Italian products, territorial acquisition in order to settle Italians under the political protection of the nation, and cultural expansion in terms of Italian literary, artistic, and scientific production. But all this required the availability of an abundant and growing population, the "fundamental biologic force" of the nation.

Thus, more than a dozen years before Mussolini's speech of May 26, 1927, all the elements of Fascism's demographic policies had appeared in the writings of Roberto Michels, Corrado Gini, and Alfredo Rocco, three men who were to exercise documented influence on Mussolini throughout the

273

entire period in question. Spengler's views may have reinforced Mussolini's convictions concerning complex demographic issues, but those views were certainly not the source of Mussolini's convictions. Nor had Mussolini concealed his convictions between 1915 and 1927. There were recurrent allusions to the problems of Italian outmigration and Italian population density.

Mussolini had clearly committed himself to the principle that Italian outmigration, under the prevailing conditions, was to be deplored. As early as 1925, furthermore, he had established institutions that would service the needs of Italian mothers and their offspring. It was in that year that the *Opera nazionale per la protezione della maternità e dell'infanzia* was founded. At almost the same time, the "Battle for Grain" was undertaken to improve the support capabilities of the peninsula, to accommodate the resident population, and free the nation from the importation of foreign grain. All these efforts, conjoined with the program of intensive industrial development, were clearly undertaken with the future population policies of the regime in mind.

Certainly the restrictions on emigration imposed by the United States acted as a catalyst. But such restrictions simply emphasized, for Fascists, the conditions surrounding Italian outmigration. Michels had early indicated that Italians arrived in foreign shores under onerous political and moral disabilities. Both nationalists like Corradini and syndicalists like Rossoni recognized that Italians were regularly, and almost everywhere, treated like the "Negroes of Europe."

By 1927 Fascist Italy had enjoyed a period of accelerated industrial growth and economic modernization. Fascists were prepared to implement the demographic policies long implicit in their political program. Those policies were simple restatements of convictions long entertained by nationalists and ultimately by syndicalists. There is nothing in Mussolini's speech of 1927 that was not present in the writings of Michels, Gini, and Rocco more than a dozen years before.

In the "Discorso dell'Ascensione" of 1927 Mussolini outlined a general population program for the peninsula. At its very commencement, Mussolini indicated that the regime would make no concessions to liberalism. The state planned to systematically intervene in every aspect of national life in order to forestall "national suicide." First of all, the state would create institutions to enhance and insure the physical well-being of the nation. It would emphasize, redevelop, and further its health programs, its programs against alcoholism, tuberculosis, and malaria. But more than that, the nation required demographic strength to face the challenges of the future. Mussolini warned that between 1935 and 1940 the future of Europe would be decided by cataclysmic events. If Italy's voice was to be heard and its rights assured, Italy would have to face that challenge with numbers, with an abundant population to support an army which might face opponents that could marshall hundreds of millions against it.[54]

Fascism and "Ruralization"

The immediate problem Italy faced, Mussolini reminded his audience in 1927, was that of a declining population. It was evident that the increasing urbanization of Italians was negatively affecting the collective birthrate. All the available evidence indicated that urban centers, those cities of half a million or more inhabitants, were centers of declining human reproduction. Only outside the urban centers was the Italian population reproducing itself in sufficient numbers to insure demographic increase. As a consequence, every effort was to be made to restrict the depopulation of the countryside.

These proposals were not in the least unusual. They are to be found in Gini's volume of 1912. That they were advocated in 1927 was probably conditioned by the contingent fact that 1927 saw a notable increase in unemployment. In 1926 the registered unemployment was approximately 114,-000. By 1927 it had increased to 278,000. While this was not a dangerous level of unemployment, it did present political problems for a regime that had only firmly established itself two years before. Gini had early warned that urban centers would be staging areas for political unrest during periods of rural depopulation. As a consequence, 1927 revealed itself as an opportune time to restrict the urbanization of Italians. As early as 1926, prefects could restrict the migration of members of the rural population into urban areas by ordering them to return to their native residences if they could not produce evidence of immediate employment.

Mussolini's restrictions on the growth of urban centers was thus a product of long-range political commitments as well as immediate concerns. Many significant programs of the regime, were introduced under the pressures of immediate circumstances, but this does not mean that the programs were simply *ad hoc* responses to such necessities. Throughout this entire period Mussolini's central and irrepressible concern was with the secular decline in the nation's reproductive rate.[55] The concern with controlling the political effects of unemployment, while important, was not the motive behind "ruralization."

Nonetheless, it was this latter concern that prompted the elaborate program of rural public works. Its purpose, however, was twofold: to reduce growing unemployment and to stabilize Italy's rural population in an environment conducive to higher reproductive rates. Eighteen hundred projects were planned, involving some six million hectares, almost one third of the total land surface of the peninsula. In 1928 the "bonifica integrale," the integral development and modernization of agricultural regions, was implemented. Arrigo Serpieri, an agricultural expert and former socialist, was put in charge of a program that employed about 600,000 workers in the decade between 1928 and 1938. The direct and indirect effects of these employments clearly reduced the impact of unemployment (critics sometimes neglect the Keynesian "multiplier effect" when they reflect on the relatively small numbers of men directly employed in these undertakings).[56]

By 1938 approximately two and a half million hectares had been made the object of developmental investment, either directly by the state, or subventionized by the government. Of the total land surface so treated, there was a marked improvement in agricultural yield on approximately ten percent of the land, about 250,000 hectares. A further 100,000 hectares were improved by effective irrigation. The remainder of the improvement had marginal productivity effect. At the same time, many rural roads were restored and new ones constructed, and water systems were maintained, improved, and expanded. There were some regions, like the Pontine Marshes, where, after development, productivity was not impressive and where extensive land areas remained grass meadows. But creating meadows out of the Pontine region, rather than allowing it to remain marsh land, had something to recommend it.[57]

There is a vast literature devoted to the "bonifica integrale" and the merits or demerits of the program, its realizations or its failures. The fact is that the program, however well or ill-conceived, however successful or unsuccessful, was part of a general ideological framework that can be traced to the very foundations of Fascism. However much governed by contingencies, the development of the agricultural regions of Italy was part of the demographic policies of Fascism that Mussolini had already anticipated before the seizure of political power.

This was the context in which Mussolini spoke of the "ruralization" of Italy. That Mussolini addressed himself to ruralization is sometimes seen to represent a form of reactionary utopianism, an effort to turn back the clock to a pre-industrial time.[58] While there were Fascist enthusiasts who wrote tracts that sounded very reactionary utopian,[59] it is evident that Fascism's program of ruralization was never intended to curtail industrial development and economic modernization. In a special conference devoted to the issue of ruralization and demography, Michels made it quite clear that industrialization was an integral and necessary aspect

277

of Fascism's demographic program. For Michels, "the population problem [was] inextricably linked with the productive capacity of the economy." Any increase in reproductive rates of the nation would have to be coupled with a collateral increase in the nation's economic productivity. Those nations with increasing population densities could only sustain their populations through intensive industrialization.[60]

Michels, like most sober Fascists, saw no difficulty in restricting the growth of cities and their dysgenic effects, and continuing industrialization of the peninsula. The anticipation of a secular increase in population necessarily required the modernization of the agricultural sectors of the economy, and the emphasis on the development of the nonindustrial regions served that purpose. Increased agricultural yields were required for a balanced program of modernization.

But more than that, Michels argued that intensive industrialization did not necessarily require the uncontrolled expansion of urban centers. It was not true that modern industry demands populations massed in a limited number of population centers. Michels recognized that such a process, historically, had attended industrialization, but he argued for alternatives. Michels, like many other Fascists, spoke of decentralizing industrial production—always with a concern for industrial efficiency. A program of urban decentralization might well be undertaken that need not jeopardize the continued "intensification of agricultural and industrial production."[61] In effect, Michels argued that Fascism's concern with ruralization in no sense implied "a departure from a sane and effective agricultural and industrial productive policy."[62]

This was how some of the more important Fascist architects and urban planners understood ruralization. Giuseppe Pagano, for instance, a ranking party member during the regime, director of the arts section of the *Scuola di mistica fascista* (a training school for party cadre), and one of Italy's most important architects, spoke of directing the growth of industrial cities "horizontally," developing "satellite communities" of industrial workers living outside the congested center cities. Such communities of twenty-five to fifty thousand inhabitants would provide workers for the center cities, but would preserve the qualities of openness and greenery that dense urban living precluded. Buildings in such service communities would be low to allow maximum infiltration of sunlight in order to reduce the threats of tuberculosis, and unsanitary and unhealthy conditions. A "green belt" would be preserved between the center city and the satellite communities. None of this would impair industrial efficiency nor prejudice economic modernization and development.[63]

The point here is not that the regime accomplished all this. What is at issue is what the concept ruralization meant for the regime. It is clear that it did not mean an antimodern utopianism or a return to the home crafts and agriculture of the premodern period. In fact, the problems addressed by ruralization are characteristically modern problems, and have been so recognized by post-Fascist commentators.[64] They were so recognized at the time by foreign commentators.[65] Ugo Spirito's article devoted to just this kind of an analysis of ruralization and its relationship to industrialization, was an early but not idiosyncratic statement of the position assumed by Fascist intellectuals in the professional, rather than the popular, doctrinal literature. Renzo De Felice counts Spirito's essay a "searching and courageous critique" of the policies of the regime, when in fact it was simply an early statement of what Fascists understood by depopulating the urban centers and ruralizing Italy.[66]

Where the regime actually undertook the planned development of cities—in the 80,000 hectares (800 square kilometers) of the drained marshland of the Pontine—the cities took on many of the proposed features of ruralized communities. The populations of Littoria, Sabaudia, Pontinia, Aprilia, and Pomezia were severely restricted. By the beginning of the Second World War, Littoria, founded in 1932, had a population of approximately 20,000 and was a center of light industry as well as an agricultural region. Sabaudia remained small—founded in 1933—its population was a scant 5,000 in 1936. In Pontinia, founded in 1934, there were 4,000 inhabitants by 1936. Aprilia was founded on the eve of the war which destroyed it, and Pomezia became an industrial satellite city of Rome.

Much has been written in this regard concerning the building program of Fascism, and it cannot be our purpose here to review that literature. The general outlines, however, are clear. Between 1931 and 1935 about one quarter of the national budget (about the same percentage devoted to defense spending) was disbursed for public works, of which building construction constituted a significant proportion.[67] In the capital deficient Italian economy, the major portion of building funds was employed in the public service areas, the construction of summer camps for children, post offices, railway stations, as well as bureaucratic offices and political headquarters. The relatively small sums disbursed for the construction of public housing were, nonetheless, larger than those provided by any pre-Fascist government.

Fascists, themselves, recognized that housing conditions in Italy were shockingly deficient.[68] Equally evident seem the reasons for the deficiencies and the difficulties in ameliorating them. First and foremost, there was the evident magnitude of the problem: Italy's housing problem had been exacerbated by rapid population growth for almost a century. Secondly, there was a scarcity of investment capital, with priority given to modernization and development of the economy. Thirdly, the existence of private property, and the associated special interests, generated resistance to any state housing plan. So emphatic, in fact, was the conflict between private and collective national interests that many Fascists advocated a nationalization of housing.[69] Added to these was a fourth, and not minor, problem. The extensive bureaucratization of the *Istituti per le case popolari*, the parastate agencies charged with attempting to solve the housing problem, made those agencies increasingly less responsive and consequently less effective.

Ruralization was an integral part of Fascism's demographic program. It was implied in the policy of deurbanization, itself undertaken to maintain as high a birthrate for the Italian population as possible. It did not imply an abandonment of economic modernization and industrialization. Taken together, the concern for industrialization and economic modernization, autarchy, the attempt to foster a high rate of demographic expansion, the contingent ruralization to sustain that population growth, and the subsequent search for adequate resource and living space, all constitute a reasonably coherent long-term political program having its own internal logic, and prefigured in the first expressions of Fascist ideology.

Fascism and "Antifeminism"

In recent professional literature Fascist "antifeminism" has become a frequently recurrent concern.[70] The appearance of women's liberation movements and the disposition to identify Fascism with reaction have proven to be powerful incentives to take up the issue and exploit it as fully as possible. We have even witnessed the resurfacing of all the silliness of Wilhelm Reich's "sexpol," the effort to explain complex and eminently contemporary political behaviors in terms of "genital frustrations" and the six-thousand-year existence of the "paternalistic, authoritarian family."[71] The current preoccupation with sex, the appearance of an aggressive women's movement, and the commonplace conviction that identifies Fascism with reaction all manifest themselves in an account that appeals to the most pervasive contemporary prejudice.

For all that, it would seem that a plausible account of Fascist antifeminism could be provided without recourse to the dubious theoretical machinery of orthodox or unorthodox Freudianism. Moreover, whether Fascist policies were "re-

281

actionary" tends to turn on how one defines the term. That Fascist antifeminism was a contingent consequence of other policies seems to be evident.

Fascists were not antifeminists, *per se*, a fact which suggests that any effort to explain their postures via some constant notions of sexual frustration, latent homosexuality, or capitalist oppression is eminently implausible. Fascist policies concerning women were the products of a number of contingent circumstances and probability assessments. In effect, antifeminism was not endemic or essential to the Fascist persuasion.

As early as 1903, for example, Michels displayed public sympathy for the women's liberation movement.[72] The Futurists under F. T. Marinetti, who were to pass directly into Fascist ranks, advocated a radical equality of the sexes. They spoke of monogamy as a form of "bourgeois barbarism" that was rendered tolerable only because adultery provided a requisite "safety valve." They spoke of the "cretinism" that made women the "slaves" of men in lifetime dependency. They advocated state hostels for children in the effort to free women from stultifying household chores. They spoke of easy divorce and easy abortion to lift the burden of monogamy from both sexes.[73]

Michels' volume, *Sexual Ethics*, published in German in 1911 as *Die Grenzen der Geschlechtsmoral*, was clearly supportive of women's liberation.[74] Michels spoke of the subjugation of women in marriage, and of their exploitation by men in a multiplicity of social, economic, and political circumstances.

In their program of 1919, the Fascists advocated suffrage rights for women, and in 1922 Fascists could still allude to the Statute of Carnaro, instituted by Gabrielle D'Annunzio during the occupation of Fiume, as a prefiguration of Fascism. In that Statute (Declaration Twelve) it was insisted that "all citizens, irrespective of sex, have complete rights in the pursuit of employment in industry, the professions, arts and crafts." In November 1922, one month after the March on Rome, A. O. Olivetti reaffirmed the Fascist commitment to the equal rights declaration of the Statute.[75]

Mussolini, himself, gave little public evidence of overt antifeminism, when one takes into account his dispositional diffidence concerning people in general. He was not, for example, an enthusiast for female suffrage because he had very little regard for bourgeois suffrage rights in general. Women's suffrage would serve little purpose, because he saw little purpose in suffrage as it was practiced in parliamentary democracy.[76] Mussolini anticipated a suffrage system predicated on the professional or occupational vote, rather than suffrage exercised by individuals as abstract citizens. As a consequence, he was not an enthusiast of women's suffrage rights because he anticipated a revision in suffrage rights in general. When the issue arose with respect to administrative elections, he, in fact, supported women's suffrage rights, not because he conceived such rights to be either just or an extension of legitimate rights, but because he thought such extension would have very little consequence.

When the International Alliance for Female Suffrage was hosted by the regime in Rome, in May 1923, Mussolini anticipated no difficulty in according women the right to vote. Women would bring to the vote their "fundamental traits" of "measure, equilibrium and wisdom." At the same time, Mussolini committed himself to the program of economic, spiritual, and moral elevation of women.[77] At the end of the same month, at the women's congress in Venice, Mussolini repeated that extension of voting rights to women would constitute no difficulty for the regime. He went on to indicate that he was convinced of the importance of women in every social, economic, and political endeavor. He spoke of their "preponderant" influence in determining the destiny of society.[78]

In May 1925, when the Italian legislature was locked in debate concerning the extension of the franchise to women in administrative elections, Mussolini personally intervened in order to assure passage of the legislation. He insisted that

283

as a mass-based party, Fascism could not logically resist suffrage. He paid tribute to the contribution made by women to the movement and to the Fascist revolution. The right to vote was only a modest compensation.

In the context of his discourse, Mussolini dismissed the suggestion that women were inferior, and simply maintained that they were "different." He did add, quite gratuitously, that he, personally, thought women lacked a "power to synthesize" and therefore were incapable of "broad creativity." Whatever that might have meant to him at the time, he indicated that the contemporary developments of industry made women's alienation from traditional household-oriented roles a predictable eventuality. He anticipated female participation in "every sector of human activity." He spoke of women as teachers, lawyers, professors, and doctors, and went on to say that such a process was not the consequence of caprice, but a necessary result of a hundred years of economic development.

He concluded with praise for women in terms of their contributions to the Italian war effort during the world conflict of 1914-1918. He argued that because Fascists had committed themselves to the mobilization of women for any future conflict, they were committed to give them full political rights.[79] Through Mussolini's intervention, the subject legislation was passed. Shortly thereafter, for reasons that had nothing to do with the extension of voting rights to women, the procedures for administrative elections were substantially changed and the positions became appointive. Women's suffrage, in that instance, became a dead letter. Before the general issue of women's rights resurfaced, a great many things had changed, and Fascist policy became characterized by the antifeminism of which so much is made.

Until 1925 there was little in Fascist ideology or Fascist policy that could be identified as essentially antifeminist. In a Latin country with a long tradition of male dominance, Fascist dispositions were at least mildly progressive. Certainly there was little in the orthodox socialism of Italy that made it aggressive in the insistence upon women's rights.[80] The issue of women's rights was of marginal interest (with some notable exceptions) to the entire Italian revolutionary movement.

By 1927 the situation had materially altered. Not only had Mussolini embarked upon an explicit population policy predicated on large families, but unemployment had begun to become a constant concern. In 1928 Mussolini wrote an introduction to a volume by Richard Korherr in which he more systematically took up themes broached in his speech of May 1927 concerning the declining birthrate in Europe. In that introduction he repeated the warnings contained in the "Discorso dell'Ascensione." He alluded to the high birthrate of China and Russia as posing threats to Europe by the end of the twentieth century and, as a consequence, took emphatic objection to the "neomalthusianism" that advocated an artificial restriction on reproduction. He spoke of Italy's declining birthrate and its special obligation to retard the process. Once again, he associated an indisposition to reproduce with increasing urbanization, and advocated deurbanization and ruralization.[81]

At the same time, several related themes made their appearance, to recur constantly in Fascist propaganda throughout the remaining years of the regime. In the same book for which Mussolini wrote the introduction, Korherr argued that one of the "roots" of the collapse of the family as the principal "embryonic cell" of the social organism was the "emancipation of women." The "liberated woman" demanded "rights," the right of independence and the implied right of facile divorce, the right to "her own body" and the implied right of abortion, all of which undermined the foundation of a stable and prolific family—the harbinger of the biologic "death of peoples."[82]

With the collapse of the Italian economy in the international crisis of 1929, all these elements coalesced to produce the ideological and legislative orientations that came to constitute the Fascist policy on women. By 1932 there were

285

over one million Italians registered as unemployed. Irrespective of extensive public works programs and the reduction in per capita hours, the rate of unemployment did not begin to abate significantly until 1935. In the interim, the Fascist position with regard to women hardened into a set of convictions, buttressed by legislation, that gave the ideology the cast by which it is now identified.

Given the commitment to the monogamous family as the best vehicle for large and disciplined families, conjoined with the conviction that the emancipation of women constituted a primary cause in the "voluntary limitation in the number of pregnancies," the termination of unwanted pregnancies, and relatively late marriages, Fascist ideologues argued that the movement to emancipate women was counterrevolutionary. Women should be inured to roles that were complementary, rather than competitive, to those discharged by men. Women should be trained to fulfill their "natural" responsibilities as wives and mothers. To that end, they should be discouraged from pursuing "masculine" professions and preoccupations. Their education should be designed to prepare them for their life tasks. Females should be trained in the youth organizations of the party and in public institutions, in child care, general pediatrics, and the "homemaking sciences."[83] In 1935 the female members of the Fascist university organizations were urged not to consider their goals to be "the displacement of men from professions or employment," but rather, as educated women, to anticipate their roles as mothers and helpmates to their husbands in marriage and in work.[84]

Although there was a gradual increment in the number of women enrolled in universities during the Fascist period (rising from ten percent in 1922 to sixteen percent in 1936), there was little positive encouragement and considerable discouragement. As the depression deepened there was a systematic effort to discourage female employment. Under all these pressures, there was an increasingly concerted effort to restrict women to traditional social roles. In his interview with Helene Gosset, Mussolini recognized that the times compelled many women to seek employment outside the home, but, he stipulated, "a woman's place, in the present as in the past, is in the home."[85] Women formally enrolled in Fascist organizations were expected to perform traditional social functions such as voluntary service for social welfare agencies and for party institutions. While females participated in competitive sports, such activities were always undertaken with special regard for their specific national task: the bearing of children.[86]

What resulted was the familiar syndrome of attitudes toward women that seem to be particularly characteristic of Latin cultures. Women were exalted as mothers, but expected to evince little interest in politics or other "masculine" concerns. While women literally incarnated the "future of the race," and were the immediate service agents for the "biologic strength" of the nation, they were not expected to concern themselves with affairs outside the home.

Mussolini himself seems to have always personally (rather than publicly) entertained a clear measure of disdain for women in general. In an interview early in the Fascist period he said that "women are the tender, gentle influence that represents a pleasant parenthesis in a man's life, the influence that often aids a man to forget his trials and fatigue, but that leaves no lasting trace. . . . Women are a charming pastime, when a man has time to pass, a means of changing one's trend of thought; but they should never be taken seriously, for they themselves are rarely serious. . . . My wife and my family are my dearest possessions, but so greatly do I treasure them, that I keep them apart from my day, to rest."[87] In 1932, in his conversations with Emil Ludwig, Mussolini maintained that "women should be passive," and then struck out "be passive" in the page proofs and replaced it with "obey." He went on to add that he was opposed to "any type of feminism." "Naturally," he went on, "[a woman] must not be a slave, but . . . in our state women must not count."[88]

287

Whatever importance one attributes to Mussolini's personal opinions, it is reasonably clear that Fascist policy on women was dictated by several very impersonal concerns. The ideological foundation of the policy was the determination to make Italy a ranking power in a competitive world composed of powerful potential enemies. Italy required a population of sixty million souls if it were to face such competitors during the second half of the twentieth century. The subsequent policy toward women was the product of this determination and the fact that Italy, between 1880 and 1922, suffered a decline in births from 37.8 per thousand to 30.2 per thousand. This, conjoined with the conviction that feminism, the emancipation of women, was a significant causal factor in that decline, bred the subsequent policy. The increasing unemployment after 1927 exacerbated the antifeminist tendency.

The logic of just such a policy was already evident among nationalists long before their fusion with Fascism. In 1914, as a case in point, Alfredo Rocco spoke before the *Circolo femminile di cultura* in Rome, and addressed himself to the problem of an increasingly insistent feminism that had begun to make its appearance in northern Europe. His objections to feminism were the same objections that were to characterize Fascism after 1927. The principal threat posed by feminism was the "voluntary limitation on reproduction" that it fostered. The consequence for the nation was a weakening of its economic and military potential at a time when Italy was preparing to face some of the most formidable opponents in its entire history.[89] "Numbers," Rocco insisted, "constituted the ultimate strength of the race."[90]

All the elements of the subsequent Fascist position, in fact, were already present in Rocco's articles of 1914. Mussolini, at that time, had not yet formulated his own position. He still shared Michels' conviction that a responsible voluntary restriction of births might very well be recommended.[91] For some period thereafter the revolutionary syndicalists (as well as the Futurists) continued to entertain reservations concerning any explicit antimalthusianism. Only the conjunction of political aspirations, the clear evidence of a declining birthrate, and the increasing threat of large-scale unemployment, produced Fascism's overt commitment to antifeminist policies. There were, of course, a number of subsidiary factors that influenced Fascist beliefs and Fascist legislation. There was the "Latin tradition" concerning reproduction and the role assignment of women in society. There was also the undeniable influence of the Catholic Church, and finally, there was the influence of Sorel's emphasis on the family in restoring the moral character to contemporary society.[92]

The potential for this kind of social policy was, however, already present when the first syndicalists opted for the defense of their proletarian nation against the plutocratic enemy. The central argument that can be traced from 1911 until the extinction of the regime was that Italy, as a retarded industrial nation, devoid of resources and circumscribed in space, had one undeniable resource advantage over the capitalist powers: its abundant population. The privileged powers had a fatal weakness: a decline in population. With declining numbers, such nations would find it increasingly difficult to sustain their military, colonial, or economic power. They would ultimately lack the manpower requisite to the defense of colonial empires covering millions of square kilometers. Increasing competition for export outlets would compound the difficulties of a shrinking internal market. Italy, on the other hand, sustaining a program of forced industrialization and rapid modernization, and maintaining a high reproductive rate, would ultimately find itself in a position to alter the world distribution of power, and thereby resolve its critical resource problems. The demographic policies of the regime were knit into the fabric of the general political program of Fascism.[93] If such an arduous program was to have any prospect of success the entire population of the peninsula would have to be committed to a work and sacrifice ethic. The regime explicitly rejected individual or collective material satisfaction as political, social, or economic motives.[94] Workers were expected to remain satisfied with controlled wage rates in an expanding economy. Capitalists were expected to sacrifice profits for autarchic development, and political control for state intervention. Citizens, in general, were admonished to sacrifice and serve, youth to "joyously obey," and women to "go forth and multiply."

In this context Fascism's social welfare legislation served to compensate the working masses for their sacrifice. There can be little doubt that the social welfare program produced a number of benefits. Even Piero Meldini, so arch a critic of the regime, alluded to the "progressive" character of Fascist social welfare legislation.[95] The legislation seems to have reduced the resistance to the regime on the part of those who were compelled to sacrifice most in the service of its long-range programs.

As for the demographic program, the ruralization of the peninsula, and the effort to revive the traditional female virtues, they all appear to have been unsuccessful. Italy's birthrate continued to decline during the years of the regime. If the birthrate was 27 per thousand in 1927, it fell to 26.1 per thousand in 1928, to continue to decline to 23.4 per thousand in 1934, and 22.2 per thousand in 1936. At that point, Fascist intellectuals were prepared to recognize the failure of the enterprise.[96] There was hardly more success in the efforts to ruralize the peninsula. With the exigencies created by the war in Ethiopia, Spain, and ultimately on the Continent itself, and the attendant difficulties in any attempt to decentralize industry, the concentration of population in the industrialized urban centers continued at an almost uninterrupted rate.[97]

Fascism's effort to resolve the crisis of the family by reinforcing women's historic roles as wives and mothers hardly seems to have met with more success. In 1938, a survey conducted among Italian schoolgirls between the ages of sixteen and eighteen, revealed only a small minority interested in homemaking as a lifetime preoccupation.[98] Fascism may have been instrumental in removing women from the job market (the percentage of Italian women involved in extradomestic employment declined from 30 percent of the labor force in 1920 to 19 percent in 1931), but the statistics are not unequivocal. Most industrial countries had experienced a decline in the employment of women after 1900. In Italy, Fascist policy may have contributed to this decline, but it is in no ways certain. On the other hand, in certain employment areas like teaching or in the fine arts, the number of women employed increased significantly during the Fascist period.[99] All of which suggests that Fascist antifeminism was not particularly successful and/or may not have been pursued with any special application. In any event, Fascist antifeminism was, at best, a subsidiary concern of Fascist social policy, and made its appearance largely as a consequence of concerns with a declining birthrate and rising unemployment.

With all this as background, it is instructive to consider the social policies of Marxism in power. All of us have been traditionally led to believe that here, if nowhere else, the differences between Fascism and Marxism should be most pronounced. Actually, the differences that obtain do little to mark an essential difference between the two systems, and tell us something about their sustained similarities.

The Social Policies of Bolshevism

If there was one single political myth that animated the organizational and insurrectional activities of the Bolsheviks, it was the commitment to the satisfaction of the material needs of the world proletariat. The anticipated revolution was to resolve the most fundamental requirements of the working classes, and the Bolsheviks charged themselves with the tutelary obligation of discharging that responsibility. From the very earliest years of the Soviet government, social welfare became one of its central preoccupations. Health, disability, old age, unemployment, and maternity insurance very rapidly distinguished Soviet policy from that of other

291

countries, however progressive. Even during the Stalinist period, the concern for social welfare characterized much of Bolshevik legislation. The Soviet Union had every ideological reason for embarking on just such a program.[100] One would have expected nothing less from the "dictatorship of the proletariat."

With the advent of the developmental program inaugurated in 1928, however, social welfare legislation was employed not only as a socialist effort to ameliorate the lot of the working class, but as a means "to promote further increases in the productivity of labor on the basis of the general plan for the industrialization of the country." In November 1930, the Seventh All-Union Conference of Labor Agencies was informed that "social insurance agencies must so readjust themselves, so reorganize their work, as by their practical operation to advance to the highest degree the successful accomplishment of social construction and the improvement of work discipline."[101] Soon the official position was expressed in the following fashion: "The task of social insurance lies in the many-sided, unremitting daily struggle for increasing the yield of labor. . . . This must be the chief content of social insurance work. . . . This is their foremost duty, and by its execution their performance will have to be judged."[102]

In the effort to reduce labor turnover, for example, welfare benefits were tied to the length of service at the last place of employment. Comprehensive illness compensation would be paid only to those workers who could prove that they had been employed for more than three years and for more than two years at their current place of employment. Length of employment was made a critical criterion for admission to health resorts, sanatoria, and convalescent homes. Special provisions were instituted for workers with high productivity records and those in industries critical to the developmental program.

By 1933 the periodical of the Social Insurance Council

of the Soviet Union could insist: "Social insurance legislation must become a powerful stimulus for increasing the yield of labor, for developing socialist competition and shock work on the largest possible scale." Whatever the principal initial motive may have been for the complex array of social welfare legislation in the Soviet Union, by the mid-thirties it was clear that its principal intent was the stimulation of labor productivity in the service of the Stalinist developmental and autarchic program. Moreover, as in the Fascist case, the entire program was funded by a policy of controlled consumption—with real wages in the Soviet Union declining precipitously after 1928 with the beginning of Stalin's industrialization efforts. Between 1930 and the conclusion of the Second World War, irrespective of impressive production increments, the purchasing power of the Soviet worker was never near the level attained in 1928.[103] If anything, Soviet workers made less gains, in terms of real wages, than did their counterparts under the Fascist regime.

In retrospect, it seems evident that Soviet social welfare policies served essentially the same instrumental purposes as those of Fascist Italy. Initially, the programs were calculated to accommodate the working class to the regime. Subsequently, the welfare policies were employed to service the needs of national development by gearing benefits to productivity and stability of employment. Such policies further served to maintain a reasonably healthy, abundant, and productive labor supply. Finally, the entire costs of the programs were borne through a system of forced savings and controlled consumption.

None of this is surprising. As the Soviet Union assumed more and more of the social, economic, and historic obligations anticipated by the revolutionary syndicalists of Italy, the Bolsheviks fashioned institutions and policies that increasingly resembled those of Fascism. This is perhaps nowhere more evident in the Soviet Union than in the social policies concerning the family.

Bolshevik Demographic Policies

As was the case with Fascist ideology, the problem of the socialist family in the Soviet Union was intimately connected with a general demographic policy. The concern with the emancipation of women was inextricably interwoven with the problem of population growth, although socialist ideologues traditionally treated both subjects as though they were, for all intents and purposes, independent. In fact, the experience of the Soviet Union tends to establish their interconnection. Once women's liberation becomes contingent on the realization of more primary goals—in this case the rate of population growth—family structure, itself, becomes instrumental to more fundamental purpose.

When the Soviets came to power in 1917 they had not yet traversed the critical phases of syndicalist reassessment. They still remained fundamentally internationalist. They expected, as we have seen, a worldwide revolution to provide the developed industrial base for socialist policies. They perceived the problem of population from the same internationalist perspective, not in terms of national realities, but from the point of view of a global system of socialist redistribution. In this regard, they had not moved far from the position first articulated by Engels in 1844. At that time Engels had deplored "Malthusianism," the voluntary restriction of births, as an egotistically motivated, bourgeois rationalization that obscured the realities of capitalist maldistribution. For Engels, the insistence that overpopulation might be a real problem was a certificate of destitution for the capitalist system. Engels maintained that "the productive power at the disposal of mankind is immeasurable. The productivity of the land can be infinitely increased by the application of capital, labor and science."[104] All that would be required to eliminate overpopulation would be the effective application of science, capital, and labor to agricultural pursuits, and the unobstructed distribution of the subsequent abundance. As late as 1895,

Engels insisted that it was not population that is pressing on the means of subsistence, but "the means of subsistence that is pressing against the population."[105]

Given this optimistic appraisal of the population problem, Engels could talk easily of "a large family" being a "desirable gift to the community," and of the necessity to destroy the bourgeoisie because "bourgeois social relations" were inhibiting the natural and desirable growth of population.[106] He went on to confidently assert that "we are forever secure from the fear of overpopulation."[107]

These notions became commonplace in the orthodox literature of classical Marxism.[108] August Bebel, in fact, went so far as to suggest that fears of overpopulation invariably attended periods of social decline.[109] Only a disintegrating social system seeks to restrict the natural growth of population. In a curious sense, the Bolsheviks inherited, for manifestly different reasons, an opposition to neomalthusianism not unlike that of the revolutionary syndicalists and nationalists during the incubation period of Fascism.

The fact that the Bolsheviks inherited so optimistic an assessment of the problem led to an easy disassociation of the problems of the family and of female emancipation from the entire issue of population growth rates. There is no indication that the principal theoreticians of the first Bolshevism ever conceived of a connection between family structure, the social position of women, and the rate of population growth. They understood population growth rates to be exclusively a function of the "growth of the productive forces."[110] Given this conviction, society would destroy "bourgeois marriage" and "domestic drudgery," and proceed to the subsequent "liberation of women" without regard to the "population problem."[111]

The first Bolshevik legislation on marriage reflected these dispositions.[112] In the Soviet Code of 1918 facile marriage and equally facile divorce were hailed as essential moves in the direction of women's liberation. The termination of unwanted pregnancies was made easy as well. Conjoined with these regulations, the female right to equal employment provided the foundations for the equality of the sexes.

Of all the regulations governing women, the regulation governing their employment in labor was the one most religiously adhered to. The reasons are not far to seek. Between 1917 and 1920, the famine conditions in the Soviet Union precipitated a migration from the urban areas to the countryside, with a corresponding shortage of labor in the cities. The number of workers in heavy industry had fallen from almost three million in 1913 to about 1,602,000 in 1922. It was in this context that Trotsky spoke of the "mobilization" and "militarization" of all labor, male and female without distinction, and it was in this context that females were increasingly drawn as equals into the labor force. Women workers became more and more common throughout industry, often undertaking the most arduous and taxing labor. When, in the late twenties, Stalin undertook the accelerated industrial development of Russia, the demand for labor further increased, and the wives and children of urban workers were registered, and under pain of penalty, were by and large compelled to accept industrial employment.[113]

The Soviet Union was, in effect, never faced with the problem of large-scale unemployment, and as a consequence sought out women, particularly in the cities (where their employment would not require further home construction or an increase in social services) to fill imperative developmental needs. As a consequence, Soviet legislation on equal employment rights for women was applied with considerable diligence. How progressive such legislation would have remained under other circumstances is difficult to divine, particularly when one considers the remarkable reversals in legislation governing divorce and abortion under the pressure of changing circumstances.[114]

The legislation concerning the Soviet family underwent the first changes as early as 1926. Under the new dispensation changes were introduced to offset the negative impact of the first efforts at family regulation. Between 1918 and 1926, it had become painfully evident that an irregular and unstable family life was burdening the Soviet state with the expensive responsibilities of hundreds of thousands of unwanted and frequently delinquent children. More than that, the difficult economic conditions increased the indisposition to have children, and the population growth rate in the Soviet Union registered a marked decline. In Moscow the birthrate declined from 31.7 per thousand to 24.5 per thousand between 1913 and 1928. In Leningrad the reproductive rate fell to 22.1 per thousand. In the Ukraine the absolute number of live births fell from 1,176,000 in 1925 to 1,039,-000 in 1928, a decline of 137,000 in a three-year period.[115]

By the mid-thirties, as a consequence, Soviet ideologues were reminding Russians that the Soviet Union "had need of people."[116] Soviet specialists revealed alarming statistics concerning the frequency of abortion. In the Ukraine the 90,000 abortions of 1924 had increased to the 156,000 of 1926. In Leningrad, the 7.5 percent abortion rate of 1912 had increased to 50 percent in 1926. In Kiev the abortion rate had increased from 16 percent in 1923 to 42 percent in 1925. In Starobelsk the abortion rate of 51.1 percent of 1924 had increased to 97.5 percent in 1926. In Moscow there were three times as many abortions as live births in 1934.[117]

In 1936 the Soviet Union passed new regulations concerning divorce and abortion. Divorce was made increasingly difficult and abortion was proscribed. In 1935 the neglect of children was made a punishable offense by law. In substance, the new legislation was advertised as restoring to women the "joys of maternity" and the "socialist responsibility" of family maintenance. Trotsky, from exile, denounced these new decrees as a "Fascist restoration" of the "bourgeois family." The legislation was designed to reestablish the stability, integrity, and fecundity of the monogamous family. Provisions were afforded for large families, and abortion was made a criminal offense.[118] By 1944 Stalin had abandoned all pretense, and legislation offered financial and welfare benefits to prolific mothers in the effort to increase Russia's rate of population growth. An honorary title "Heroine-Mother" and the order of "Mother's Glory" were created, and a decoration, the "Medal of Motherhood," was provided for those women who produced children in abundance.[119]

Fascists were not slow to point out the analogues with Fascist legislation.[120] The Bolsheviks were attempting to re-establish the integrity of the monogamous family as the most effective agency for the maintenance of a high birthrate. It was to this end that Stalin's Supreme Soviet insisted that the "strengthening of the family has always been a major task of the Soviet state."[121] Women were no longer to be liberated from the obligations of childbirth and domestic duties. Moreover, they were expected to assume the added burden of laboring for the development of the socialist community. The confluence of developmental and demographic needs produced the Soviet regulations concerning the family. Just as Fascist legislation, the product of significant unemployment and a declining birthdate, produced Fascist anti-feminism, the Soviet concern for national development, the preoccupation with a declining birthrate, and the prevailing labor shortage, produced Soviet "quasi-feminism." Whatever their manifest differences, both policies were very largely a function of contingent circumstances to which, in the Soviet case, ideological commitment was forced to submit.

In both the Fascist and the Bolshevik systems, specific social policies can best be understood as the consequence of the intersection of ideological, contingent, instrumental, and prudential concerns. The distinction between the two systems, in these cases, seems to reside in Fascism's clear commitment to national development before the revolution. In the Bolshevik case there was, initially, no such similar ideological concern. Social welfare legislation, decrees concerning the family, and the dedication to women's liberation were general stock-in-trade concerns of European socialism. Only with Stalin's decision to undertake industrial development in an autarchic environment did the priorities of the revolutionary socialist program for the Soviet Union become apparent. Not only were labor organizations domesticated, consumption controlled, and state authority reinforced and expanded, but the military necessities of defense and aggression recommended a population policy that would foster and sustain rapid population growth. As a consequence, social welfare legislation and the legislation devoted to women underwent corresponding involution. Social welfare legislation was pressed into the service of increased productivity and women were assigned the sometimes conflicting roles of man's equal in work responsibilities and of dutiful mother of his abundant children. It was not the essential antifeminism of Fascism that distinguished it from the quasi-feminism of the Soviet Union. It was rather the unemployment rate in the one country, and the labor scarcity in the other, that shaped legislation. In any case, the central concerns of both systems turned on the creation of industrially advanced and densely populated national communities that could face any challenges that might be tendered by more fortunately circumstanced powers.

NINE

FASCISM AND DEVELOPMENT IN
COMPARATIVE PERSPECTIVE

Throughout the discussion thus far, regular allusion has been
made to the similarities shared by Bolshevism and Fascism
as political systems. Both have been characterized as developmental regimes bent on the modernization and industrialization of their respective national communities. Involved
in substantially the same processes, both regimes created
analogous strategies and analogous institutions to service
them. Granted all the differences in history, national culture,
the accession to power, resource capabilities, geographic
extent, population density, and relationship to other nations,
both systems came to share remarkable similarities recognized by bourgeois economists and social scientists, as well
as by commentators of both Marxist and Fascist persuasion.

Discussions such as these are, of course, always fraught
with peril. One places emphasis on similarities and neglects
differences. And similarities, John Kautsky has warned us,
are always in the eye of the beholder.[1] What constitutes a
significant or essential similarity for one becomes a superficial and nonessential similarity for another.

Similarities in political and social science are generally
sought out to support some interpretive argument, or as the
basis for empirical generalizations. The business of social
science, in fact, is the searching out of just such similarities
—precisely to serve such purposes—for social science is
predicated on a regularity analysis of complex and seemingly
unique sequences of events. The fact that everything in the

300

natural and social universe is, in some sense, unique is not enough to discredit the effort to identify, isolate, code, and employ significant similarities. Every tree and shrub, every insect and fish, every nation, and every human being, is unique in a clear and indisputable sense. But botany and entomology, ichthyology, and political and social science proceed to categorize, classify, and generalize on the basis of what are conceived to be fruitful similarities. The similarities employed will be selected for theoretical reasons, to enhance, at first, our preliminary understanding and, ultimately, to afford explanatory, and predictive leverage.[2]

It is fairly obvious that the social sciences have made only preliminary moves in the direction of comprehensive theoretical understanding of the complex behaviors that govern political and social life. But however preliminary, these moves involve intricate comparative judgments that find expression in numerous classificatory schemata.

Like all such preliminary attempts, these efforts involve considerable cognitive risks. Political regimes can be accommodated in any number of mutually exclusive classificatory schemata. Every classification involves the selection of a few relatively abstract features that serve as sorting criteria. As long as no generally accepted theory serves as a guide to sorting criteria, many alternative criteria and, hence, alternative classifications, remain possible. Bats are not birds and whales are not fish, but only because we have a standard body of theory at our disposal that excludes common-sense criteria. For many intelligent laymen, bats will continue to be birds, and whales will continue to be fish. For many laymen, any animal that flies is a bird, and any that inhabits the sea is a fish.

When we deal with complex political phenomena we find ourselves circumstanced like intelligent laymen bereft of comprehensive theory. Fascists were anti-Marxist and Marxists are anti-Fascist; consequently, their respective regimes must be fundamentally different. To suggest that a Marxist regime and a Fascist regime shared more than superficial

301

similarities outrages common sense. For all that, we have argued just that. We have argued, in effect, that for all its commonsensical unlikelihood, whales and bats are mammals, and Fascism, like Stalin's Bolshevism, was a developmental dictatorship.

That bats and whales are not identical—and that Fascism and Bolshevism are not identical—hardly requires argument. What we have attempted is not the identification of Fascism and Bolshevism, but rather what G. Lowell Field calls "experimental naming," a preliminary attempt at theoretically significant classification.[3] Since political science in particular, and social science in general, possess very few generally accepted theories, the best that can be said for any such preliminary classification is that one can make a reasonable case for its plausibility, and that the plausible classification has some heuristic merit. Since social science possesses few theories with which any classificational schema might be expected to mesh, little more than heuristic utility can be required of such preliminary and experimental efforts.

Having granted all that, there are enough insights in the professional literature that make the effort to classify Fascism and Bolshevism as members of the same set, or subset, of political regimes of considerable heuristic interest. A similar search for sustained and theoretically interesting similarities between political systems has led other professionals to explore and compare systems as different as that of Mexico and the Soviet Union, Nkrumah's Ghana and the Soviet Union, Kemal Ataturk's Turkey and National Socialist Germany.[4] Whatever the cognitive yield of such efforts, the point is that comparative politics cannot restrict itself exclusively to the exploration of intuitively plausible or common-sense similarities. For decades Fascism (however Fascism is construed) and Marxism (however Marxism is construed) have been intuited as mutually exclusive. The folk wisdom of political and social science has insisted upon the irrepressible essential differences presumed to obtain between them. The point of the present exercise is to suggest that whatever differences distinguish Italian Fascism from its Bolshevik contemporary, these differences are not as interesting or theoretically significant as their shared similarities.

Fascism and Development

The term "development" is used here to refer to a comprehensive process of socioeconomic change that includes emphatic attitudinal and institutional alterations requisite to the creation of a modern productive system.[5] Development refers to both modernization—the secularization of belief systems, the invocation of scientific techniques for the resolution of problems, the urbanization of populations, increments in literacy, the reduction of parochialism and regionalism, and the expansion of information and communications systems—and industrialization—the employment of technological innovation to enhance per capita productivity, the spread of commerce, and the expansion and diversification of manufacturing and extractive plants, as well as the steady and sustained growth of the gross national product.[6] Conjoined with development understood in this broad sense is political development, the increased regulative and extractive capability of the state.

In general, it can be said that development in the twentieth century (as distinct from development prior to that time) has been attended by a correlative increase in the regulative and extractive capability of the central state. Where a case can be made that centralization of resource mobilization and allocation and economic planning impaired economic development in the eighteenth and nineteenth centuries,[7] such structural features seem to foster (or at least attend) development in the twentieth.

What this implies for developmental politics is interesting. When Marx and Engels addressed themselves to the future role of the state, they conceived of its "withering away." In the postindustrial society they anticipated, there would be no function that the state, *per se*, might discharge.

303

Economic activity in the anticipated postrevolutionary society would be undertaken by the voluntary association of free productive communes. Initially, this seems to have been Lenin's vision of the future of the Bolshevik state. Very quickly, however, all that changed. Under the pressures generated by development within an insulated economy, the Bolshevik "workers' state" took on all the institutional features of a complex bureaucratic apparatus capable of closely regulating the social, political, and economic subsystems of the nation, as well as extracting from the general population all the capital, skill, and labor resources necessary for sustained industrialization. From 1917 through the thirties the regulative and extractive capabilities of the Bolshevik state increased exponentially.

It has been argued that all developing systems increase their regulative and extractive capabilities in order to insure the resources necessary for regular expansion. The distinction seems to be between liberal systems that modernized and industrialized by and large in the nineteenth century when centralization was largely dysfunctional because of logistic, communications, and information shortfall, and those hegemonic systems that have modernized and industrialized in the twentieth century, when logistic, communications, information, and control capabilities have made centralization a functional adjunct to the process.

During the first decade of the present century, Italy's revolutionary syndicalists advocated economic and political decentralization in much the same spirit as that which animated Marx and Engels before the turn of the century. But by the advent of the First World War, most syndicalists had come to recognize the functional importance of the state as a centralizing, integrative, and managerial agency. By that time, the economic development that had begun in Italy before the turn of the century was seen largely in terms of industrialization, a process which, in itself, required extensive regulation and, ultimately, a commensurate increase in extractive capabilities. By 1921 Panunzio and Rossoni regularly alluded to just such functional requirements.

By the mid-twenties the practice in the Soviet Union, so much at variance with Marxist theory, confirmed the judgments of the revolutionary national syndicalists. The Soviet regime exercised control over, and extracted resources from, its population to a degree that would have been unthinkable even under the Czars. "Everyone possessing any skill or knowledge or simple muscle power was pressed into service, willing or not," Alfred Meyer recounts. "The workers, in whose name the regime claimed to govern, were forced to work under unbelievably hard conditions. Control over many economic enterprises, which they had seized in the early months of the revolution, was wrested from their hands, and their unions were subjected to the command of the party."[8] By the commencement of the first five-year plan, the regulative and extractive capabilities of the Soviet system had reached a level perhaps unattained by any other governmental authority in history.

One of the most characteristic features of development, particularly during the industrialization phase, is the enormous cost to the working masses. Recently, Roger Hansen has indicated that there is no "clear evidence that economic development can be achieved in any society without sustained sacrifices on the part of the lower income groups."[9] It is reasonably clear that controlled consumption must be invoked to underwrite the high costs of modernization and industrialization.[10]

Whatever political form developmental regimes assume, they are all faced with the problem of extracting from the general population the resources necessary for the construction of a modern infrastructure—roads, communications media, and educational facilities—as well as those involved in expanding productive plants and providing the requisite technology. Mass-mobilizing regimes face special problems in such circumstances. Masses must be marshalled, and effectively integrated—"domesticated"—inured to sustained and demanding enterprise. To achieve these ends as quickly and as efficiently as possible, masses must be infused with a work, sacrifice, and obedience ethic, the dictatorship's functional analogue of the protestant ethic so successful during the more leisurely development of northern Europe and North America. All of which implies regulative and extractive efficiencies of a high order.

With the expansion of the regulative and extractive capabilities of revolutionary developmental government, there is a necessary, and concurrent, expansion of propaganda efforts. Entire populations are to be infused with the ideology of the revolution. Masses must be animated by messianic invocations, the noneconomic incentive necessary to sustain protracted and demanding collective enterprise. "Symbolic capability" grows conjointly with regulative and extractive efforts.[11] As long as the material benefits available for distribution remain limited, noneconomic supplements are required to offset the demands of a newly mobilized population. Moreover, developmental regimes that are revolutionary in origin, lack the legitimacy of established regimes. As a consequence, they develop elaborate "charter myths" to legitimize their rule. Such systems tend to become "ideocracies," political polities sustained by exclusive and messianic belief systems.

Such regimes charge themselves with the obligation of integrating all the segments of a society behind the developmental enterprise. Often these efforts find expression in a hierarchical and monolithic political system which maximizes regulative, extractive, and symbolic capabilities. The accompanying ideology develops "religious" features: the employment of ritual, symbolic exchanges, hagiographies, and sustained chiliastic preoccupations. Often, if not always, the leader of the movement takes on charismatic properties and becomes the incarnation of the goals of the revolution.[12] The leader becomes the "Duce," the "Lider massimo," the "Osagyefo," the "Vozhd." The leader is spoken of as "our father, teacher, our brother, our friend, indeed our very lives, for without him we would no doubt have existed, but we would not have lived; there would have been no hope of a cure for our sick souls, no taste of glorious victory after a lifetime of suffering. What we owe him is greater even than the air we breathe."[13]

Where such ideal motives fail to effect integration and domestication, one can expect the expansion of police powers. Any regime possessed of the most minimal political competence would employ both ideal and coercive powers in a measure understood to be appropriate in each special circumstance.

Among the most effective ideological symbols exploited by developmental regimes, the "nation" has taken a preeminent place. That this should be the case is easily comprehensible. Before the turn of the century, classical Marxists recognized the nation-state as the most appropriate vehicle for economic modernization and development. In our own time, given the differential distribution of resources, technology, political power, modernization, and development itself, developing nations have generally assumed that modernization and industrialization must proceed largely within the confines of their oppressed nation-state, under the political hegemony of a nationalist leadership. In this regard, Robert Ward has labelled "popular identification with the nation" as "one of the most operationally crucial aspects" of the political culture of development.[14] In his earliest essays on economic growth, Walt Whitman Rostow indicated the functional role of nationalism in the process of comprehensive development.[15] Nationalism has become, in fact, characteristic of contemporary developing systems.[16] The literature devoted to economic and political development is filled with references to modernization and industrialization as necessary for "national self-realization."[17] Under the impetus of nationalist aspirations, priorities are accorded domestic enterprise, generally accompanied by a redirection of

307

export trade in the effort to escape the dependency on more advantaged trading partners, a relationship (correctly or incorrectly) understood as impeding effective development.[18]

As revolutionary and developmental elites assume more and more obligations—regulative, extractive, symbolic, pedagogical, tutelary, and managerial—specialized and diversified bureaucracies can be expected to develop. Government is obliged to discharge not only its characteristic functions—the maintenance of law and order and internal and external security, the provision and administration of a national legal system, as well as the implementation of viable fiscal programs—but must undertake other, highly specialized activities.[19] Government ceases to be preoccupied solely with executive functions and assumes more and more directive and managerial activities.[20] Not only does government charge itself with increasingly onerous and complex tasks of population management and integration, it must channel collective energies into ambitious programs of modernization and industrialization to catch up with more favored industrialized nation-states. Moreover, it must frequently undertake such tasks in circumstances characterized by impressive capital scarcity. J. Fei and G. Ranis, in fact, identify the lack of capital as the "most important handicap" that developmental regimes must face in their efforts to develop retarded economies.[21]

The nonavailability of investment capital constitutes the grounds for strict population management, the inculcation among the masses of ideological or moral incentives, as well as for an effective police backup for the hegemonic system. Without the institutional framework in which all these functions can be discharged, neither the accumulation of necessary capital nor its successful administration can be achieved.[22]

Each developmental regime, of course, finds itself involved in a multiplicity of contingencies which will significantly influence its overt behavior. If the developmental regime accedes to power in a power vacuum after a lost or an extended civil war, its political and institutional development can take place with less constraints than if it comes to power encumbered by nonmovement allies, or under the controlling influence of its former colonial masters. Whatever the case, the general functional requirements with which such regimes must contend produce an identifiable similarity among them.

Given the rehearsal of the functional requirements of general development, few commentators have failed to recognize Bolshevism as a "modernizing movement."[23] If such is, in fact, the case, and the Soviet Union is a member of an inclusive class of developmental regimes that includes, among others, the underdeveloped countries of the third world,[24] we find ourselves possessed of a very general classificatory schema that distinguishes developed and developing from traditional systems. Where Italian Fascism, not to speak of generic fascism, might fit in such a preliminary schema, is problematic, to say the very least. Fascism has been treated, in general, as a kind of parenthesis in history, an interval in the history of Europe between the wars, having little connection with anything that followed.

Recently, however, there has been some suggestion of change. In the immediate past, Otto-Ernst Schueddekopf identified Italian Fascism as a "dictatorship for development."[25] Earlier still, Mary Matossian characterized Mussolini's Fascism as animated by an "ideology of delayed industrialization," a belief system calculated to husband the population of Italy from the stage of first industrialization to its conclusion.[26] If, in fact, Fascism was a developmental regime, and its ideology a developmental belief system, could it not be accommodated in our preliminary schematization without theoretical tension?

Anthony Joes has suggested just such a possibility. He has intimated, as a consequence, that fascism as well as communism might well be on the agenda for the developing nations of the third world[27]—a possibility that would restore lines of continuity broken by the disposition to treat Fascism (or fascism) as an idiosyncratic episode in the history

309

of Europe. One might have expected John Kautsky, who has made herculean efforts to synthesize Marxist regimes into just such an analysis through their identification as "modernizing," to have welcomed the suggestion. Unhappily, Kautsky has chosen to reject such a possibility.[28] The reasons for his rejection offer some instructive insights into the study of Fascism from a comparative perspective.

Kautsky's argument proceeds in the following fashion. He argues that at some time in the first stages of development, there are occasions when a balance is struck between some of the traditional elements of the changing society and its modernizers. On these occasions, the aristocracy, attempting to restore its positions of privilege, but unable to reestablish itself without political allies, searches out political elements that might assist as janissaries in a "last stand against the political consequences of industrialization." The plebian allies of the aristocracy are fascists, and although fascists are concerned with industrialization—in fact, "it is industry that furnishes the very *raison d'être* of fascist regimes"—they, like their patrons, "fear the political consequences of industrialization, particularly . . . the political mobilization and organization of industrial labor."[29] Fascism, then, according to this argument is granted a grudging place within the developmental regimes. It is a schizophrenic developmental system committed to the defense of the most retrograde elements of modern society: the aristocracy.

Now there is just enough truth in this argument to make it exceedingly popular.[30] But the semblance of truth notwithstanding, such an account is, at best, implausible. Norman Kogan was not the first to suggest its principal drawbacks. If fascism, as an ally of the aristocracy, sought to politically demobilize the working classes, we are embarrassed to explain why the Bolsheviks, without aristocratic preoccupations, were equally energetic in domesticating the working classes of the "dictatorship of the proletariat." The Bolshevik trade unions were no less hierarchically controlled agencies of the state than were the Fascist syndicates.[31] If both regimes were so assiduous in controlling just this feature of industrialization, it is conceivable that both sought solution to the same problem. If Bolshevism's purpose was to effectively integrate labor in the demanding national developmental enterprise upon which it had embarked, no less might be said of Fascism. Rather than serving the purposes of the aristocracy, it seems perfectly plausible that Fascism's control of labor through a mixture of myth-mongering, overt and subtle coercion, and a display of social welfare concerns, was instrumental to its overall developmental needs. The fact that Fascism had accepted aristocratic elements as passive allies in its struggle for power would then be a contingent, rather than an essential, feature of its labor policies.

Certainly the aristocratic elements of the traditional society persisted into the Fascist period, and they were notably absent in the Bolshevik case. But their presence or absence might well constitute nothing more than an historic irrelevance in terms of Fascism's general developmental program.

The Fascists, as distinct from the Bolsheviks, found themselves in a political environment in which many elements of the pre-Fascist polity (including the aristocracy) still enjoyed considerable political power. There is little to suggest that Fascism could have embarked upon its developmental program, much less acceded to power, without making accommodations for those still vital elements. It is clear that Fascism, prior to the March on Rome, recognized the need of nonmovement allies. With equal clarity Fascists understood that a protracted class war could only impede their program, just as it had impeded the Bolshevik program. The difference was that the Fascists understood their historic charge—the rapid modernization and industrialization of a retarded socioeconomic system—while the Bolsheviks were still hobbled by the commitment to an inappropriate form of Marxism designed for revolution in a postindustrial environment. All of which suggests that it was not the defense of aristocratic privilege that governed Fascism's efforts to domesticate labor. Fascism, like Bolshevism, sought to reduce

311

the wage and resource demands any free and aggressive labor movement might make on a capital-scarce developing system.

To suggest that the defense of the aristocracy was among the political intentions of Fascism is belied by every piece of historic evidence available. While some elements of the aristocracy might have found Fascism among the least threatening of the alternatives open to them, there is no evidence that they welcomed its advent or exercised any appreciable influence over its political evolution. The aristocracy seems to have served Fascism as a vehicle for capital accumulation. The profits of the landed aristocracy were turned to developmental account by the regime, often disbursed in the modern sectors of the economy. Traditional elements were, in effect, compensated for their loss of political power, but there is little indication that the regime defended the aristocracy.[32]

The misalliance between the aristocracy and Fascism was a contingent historic circumstance rather than an essential feature of the regime. It was a misalliance both were to grievously regret. The aristocracy, with its strong anglophile sympathies, impaired the Fascist war effort in time of crisis, and abandoned Fascism, without regret, as soon as it was politically feasible and other alternatives made themselves available.

Kautsky himself has come to recognize that modernizers, even Marxist modernizers, show every disposition to league themselves not only with industrial capitalists when the developmental program requires such an alliance, but they are equally disposed to enter into accord with aristocratic and feudal elements when necessary. Marxists have shown themselves prepared to defend "the rights of patriotic landlords" and make common cause with the "liberal" aristocracy when any alternative might threaten their developmental program.[33]

In effect, what is essential for all mass-mobilizing, developmental regimes is not their respective class bases, but their developmental program, and that is governed by functional requirements. These regimes must domesticate labor to an economy of high productivity but minimal consumption. To that end, they will try to orchestrate consensus, inspire confidence through the invocation of national myths and appeals to the providential leader. They will have to attract entrepreneurial and technological talent in a seller's market. To do so they will variously advocate class collaboration, make the "national bourgeoisie" part of the "people's democratic dictatorship," pay differential wages, or differentially distribute power and welfare benefits. Historical, cultural, and sociopolitical circumstances will influence, if not determine, how each modernizing regime effects its purposes and which social elements it will accept as allies. Kautsky, himself, in discussing Marxist developmental dictatorships maintains that just these realities reveal how Marxists have exposed themselves as a party "composed of an elite of intellectuals representing no given social class but seeking a base for the realization of its ambitions in any class from which it can draw support."[34] His argument concludes with the conviction that "Communist parties in underdeveloped countries want to cooperate with the capitalists [and the aristocracy, if necessary] because they need them for industrialization. And this simply makes no sense in Marxist terms."[35] Bolshevism, in effect, was not "the ideology of an industrial proletariat," but the rationale of a "group in quest of political power and in search of a shortcut to industrialization."[36] No less could be said of the revolutionary syndicalist and nationalist elite that sought to force Italy to the stage of industrial maturity.

That the national syndicalists and nationalists of Italy had a clearer conception of the historic tasks they had set for themselves does them no discredit. The distinction can be no better articulated than in the words of Kautsky himself:

While the Bolsheviks retained the vocabulary and concepts associated with their prerevolutionary ideology, that ideology did not guide their policies during and after the Revolution, much as they thought that it should and did. Being a product of industrially advanced Western Europe

313

and focusing on the role of a powerful industrial proletariat, Marxism could not serve as a guide to effective political action in underdeveloped Russia. To a large extent, then, the Soviet regime's policies were not a result of Marxist ideology elaborated and defined before the Revolution, but, on the contrary, communist ideology tended to be a product of Soviet policies which responded to the conditions the regime in fact confronted.[37]

The revolutionary syndicalists of Italy, on the other hand, had traversed all the stages that Bolshevism endured under the pressure of circumstances, before their accession to power. Even prior to their assumption of responsibilities as the ideologues of Fascism, the revolutionary syndicalists had subjected classical Marxism to a studied critique. As a consequence, they had radically altered the character and complexion of the Marxism they had inherited, and created an ideology of rapid modernization and industrialization suitable for a national community suffering all the handicaps of retarded development. Their principal spokesmen anticipated that in the service of rapid development they would be required to furnish a declassed and nationalist, vanguard elite that would dominate the entire process. To further their program, they anticipated the domestication of labor, the imposition of a work and sacrifice ethic, class collaboration, the orchestration of consensus, and the expansion of a dynamic, interventionist, and hegemonic state. With rare prescience they anticipated the advent of a charismatic and heroic leader who would incarnate the process. In point of fact, of all the developmental dictatorships of the twentieth century, Fascism, inspired largely by the ideology of revolutionary national syndicalism, was perhaps the most prescient, explicit, and frank. It represented a paradigm instance of that class of mass-mobilizing developmental dictatorships that have invested much of our century.

Each developmental regime, of course, faces unique historic circumstances. Some attempt to negotiate the process of development under polyarchic or pluralistic auspices. Access to foreign sources of investment capital or a unique endowment of subsoil resources might shape liberal political strategies. Others with extremely fragile communications and political infrastructures may succumb to the dominance of military rule. Still others, because of peculiar local or international circumstances, may make developmental effort under modernizing aristocracies. But there clearly seems to be a subset of developmental regimes that can best be characterized as mass-mobilizing, single-party dictatorships, which includes heretic Marxist polities as diverse as Bolshevism, Maoism, and Italian Fascism. However different these regimes are in terms of the age structure, social class, geographic provenience, educational and occupational origins of their leadership and membership,[38] the tasks they assume, and the strategies and institutions that attend them, bear a remarkable family resemblance. These resemblances have not been lost on bourgeois, Marxist, and Fascist commentators alike. That Anglo-American analysts have chosen to neglect them is probably a consequence of our serious neglect of Fascist ideology,[39] and the almost complete absence, in English, of any serious study of Fascist economic policy. Only recently has Alan Milward provided an account of Fascist economics that goes some considerable distance in redressing the inadequacies of earlier renderings.[40] Anglo-Americans have been surprisingly slow to accept what even the most committed Marxists have been prepared to acknowledge for some time. Recently, the Marxist Nicos Poulantzas wrote, for a French audience, that in Fascist Italy "industrial recovery between 1922 and 1929 was the strongest in capitalist Europe. . . . [and] the recovery after the crisis was quite spectacular." Fascism, he continued, "really represented a development of capitalist forces of production. . . . It represented industrial development, technological innovation, and an increase in the productivity of labor." Fascism was, in fact, a victory of the indigenous forces of modernization and development over the landed aristocracy and banking capital

315

with its multiple links with international plutocracy. The results, as a consequence, were reflected not only in industrialization but in the modernization of agriculture where there were "some spectacular results."[41]

However much the identification of Italian Fascism as a developmental regime may strain the collective folk wisdom of traditional political science, that recognition recommends itself to our consideration. It provides a preliminary classification system far less paradoxical than those produced by conventional wisdom. When Organski suggested that Mussolini was disposed to involve Italy in wars of one or another sort, and yet, in defense of the traditional elements of the community, he suppressed industrial development, the necessary material precondition for waging war, we are left with an irrepressible sense that something has gone wrong in the analysis. The effort to identify Italian Fascism as conservative, reactionary, and antimodern has produced little more than a tissue of implausibilities.[42]

John Kautsky has argued that, for all their evident differences, the Bolshevik and Mexican revolutions shared important functional similarities. Both are revealed as having generated developmental systems that sought to satisfy the requirements of modernization and industrialization. A better case, it would seem, could be made for Italian Fascism as a developmental system—supported by an ideology rooted in classical Marxism, but adapted to the demands of contemporary development. When Fascists spoke of "economic expansion," the "need to industrialize," "accumulate capital," "rationalize the means of production," introduce "technological innovation" to increase *per capita* production, expand the "managerial functions" of the state, modify traditional attitudes toward organization, and integrate labor under the "unitary discipline of the state corporations," they were clearly speaking the language of developmental politics.[43] The program, judged by purely economic criteria, produced good results.[44] That the costs of development fell most heavily on the subaltern classes, and included the loss of political liberty, does nothing to detract from the characterization of Fascism as a developmental regime. As we have seen, *all* developmental systems transfer the costs of the process to the working masses, and many tend to suppress liberty.

The treatment of Fascism as a modernizing movement places the entire phenomenon once again in the mainstream of contemporary discussion. The treatment of Italian Fascism (if not generic fascism) as a case apart, unique in some special sense, has produced only confusion, perplexity, and discontinuity. The treatment here has been largely within the general confines of the politics of development. Fascism has been viewed all but exclusively in just such a context. This is not to deny that Mussolini's Fascism had unique features that merit special treatment in their own regard. Rather, what has been attempted is: the treatment of Fascism as an instance of mass-mobilizing dictatorship, suggesting something of its relationship to Bolshevism (often treated as a unique subject in its own right), within the confines of a study of modernization and industrialization. Purchased by such an effort, presumably, is a more satisfying preliminary understanding of an entire range of issues, hitherto treated as discrete and incommensurable. So conceived, Mussolini, Panunzio, Michels, and Olivetti would enter the lists with Lenin, Stalin, Trotsky, Mao, Ho, Castro, Sun, Sukarno, Nasser, and Nkrumah as members of the class of revolutionary modernizers, all different in their various ways, but all united in a central enterprise that has preoccupied political energies in special fashion throughout the twentieth century.[45]

Revolutionary modernizers have created political systems that often responded in singular ways to the contingent and special needs of their specific time and place. But of all developmental regimes, Fascism exemplified the constellation of traits that mark it as a paradigm of twentieth century mass-mobilizing, developmental dictatorship. More than that, its ideology was clearly fashioned to satisfy the needs of such a contemporary dictatorship. Unlike Bolshevism, jerry-built to respond to needs pressed upon the regime, Fascism largely

317

anticipated its enterprise. Contemporary Marxist developmental dictatorships now display the entire syndrome of traits that, at one time, distinguished Fascism from its more orthodox competitors. Marxist revolution is now modernizing, industrializing, and national, uniting all patriotic elements (including the national bourgeoisie and at times the patriotic aristocracy) under the auspices of a hierarchic, hegemonic party identified with the state, and enjoying the sure guidance of the providential, charismatic leader. The style of this subset of developmental regimes has become increasingly moralistic and military, with devotion, struggle, obedience, faith, and sacrifice their cardinal virtues. The enemy has become not the native capitalists, but the foreign imperialists, the contemporary analogue of Fascism's plutocratic opponents. All the appurtenances of these regimes—the massive propaganda requirements, the orchestrated consensus, the populism, the demonstrations, flags, rituals, the religious devotion to the exemplary leader, the solidarist dispositions, the complex bureaucracies, the messianism—were all prefigured in Fascist ideological literature long before Bolshevism revealed itself a member of this subset of developmental regimes.

All developmental regimes share common, and consequently general, characteristics, just as all mass-mobilizing, developmental dictatorships share common, and equally general, characteristics. We have been sufficiently warned that in choosing to emphasize such common species traits one cannot be understood to have dealt with the undeniably distinct traits that distinguish one regime from another. Each developmental regime is different if one chooses to dwell on its specific properties, just as all fall in the same classification if one chooses to mark their general similarities.[46]

That some developmental regimes share significant similarities is effectively borne out by the treatment they have been accorded in the literature devoted to totalitarianism. And it is to this issue that we can now profitably turn our attention.

Fascism and Totalitarianism

For all the criticism levelled against the concept "totalitarian," it remains remarkably vital.[47] The concept appears and reappears in the professional and lay literature with impressive frequency. Recently, Juan Linz has insisted on its utility, and Leonard Shapiro has restated the case for its continued employment.[48] In fact, the use of the concept constitutes a cognitive convenience, a preliminary "experimental naming" of a class of political systems sharing what seem to be a number of overt, behavioral similarities. However much the concept may have been exploited for propaganda purposes in cold war circumstances, the similarities upon which the concept is parasitic were identified long before the period following the Second World War.[49]

Linz has offered a lexical definition of totalitarianism that includes the following elements: (1) an ideology, (2) a single mass party and mobilizational organizations, (3) hegemonic power with political decision making concentrated in a single individual, or a small group, that is not constitutionally responsible to an electorate and cannot be displaced by institutionalized, peaceful means.[50] For our purposes, such a characterization is sufficiently broad to sustain discussion. It is a definition similar enough to that originally proposed by Carl Friedrich and Zbigniew Brzezinski to establish the continuity of the concept over the last decade.[51] The postwar efforts, beginning with Vittorio Zincone's *Lo stato totalitario*, through J. L. Talmon's seminal *The Origins of Totalitarian Democracy*, have all helped define and lend substance to the elements of totalitarianism.[52]

It is clear that for all the persistence and continuity of the concept, "totalitarian," it is as abstract, porous, and as open-textured as the concept "modernization." Each author will use it in a variable and sometimes idiosyncratic manner. Some, like Hannah Arendt, will emphasize the terror that has often distinguished totalitarian systems, while others will

319

treat terror as a contingent, rather than an essential, feature of such regimes. Some treat the continuity of ideas as central to their analysis, while others emphasize institutions.[53] Any number of variations can be played on an indeterminate number of constituent themes.

For all that, the same thing can be said of totalitarianism as might be said about class. The effort, by social scientists, to produce a generally accepted definition of "class" has been a notable failure—but no one is seriously prepared to argue, as a consequence, that classes do not exist. Similarly, definitional problems of the same order and magnitude prompt only the most heroic to deny the existence of something called "modernization."

It has been suggested that we find ourselves embarrassed by a lack of a common definition concerning all these concepts because we do not have a formal theory of politics or society. As a consequence, we must be content with an informally articulated set of plausibilities. We couch our accounts in academic language, a style necessarily dependent on stipulative and lexical definition. Such definitions are inevitably tailored to the purposes of their authors. They cannot be spoken of as literally true or false, but rather as appropriate or inappropriate, plausible or implausible, suggestive or sterile, insightful or opaque, all characterizations that evidence their intrinsic (even if principled) relativity. Selecting one of the many stipulative definitions to be found in the literature involves judgment, and turns on the respective purposes entertained by each author. One can, of course, invoke formal criteria of adequacy: internal consistency, for example; and one can attempt to map such definitions over empirical reality by operationalizing notions such as the "concentration of power," and the presence or absence of "ideology." But the first, and formal criterion serves only negative purposes, and the second, empirical criterion, involves access to data that is more often than not unavailable or nonexistent. We know, for example, almost nothing definitive concerning the decision-making processes governing

Fascist policies. For all the work on the relationship between the leaders of Italian industry and Mussolini, there is actually very little unequivocal evidence that would define the conditions governing the exercise of power in the Fascist state.[54] Furthermore, even though the best scholarship makes a compelling case for Mussolini's preponderant control over the system,[55] we still must decide if that control was sufficient to satisfy the requirements of totalitarian power.

In this regard, Linz has argued, persuasively, that the existence of vital non-Fascist components—the military, the Church, and the organized business community—within the Fascist system created a "limited pluralism." Mussolini was forced, in view of these circumstances, to exploit the tensions between a plurality of social components in the effort to implement his (oftentimes faulted) program.[56] Nonetheless, Zincone could identify Italian Fascism as totalitarian, focusing on its intentions as well as a constellation of selected traits, and J. Lucien Radel could include Fascism in a volume devoted to totalitarianism, while acknowledging some trepidation because of the "prismatic" character of the regime.[57] Linz, for his part, simply identified Mussolini's system as pretotalitarian.

For our purposes, we have characterized Mussolini's regime as a mass-mobilizing, developmental dictatorship, animated by clearly totalitarian intentions, but confined by the existence of still vital and reasonably powerful nonmovement allies. Although Fascism was capable of neutralizing the Church to an appreciable degree, it had far less success with the organized business community, which it critically needed for its developmental program. It had equally little success with the established military hierarchies, important in Fascism's international program, which operated throughout the tenure of the regime with considerable independence.[58]

Recognizing all that, it is clear that Fascism was not a traditional authoritarian regime. However apathetic the masses of the peninsula may have been, for example, there was a systematic and totalitarian effort to marshall them into party

321

organizations, and there was some considerable success in orchestrating the consensus necessary to the arduous process of modernization and industrialization. Fascism extracted from its population the enormous capital and labor resources for a reasonably effective program of development—a capability few traditional authoritarian systems have been able to match. That this was done with remarkably little coercion is testimony to both Fascism's totalitarian mobilization as well as to the relative independence of its nonmovement allies.[59] Because a constellation of comparatively independent social elements provided the effective support base of the regime, it could not move aggressively against any one of them (regardless of its totalitarian ideology) without threatening the disintegration of the coalition. It is unlikely, furthermore, that any of the politically important population elements would have continued to feel secure if Fascism undertook repressive activities totally uncontrolled by law or devoid of restraint. Such circumstances would have generated anxiety levels that might well have alienated critical nonmovement support. For such prudential reasons the regime's purges were modest quasi-totalitarian affairs, its secret police surprisingly mild, its insistence on ideological intransigence more often honored in the breach than respected in adherence. When one considers the bestiality of the purges and the successive waves of revolution that darken the history of the Soviet Union and China, the "Special Tribunals" and the "permanent revolution" of Italian Fascism pale into virtual insignificance.

All these features seem to be related to the historic conditions surrounding the occasion of Fascism's accession to power. Political circumstances, as well as Fascism's assessment of the intrinsically bourgeois obligations of the revolution, conspired to produce a "diarchic" or "prismatic" political regime. Because Italian Fascism was never able to completely domesticate nonmovement allies in characteristically totalitarian fashion, Fascists could never act with the independence of Bolsheviks. Any massive program of suppression—mass executions or mass incarceration—would disturb the delicate balance of forces within which Fascism operated.

Moreover, Mussolini's recognition of the functional importance of the entrepreneurial, managerial, and bureaucratic bourgeoisie to the revolution rendered the development of a specifically totalitarian Fascist ruling class an unlikely probability. Rarely, for example, were Fascists prepared to sacrifice what they thought to be expertise for political enthusiasm. Entrepreneurs, technicians, and experts, even though not members of the party, were invited to join the Fascist government as long as they were not overtly opposed to the regime. Which did not mean that Fascism or Mussolini totally abjured political criteria in the evaluation of even the most influential nonmovement individuals. The painful history of Gino Olivetti, one of the most important leaders of the powerful Confederation of Italian Industrialists, whom Mussolini forced into ignominious exile, is evidence enough for that.

In general, though, Fascism was rather casual in exacting ideological commitments from its functionaries and, therefore, the regime never developed its own fully committed ruling class. After the destruction of the regime, as a consequence, the functionaries that had served Fascism simply transferred their allegiance to the successor regime without appreciable intellectual or moral tension.[60] They had been sufficiently effusive in their support of the regime to ensure their job security. With the change of regimes, they were sufficiently effusive in support of the successor system to provide for their job continuity.

The apolitical entrepreneurial and technical allies of Fascism provided the base for the relative independence of the magistrature, insulation for afascists in the armed forces, as well as a defense capability for a modest form of political dissidence. As a consequence, Fascism, which had put together the first, and what is perhaps the most coherent, rationale for totalitarianism in the twentieth century, had to content itself with a system that fell considerably short of its ideals. Bolshevism, on the other hand, with all its talk of liberation, its "Stalin Constitution" which protected the rights of free speech and free association produced, in reality, a totalitarianism unmatched in our century.

The differences between totalitarian systems can be pursued in any number of directions, and with considerable, if variable, profit. Alexander Groth has suggested that an analysis of the various groups that influenced the determination of policy within such regimes would be instructive.[61] Frederic Fleron has suggested that totalitarian systems must be disaggregated in order to obtain some empirical understanding of how they actually operated.[62] Jeremy Azrael's study of the influence of the managerial class in the Soviet Union is, at least in part, the fulfillment of such an analysis.[63]

All of which is unobjectionable. Nonetheless, however assessed, there remains a class of political systems that display a marked family resemblance captured in their identification as totalitarian. A totalistic political ideology that functions as a surrogate religion, a single-party system that countenances no formal opposition, a hegemonic and mobilization system that culminates in a minority leadership or in the charismatic rule of a single providential leader, monopolistic control over the means of education, communication, and coercion, an elaborate bureaucratic infrastructure that directly or indirectly controls the nation's economy, and an invasive system that erodes the privacy of individual lives— all conjoined with the modern technology capable of effecting such elaborate purpose—suggest a political system new to the twentieth century, having no real counterpart in the past. Within the class of such systems any number of distinctions can, and must be, traced, if we are to attempt to be true to the complexities of empirical reality. But mammals are mammals no matter what differences distinguish bats from whales. And Fascism was more like Bolshevism than it was like parliamentary polyarchies or traditional authoritarianism.

Fascism and Bolshevism were political systems developed

in response to special crisis conditions in our century. They both found their origins in an heretical form of Marxism. Both were as different from the classical Marxism of Marx and Engels as both were similar in their principal goals, institutional features, and overall political intentions. Both were national responses to developmental retardation in a world of powerful, industrialized states. Both adapted themselves to the bourgeois and national tasks of modernization and rapid industrial development. Both sought, with a manifestly different measure of success, to create a great power out of the latent potential of their industrially disadvantaged national communities.

In substance, developmental demands and totalitarian systems can, under as yet unspecified and indeterminate conditions, intersect. Some developmental systems can take on some or all the attributes of totalitarianism. That such features should surface in such unlikely environments as China and Cuba constitute evidence that developmental systems can still be expected to assume some or all the principal features of totalitarianism. How one chooses to refer to such systems—fascistoid, fascist, or socialist—seems more a matter of personal taste and preference than of substance. To avoid the noncognitive, and correspondingly invidious, connotations attached to any or all these terms, one might refer to such a class of regimes as mass-mobilizing developmental dictatorships which feature totalitarian traits.

Fascism was a paradigm instance of the class. Its modernizing and industrializing characteristics are now reasonably well established.[64] Subsequent members of the class have taken on a significant number of those features first overtly displayed by Fascism. Contemporary Marxists, like Fascists, are disposed to recruit wherever and from whatever classes they can.[65] That Mao, in his time, identified the national bourgeoisie, the entrepreneurial capitalists of China, with the revolutionary people, and thereby conceived of them as allies in socialist construction, has not escaped the notice of other Marxists.[66] That he basked in a cult of personality, advocated class collaboration among the people, opposed what he called "economism," the arbitrary increase of wages and benefits at the expense of capital resources necessary for autarchic development, and that he entertained national rather than international aspirations has, understandably, led some of the same Marxists to identify his regime as fascist.[67]

The invocation of such a characterization obviously serves polemic purposes, but the credibility of such an allusion derives from the fact that some of the most important socialist systems have taken on many of those traits anticipated by the heretical national syndicalists of pre-Fascist Italy. It was national syndicalism that produced the rationale for the nationalist and mass-mobilizing developmental dictatorship put together by Fascism. More than that, national syndicalists anticipated, as early as 1922, that such dictatorships might very well develop into that system we now identify as totalitarian.

History has compelled us to recognize that mass-mobilizing, developmental dictatorships can evolve (or devolve as one chooses) into one or another form of totalitarianism in the demanding effort to force-draught a nation through the several stages of modernization and industrialization. In this respect, both Fascist Italy and Bolshevik Russia began to take on totalitarian species traits during their respective drives to industrial maturity, after the first stages of modernization had been traversed under alternative political auspices. Other nations, that find themselves at still more primitive levels of development, have found some form of totalitarianism equally well suited to their purposes. Still others, like National Socialist Germany, found totalitarianism appropriate to the resolution of postindustrial problems only indirectly related to late industrialization. But the rare appearance of totalitarianism in postmodern and postindustrial society suggests that such an eventuality is the product of only the most unusual circumstances. The most suitable ambience for the manifestation of totalitarianism, in whatever form, seems associated with the collective effort to rapidly develop retarded socioeconomic systems.

Roberto Michels had suggested as much as early as 1926 when he alluded to the special circumstances characteristic of developmentally retarded nations. Such disadvantaged communities suffer collective psychological disabilities conducive to the appearance of mass-mobilizing movements. These movements are informed by national and nationalist purpose and are capable of extracting labor and enterprise through mythic language which provides the symbolic assurances necessary for populations suffering energy, resource, and capital shortfall. Michels expected, in fact, that a vast process of modernization and industrialization would affect most, if not all, peoples afflicted by retarded development. He spoke of an anticipated Chinese, Black, and Latin American modernization and industrialization.[68]

That such developmental systems might very well take on the defining traits of Fascism was recognized by Fascist ideologues throughout the interwar years.[69] Renzo Bertoni, for example, in a book heralded by Mussolini, himself, argued that the processes of intensive development required that systems like Bolshevism, whatever their putative ideological persuasion, must ultimately adopt the most critical features of Fascism.[70] In our own time, irrespective of the reservations bruited by such eminent critics as John Kautsky, some have recognized the same requirements in the developmental efforts surfacing in Africa and Latin America.[71]

National syndicalists, and Fascists, recognized that the ideology of Fascism constituted a rationale for a political system well adapted to nations making the transit to industrial maturity. They recognized that under such conditions mass-mobilizing systems might well display totalitarian properties. Since that time, we have observed so many developmental regimes divest themselves of the institutional and political appurtenances of liberal pluralism that such assessments cannot be summarily dismissed. One-party states,

327

with their charismatic leaders, their exacerbated nationalism, their mobilizational strategies, their inculcated civic virtues of work, sacrifice, and obedience, their orchestrated populism, and factitious democracy, as well as their military posturing, have become sufficiently abundant to suggest not only a functional connection between development and totalitarianism but their probable future coincidence. Fortunately, the mix that supports the full maturation of such tendencies is apparently rare and complex enough to preclude anything like the general or inevitable advent of modernizing totalitarianism. Developmental regimes take on such a multiplicity of intermediate forms that we have little leverage on adequate classification, much less predictive advantage. The tendencies, however, and the probable connection between development and totalitarianism, are sufficiently evident to provide us a sense of continuity, relating the experiences endured by Italy during the interwar years and the politics now so prevalent in the modernizing nations of the contemporary world. More than that, all this suggests that we have something to learn from the arguments articulated by the national syndicalists of Italy, who not only provided the charter rationale for Mussolini's Fascism, but produced the first heretical Marxism as well. They, more than anyone else, provided the intellectual substance for what Ernst Nolte has aptly identified as the first "totalitarian national development dictatorship."[72] The shape of things to come were, in impressive measure, prefigured in their heretical socialism.

Conclusions

The history of our times suggests that Marxism has survived into the twentieth century only in the form of an heretical belief system that makes of Karl Marx a prophet of rapid modernization and industrialization. Marx is seen as the patron saint of mass-mobilizing, developmental dictatorships. All of which is very curious.

That Marx never conceived of himself in such guise is obvious in everything he wrote. Marx and Engels understood themselves to be spokesmen for a revolution to be undertaken in postindustrial environments—a revolution that would constitute "the act of the dominant peoples 'all at once' and simultaneously, which presupposes the universal development of productive forces."[73] Both Marx and Engels assumed that the revolution would follow the "universal development of productive forces" that would be accomplished under the auspices of the entrepreneurial bourgeoisie. For Marx, it was the "bourgeois period of history" that was charged with the historic obligation of creating "the material conditions of a new world."[74]

Both Marx and Engels clearly understood national liberation, nation-building, and development to be the responsibilities of the bourgeoisie. As a consequence, the revolutions they anticipated in the underdeveloped regions of the globe were not to be socialist, but bourgeois, revolutions.[75] Socialist revolution was on the immediate agenda of only the advanced industrial countries suffering all the disabilities of postindustrialization: crises of overproduction, vast armies of the industrial unemployed displaced by the extensive exploitation of machine labor, the concentration of the vast majority of men into the ranks of the industrial proletariat, the capital saturation of significant sectors of the economy.

By the first decade of our century all this had become increasingly transparent to the revolutionary syndicalists of the Italian peninsula. It became more and more obvious to them that classical Marxism had very little to say that was immediately relevant to their situation and to the situation of peoples similarly circumstanced. It soon became evident to those same syndicalists that revolutionaries, on pain of abject passivity, would have to involve themselves in the discharge of bourgeois tasks. As early as 1911, when he was but twenty-eight, the young Mussolini could suggest that a "new and youthful bourgeoisie" might make effective allies for a revolutionary movement in a retarded industrial environment.[76] Socialists, Mussolini and the syndicalists argued, would have to do some of the work of the bourgeoisie. Conversely, the bourgeoisie would have to do some of the work of socialism.

In fact, neither Marx nor Engels had precluded such an eventuality. Both had granted that Bismarck, for example, the "representative of the bourgeoisie," succeeded in doing "a bit" of socialism's work. Both Marx and Engels saw development in the future of every underdeveloped country that possessed its material prerequisites. "The country that is more developed industrially only shows, to the less developed, the image of its own future," Marx advised those revolutionaries that followed him. Moreover, the process was one which resulted "from the natural laws of capitalist production"—laws, which, as "tendencies," worked "with iron necessity towards inevitable results." Every nation must learn from others, but no nation can "clear by bold leaps, nor remove by legal enactments, the obstacles offered by the successive phases of its normal development."[77]

Given such an account, it could be argued that any individual or agency that fostered such normal development of the inevitable process could only be progressive, and perform some of socialism's work. Since that development, process, and work included the "primitive accumulation of capital" to fuel development within the politically defined nation-state, under the auspices of a directive minority employing all the machinery of state power, any revolutionary movement prepared to assume these bourgeois responsibilities would be involved in socialism's labors.

The revolutionary national syndicalists who put together the entire rationale for nationalist, mass-mobilizing, developmental dictatorship under single-party auspices, conceived of their historic obligations in just such fashion. And what was the heresy of yesterday has now become the new Marxist orthodoxy. "Socialist transformation" has come to mean rapid industrial development, and "primitive socialist accumulation" takes place within the oppressed and proletarian nation united against imperialist and capitalist powers. In the train of these developments, the elitist unitary party, the "all-peoples' state," the charismatic leader, the military style, the propaganda, and the work and sacrifice ethic, all follow effortlessly.

When the revolutionary syndicalists of Italy identified the nation-state as the appropriate vehicle of the revolution, they were denounced as having abandoned the substance of Marxism. Today, every Marxist recognizes the revolutionary character of nationalist appeal. Recently, J. P. Nettl has argued that "in the context of developing countries" the distinction between "nationalism" and "socialism" is "meaningless,"[78] a premise upon which national syndicalism had insisted more than fifty years ago. All contemporary Marxists mobilize masses around the symbols of nationalism in the service of intensive and extensive development. Thomas Greene, in fact, has generalized that "where nationalism has not been an issue in revolutionary mobilization . . . the movements have been doomed to narrow class-based appeal and, consequently, political insignificance." He concluded that "Marx himself would appreciate the irony of apparently class-based movements depending on nationalist passions for their revolutionary power,"[79] when, in fact, both Marx and Engels were prepared to recognize the efficacy (as well as the theoretical legitimacy) of an appeal to just such passion when the revolution found itself charged with the responsibilities of bourgeois tasks.

All this was clearly anticipated decades ago by the revolutionary national syndicalists who provided Fascism its belief system. They were the advocates of a new nationalism that would animate proletarian nations in their struggle against the dominant plutocracies. They were the first advocates of a united front of all revolutionary classes, including the national or productive bourgeoisie, against the feudal remnants in their own society and the imperialist oppressor from without. They were the first to insist that only modernization and industrialization could save the nation. They were the first

331

developmental revolutionaries to recognize the serviceability of the national entrepreneurial bourgeoisie. They insisted on the fucntional necessity of an elaborate state apparatus. They acknowledged the need for reeducation, even coercion, in the governance of masses as yet only dimly conscious of their historic needs. They were the first to make frugality, thrift, discipline, work, sacrifice, and obedience revolutionary virtues.

Today the Maoists tell us that they will mobilize not the proletariat, but the "people," and the people include "the working class, the peasantry, the urban petty bourgeoisie, and the national bourgeoisie." All must be united in the effort to "modernize," and modernization is calculated to "save China." Only through such a process, Maoists insist, can the nation win the struggle to be "treated as an equal" by "imperialist" powers. To service these needs "state power" must be maintained and enhanced. It is the state which will "systematically solve the problems of industrialization." That solution involves the active participation of the entrepreneurial bourgeoisie, whose interests the revolutionary "state power" will "protect."[80]

All of this was said before, and with considerably more intellectual coherence, by the revolutionary national syndicalists of Italy. When Soviet critics characterize Maoism as "bourgeois-nationalistic," "petty-bourgeois revolutionism," and "Bonapartism," they are repeating objections long ago bruited against national syndicalism and subsequently against Fascism.[81] The Soviets view the "sinification of Marxism" as an effort to "adapt" Marxism to "nationalistic schemes and aims,"[82] objections similarly raised against national syndicalism and Fascism. The Soviets lament the "military-bureaucratic degeneration," the systematic inculcation among the "masses" of "subservient obedience," the "ideological fanaticism," the "anti-intellectualism," the "subjectivism," and "voluntarism," the program of controlled consumption, the effort to relocate "surplus population" on "foreign territory," and the disposition to create an autarchic economy "behind the Great Wall," that have come to characterize the Chinese revolution.[83] That, as a consequence, the Soviets should find that "the Maoist approach in no way differs from fascism"[84] is not in the least surprising. Nor is it surprising that the Maoists, in turn, should find the Soviet Union a "fascist dictatorship,"[85] rehearsing the same catalog of characteristics the Soviets have employed to license a similar charge against Maoism.

Divested of hyperbole and shorn of polemics, such charges refer to those characteristics that have become characteristic of mass-mobilizing, developmental regimes animated by totalitarian aspirations. They are characteristics anticipated by the men who were to become the ideologues of Fascism at the very commencement of the revolutionary epoch in which we find ourselves still embroiled. In the mid-thirties, when Roberto Michels attempted a stenographic reconstruction of the history of the working-class movement in Italy, he traced Fascism's origins to the heretical Marxism of revolutionary syndicalism. It was that Marxism, "latinized" to satisfy the national and economic requirements of a "poor and proletarian" nation, that provided the substance of Fascism. "Fascism," Michels insisted, "cannot be understood . . . without an appreciation of Marxism—not only because of its historical connection . . . but also in so far as there remain vital points of contact between them."[86] However obscured by time, ignorance, prejudice, and historic circumstances, those vital points of contact remain. That connection and those points of contact were, and are, a function of the general prerequisites and requisites of modernization and development in our time. That such ideological, institutional, and structural similarities persist among an entire class of regimes remains testimony to the historic, social, and economic significance of national development in the twentieth century. All of which makes the neglect of the thought of heretical Marxists like Sergio Panunzio, A. O. Olivetti, and Roberto Michels, and the system they assisted in engineering, lamentable. Such men spoke to the pervasive needs of their time, needs which still seem to persist in large areas of the globe. That, today, men who attempt to speak to those needs should articulate belief systems that contain significant elements of that ideology first formulated before and during the First World War need not have been totally unanticipated. That the systems they engineer should share similarities with that system fostered by revolutionary national syndicalism should not have been totally unforeseen. That we have succeeded, somehow, in obscuring all the lines of continuity that connect these processes has left us all suffering considerable intellectual disadvantage.

NOTES

Preface

1. A. James Gregor, *The Ideology of Fascism*, p. xii.

2. See A. James Gregor, "Storiografia e relatività della storia," in Marcel De Corte, et al., *La libertà dello storico fra storia e politica* (Rome: Volpe, 1976).

3. Richard Collier, *Duce!*, p. 37.

4. Cf. Francesco Bonavita, *Mussolini svelato* and Alessandro Lessona, *Un ministro di Mussolini racconta*.

5. Antonio Trizzino, *Mussolini ultimo*.

6. Renzo De Felice, *Fascism*, p. 36.

7. Renzo De Felice, *Mussolini il rivoluzionario*, p. 40.

Chapter One. The Ambiguous Legacy

1. Karl Marx and Friedrich Engels, *Werke*.

2. Cf. Otto Ruehle, *Karl Marx*, pp. 362f.; Engels' letter to F. A. Sorge, September 16, 1886, *Werke*, xxxvi, 532; letters of April 29, 1886 and January 29, 1886, ibid., 476-80, 431.

3. Marx, letter to Engels, August 10, 1869, *Werke*, xxxii, 360.

4. Cf. A. James Gregor, *Survey of Marxism*, chap. 2; Norman Levine, *The Tragic Deception*.

5. "Tout ce que je sais, c'est que ne ne suis pas Marxiste," as reported in Engels' letter to C. Schmidt, August 5, 1890, *Werke*, xxvii, 436; cf. Isaiah Berlin, *Karl Marx*, p. 251.

6. Cf. Peter Gay, *The Dilemma of Democratic Socialism*, p. 68.

7. Eduard Bernstein, *Die Voraussetzungen des Sozialismus und die Aufgaben der Sozialdemokratie*. There is a partial Eng-

lish translation available as *Evolutionary Socialism* (New York: Schocken, 1961).

8. Georg von Vollmar, *Ueber die naechsten Aufgaben der deutschen Sozialdemokratie.*

9. Friedrich Engels, introduction to "The Class Struggles in France 1848-1850," in Marx and Engels, *Selected Works*, I, 122f., 125.

10. Ibid., pp. 126f., 128f., 130.

11. Ibid., pp. 136f.

12. Ibid., p. 118.

13. These were later published by Bernstein in his *Dokumente des Sozialismus*, II, 65ff.

14. Engels to Bloch, August 5, 1890, in Marx and Engels, *Selected Correspondence*, pp. 498-500.

15. Ibid., p. 500.

16. Engels letter to Schmidt, October 27, 1890, Ibid., pp. 504ff.

17. Cf. Eduard Bernstein, *Wie ist wissenschaftlicher Sozialismus moeglich?*

18. Cf. Eduard Bernstein, *Der Sozialismus einst und jetzt*; Christian Gneuss, "The Precursor: Eduard Bernstein," in Leo Labedz, ed., *Revisionism*, pp. 31-41. See particularly the comments of Georges Sorel, *Les polémiques pour l'interprétation du Marxisme*, pp. 15ff.

19. Cf. Samuel H. Baron, *Plekhanov*, p. 168.

20. Cf. Engels' introduction of 1892 to his *The Condition of the Working Class in England in 1844*, pp. xviif.

21. Karl Marx, *Capital*, III, 862f.

22. Ibid., I, 8f.

23. Friedrich Engels, *Ludwig Feuerbach and the End of Classical German Philosophy*, in *Selected Works*, II, 389f.

24. Baron, *Plekhanov*, pp. 172f.

25. Georgii Plekhanov, *The Development of the Monist View of History*, pp. 54, 126, 134.

26. Georgii Plekhanov, *The Role of the Individual in History.*

27. Ibid., p. 27.

28. Karl Marx and Friedrich Engels, *The Holy Family*, p. 53. Italics supplied.

29. Plekhanov, *The Role of the Individual*, pp. 44, 55, 60.

30. Vladimir I. Lenin, "What the 'Friends of the People' Are, and How They Fight the Social Democrats," *Collected Works*, I, 129-332.

31. Ibid., p. 166. Italics supplied.

32. Marx, *Capital*, I, 18.

33. Lenin, "Review: *Karl Kautsky, Bernstein und das sozialdemokratische Programm. Eine Antikritik*," *Collected Works*, IV, 194.

34. Lenin, "What the 'Friends of the People' Are," *Collected Works*, I, 166.

35. Cf. Marx, *Grundrisse der Kritik der politischen Oekonomie*, pp. 631-643; *Capital*, III Pt. 3, chaps. XIII, XIV. See Joseph M. Gillman, *The Falling Rate of Profit*, and Domenico Settembrini, *Socialismo a rivoluzione dopo Marx* (Naples: Guida, 1974), chap. 1.

36. Engels, *The Condition of the Working Class*, p. 295.

37. F. Saverio Merlino, *Pro e contro il socialismo*.

38. Cf. Roberto Michels, *Storia del marxismo in Italia*, pp. 111f.

39. Antonio Graziadei, *La produzione capitalistica*. Cf. Roberto Michels, *Storia critica del movimento socialista italiano*, pp. 265ff.

40. Bernstein, *Wie ist wissenchaftlicher Sozialismus moeglich?*, p. 40.

41. Filippo Turati, "L'estetismo catastrofico dei sindacalisti e l'equivoco integralista," *Le vie maestre del socialismo*, p. 79. Cf. Roberto Michels, "Die Entwicklung der Theorien im modernen Sozialismus Italiens," in Enrico Ferri, *Die revolutionaere Methode*, pp. 29f.

42. Cf. Arturo Labriola, "Pro e control il socialismo: Critica di F. S. Merlino," *Critica sociale*, 7, No. 14 (July 16, 1897), "Il congresso di Firenze," *Riforma sociale*, 6, No. 3 (1896); Enrico Leone, "Il neo-liberismo," *Rassegna popolare del socialismo*, 5 (1899).

43. Cf. the reports of Roberto Michels, "Fra due congressi," *Avanti!*, 6, No. 2097 (October 8, 1902), and *Storia del marxismo in Italia*, pp. 132-38.

44. For the purposes of exposition the major works of Arturo Labriola and Enrico Leone are the following: Arturo Labriola, *Riforme e rivoluzione sociale* (Milan: SEM, 1904)

with a second revised edition Lugano: Avanguardia, 1906. References in this chapter will be to the third edition, Naples: Partenopea, 1914. Enrico Leone, *Il sindacalismo* (Milan: Sandron, 1907). Chapter references will be to the second revised edition, Milan: Sandron, 1910.

45. Sergio Panunzio, "Socialismo, sindacalismo e sociologia," *Pagine libere*, I, Nos. 3-4 (1907), 173; Leone, *Il sindacalismo*, p. 138.

46. Labriola, *Riforme e rivoluzione sociale*, p. 216.

47. Ibid., p. 220; Angelo O. Olivetti, *Questioni contemporanee* (Naples: Partenopea, 1913, second edition of *Problemi del socialismo contemporaneo* of 1906), pp. 208-213; cf. Roberto Michels, *Il proletariato e la borghesia nel movimento socialista italiano*, particularly pp. 365-377.

48. Marx and Engels, "Zirkularbrief," *Werke*, XXXIV, 407f.

49. Marx, "The Civil War in France," *Selected Works*, I, 473-545.

50. Engels' introduction to "The Civil War in France," *Selected Works*, I, 482-485; cf. Leone, *Il sindacalismo*, p. 91.

51. Olivetti, *Questioni contemporanee*, pp. 219-222.

52. Marx, "Lohn, Preis und Profit," *Werke*, XVI, 152.

53. Cf. Domenico Settembrini, *Due ipotesi per il socialismo in Marx ed Engels*, particularly p. 292, for a discussion of Marx's views of parliament; cf. Michels, *Storia del marxismo*, p. 59.

54. Cf. Marx, "Der Prozess gegen den Rheinischen Kreisausschuss der Demokraten," *Werke*, VI, 256f.; cf. Labriola, *Riforme e rivoluzione sociale*, p. 160.

55. Cf. Michael Evans, *Karl Marx* (Bloomington: University of Indiana Press, 1975), p. 131.

56. Engels' introduction to his *The Condition of the Working Class*, pp. xii-xiv; compare Labriola, *Riforme e rivoluzione sociale*, p. 111 n. 2.

57. Marx and Engels, "The Manifesto of the Communist Party," *Selected Works*, I, 65.

58. Marx and Engels, "Sieg der Kontrerevolution zu Wien," *Werke*, V, 457. Cf. Labriola, *Riforme e rivoluzione sociale*, pp. 139f.

59. Leone, *Il sindacalismo*, pp. 213-220; cf. Olivetti, *Questioni contemporanee*, pp. 154-165.

60. Cf. Georges Sorel, *Saggi di critica del marxismo*, p. 253; Leone, *Il sindacalismo*, pp. 223-231.

61. Plekhanov's criticisms are conveniently collected in Georgii Plekhanov, *Sindicalismo y marxismo*. Leone responded to Plekhanov in his "Critici e libellisti del sindacalismo," *Divenire sociale* (1908); Arturo Labriola responded in his *Contro G. Plekhanov e per il sindacalismo* (Pescara: Abruzzese, 1909). Cf. Arturo Labriola's comments in *Riforme e rivoluzione sociale*, pp. 135f., and Michels, *Storia del marxismo*, pp. 65f. n. 1.

62. Cf. Olivetti, *Questioni contemporanee*, pp. 209f.

63. Cf. Louis Levine, *Syndicalism in France*.

64. Cf. Roberto Michels, "Eine syndikalistisch gerichtete Unterstroemung im deutschen Sozialismus (1903-1907)," *Festschrift fuer Carl Gruenberg* (Leipzig: Hirschfeld, 1932).

Chapter Two. The First Revolutionary Socialist Heresy

1. References will be made to the second edition of this work, entitled, *Studio su Marx*. The second edition is identical to the first, with the exception of some additional explanatory footnotes.

2. In this regard, cf. A. James Gregor, *A Survey of Marxism*, pp. 6-16, and "Marx, Feuerbach and the Reform of the Hegelian Dialectic," *Science and Society*, 29, No. 1 (Winter 1965).

3. Labriola, *Studio su Marx*, pp. 41, 44, 62.

4. Marx, "Theses on Feuerbach," in Marx and Engels, *The German Ideology*, p. 646.

5. Marx, *The Economic and Philosophic Manuscripts*, pp. 104f.

6. In the *Grundrisse* Marx expressed this conviction in the following way: "The human being is in the most literal sense *a political animal*, not merely a gregarious animal, but an animal which can individuate itself only in the midst of society" (p. 84).

7. "It is natural necessity, essential human properties, however alienated they may seem to be, and interest that hold the members of civil society together." Karl Marx and Friedrich Engels, *The Holy Family*, p. 163; cf. pp. 56, 60. Cf. Arturo Labriola, *Studio su Marx*, p. 164.

8. Cf. Labriola, *Studio su Marx*, p. 46.

9. Marx and Engels, *The German Ideology*, p. 37.

10. Cf., for example, Thomas G. Masaryk, *Philosophischen und sociologischen Grundlagen des Marxismus*, pp. 155f., and Georges Sorel, *Saggi di critica del Marxismo*, p. 48.

11. Cf. Labriola, *Studio su Marx*, pp. 120f.

12. As early as 1899, Paolo Orano wrote his *Il precursore italiano di Carlo Marx* in which he devoted considerable space to the social science and social psychology of historical explanation. Cf. his *La logica della sociologia* and his *La società-organismo ed il materialismo storico*.

13. Paolo Orano, *La psicologia sociale*; Angelo O. Olivetti, "La problema della folla," *Nuova antologia*, 38, No. 761 (September 1, 1903).

14. The principal works of Gabriel Tarde are *Social Laws* and *The Laws of Imitation*; those of Gustave Le Bon, *The Crowd* and *The Psychology of Socialism*.

15. There is a brief exposition of Panunzio's syndicalist convictions in Leonardo Paloscia, *La concezione sindacalista di Sergio Panunzio*.

16. Sergio Panunzio, *Il socialismo giuridico*.

17. Cf. Ibid., pp. 4f.

18. Years later, when Karl Kautsky attempted to provide an account of the psychological regularities governing social life in his *Die materialistische Geschichtsauffassung*, the sections devoted to the psychology of social life were completely innocent of references to the works of Marx and Engels, suggesting that there was little there that would contribute to the enterprise. Even Nikolai Bukharin's *Historical Materialism* could appeal to very few references to the Marx corpus to document his interpretation of social psychology.

19. Panunzio, *La persistenza del diritto* p. 18. Cf. in this context, Sorel, "Le idee giuridiche nel Marxismo," *Saggi di critica del Marxismo*, pp. 189-223. Marx frequently spoke of the "morality" and "law" of the dominant classes as becoming a "means" for effecting the control of the "oppressed." He nowhere explains how the oppressed come to passively accept the morality and/or law of their oppressors. Cf. Marx and Engels, *The German Ideology*, p. 461.

20. Orano, *Psicologia sociale*, chap. 2. Cf. also Orano's long disquisition on the psychosocial laws of Gabriel Tarde, ibid., chap. 4.

21. Panunzio, *Socialismo giuridico*, pp. 60 n. 1, 221 n. 1.

22. Cf. Panunzio, "Socialismo, sindacalismo e sociologia," *Pagine libere*, 1, Nos. 3, 4 (1907), 170, 232; *Socialismo giuridico*, pp. 60, 195, *La persistenza del diritto*, pp. xviii, 27, 34, 260, *Sindacalismo e medio evo*, p. 68. Panunzio was familiar with Gumplowicz's *Grundriss der Sociologie* and *Die sociologische Staatsidee*. The *Grundriss* is available in a convenient English edition as *Outlines of Sociology*.

23. Cf. Panunzio, *La persistenza del diritto*, p. xiv.

24. Cf. the discussion in Panunzio, the preface to *Il diritto e l'autorità*.

25. Panunzio, like most of the syndicalists, accepted the Sorelian distinction between establishment force and revolutionary violence. This distinction, as we shall see, was to be critical to Panunzio's thought. Cf. Panunzio, *Il concetto della guerra giusta*.

26. Engels, "On Authority," in *Selected Works*, I, 635f.

27. Panunzio, *Sindacalismo e medio evo*, pp. 31f.; "Socialismo, sindacalismo e sociologia," pp. 177, 231, 238 n. 2.

28. Panunzio, *Sindacalismo e medio evo*, p. 89, "Socialismo, sindacalismo e sociologia," pp. 179-181, 233, 234-236. Angelo O. Olivetti, *Questioni contemporanee*, pp. 32f.

29. Panunzio, *Sindacalismo e medio evo*, pp. 102f., 109.

30. Cf. Labriola, *Studio su Marx*, pp. 113-130.

31. Cf. for example, Panunzio, *Sindacalismo e medio evo*, p. 31 and A. James Gregor, *The Fascist Persuasion in Radical Politics*, pp. 146f., *The Ideology of Fascism*, chap. 2.

32. Vittorio Racca, introduction in Sorel, *Saggi di critica del Marxismo*, pp. xix, xxii, xliii.

33. Roberto Michels, *La sociologia del partito politico nella democrazia moderna* (Bologna: Il Mulino, 1966). The first edition of this classic appeared in 1911 in German and in 1912 in Italian. An English edition is available as *Political Parties*.

34. Roberto Michels, "Begriff und Aufgabe der Masse," *Das freie Wort*, 2 (1903), 410. Cf. Olivetti, *Questioni contemporanee*, p. 44.

35. Roberto Michels, *Il proletariato e la borghesia nel movi-*

341

mento socialista italiano, pp. 8 f.; cf. Roberto Michels, "Le syndicalisme et le socialisme en Allegmagne," in *Syndicalisme & socialisme* (Paris: Rivière, 1908), pp. 21-28.

36. Cf. Michels, *Il proletariato e la borghesia*, pp. 363-374.

37. Michels, "La fatalità della classe politica" originally published in *Riforma sociale* 17, No. 2 (1908) and reproduced in *Studi sulla democrazia e sull'autorità*, pp. 1-28.

38. Cf. Michels' discussion in "L'uomo economico e la cooperazione," *Saggi economico-statistici sulle classi popolari*, which appeared originally in 1908. These themes remained constant in Michels' subsequent work and were developed in his "Intorno al problema della solidarietà e della formazione delle caste," *Problemi di sociologia applicata* (Turin: Bocca, 1919).

39. Michels, "La democrazia e la legge ferrea delle elites," originally published in 1909 and reproduced in *Studi sulla democrazia e sull autorità*.

40. Michels, *Storia del marxismo, in Italia*, preface.

41. Cf. Michels, "A proposito di socialismo illusorio," *Avanguardia socialista*, 2, No. 88 (1904).

42. Giuseppe Prezzolini, *La teoria sindacalista*, p. 95.

43. Olivetti, "I sindacalisti e la elite," *Pagine libere*, July 1, 1909.

44. Cf. Labriola, *Studio su Marx*, pp. 212-220.

45. Cf. Michels, "Der ethische Faktor in der Parteipolitik Italiens," *Zeitschrift fuer Politik*, 3, No. 1 (1909), " 'Endziel,' Intransigenz, Ethik," *Ethische Kultur* 11, No. 50 (December 12, 1903); Olivetti, "Presentazione," *Pagine libere*, December 15, 1906, "La soluzione pratica della crisi del socialismo," December 1, 1907 "Sindacalismo e nazionalismo," in *Pro e contro la guerra di Tripoli* (Naples: Partenopea, 1912); "Giovinezza e rivoluzione," *Gioventù socialista*, September 1911; Panunzio, *Sindacalismo e medio evo*, pp. 11, 28, 89, 101.

46. Michels, "Intorno al materialismo storico," *Riforme sociale*, October 1914, p. 846.

47. Marx and Engels, "Address of the Central Committee to the Communist League," *Selected Works*, I, 109-117. Cf. Enrico Leone, *Il sindacalismo*, pp. 137f.

48. Cf. the comments of Boris Nikolaevskij and Otto Maenchen-Helfen, *Karl Marx*, pp. 240 f.; Domenico Settenbrini, *Due ipotesi per il socialismo in Marx ed Engels*, pp. 241-244; see also

Michael Lowy, *La teoría de la revolución en el joven Marx*, chap. 4.

49. Marx, *The Poverty of Philosophy*, p. 196. Cf. Leone, *Il sindacalismo*, p. 127.

50. Benito Mussolini, "La teoria sindacalista," *Opera omnia*, II, 125. Cf. Arturo Labriola, *Riforme e rivoluzione sociale*, pp. 13f., 142ff.

51. Mussolini, "La teppa," and "Karl Marx," in *Opera*, I, 92, 103f.

52. Mussolini, "Prefazione a 'Il socialismo rivoluzionario,' " "Il congresso di Brest," *Opera*, V, 92, 175; cf. "Il valore attuale del socialismo," *Opera*, VI, 182.

53. Prezzolini, *La teoria sindacalista*, pp. 95, 179-181; Mussolini, "La teoria sindacalista," *Opera*, II, 128. Cf. Michels, *Storia del marxismo in Italia*, pp. 121f.

54. Olivetti, "I sindacalisti e la elite."

55. Michels, *Storia del marxismo in Italia*, p. 71; cf. Michels, *Storia critica del movimento socialista italiano*, pp. 2f., 72, 215, 223-231 and Olivetti, "Presentazione."

56. Mussolini, " 'Prepariamo l'avvenire d'Italia,' " *Opera*, I, 185-189.

57. Cf. Michels, *Il proletariato e la borghesia*, pp. 14-17, 68-83, passim.

58. Cf. Ibid., p. 395.

59. Mussolini, "Socialismo e movimento sociale nel secolo XIX," *Opera*, I, 44f.

60. Olivetti, "I sindacalisti e la elite" and "Rivoluzione liberale," *Pagine libere*, December 1906; cf. Renato Melis, ed. *Sindacalisti italiani* (Rome: Volpe, 1964), pp. 172, 192f.

61. Engels, introduction to Marx's "The Class Struggles in France 1848-50," *Selected Works*, I, 125; cf. Sorel, "I tre sistemi storici di Marx," in *Saggi di critica del marxismo*, p. 253.

62. Labriola, *Riforme e rivoluzione sociale*, pp. 132f.

63. Ibid., p. 136; Marx, *Poverty of Philosophy*, p. 196.

64. Marx to Carlo Cafiero, July 29, 1879, *Werke*, XXXIV, 384. Compare "Lettera di Marx a Cafiero," Carlo Cafiero, *Compendio del capitale*, p. 10.

65. Leone, *Il sindacalismo*, pp. 143ff.

66. Olivetti, *Questioni contemporanee*, pp. 122f.

67. Georges Sorel, "The Decomposition of Marxism," in

Irving Louis Horowitz, *Radicalism and the Revolt Against Reason*, pp. 240f.

68. Cf. Georgii Plekhanov's comments in *Sindicalismo y marxismo*, pp. 11f., 15.

69. Panunzio, *Il sindacalismo e medio evo*, pp. 128f.

70. Ibid., pp. 130f.

71. Ibid., p. 132.

72. Marx, *Capital* (Moscow: Foreign Languages, 1954), I, 10.

73. Lenin, "What Is To Be Done?" *Collected Works*, V, 370f., 375.

74. Ibid., p. 369.

Chapter Three. The First National Socialism

1. Benedetto Croce, "La morte del socialismo," *La Voce*, February 9, 1909, reproduced in *Cultura e vita morale*, pp. 150-159.

2. Karl Marx and Friedrich Engels, *The German Ideology*, p. 76.

3. Engels to Marx, August 15, 1870, *Selected Correspondence*, pp. 294f.

4. Engels, "Po und Rhein," *Werke*, XIII, 227-268.

5. Ibid., 267.

6. Cf. Engels, "Democratic Panslavism" and "Hungary and Panslavism," in Paul W. Blackstock and Bert F. Hoselitz, eds., *The Russian Menace to Europe*. See Jorge E. Spilimbergo, *La revolucion nacional en Marx*.

7. Cf. the discussion in Norman Levine, *The Tragic Deception: Marx contra Engels*, chap. 5.

8. Arturo Labriola, *Studio su Marx*, p. 213.

9. Roberto Michels, "Der Internationalismus der Arbeiterschaft," *Ethische Kultur*, 13, No. 15 (August 1, 1904).

10. Roberto Michels, "Le Patriotisme des Socialistes Allemands et le Congrès d'Essen," *Le Mouvement Socialiste*, 3rd ser. 10 and 12 (1908).

11. Benito Mussolini, letter dated February 26, 1905, *Opera omnia*, I, 216.

12. Mussolini, "Per Ferdinand Lassalle," ibid., 66.

13. Mussolini, "Il Trentino veduto da un socialista," *Opera*, XXXIII, 151-213.

14. Mussolini, "Ciccaiuolo," *Opera*, II, 203.

15. Arturo Labriola, *Le tendenze politiche dell'Austria contemporanea*, particularly p. 48.

16. Mussolini, "Giovanni Huss il veridico," *Opera*, XXXIII, 273-327.

17. Angelo O. Olivetti, "Carrezze Austriache," *Pagine libere*, December 1, 1908.

18. Olivetti, "Sindacalismo e nazionalismo," *Pagine libere*, February 15, 1911.

19. Cf. Wilfried Roehrich, *Robert Michels*, p. 9.

20. Engels, introduction to Marx, "The Class Struggles in France," *Selected Works*, I, 125, 127f.

21. Olivetti, "L'altra campana," *Pagine libere*, November 15, 1911.

22. Olivetti, "Ribattendo il chiodo," in *Pro e contro la guerre di Tripoli* (Naples: Partenopea, 1912), pp. 11-27.

23. Olivetti, "Le domande dell'inchiesta sul nazionalismo," in A. Salucci, ed., *Il nazionalismo giudicato* (Milan: Moderno, 1913).

24. Roberto Michels, *L'imperialismo italiano*, pp. v-vii.

25. Ibid., p. 92 n. 4. Arturo Labriola, *La guerra di Tripoli e l'opinione socialista* (Naples: Scintilla, 1912), pp. 19, 114.

26. For Engels, the Turks were a "thoroughly degenerate nation," doomed to succumb to some "vital people." Engels, "Hungary and Panslavism," in Blackstock and Hoselitz, *The Russian Menace to Europe*, pp. 62f.

27. In this regard, cf. Michels' comments in *L'imperialismo italiano*, pp. 178f.

28. Michels, "Zur historischen Analyse des Patriotismus," *Archiv fuer Sozialwissenschaft und Sozialpoltik*, 36, Nos. 1 and 2 (1913).

29. Cf. Michels, "Zum Problem: Wirtschaft und Politik," in *Probleme der Sozialphilosophie* (Leipzig: Teubner, 1914).

30. Cf. Sergio Panunzio, "Il lato teorico e il lato pratico del socialismo," *Utopia*, 2, Nos. 7-8 (May 15-31, 1914), p. 201. In this context read his later *Diritto, forza e violenza*, p. 43.

31. Sergio Panunzio, "Il socialismo e la guerra," *Utopia*, 2, Nos. 11-12 (August 15-September 1, 1914), p. 324.

32. Cf. Massimo Rocca, *Come il fascismo divenne una dittatura*, p. 40.

33. Mussolini, "La settimana rossa," *Opera*, VI, 263.

34. Panunzio, "Il socialismo e la guerra," 323f.

35. Angelo O. Olivetti, "Ricominciando . . . ," "Salutatemi i pacifisti," *Pagine libere*, October 10, 1914.

36. Mussolini, "I termini del problema," *Opera*, VII, 13-15.

37. Roberto Michels, "La guerra europea al lume del materialismo storico," *Riforma sociale*, 3rd ser. 25 (1914).

38. Cf. Antonio Gramsci, "Alcuni temi della quistione meridionale," *Scritti politici*, pp. 730f., for a discussion of the relationship of Mussolini with some of the principal theoreticians of syndicalism.

39. Cf. Renzo De Felice, *Mussolini il rivoluzionario*, pp. 245-247.

40. Sergio Panunzio, "Principio e diritto di nationalità," reprinted in *Popolo nazione stato*, pp. 60, 101.

41. Ibid., p. 74.

42. Cf. his comments in Panunzio, "La questione sindacale," in *Stato nazione e sindacati*, pp. 180f.

43. Cf. Panunzio, *Il concetto della guerra giusta*, p. 50 n. 1.

44. Ibid., p. 62, "Il lato teorico," p. 201.

45. Panunzio, *Sindacalismo e medio evo*, pp. 19, 28f.

46. Cf. Panunzio, *Il concetto della guerra giusta*, p. 53, "Il lato teorico," pp. 201f.

47. Cf. Panunzio, *Il concetto della guerra giusta*, pp. 57f. n. 5, 59, 68f. n. 1.

48. Ibid., p. 61.

49. Cf. Panunzio, *Sindacalismo e medio evo*, pp. 18, 53, 81f. n. 1, "Principio e diritto di nazionalità," p. 71.

50. Mussolini, " 'Tu quoque', Jouhaux?" *Opera*, XI, 356-360.

51. The best single exposition of Corridoni's thought is to be found in Ivon De Begnac, *L'arcangelo sindacalista* (*Filippo Corridoni*); see also Vito Rastelli, *Filippo Corridoni*.

52. Cf. Filippo Corridoni, *Sindacalismo e repubblica*.

53. Roberto Michels, "Appunti sulla sociologia di Vilfredo Pareto," *Nuova antologia* 192 (November-December, 1917), pp. 393-395.

54. Cf. Michels, "Intorno al problema della psicologia della

borghesia nei diversi aggregati nazionali," in *Problemi di sociologia applicata* (Turin: Bocca, 1919), p. 187.

55. Cf. Ibid., pp. 173-177.

56. Cf. Mussolini, "L'armée nouvelle," *Opera*, VIII, 124.

57. Mussolini, "Patria e terra," *Opera*, X, 55.

58. Mussolini, "Tra il segreto e il publica," *Opera*, X, 139.

59. Mussolini, "Per la consegna della bandiera alla batteria 'Cesare Battista,' " and "La politica delle organizazioni operaie," *Opera*, XI, 18, 354.

60. Mussolini, "Battisti," *Opera*, IX, 44.

61. Mussolini, "Onori ai operai," *Opera*, X, 24.

62. Mussolini, "L'attimo che fugge," *Opera*, IX, 150.

63. Mussolini, "Resistere per vincere," *Opera*, X, 195.

64. Mussolini, "L'offerta," *Opera*, X, 15.

65. Mussolini, "La data," *Opera*, XI, 370; cf. "Il discorso di Wilson," *Opera*, XI, 385.

66. Mussolini, "Direttive," *Opera*, IX, 259.

67. Mussolini, "Produce per vincere," *Opera*, X, 100, "Il fucile e la vanga," "Consensi," *Opera*, XI, 35, 348.

68. Mussolini, "La vittoria fatale," *Opera*, XI, 86.

69. Mussolini, "Patria e terra," *Opera*, X, 56; cf. "Scoperte," *Opera*, XI, 288. These ideas are to be found in Corridoni's *Sindacalismo e repubblica*. Filippo Corridoni, along with Sergio Panunzio, was one of Mussolini's intimates during this period. In *Sindacalismo e repubblica*, Corridoni referred to Italy as being in "swaddling clothes from an economic point of view" (p. 19). Italy remained at a "preindustrial level" (p. 20). As a Marxist, Corridoni recognized the necessity of technological and industrial development if any socialist program was to be seriously contemplated. In his judgment, revolutionaries were obliged to undertake the rapid "industrial development" of the peninsula (p. 22). Marxism required completion of the "bourgeois mission" of national integration and economic and industrial development. "What we are required to do," Corridoni insisted, "is to assist the bourgeoisie—if necessary—to compel the bourgeoisie with steel and the application of force to complete its historic mission as rapidly as possible" (p. 26). Nations that undertake late industrialization face special problems if they are to effectively compete with those already advanced (p. 32). In the case of late

347

industrialization, the bourgeoisie may prove to be incompetent and the proletariat inept (pp. 37-39, 41). The population of Italy was, in Corridoni's judgment, too afflicted with individualism, too egocentric, and too provincial, to automatically assume the sacrifice and the obligations entailed in a program of intensive development (p. 46). Italy, which had only begun its program of modernization, required will, dedication, and organization (p. 48). Italy, which found itself "in essentially precapitalist circumstances," afflicted by a lack of initiative and organization, needed a revolutionary propulsive force to complete the mission of the twentieth century (p. 55). The bourgeoisie, "stalled in its economic development" must be compelled to complete the process (p. 70). After the process was completed, Italy would be fully industrialized and possessed of a mature and responsible working class (Corridoni's "Political Testament" in *Sindacalismo e republica*, pp. 110f.).

70. Mussolini, "Divagazione," *Opera*, XI, 270f.

71. Mussolini, "Il fucile e la vanga," *Opera*, XI, 35.

72. Mussolini, "Popolo e borghesia," *Opera*, VIII, 71.

73. Mussolini, "Novità," "Consensi," *Opera*, XI, 243, 348f.

74. Mussolini, "Il mio collaudo sullo 'SVA,' " *Opera*, XI, 171.

75. Engels, "Democratic Panslavism," in Blackstock and Hoselitz, *The Russian Menace to Europe*, p. 71.

76. Engels, "Der daenisch-preussische Waffenstillstand," *Werke*, V, 395.

77. Engels, "French Rule in Algeria," in Shlomo Avineri, ed., *Karl Marx on Colonialism and Modernization*, p. 43.

78. Mussolini, "Orientamenti e problemi," *Opera*, XI, 283f.

79. Michels, "Der patriotische Sozialismus oder sozialistische Patriotismus bei Carlo Pisacane," in Carl Gruenberg (ed.), *Archiv fuer die Geschichte des Sozialismus und der Arbeiterbewegung* (Leipzig: Hirschfeld, 1914).

80. Cf. Curzio Malaparte, *Europa vivente*, pp. 337f., 348-353, 381.

81. Ibid., pp. 384, 390-395.

82. Cf. Ibid., pp. 432f.

83. Max Hirschberg, "Bolschewismus," *Archiv fuer Sozialwissenschaft und Sozialpolitik* 48 (1920-1921), pp. 3-5.

84. Engels, *The Peasant War in Germany*, p. 135.

85. Engels, "Russia and the Social Revolution," in Blackstock and Hoselitz, *The Russian Menace in Europe*, p. 205.

86. Vladimir I. Lenin, "Two Tactics of Social-Democracy in the Democratic Revolution," *Collected Works* IX (1962), 48-50.

87. See Torquato Nanni, *Bolscevismo e fascismo al lume della critica marxista*. The entire volume merits reading, but chapters 1-6, 11-13 deserve special attention.

Chapter Four. The Program of Fascism

1. In this regard, cf. Emilio Gentile, *Le origini dell'ideologia fascista*, chaps. 2 and 4, and Adrian Lyttelton, *La conquista del potere*, p. 67.

2. Benito Mussolini, "Dottrina del fascismo," *Opera*, XXXIV, 122.

3. Renzo De Felice suggested that Fascism was in the "radical" tradition and succeeded in scandalizing the Italian (and Anglo-American) reading public. Cf. Renzo De Felice, *Intervista sul fascismo*, pp. 104f.

4. Lyttelton, *La conquista del potere*, p. 67.

5. I have developed the prewar convictions of the young Mussolini in some detail in my *The Young Mussolini and the Intellectual Origins of Fascism* (Berkeley and Los Angeles: University of California Press, 1979).

6. Mussolini, "L'impresa disperata," *Opera*, VI, 49.

7. Cf. *Utopia*, 1, No. 2 (December 10, 1913), p. 30.

8. For a dramatic statement of this conviction, cf. Mussolini, "Le ragioni del cosidetto 'pacificismo,'" *Opera*, V, 134.

9. Cf. Mussolini, "Il programma del partito socialista," and "Un blocco rosso?" *Opera*, V, 328, VI, 86.

10. Mussolini, "Ricordando," *Opera*, V, 71.

11. Cf. Mussolini, "Il socialismo oggi e domani," *Opera*, VI, 41. I have elsewhere developed this theme in more detail; cf. *The Ideology of Fascism*, pp. 100-105 and chap. 5 of *The Young Mussolini and the Intellectual Origins of Fascism*.

12. Mussolini, "La filosofia della forza," *Opera*, I, 175.

13. Mussolini, "L'uomo e la divinità," *Opera*, XXXIII, 22.

14. Mussolini, "La filosofia della forza," *Opera*, I, 175; cf. "Fra libri e riviste," *Opera*, II, 248f.

15. Mussolini insisted on economic development from the first commencement of his political writings. This quotation is from a speech he made as one of the principal leaders of the Socialist party. Mussolini, "Il valore storico del socialismo," *Opera*, VI, 82.

16. Mussolini, "Pace tedesca, mai!," *Opera*, VIII, 272; cf. "E in piu . . . ," "L'episodio di Parigi," "L'ora dei popoli," *Opera*, IX, 20, 33, 118, "Trincerocrazia," *Opera*, X, 140-142, "La vittoria fatale," "L'ora presente," *Opera*, XI, 85f., 143, 145.

17. All of these themes have been developed more fully in my *The Young Mussolini and the Intellectual Origins of Fascism*.

18. Cf. A. James Gregor, "Fascism and Modernization," *World Politics* 24, no. 3 (July 1974).

19. Cf. Mussolini, "Atto di nascita del fascismo," *Opera*, XII, 321-327.

20. Cf. Franco Gaeta, *Nazionalismo italiano*, p. 203.

21. Herbert Schneider, *Making the Fascist State* (New York: Oxford University Press, 1928), p. 145.

22. Enrico Corradini, "Sindacalismo, nazionalismo, imperialismo," *Discorsi politici* (*1902-1923*), pp. 59f., cf. pp. 51-69.

23. Alfredo Rocco, "Il problema economico italiano," *Scritti e discorsi politici*, I, 13-19.

24. Rocco, "La soluzione nazionale," ibid., 21-25.

25. Cf. Corradini, "Il nazionalismo e i sindacati," *Discorsi politici*, pp. 419-426; Rocco, "Crisi dello stato e sindacato," and "Programma politico nazionale," in *Scritti e discorsi politici*, II, 631-645, 653f.

26. In this regard, cf. Karin Priester, *Der Italienische Faschismus*, pp. 203, 212, 216, 225, 227, 231, 243.

27. Enrico Corradini, *La marcia dei produttori*, pp. viii-ix, 6; cf. Giacomo Pavoni, *Enrico Corradini nella vita nazionale e nel giornalismo*, p. 101.

28. Cf. Vincenzo Amoruso, *Il sindacalismo di Enrico Corradini*, pp. 17, 55f., 58, 61, 79f., 91.

29. Cf. Rocco, "Dalla vecchia alla nuova Italia," *Scritti e discorsi politici*, II, 545-567.

30. Cf. Corradini, "Principii di nazionalismo," *Discorsi politici*, pp. 100f. and "Le nazioni proletarie e il nazionalismo,"

ibid., pp. 104-118; "Le nuove dottrine nazionali e il rinnovamento spirituale," ibid., pp. 199-209.

31. This was essentially the argument advanced by Arturo Labriola as early as Italy's involvement in the war in Tripoli. Cf. "L'Europa contro l'Italia," in Giulio Barni, et al., *Pro e contro la guerra di Tripoli*, pp. 55-61.

32. Angelo O. Olivetti, "Nazione e classe," *L'Italia nostra*, May 1, 1918.

33. Olivetti, "Ripresa," ibid.

34. Olivetti, Letter to the Unione Italiana del Lavoro, June 8, 1918, in *Battaglie sindacaliste* (typescript ms.), p. 121.

35. Olivetti, "Ripresa," *Pagine libere*, February 15, 1920.

36. Mussolini, "Dopo l'adunata proletaria di Genova," *Opera*, XI, 21-22.

37. Mussolini, "Il fucile e la vanga," and "Divagazioni pel centenario," ibid., 35, 47.

38. Mussolini, "Dopo quattro anni," ibid., 55.

39. Mussolini, "Osare!" ibid., 120-122.

40. Mussolini, "Francia e Italia," ibid., 199.

41. Mussolini, "Idee e propositi durante e dopo la guerra," ibid., 265.

42. Mussolini, "Orientamenti e problemi," ibid., 282-284. Cf. "Scoperte," ibid., 288-290.

43. Cf. Mussolini, "Discussioni attorno alla nostra politica estera," ibid., 295.

44. Mussolini, "Divagazione," ibid., 341f. Cf. " 'Tu quoque,' Jouhaux?", ibid., 356ff.

45. Mussolini, "La data," ibid., 370.

46. Sergio Panunzio, "Un programma d'azione," *Il rinnovamento*, 1, No. 2 (March 15, 1919).

47. Cf. Panunzio, "Una forza," written in April 1918, "La rappresentanza di classe," written in August 1919; "Contro il regionalismo," written in September 1921, and "Il sindacalismo nazionale," written in November 1918, collected in Sergio Panunzio, *Stato nazionale e sindacate*.

48. In this regard, cf. Sergio Panunzio, "Origini e sviluppi storici del sindacalismo fascista," in Luigi Lojacono ed., *Le corporazioni fasciste*, pp. 45-67.

49. Cf. Panunzio's introduction to Romolo Ronzio, *La fusione del nazionalismo con il fascismo*.

50. Cf. C. Curcio, "Sindacalisti e nazionalisti a Perugia fra il 1928 e il 1933," *Pagine libere*, December 1956.

51. Panunzio, "Un programma d'azione," p. 83.

52. Olivetti, "Ripresa," *Pagine libere*, February 15, 1920, "Ripresa," *Italia nostra*, May 1, 1918, "Nazione e classe," ibid. Cf. "Sindacalismo nazionale," *Il Resto di Carlino*, April 13, 1922.

53. Panunzio, "Una forza," *Giornale del Mattino*, April 28, 1918, reproduced in *Stato nazionale e sindacati*, pp. 33-35, and "La rappresentanza di classe," in ibid., p. 37.

54. Cf. Panunzio, *Introduzione alla società delle nazioni*, pp. 39ff., 45f., 51f.

55. Ibid., p. 60.

56. Mussolini, "Il Trentino veduta da un socialista," in *Opera*, XXXIII, 189, 191.

57. Mussolini, "Divagazioni pel centenario," *Opera*, XI, 46f.

58. Cf., for example, Massimo Rocca (Libero Tancredi), "L'errore di Sorel," *Gerarchia*, June 1922, reprinted in Rocca, *Il primo fascismo* (Rome: Volpe, 1964), pp. 77f.

59. Olivetti, "L'altra campana," in Barni, *Pro e contra la guerra di Tripoli*, p. 121, and "Postilla a 'Socialismo e guerra sono termini antitetici? Ancora per la neutralità' di Aroldo Norlenghi," *Pagine libere*, March 20, 1915.

60. Edmondo Rossoni, *Le idee della ricostruzione*, pp. 5-11; cf. pp. 17f., 30-33.

61. Ibid., p. 52, 56, 60f.

62. Ibid., pp. 74f., 77.

63. Panunzio, *Lo stato di diritto* (Ferrara: Taddei, 1922), chap. 6.

64. Panunzio, *Che cos'è il fascismo, Lo stato fascista*.

65. Panunzio, "Stato e sindacati," *Rivista internazionale di filosofia del diritto*, 3 (January-March 1923).

66. Panunzio, *Il sentimento dello stato*.

67. Panunzio, *Teoria generale dello stato fascista*.

68. Olivetti, *Il sindacalismo come filosofia e come politica*.

69. Olivetti, *Lineamenti del nuovo stato italiano* (Rome: Littorio, 1930).

70. Cf. Guido Nozzoli, *I ras del Regime*, p. 169. Cf. Dino Grandi, "Il mito sindacalista," in *Giovani*, p. 220.

71. Grandi, "La guerra non risolverà nulla," *L'Azione*, De-

cember 6, 1914, in *Giovani*, pp. 38-43; cf. "In vedutta," *La libertà economica*, July 26, 1919, and "La coscienza nazionale," in *Giovani*, pp. 85f., 95f.

72. Grandi, "Lettera a un socialista," *Resto di Carlino*, September 11, 1920, in *Giovani*, pp. 224f.

73. Olivetti, "Risposta ad una lettera aperta di Tommaso Sorricchio," *Pagine libere*, June 30, 1921.

74. Olivetti, "Terno secco," *Pagine libere*, April 25, 1920.

75. Olivetti, "Il mito comunista, la realità sindacale," *Pagine libere*, March 15, 1920.

76. Mussolini, "Da Stuermer a Lenine," "Viva Kerensky!" "Il 'morale,' " "Impudenza e mistificazione," *Opera*, IX, 74-76, 78, 82f., 109-111 and "Nell'attesa," *Opera*, X 20.

77. Mussolini, "Antologia di documenti," *Opera*, XIII, 6-8.

78. Cf. Mussolini, "Il ricatto dei vinti," ibid., 10f.

79. Mussolini, "Triplice condanna," ibid., 77-79.

80. Mussolini, "Un appello alla solidarietà per gli scioperanti metallurgici aderenti all'U.S.M.," ibid., 348.

81. Mussolini, "Crepuscolo," *Opera*, XIV, 69.

82. In this regard, cf. Vladimir I. Lenin, "The Revolutionary Phrase," *Collected Works*, XXVII, p. 27 and "Political Report of the Central Committee, March 7, 1918," ibid., pp. 95, 98f., "Report on the Ratification of the Peace Treaty," ibid., p. 188.

83. Lenin, "Resolution on War and Peace," ibid., p. 118.

84. Lenin, "Speech Against Bukharin's Amendment," ibid., p. 147.

85. Lenin, "Original Version of the Article 'The Immediate Tasks of the Soviet Government,' " ibid., pp. 211, 212f., 215, 217.

86. Lenin, "The Immediate Tasks of the Soviet Government," ibid., pp. 237-277.

87. Cf. Lenin, "Report on the Immediate Tasks of the Soviet Government," ibid., pp. 281-313.

88. Lenin, "Six Theses on the Immediate Tasks of the Soviet Government," ibid., pp. 314-317.

89. Cf. Lenin, "Fourth Anniversary of the October Revolution," *Collected Works*, XXXIII, 51-59, "Our Revolution," ibid., pp. 478ff.

353

Chapter Five. The Political Economy of Fascism

1. This is the thrust of Giacomo Matteotti's *The Fascisti Exposed*, pp. 14-30.

2. Cf., for example, Pietro Grifone, *Il capitale finanziario in Italia*; Ernesto Rossi, *Padroni del vapore e fascismo*; Rajani Palme Dutt, *Fascism and Social Revolution*; Daniel Guerin, *Fascism and Big Business*.

3. Sergio Panunzio, "Un programma d'azione," *Il rinnovamento*, 1, No. 2 (March 15, 1919), p. 85; cf. Edmondo Rossoni, *Le idee della ricostruzione* pp. 5f.

4. Cf. the "Programma del PNF (1921)," in Renzo De Felice, *Mussolini il rivoluzionario*, pp. 756-763.

5. Cf. Giovanni Preziosi, *Cooperativismo rosso piovra dello stato* and *Uno stato nello stato*.

6. Maffeo Pantaleoni, *Bolcevismo italiano*, pp. 212f.

7. Sergio Panunzio, *Lo stato di diritto*, pp. 153-157.

8. Cf. Sergio Panunzio, "Che cos'è il liberalismo?" in *Stato nazionale e sindacati*, pp. 198f.

9. Cf. Alessandro Roveri, *Le origini del fascismo a Ferrara (1918-1921)*, p. 71.

10. For an account of the development of Italian nationalism, cf. Paola Maria Arcari, *Le elaborzioni della dottrina politica nazionale fra l'unità e l'intervento (1870-1914)*, II, pp. 841-856; Franco Gaeta, *Nazionalismo italiano*, chap. 2.

11. Nazareno Mezzetti, *Alfredo Rocco nella dottrina e diritto della rivoluzione fascista*, p. 42; Paolo Ungari, *Alfredo Rocco e l'ideologia giuridica del fascismo*, p. 29 n. 15.

12. Alfredo Rocco, "Il problema economico italiano," *La Tribuna*, January 13-14, 1914, in *Scritti e discorsi politici*, I, 13-25.

13. Rocco, "Economia socialista, economia liberale, economia socialista e economia nazionale," *Rivista delle società commerciale*, 4, No. 1 (April 1914), ibid., 29-58.

14. Rocco, "Il congresso nazionalista di Roma," (March 16, 1919), in ibid., II, 475-491.

15. "Il programma nazionalista," ibid., 494-506; cf. Rocco, "La politica finanziaria," *Politica*, 1, No. 1 (1918).

16. Rocco, "L'ora del nazionalismo," *Scritti e discorsi politici*, II, 507-517.

17. Rocco, "La situazione interna italiana," ibid., p. 617; cf. Ettore Alasia, "La situazione economica," *Politica*, 1, No. 1 (1918).

18. Rocco, "Programma politica nazionale," ibid., pp. 656f., 658, and "Indirizzo di risposta al discorso della corona," ibid., 669.

19. These specifics appear as early as his "Indirizzo di riposta," ibid., pp. 669-674. Cf. "Politica e finanza," and "Il principio economico della nazione," ibid., pp. 689-691 and pp. 717-724.

20. This was already evident in Rocco's "Il problema economico nazionale" of 1914. Cf. ibid., pp. 22f.

21. Cf. Rocco, "Economia socialista, economia liberale," ibid., pp. 40, 47.

22. In this regard, cf. Giorgio Rumi, *Alle origini della politica estera fascista*, chap. 1. For a Fascist expression of these themes, cf. "Genova," *Italia nuova*, April 15, 1922. In 1921 Mussolini insisted that an independent foreign policy could only be possible with a maximum degree of economic self-sufficiency for the nation. Cf. Mussolini, "Il fascismo nel 1921," *Opera*, XVI, 102f.

23. Cf. Rocco, "Che cosa è il nazionalismo e che cosa vogliono nazionalisti," *Scritti e discorsi politici*, I, p. 72; Rocco and Maurizio Maraviglia, "Il programma nazionalista," in Alfredo Francesco Perfetti, ed., *Il nazionalismo italiano*, pp. 119f., 127-129; Enrico Corradini, *L'unità e la potenza delle nazioni* (Florence: Vallecchi, 1922), pp. 228-244. Compare Mussolini, "Discorso di Piazza Belgioioso," and "Salandra," *Opera*, XVI, 300, 320.

24. Cf. Rocco, "L'ora del nazionalismo," "Il dovere dei giovani," "Manifesto di 'Politica,'" in *Scritti e discorsi politici*, II, 511-513, 524f., 541ff.

25. Emilio Gentile (*Le origini dell'ideologia fascista*, pp. 149-154) has argued that Fascism, at its origin, "advanced no theory of imperialism." As a matter of fact, it is clear that Mussolini, as early as 1918, had entertained a clear conviction that "imperialism" and "expansion" was a "law of life." (Cf. Mussolini, "Primo dell'anno prima divagazione," *Opera*, XII, 100f.; "Discorso di Cremona," *Opera*, XV, 184f.) At the founding meeting of the Fascist movement, Mussolini had referred to

355

Italy's resource and population problems as capable of resolution only through a more equitable distribution of the world's resources and the world's space. (Cf. Mussolini, "Atto di nascita del fascismo," *Opera*, XII, 323f.; "Discorso di Cremona," *Opera*, XV, 185.) In the beginning of 1921, Mussolini spoke candidly of creating an "empire" for Italy which would satisfy its space and resource requirements (Mussolini, "Il fascismo e i problemi della politica estera italiana," *Opera*, XVI, 158f.). Giorgio Rumi has reviewed the earliest Fascist commitments and the affinities between Fascist and nationalist economic policy are transparent. (Cf. Rumi, *Alle origini della politica estera fascista*, chap. 1.) For Rocco's analysis of the rapprochement of nationalism and Fascism, cf. Rocco, "Il fascismo verso il nazionalismo," *Scritti e discorsi politici*, II, 694-699.

26. As early as 1918 the nationalists welcomed Mussolini's appeal to the "producers" of the "New Italy" as a harbinger of a national economic policy that would fulfill nationalist demands. Cf. "La verità è in cammino," *L'idea nazionale*, August 4, 1918, in Franco Gaeta, ed., *La stampa nazionalista*, pp. 551-553.

27. For the polemic between Fascists and nationalists concerning this issue cf.: Agostino Lanzillo, "La guerra e le imposte," *Popolo d'Italia*, July 31, 1918 and Gian Luigi Franchi, "Pilastri sulle nuvole," *L'idea nazionale*, July 31, 1918, ibid., pp. 116-119.

28. Rocco, "Il principio economico della nazione," *Scritti e discorsi politici*, II, 717.

29. Cf. Rosario Romeo, "La rivoluzione industriale dell'età giolittiana," and Alberto Caracciolo, "La grande industria nella prima guerra mondiale," in Alberto Caracciolo, ed., *La formazione dell'Italia industriale*, pp. 115-134, 163-222.

30. In this regard, Mussolini's judgments were explicit. Mussolini, "I diritti della vittoria," "Rilievi elettorali," "Fascismo e terra," *Opera omnia*, XIV, 53, 69, and XVI, 170.

31. Cf. Rosario Romeo, *Breve storia della grande industria in Italia*, pp. 134f.

32. Cf. Bruno Caizzi, *Storia dell'industria italiana*, pp. 457f.

33. In this regard, see Pareto's comments in the appendix to *Trasformazioni della democrazia* (Rocca San Casciano: Cappelli, 1964).

34. Shepard Clough's insistence that prior to the March on Rome "what [Fascist] policies would be had not been made

clear" is, at best, only partially true. Shepard Clough, *The Economic History of Italy*, p. 222.

35. Cf. Lello Gangemi, *La politica finanziaria del governo fascista*, pp. 3-15.

36. Cf. Siro Lombardini, "Italian Fascism and the Economy," in Stuart J. Woolf, ed., *The Nature of Fascism*, p. 157; Ester Fano Damascelli, "La 'Restaurazione antifascista liberista': Ristagno e sviluppo economico durante il fascismo," in Alberto Aquarone and Maurizio Vernassa, eds., *Il regime fascista*, pp. 289, 293.

37. William G. Welk, *Fascist Economic Policy*, p. 161; Giuseppe Volpi di Misurata, "Hydro-electric Development in Italy," in Tomasso Sillani, ed., *What Is Fascism and Why?*, p. 296; Romeo, *Breve storia*, p. 136.

38. Antonio Stefano Benni, "The Industrial Growth of Fascist Italy," in Sillani, *What Is Fascism and Why?*, p. 292. Angus Maddison gives essentially the same results with his standardized figures of "Total Volume Output." Cf. Angus Maddison, *Economic Growth in the West*, p. 202.

39. Cf. Piero Melograni, *Gli industriali e Mussolini*, pp. 302-304; Oddone Fantini, *La politica economica del fascismo*, pp. 37-42.

40. Maddison, *Economic Growth in the West*, p. 232.

41. Franz Borkenau, "Zur Soziologie des Faschismus," in Ernst Nolte, ed. *Theorien ueber den Faschismus*, p. 165.

42. For a synopsis of the legislation involved, cf. Salvatore La Francesca, *La politica economica del fascismo*, pp. 15ff.

43. Cf. Mussolini, "Proroga dei lavori parlamentari e plauso al presidente della camera," and "Per l'insediamento del comitato permanente del grano," *Opera*, XXI, 356, 372-373.

44. For a summary discussion of these programs, cf. Riccardo Festa Campanile and Romeo Fittipaldi, *Mussolini e la battaglia del grano*. A detailed account can be found in *I progressi dell'agricoltura italiana in regime fascista* (Rome: Ministero dell'agricoltura e delle foreste, 1934).

45. Luigi Salvatorelli and Giovanni Mira, *Storia d'Italia nel periodo fascista*, p. 561.

46. Clough, *Economic History of Italy*, p. 242.

47. In this regard, cf. the critiques of Carl Schmidt, *The Plow and the Sword;* Jon S. Cohen, "Un esame statistico delle

opere di bonifica intraprese durante il regime fascista," in Gianni Toniolo, ed., *Lo sviluppo economico italiano 1861-1940*, pp. 351-372.

48. Gangemi, *Politica finanziaria*, p. 26; Leopoldo Viali, *Studi di economia, politica amministrazione e finanza*, pp. 208 f.

49. Mussolini, "Discorso di Pesaro," *Opera*, XXII, 196-198.

50. The most detailed treatment of this is found in Renzo De Felice, *Mussolini il fascista*, II, chap. 3.

51. In this regard, see the comments of Paul Einzig, *Economic Foundations of Fascism*, pp. 78f.

52. Arnaldo Mussolini is often neglected in discussions of Fascist ideology or Fascist economic policy, but his writings in the *Popolo d'Italia* are not only intelligent and insightful, they often anticipate the overt political acts of the government. Mussolini had great confidence in his brother's judgment. With regard to the development of the second phase of Fascism's economic policies, see Arnaldo Mussolini's essays in which both Fascist control of the economy and economic autarchy are anticipated. Arnaldo Mussolini, *Scritti e discorsi di Arnaldo Mussolini*, IV, "La lotta per la produzione (1925-1931)."

53. Caizzi, *Storia dell'industria italiana*, pp. 466f.; cf. also tables 15 and 16 in Welk, *Fascist Economic Policy*, pp. 166f.

54. Cf. Giampiero Carocci, "Appunti sull'imperialismo fascista negli anni '20," in Aquarone and Vernassa, *Il regime fascista*, particularly pp. 415-421.

55. Cf. A. Borghesani, *Le materie prime* (Rome: Littorio, 1927).

56. Celestino Arena, *L'espansione economica in regime corporativo*, p. 107.

57. For a detailed treatment of this period, cf. Giampiero Carocci, *La politica estera dell'Italia fascista, 1925-1928*.

58. Giampiero Carocci, "Appunti sull'imperialismo fascista negli anni '20," p. 422. Cf. Roberto Michels, "La politica demografica," Gerhard Dobbert, ed., *Economia fascista*, pp. 85f.; and Rumi, *Alle origini della politica estera fascista*, pp. 11f.

59. Felice Guarneri, *Battaglie economiche*, I, p. 285.

60. For a representative volume, cf. Arena, *L'espansione economica*.

61. Cf. Ibid., pp. 9-30, 57-67, 95-123.

62. For a discussion of the structure and control features

of these agencies, cf. Giulio Scagnetti, *Gli enti di privilegio nell'economia corporativa Italiana*, pt. 1, chap. 5.

63. For a discussion of the development of controls, cf. Ferdinando Di Fenizio, *L'economia di guerra come economia di monopoli* (Milan: Ambrosiana, 1942).

64. Cf. Mussolini, "Discorso per lo stato corporativo," *Opera*, XXVI, 86-96, and "Il piano regolatore della nuova economia italiana," *Opera*, XXVII, 241-248. Umberto Renda identified these speeches as the explicit doctrinal bases of the autarchic program. Cf. Umberto Renda, *L'autarchia nell'Italia fascista*, p. 11.

65. Mussolini, "Il piano regolatore," *Opera*, XXVII, p. 247.

66. Cf. in this regard the attempt to attribute Italy's autarchic policy to the response to the sanctions of 1935 in Raffaello Riccardi, *Economia fascista*, pp. 20f., but see the Fascist counterassertion in Renda, *L'autarchia nell'Italia fascista*, pp. 10f., and Settimo Mobilio, *Il fascismo in marcia*, pp. 129-150.

67. Cf. La Francesca, *La politica economica del fascismo*, pp. 74f. Di Fenizio, *L'economia di guerra*, identified the policy decisions of 1934 as marking the commencement of this period. In effect, these decisions inaugurated the final phase of the Fascist economic program.

68. Cf. Romeo, *Breve storia*, pp. 168f.

69. Ibid., p. 173; cf. Roland Sarti, *Fascism and the Industrial Leadership in Italy, 1919-1940*, pp. 118-125.

70. Cf. the discussion in Giovanni Balella, ed., *L'industria dell'Italia fascista* (Rome: Usila, 1940); compare La Francesca, *La politica economica del fascismo*, pp. 92-96; and Caizzi, *Storia dell'industria italiana*, pp. 488-512.

71. Cf. Caizzi, *Storia dell'industria italiana*, pp. 488-512.

72. Cf. Sarti, *Fascism and the Industrial Leadership*, pp. 104f.

73. Alexander Galkin, "Capitalist Society and Fascism," *Social Sciences* (Moscow), II (1970), 30. Roberto Michels spoke of capitalists as "state functionaries" under Fascism. Cf. Roberto Michels, "Un pensiero sul corporativismo," *La rivoluzione*, 1, No. 5 (1934), 8.

74. Cf. Carlo De Biase, *L'impero di "faccetta nera,"* pp. 15f; Arnaldo Pellegrineschi, *Etiopia*.

75. Maddison, *Economic Growth in the West*, p. 202, ap-

pendix A. Compare Nicos Poulantzas, *Fascism and Dictatorship*, pp. 99 and 119.

76. Ibid., pp. 231-233, appendix H.

77. The Fascists produced an inordinate amount of literature on this subject. I have found the following of particular interest in the context of the present account: Vito Beltrani, *Il problema delle materie prime*; Raffaele Conti, ed., *Il convegno di Pisa e la premesse per un ordine economico nuovo*; L. Fontana Russo, *Preparazione e condotta economica della guerra*, particularly pp. 287-301; A. Messineo, *Spazio vitale e grande spazio* Lauro Mainardi, *Mazionalità e spazi vitali*; Gaetano Napolitano, *Premesse economiche dell'espansione corporativa*. Cf. particularly, Raffaello Riccardi, *La collaborazione economica europea*, pp. 127-131.

78. Mussolini, "Pensieri Pontini e Sardi," *Opera*, XXXIV, 288.

79. Vladimir I. Lenin, "Political Report of the Central Committee," *Collected Works*, XXVII, 95.

80. Lenin, "Report on the Ratification of the Peace Treaty," Ibid., 188.

81. Lenin, "Original Version of the Article 'The Immediate Tasks of the Soviet Government,' " Ibid., 204, 206f., 211-213.

82. Ibid., 217; cf. Lenin, "The Immediate Tasks of the Soviet Government," Ibid., 257-259.

83. Lenin, "Report on the Immediate Tasks of the Soviet Government," Ibid., 293.

84. Joseph Stalin, *Collected Works*, XIII, 41.

85. Eugene Preobrazhenskii, *La nuova economica*, pt. 2.

86. Cf. Abram Bergson and Simon Kuznets, eds., *Economic Trends in the Soviet Union*, p. 355.

87. Janet Chapman, *Real Wages in Soviet Russia Since 1928*, p. 166.

88. Leon Trotsky, *Terrorism and Communism*, p. 170.

89. Stalin, "Report to the Eighteenth Congress of the CPSU (B)," *Problems of Leninism*, pp. 790-803; cf. Danilo Zolo, *La teoria communista dell'estinzione dello stato*, introduction.

90. Stalin, "La situazione interna dell'Unione Sovietica," in Lisa Foa, ed., *L'accumulazione socialista*, pp. 270f.

91. Cf. Isaac Deutscher, *Stalin*, pp. 284f., 340-343.

92. Cf. the discussion in Robert V. Daniels, *The Nature of Communism*, pp. 191-199.

93. Alexander Gerschenkron, *Economic Backwardness in Historical Perspective*, p. 150.

94. Leon Trotsky, *The Revolution Betrayed* (Garden City: Doubleday, Doran, 1937), p. 278.

95. Bruno Rizzi, *La lezione dello Stalinismo*, pp. 46, 95f.

96. Agostino Nasti, "L'Italia, il bolscevismo, la Russia," *Critica fascista*, 15, No. 10 (March 15, 1937), 162.

97. Cf. A. James Gregor, *The Fascist Persuasion in Radical Politics*, pp. 183-185. Cf. also in this regard the interesting volume by Tommaso Napolitano, *Le metamorfosi del bolscevismo*.

98. Mirko Ardemagni, "Deviazioni Russe verso il fascismo," *Gerarchia*, 15 (July 1934), 571.

99. Cf., for example, Martin Nicolaus, *Restoration of Capitalism in the USSR*.

100. This is of course the principal theme of Milovan Djilas, *The New Class*; cf. also Leo Kofler, *Stalinismus und Buerokratie*. Jeremy Azrael, in speaking of the "post-purge" technical administrators in the Soviet Union says of them: "they display a marked tendency to view Soviet reality through the glow of their own contentment—a contentment that derives from their having been raised in affluent and privileged families, educated in the best Soviet schools, and launched by the regime upon promising careers" (*Managerial Power and Soviet Politics*, p. 163).

Chapter Six. The Labor Policy of Fascism

1. Cf. Renzo De Felice, *Sindacalismo rivoluzionario e fiumanesimo nel carteggio De Ambris-D'Annunzio*, pp. 56-59.

2. Cf. Mussolini's discussion of the affiliation in "L'ora del sindacalismo," *Opera*, XIII, 12f., and the discussion in Guido Pighetti *Sindacalismo fascista*, pp. 12-17; Mario Viana, *Il sindacalismo* (Bari: Laterza, 1923), passim; and Eduardo Malusardi, *Elementi di storia del sindacalismo fascista*, chap. 1.

3. Alceste De Ambris, "Sempre e più che mai sindacalisti: Intermezzo polemico," *Il rinnovamento*, May 31, 1919.

4. Cf. Carlo Matteotti, *Il volto economico della dittatura*

fascista, p. 31; Rosario Romeo, *Breve storia della grande industria in Italia*, pp. 127f.

5. Cf. the discussion in Mario Missiroli, *Il fascismo e il colpo di stato dell'Ottobre 1922*.

6. Cf. Angelo Tasca, *Nascità e avvento del fascismo*, chap. 6.

7. Cf. Paolo Spriano, *L'occupazione delle fabbriche*, chap. 4.

8. Mussolini, "Discorso di Dalmine," *Opera*, XII, 314-316.

9. Mussolini, "Discorso di Cremona," *Opera*, XV, 136.

10. Ibid., p. 188.

11. Mussolini, "Discorso di Trieste," *Opera*, XV, 219; cf. Ferdinando Cordova, "Le origini dei sindacati fascista," *Storia Contemporanea*, 1, No. 4 (December 1970), pp. 925-930.

12. Mussolini, "L'epilogo," *Opera*, XV, 231.

13. Mussolini, "Stanchezza o saggezza?" *Opera*, XV, 288-290.

14. Mussolini, "Fine d'anno," *Opera*, XVI, 88; Cordova, "Le origini dei sindacati fascista," pp. 930f., 940.

15. Mussolini, "Un ordine del giorno," *Opera*, XVI, 93.

16. Mussolini, "Il fascismo nel 1921," *Opera*, XVI, 101-103.

17. Mussolini, "Per essere liberi," *Opera*, XVI, 104-106.

18. Mussolini, "L'ora del fascismo," *Opera*, XV, 153.

19. Paul Corner, *Fascism in Ferrara, 1915-1925*, chaps. 6 and 7.

20. Cf. Rolando Cavandoli, *Le origini del fascismo a Reggio Emilia, 1919-1923*.

21. Claudio Schwarzenberg, *Il sindacalismo fascista*, chap. 1. For details concerning the organization of the first specifically Fascist syndicates, cf. Giorgio Alberto Chiurco, *Storia della rivoluzione fascista*, III, 87-91.

22. Edmondo Rossoni, *Le idee della ricostruzione*, p. 8; and Enzo Santarelli, *Storia del fascismo*, I, 285f.

23. Cf. Schwarzenberg, *Il sindacalismo fascista*, p. 19. Cf. Rajani Palme Dutt's comments in *Fascism and Social Revolution*, p. 119.

24. Cf. Adrian Lyttelton, *La conquista del potere*, pp. 98f.

25. Salvemini, as cited in Schwarzenberg, *Il sindacalismo fascista*, p. 19.

26. Clara Zetkin, "Der Kampf gegen den Faschismus," in Ernest Nolte, ed., *Theorien ueber den Faschismus*, p. 99.

27. Cf. Gaetano Salvemini, *The Origins of Fascism in Italy*, pp. 285f.

28. In this regard cf. Renzo De Felice, *Mussolini il rivoluzionario*, pp. 611-615; Luigi Preti, *Le lotte agrarie nella valle padana* (Turin: Einandi, 1955), pp. 422ff.; Roberto Cantagalli, *Storia del fascismo fiorentino, 1919-1925*, pp. 88f.

29. Cf. Missiroli, *Il fascismo e il colpo di stato*, pp. 108f.

30. Cf. Corner, *Fascism in Ferrara*, chap. 7.

31. Cf. Cavandoli, *Le origini del fascismo*, p. 131.

32. This was grudgingly recognized even by the Communists. Cf. Palmiro Togliatti, *Lezioni sul fascismo*, p. 122.

33. Cf. Gaetano Salvemini, "Memorie e soliloqui," *Scritti sul fascismo*, ii, 13.

34. Roberto Michels, "Ueber die Versuche einer Besetzung der Betriebe durch die Arbeiter in Italien (September 1920)," *Archiv fuer Sozialwissenschaft und Sozialpolitik*, xlviii (1920/1921), 469-503.

35. Cf. Renzo De Felice, *Mussolini il fascista*, i, pp. 367f.

36. Roberto Michels, "Der Aufstieg des Fascismus in Italien," *Sozialismus und Fascismus in Italien*, pp. 266f.

37. Cf. Emilio Gentile, *Le origini dell'ideologia fascista*, pp. 76f.

38. Sergio Panunzio, "Stato e sindacati," *Rivista internazionale di filosofia del diritto*, 3, No. 1 (January-March 1923), 1-20.

39. Sergio Panunzio, "Il socialismo, la filosofia del diritto e lo stato," *Rivista giuridica del socialismo* (1914), 65-84.

40. Panunzio, "Stato e sindacati," pp. 9, 19.

41. Ibid., pp. 19f.

42. Compare Paolo Ungari, *Alfredo Rocco e l'ideologia giuridica del fascismo* with the works of Panunzio on the same subject.

43. Cf. Angelo O. Olivetti, "Sindacalismo eroico—Ricordando Filippo Corridoni," *Augustea* (1926) in *Battaglie sindacaliste: Dal sindacalismo al fascismo* (mimeographed).

44. Cf. Angelo O. Olivetti, *Lineamenti del nuovo stato italiano* (Rome: Littorio, 1930), particularly chaps. 8-11.

45. Cf. the discussion during the "9a riunione del Gran Consiglio del fascismo," *Opera*, XIX, 172.

46. Cf. Pighetti, *Sindacalismo fascista*, pp. 23f., 250.

47. Rossoni, *Le idee della ricostruzione*, pp. vii, 5f., 9f., 17, 20f., 32, 39, 52, 56.

48. Cf., Ibid., p. 20; Pighetti, *sindacalismo fascista*, pp. 79f.

49. Pighetti, *Sindacalismo fascista*, pp. 86, 138-141, 148, 207f., 218f., 234f.

50. Ibid., pp. 156, 206-214, 236f. In this regard cf. Camillo Pellizzi, *Fascismo-aristocrazia*, chaps. 10 and 11.

51. Oddone Fantini, *La legislazione sociale nell'Italia corporativa e negli altri stati*, p. 85.

52. Mussolini, "Il primo discordo presidenziale alla camera dei deputati," *Opera*, XIX, 22.

53. Cf. Attilio Tamaro, *Venti anni di storia*, I, p. 216.

54. As cited, Schwarzenberg, *Il sindacalismo fascista*, p. 24.

55. Gianni Merlin, *Com'erano pagati i lavoratori durante il fascismo*, pp. 104f.; Vera Zamagni, "La dinamica dei salari nel settora industriale," in Pierluigi Ciocca and Gianni Toniolo, eds., *L'economia italiana nel periodo fascista*. Mussolini, before the March on Rome, had informed Italian workers that he was prepared to reduce salaries in the service of enhancing production. Cf. Mussolini, "Sindacalismo," *Opera*, XVIII, 386.

56. Cf. Alberto Aquarone, *L'organizzazione dello stato totalitario*, pp. 122-126. For Mussolini's antiliberal interpretation of the Pact of Palazzo Chigi, cf. Mussolini. "Prime basi dello stato corporativo," *Opera*, XX, 132-135. Alfredo Rocco recognized the resistance of industrialists to the monopolization of labor representatives by Fascism; cf. Rocco, "Discorso alla Camera dei deputati," *Scritti e discorsi politici*, III, 982.

57. Mussolini, "La legge sindacale," *Opera*, XXII, 91.

58. Ibid., pp. 92f.

59. Rocco, "Legge sulla disciplina giuridica dei rapporti collettivi del lavoro," *Scritti e discorsi politici*, III, 963, 965, 967.

60. Rocco, "Discorso alla Camera dei deputati," ibid., 991, 995.

61. Ibid., p. 998.

62. Suardo, as cited, Renzo De Felice, *Mussolini il fascista*, II, 283.

63. Cf. Sabino Cassese, "Corporazioni e intervento pubblico

nell'economia," in Alberto Aquarone and Maurizio Vernassa, eds., *Il regime fascista*, pp. 327-355.

64. Cf. Francesco Paoloni, *Sistema rappresentativo del fascismo*, chap. 10; Giusseppe Bottai, *Vent'anni e un giorno*, chap. 6.

65. Vincenzo Corsini, *Il Capo del Governo nello stato fascista*, pp. 190f.

66. This entire argument is developed in considerable detail in Panunzio, *Il sentimento dello stato*.

67. Panunzio, *Il diritto sindacale e corporativo*, pp. vi, 4f., 20.

68. Panunzio, *Il sentimento dello stato*, p. 94.

69. Ibid., pp. 108f., cf. pp. 119f. n. 61, and *Teoria generale dello stato fascista*, pp. 185, 437.

70. Cf., in this regard, Giulio Sapelli, *Fascismo, grande industria e sindacato*, chap. 3.

71. Mussolini, "Storia di un anno," *Opera*, xxxiv, 410. Cf. in this regard, Oddone Fantini, *La politica economica del fascismo*, pp. 47f.

72. Mihaly Vadja, "Crisis and the Way Out: The Rise of Fascism in Italy and Germany," *Telos*, 12 (Summer 1972), 12f.

73. Cf. Renzo De Felice, *Mussolini il duce*, pp. 193f. and passim.

74. Cf. Togliatti, *Lezioni sul fascismo*, p. 56.

75. Cf. Lenin, "Report to the Council of People's Commissars," *Collected Works*, xxvii, 516f.

76. Emma Goldman, *My Disillusionment in Russia*, p. 249.

77. Leon Trotsky, *Terrorism and Communism*, pp. 132f.

78. Ibid., pp. 143, 146, 147.

79. Cf. Emily Clark Brown, *Soviet Trade Unions and Labor Relations*, p. 61.

80. Cf. Maurice Dobb, *Soviet Economic Development since 1917*, p. 447.

81. Walt Whitman Rostow, *The Dynamics of Soviet Society*, p. 67.

82. As quoted, Solomon M. Schwarz, *Labor in the Soviet Union*, p. 185.

83. Ibid., p. 180.

84. Victor Serge, *From Lenin to Stalin* (New York: Pioneer, 1937), p. 58.

85. Cf. Herbert McCloskey and John E. Turner, *The Soviet Dictatorship*, pp. 502ff.

86. Harry Schwartz, *Russia's Soviet Economy*, p. 462; Marshall Goldman, *The Soviet Economy*, p. 51.

87. As quoted in Theodore H. Von Laue, *Why Lenin? Why Stalin?*, p. 196. Cf. John H. Kautsky, *Patterns of Modernizing Revolutions*, pp. 34f., Abram Bergson, *Planning and Productivity under Soviet Socialism*, pp. 17f.

88. Mirko Ardemagni, "Deviazioni russe verso il fascismo," *Gerarchia*, 14, No. 7 (July 1934), 571-573.

89. Cf. Panunzio, *L'economia mista*, pp. 64, 78; *Teoria generale dello stato fascista*, p. 10.

90. Cf. Renzo Bertoni, *Russia*, pp. 220, 223f. See also A. James Gregor, *The Fascist Persuasion in Radical Politics*, pp. 183-186.

91. René Dumont, *Socialism and Development*, p. 44.

92. Bruno Rizzi, *La lezione dello Stalinismo*, p. 38.

93. Paul Einzig, *Economic Foundations of Fascism*, pp. 107-111.

Chapter Seven. The Orchestration of Consensus

1. Nello Lazzeroni, *La rivoluzione delle coscienze*, pp. 61f.

2. Augusto Turati, *Ragioni ideali di vita fascista*, pp. 77f. The specific reference comes from a speech made by Turati in July 1922.

3. Mussolini, "Il 'fascismo,'" *Opera*, XIII, 220, "Dopo un anno: Il fascismo," *Opera*, XIV, 379, "Un manifesto dei fasci di combattimento sulla situazione," *Opera*, XV, 131.

4. See, in particular, Angelo O. Olivetti, "Il problema della folla," *Nuova antologia*, 38, No. 761 (September 1903); Paolo Orano, *La psicologia sociale*; Roberto Michels, "Begriff und Aufgabe der 'Masse,'" in M. Henning, ed., *Das freie Wort*, II (1903), 407-412.

5. Michels, *Il proletariato e la borghesia nel movimento socialista italiano*, p. 372.

6. Michels, "L'oligarchia organica costituzionale," *Riforma sociale*, 17, No. 12 (1908), reprinted in *Studi sulla democrazia e sull'autorità*, p. 3.

7. Michels, "La democrazia e la legge ferrea dell' oligar-

chia," *Rassegna contemporanea*, 3, No. 5 (1910), reprinted in *Studi sulla democrazia e sull'autorità*, p. 32.

8. Ibid., p. 41.

9. Some of these arguments appear in Michels' contemporary writings. Cf. Michels, "Einige Randbemerkungen zum Problem der Demokratie," *Sozialistische Monatshefte*, 25 (1908) and "Der konservative Grundzug der Partei-Organisation," *Monatsschrift fuer Soziologie*, 1 (1909).

10. Michels, *Political Parties*, Translated by E. and C. Paul. (New York: Dover, 1915), pp. 53, 22, 32; cf. pp. 57, 60, 205.

11. Ibid., pp. 60, 63f., 67.

12. Ibid., pp. 69, 72.

13. Ibid., pp. 235f., 237, 307.

14. Ibid., p. 407.

15. Cf. Ibid., pp. 162f., 42f., 39f. John May correctly described Michels as a "romantic revolutionist," a "scientific paternalist," who understood that pluralist organizations were "conservative" under those ordinary circumstances when revolutionary "principles" and "comprehensive theory" cannot inform the political consciousness of the masses. John D. May, "Democracy, Organization, Michels," *American Political Science Review*, 59, No. 2 (June 1965).

16. Michels, *Il proletariato e la borghesia*, p. 268.

17. Michels, "Wirtschafts- und Sozialphilosophie," *Archiv fuer Rechts—und Wirtschaftsphilosophie*, 4, No. 3 (1911), reprinted as "Intorno al problema del rapporti tra economia e politica," in *Problemi di sociologia applicata* (Turin: Bocca, 1919).

18. Michels, "La guerra europea al lume del materialismo storico," *Riforma sociale*, 25, No. 3 (1914).

19. Michels, "Appunti sulla sociologia di Vilfredo Pareto," *Nuova antologia*, 192 (November-December 1917).

20. Cf. Michels, "Intorno al problema della solidarietà e della formazione delle caste," in *Problemi di sociologia applicata*, pp. 18-22.

21. As early as 1913, Michels provided an historical analysis of the development of European patriotic sentiments. Cf. Michels, "Zur historischen Analyse des Patriotismus," *Archiv fuer Sozialwissenschaft und Sozialpolitik*, 36, Nos. 1-2 (1913).

22. Cf. Michels, *Political Parties*, pp. 226-231.

23. Cf. Michels, *Corso di sociologia politica* (Milan: IES, 1927), published in English as *First Lectures in Political Sociology*.

24. In this regard, cf. Wilfried Roehrich, *Robert Michels*.

25. Panunzio, "Il sindacalismo nationale: I," *Stato nazionale e sindacati*, pp. 102f. This essay was written in 1918 and reprinted in the 1924 edition.

26. Cf. Michels, "Faschistische Arbeitsprobleme. Die sozialen Pflichten der Unternehmer," *Koelnische Zeitung*, 106 (February 10, 1927).

27. Panunzio, *Diritto, forza e violenza*, p. 73.

28. Ibid., p. 74.

29. Cf. Ibid., pp. 48f., 50, 55f., 144, 178f., 190, 193, 204.

30. Cf. Panunzio, *Che cos'è il fascismo*, pp. 78f.

31. Cf. Panunzio, "Teoria generale della dittatura," *Gerarchia*, 14, Nos. 4 and 5 (1935), 228-236, 303-316.

32. Cf. Panunzio's essay, "Una forza," published in 1918 and reprinted in *Stato nazionale e sindacati*, p. 36, and "Politica ed educazione," ibid., p. 147.

33. Panunzio, *Che cos'è il fascismo*, p. 9.

34. Cf. Panunzio, *Teoria generale dello stato fascista*, pp. 19f.

35. Panunzio, "Teoria generale della dittatura," pp. 315f., and *Teoria generale dello stato fascista*, pp. 54, 517-520.

36. Cf. Michels, "Der patriotische Sozialismus oder sozialistische Patriotismus bei Carlo Piscane," *Archiv fuer die Geschichte des Sozialismus und der Arbeiterbewegung*, ed. Carl Gruenberg (Leipzig, 1914), pp. 222-242.

37. Cf. Adrian Lyttelton, *La conquista del potere*, pp. 633f.

38. *Codice della stampa*, ed. G. Benedetti. (Bologna: Zanichelli, 1933), pp. 26f.

39. Cf. Philip V. Cannistraro, "Burocrazia e politica culturale nello stato fascista: Il Ministero della cultura popolare," in *Il regime fascista* (edited by Alberto Aquarone and Maurizio Vernassa. Milan: Il Mulino, 1974), pp. 171f.

40. F. Monteleone, *La radio italiana nel periodo fascista* (Venice: Marsilio, 1976), p. 21.

41. Cf. Carlo Mannucci, *Lo spettatore senza libertà* (Bari: Laterza, 1962), p. 47.

42. There is good evidence that some quite prominent

journalists could ply their trade without having met such criteria, but the principle of state licensing had been established, and that seems to be the most important consideration. Cf. Alfredo Signoretti, *La Stampa in camicia nera*, pp. 10f.

43. Philip V. Cannistraro, *La fabbrica del consenso*, pp. 18f.

44. Giovanni Gentile, "Discorso inaugurale dell'Istituto nazionale fascista di cultura," *Fascismo e cultura* (Milan: Treves, 1928), pp. 46-48; cf. pp. 61, 65.

45. Balbino Giuliano, *Elementi di cultura fascista*, pp. 8, 10, 38f., 48, 72f.

46. Ibid., pp. 75-78, 95.

47. In this regard, see the content of Filiberto Mariani, *Italia fascista*. The content is not cultural, but political.

48. *La cultura fascista* (Partito nazionale fascista. Rome: Libreria dello Stato, 1936), p. 37.

49. Cf. Giuseppe Bottai, *Politica fascista delle arti*; Francesco Sapori, *Il fascismo e l'arte* and *L'arte e il duce*.

50. Cf. Gentile, "Contro l'agnosticismo della scuola," and "Discorso inaugurale," in *Fascismo e cultura*, pp. 38f., 42f., 55-58.

51. Gentile, "Continuando," and "Revisione," ibid., pp. 73, 95-98.

52. Gentile, "Il programma," ibid., p. 89.

53. Cf. *Professionisti e artisti nel primo decennale* (Confederazione nazionale sindacati fascisti prefessionisti e artisti. Rome: CNSFPA, 1932), p. 121.

54. Cannistraro, *La fabbrica del consenso*, p. 27.

55. By the time the young Fascist reached the age of 21 he should have developed a sense of "absolute and conscious obedience to every order issued by the state and by the hierarchy in the supreme interests of the Fatherland." Paride de Bella, *Cultura fascista*, p. 102.

56. G. B. Marziali, *Fascismo educatore*, p. 112.

57. Nazareno Padellaro, *Scuola e rivoluzione*, pp. 9, 23.

58. Ibid., pp. 12, 13.

59. Antonino Anile, *Lo stato e la scuola*, pp. 56f.

60. Luigi Romanini, *I principi del fascismo nel campo dell'educazione*, pp. 15, 19, 38, 50, 57, 74; cf. G. A. Fanelli, *Idee e polemiche per la scuola fascista*, p. 12.

61. Fanelli, *Idee e polemiche*, p. 18.

62. Ibid., pp. 31f.

63. A. C. Puchetti, *Il fascismo scientifico* (Turin: Bocca, 1926), pp. 16f.

64. For an extended discussion of Fascist control of the film industry, cf. C. Carabba, *Il cinema del ventennio nero* (Florence: Vallecchi, 1975).

65. Starace, as quoted, Herman Finer, *Mussolini's Italy*, pp. 486f.

66. Oddone Fantini, *La legislazione sociale nell'Italia corporativa e negli altri stati*, p. 432.

67. Cf. Fausto Pitigliani, *The Italian Corporative State*, pp. 235f.

68. Finer, *Mussolini's Italy*, p. 438.

69. Books like Luigi E. Gianturco, *Misticismo eroico*, represent the genre.

70. *Vademecum dello stile fascista* ed. Asvero Gravelli (Rome: Nuova Europa, 1939).

71. Dino Biondi, *La fabbrica del duce* (Florence: Vallecchi, 1973). There are readily available collections of representative Fascist propaganda tracts: cf. Giuliano Manacorda, *Letteratura e cultura del periodo fascista; Eia, eia, eia, alalà! La stampa italiana sotto il fascismo, 1919/1943* (Milan: Feltrinelli, 1971).

72. Cf. Enrico Ferri, *Die revolutionaere Methode*.

73. Enrico Ferri, *Mussolini Statesman*, passim.

74. Ottavio Dinale, *La rivoluzione che vince*, pp. 11, 147f.

75. Antonio Canepa, *Sistema di dottrina del fascismo*. Cf. vol. 1, pp. 90f.

76. Armando Carlini, *Filosofia e religione nel pensiero di Mussolini*.

77. *Il pensiero di Benito Mussolini*, ed. Ezio Maria Gray. Cf. Marino Parenti, *Bibliografia mussoliniana* (Florence: Sansoni, 1940).

78. Adolf Dresler, *Mussolini giornalista*.

79. Renzo De Felice, *Mussolini il duce*.

80. Michels, "Psychologie der antikapitalistischen Massenbewegungen," in G. Albrecht, et al, *Grundriss der Sozialoekonomik* (Tuebingen: Mohr, 1926), pt. 1, especially pp. 1, especially pp. 244f.

81. Cf. Michels, *Political Parties*, pp. 389, 400; *Soziologie als Gesellschaftswissenschaft* (Berlin: Mauritius, 1926), p. 52; *Umschichtungen in der herrschenden Klassen nach dem Kriege* (Berlin: Kohlhammer, 1934), p. iii.

82. Michels, *Der Patriotismus* (Munich: Duncker & Humblot, 1929), pp. vii, 1, 10f., 17, 30f., 39-41. In 1926 Michels published a long piece entitled, "Nation und Klasse," *Die Arbeit*, 3, No. 2 (February 15, 1926), in which all these themes were developed with considerable care. Cf. ibid., pt. III.

83. These convictions were apparent as early as 1913. Cf. Michels, "Zur historischen Analyse des Patriotismus," *Archiv fuer Sozialwissenschaft und Sozialpolitik*, 36, Nos. 1-2 (1913). For Michels' later accounts, cf. "Neue Polemiken und Studien zum Vaterlandsproblem," ibid., 66, No. 1 (1931) and "Patriotismus," *Handwoerterbuch der Soziologie*, ed. A. Vierkandt (Stuttgart: Enke, 1931), The latter piece appeared in Italian as "Il patriottismo," in *Atti della reale accademia de scienze morali e politiche* (Naples: Sangiovanni, 1932) and in English in Michels, *First Lectures in Political Sociology*, as a chapter on "Patriotism."

84. Michels, "La 'classe politica,' nel dopoguerra europeo," *Educazione fascista*, 10 (December 1932); "Le forze essenziali del divenire politico," *L'ordine fascista*, 12, Nos. 8-9 (1933); & "Aphorismen zum Problem der Elite," *Abendland*, 3, No. 5 (1928).

85. Michels, *Cenni storici sui sistemi sindacali corporativi* (Rome: INFC, 1936).

86. Cf. Michels, *Introduzione alla storia della dottrine economiche e politiche* (Bologna: Zanichelli, 1932); *Cenni storici sui sistemi sindacali corporativi* (Rome: Cremonese, 1936); "Osservazioni retrospettive sulla democrazia e sul consenso," *La stirpe*, 10, No. 12 (December 1932).

87. Michels, *Italien von Heute*, pp. 207-241.

88. Ibid., pp. 266-270.

89. Michels, "Some Reflections on the Sociological Character of Political Parties," *American Political Science Review*, 21, No. 4 (November 1927), esp. pp. 754, 756f., 760, 770, 771f.

90. Panunzio, *Teoria generale dello stato fascista*, pp. 577f.

91. Cf. Paolo Orano, *Il fascismo*, II, "La stampa fascista" and "Filosofia, scuola, regime."

92. Cf. Michels, "Lineamenti di storia operaia nell'Italia

degli ultimi vent'anni," *Educazione fascista*, 11, No. 10 (1933), particularly pp. 856f., and "Some Reflections on Sociological Character," pp. 770-772; Panunzio, *Teoria generale dello stato fascista*, p. 564. Mihail Manoilescu, one of the most prominent non-Italian Fascist ideologues, reviewed these affinities in his *Die einzige Partei*.

93. Rosa Luxemburg, *The Russian Revolution and Leninism or Marxism*, pp. 69, 71f.

94. Nikolai Bukharin and Eugene Preobrazhenskii, *The ABC of Communism*, pp. 232f., 244f.

95. Anatoli Lunatscharski, "Die Revolution und die Kunst," *Die Revolution und die Kunst*, pp. 27f.

96. Ibid., p. 26.

97. Andrei A. Zhdanov, "Literature," *Literature, Philosophy and Music*, pp. 7, 9, 12. Cf. Walter N. Vickery, *The Cult of Optimism*.

98. *La cultura fascista*, pp. 55f.

99. Cf. Cannistraro, *La fabbrica del consenso*, pp. 88-91.

100. René Fueloep-Miller, *The Mind and Face of Bolshevism*, p. 243.

101. Pravda, as quoted, Robert Conquest, ed., *The Politics of Ideas in the USSR*, p. 35.

102. Benjamin Moore, Jr., *Terror and Progress—USSR*, pp. 105f.

103. Robert Payne, *The Rise and Fall of Stalin*, pp. 388f.

104. G. F. Alexandrov, et al., *Joseph Stalin*, pp. 200-206.

105. Conquest, *The Politics of Ideas*, p. 67; cf. Zhdanov, *Literature, Philosophy and Music*, pp. 21-26.

106. For a critical account of these developments, cf. Stephen F. Cohen, *Bukharin and the Bolshevik Revolution*, chap. 4.

107. Nikolai Bukharin, *Historical Materialism*, pp. 207f., 264.

108. Cohen, *Bukharin and the Bolshevik Revolution*, p. 112.

109. Ibid., pp. 142ff.

110. Joseph Stalin, "Report to the Seventeenth Party Congress," *Works*, XIII, p. 374.

111. Cf. the discussion in Raymond A. Bauer, *The New Man in Soviet Psychology*.

Chapter Eight. The Social Policies of Fascism

1. Cf. the discussion in Roberto Michels, *Probleme der sozialphilosophie*, chap. 10.

2. Cf. Vilfredo Pareto, *The Rise and Fall of Elites* (Totowa: Bedminister, 1968), p. 27, and *I sistemi socialisti* (Turin: Utet, 1974), chap. 1.

3. Roberto Michels, *Soziologie als Gesellschaftswissenschaft* (Berlin Mauritius, 1926), p. 43.

4. Roberto Michels, *First Lectures in Political Sociology* (New York: Harper, 1949), pp. 26f.

5. This is the thrust of Michels' discussion in his "Il patriottismo," *Atti della Reale Accademia di scienze morali e politiche* (Naples: Sangiovanni, 1932), pp. 168-182. Cf. also "Neue Polemiken und Studien zum Vaterlandsproblem," *Archiv fuer Sozialwissenschaft und Sozialpolitik* 66, No. 1 (1931).

6. Mussolini, "Il rocatto dei vinti," *Opera*, XIII, 11.

7. Emil Ludwig, *Colloqui con Mussolini*, p. 119f.

8. Mussolini, "Ai metallurgici lombardi," *Opera*, XIX, 58. Cf. Nazareno Mezzetti, *Mussolini e la questione sociale*, pp. 163f.

9. Aldo Grechi, *Le assicurazioni sociali*, p. 100; Oddone Fantini, *La legislazione sociale nell'Italia corporativa e negli altri stati*, p. 24.

10. Ibid., pp. 24, 26.

11. Cf. Michels' report, "Le leggi sociali del Fascismo giudicate all'estero," *Lavoro d'Italia*, November 14, 1928.

12. Cf. Giuseppe Bottai, *La carta del lavoro*, pp. 194-206.

13. Celestino Arena, *Mussolini e la sua opera*, pp. 28f.

14. Mezzetti, *Mussolini e la questione sociale*, p. 38.

15. Umberto Renda, *Realizzazioni del fascismo*, pp. 77f.; cf. Gian Alberto Blanc, "L'opera nazionale per la protezione della maternità e dell'infanzia," in Tomasso Sillani, ed., *Lo stato Mussoliniano*.

16. Mario Missiroli, *Cosa deve l'Italia a Mussolini*, pp. 62 f.; *Fascist Era: Year XV* (Rome: Fascist Confederation of Industrialists, 1938), p. 56.

17. Cf. Missiroli, *Cosa deve l'Italia a Mussolini*, pp. 66f., Bruno Fornaciari, "La lotta contro la tubercolosi," in Sillani, *Lo*

stato Mussoliniano Venti Anni (Rome: P.N.F., 1942), II, pp. 252ff.

18. Herman Finer, *Mussolini's Italy*, pp. 470f.

19. Cf. Amleto Angelelli, *Principi di legislazione del lavoro*, chap. 1; Luigi Salvatorelli and Giovanni Mira, *Storia d'Italia nel periodo fascista*, pp. 568 f.; Claudio Schwarzenberg, *Breve storia dei sistemi previdenziali in Italia*, pp. 174-180.

20. Schwarzenberg, *Breve storia dei sistemi previdenziale*, pp. 178f.; cf. Renzo De Felice, *Mussolini il duce*, pp. 198f.

21. William G. Welk, *Fascist Economic Policy*, p. 105.

22. Even Gaetano Salvemini seems prepared to recognize the differences between capital availability in the United States and Great Britain and Fascist Italy. Cf. Gaetano Salvemini, *Under the Axe of Fascism*, p. 297; see chaps. 18-21.

23. Mussolini, in a letter to Bruno Biagi insisted that such programs would insure "national solidarity" among the working masses. Cf. Renda, *Realizzazioni del fascismo*, p. 79.

24. *Venti anni*, II, p. 252.

25. Mussolini, "Il discorso dell'Ascensione," *Opera*, XXII, 360-390.

26. Riccardo Mariani, *Fascismo e "città nuove"* pp. 52-54, 73-86.

27. Renzo De Felice, *Mussolini il fascista*, II, p. 379 n. 1.

28. Renzo De Felice, *Mussolini il duce*, pp. 38-42.

29. Cf. Mussolini's comments in his "Vita di Arnaldo," *Opera*, XXXIV, 144f.

30. Cf. Giorgio Rumi, *Alle origini della politica estera fascista*, pp. 11f.

31. Mussolini, "Il fascismo e i problemi della politica estera italiana," *Opera*, XVI, 159.

32. Ibid., pp. 150-152. Compare Agostino Lanzillo, *La disfatta del socialismo* (Florence: La Voce, 1918), pp. 39ff.

33. Cf. Arturo Labriola, "Lo prima impresa collettiva della nuova Italia," in Giulio Barni, et al., *Pro e contro la guerra di Tripoli*, pp. 47-61, and Libero Tancredi (Massimo Rocca), "Una conquista rivoluzionaria," ibid., pp. 183-233.

34. Michels' major writings on these subjects are to be found in *L'imperialismo italiano, Sexual Ethics* (London: Walter Scott, 1914), and "Simultaneità dei tre termini: Aumento della

popolazione, crescenza dell'immigrazione e decrescenza dell'emigrazione in Germania," *Saggi economico-statistici sulle classi popolari.*

35. Michels, *L'imperialismo italiano,* pp. 66, 70-83; *Sexual Ethics,* pp. 247f.

36. Michels, *L'imperialismo italiano,* pp. 83-89; *Sexual Ethics,* p. 246 n. 1.

37. Michels, *Imperialismo italiano,* pp. 56f.; cf. "Simultaneità dei tre termini."

38. Michels, *Sexual Ethics,* pp. 241-246.

39. Ibid., p. 249.

40. Michels, "Simultaneità dei tre termini," pp. 270f.

41. Michels, *L'imperialismo italiano,* pp. 25, 47, 48, 79, 86, 90-93, 108, 114, 125, 127.

42. Cf. A. James Gregor, *The Ideology of Fascism.*

43. Corrado Gini, *I fattori demografici dell'evoluzione delle nazioni,* pp. 34-61.

44. Ibid., pp. 38f.; cf. pp. 64f. n. 1.

45. Ibid., pp. 62-72; cf. pp. 85f.

46. Ibid., pp. 90f.

47. Ibid., pp. 93-101.

48. Ibid., pp. 102-106.

49. Cf. Alfredo Rocco, "Il problema economico italiano," *Scritti e discorsi politici,* I, 15.

50. Rocco, "Che cosa è il nazionalismo e che cosa vogliono i nazionalisti," ibid., p. 71; cf. "Il problema economica italiano," ibid., p. 22.

51. Cf. Rocco, "Lo sforzo necessario," ibid., p. 267.

52. Rocco, "Economia liberale, economia socialista ed economia nazionale," "Che cosa è il nazionalismo," ibid., pp. 54, 83.

53. Cf. Rocco, "Socialismo imperiale e pace germanica," ibid., p. 248.

54. Mussolini, "Il discorso dell'Ascensione," *Opera,* XXII, 364, 386.

55. Cf. Mariani, *Fascismo e "citta nuove,"* pp. 62f.; De Felice, *Mussolini il duce,* pp. 146f.

56. In this regard cf. Mariani, *Fascismo e "citta nuove,"* pp. 67f. and Salvemini, *Under the Axe of Fascism,* chap. 15.

57. Cf. De Felice, *Mussolini il duce,* pp. 143-145, 153f.

58. Cf. A.F.K. Organski, "Fascism and Modernization," in Stuart J. Woolf, ed., *The Nature of Fascism*, pp. 19-41; Henry A. Turner, "Fascism and Modernization," *World Politics* 24 (1972).

59. Cf. Alfredo Pino-Branca, *Riflessi storici della politica agraria fascista* (Catania: Moderno, 1930).

60. Roberto Michels, "Il problema della popolazione," in *Annali della Facoltà di Giurisprudenza*, 39, No. 5 (1927), pp. 151, 153, 156f., 171, 172.

61. Ibid., pp. 177-179, 182.

62. Roberto Michels, "La politica demografica," in Erwin von Beckerath, et al., *Economia fascista* (Florence: Sansoni, 1935), p. 105.

63. Cf. Giuseppe Pagano, "Le case 'popolarissime,' " "Il fascismo e la casa," and "L'ordine contro il disordine," *Architettura e città durante il fascismo*, pp. 359-370.

64. F. Menna, *Profezia di una società estetica* (Milan: Lerici, 1968), p. 111; cf. Cesare De Seta's introduction to Pagano, *Architettura e città*, pp. xxxvif.

65. E. W. Eschmann, "I problemi sociali," in Erwin von Beckerath et al., *Economia fascista*, pp. 68-70.

66. Ugo Spirito, "Ruralizazzione o industrializzazione?" *Archivio di studi corporativi*, 1 (1930), reprinted in *Il corporativismo*. Cf. De Felice, *Mussolini il duce*, p. 152 n. 1.

67. Cf. Salvatore La Francesca, *La politica economica del fascismo*, p. 65; De Felice, *Mussolini il duce*, p. 138 n. 3.

68. Pagano, "Case per il popolo," *Architettura e città*, p. 376.

69. Carlo Teodori, *Il fascismo e la casa*; Pagano, "Un sistema per l'accrescimento organico delle città," *Architettura e città*, pp. 356f.

70. Maria Antonietta Macciocchi, *La donna "nera"*; Piero Meldini, *Sposa e madre esemplare*.

71. Cf. Macciocchi, *La donna "nera,"* pp. 94f.

72. Roberto Michels, "Entstehung der Frauenfrage als soziale Frage," *Die Frauenbewegung*, 9, No. 3 (February 1, 1903).

73. Filippo T. Marinetti, *Teoria e invenzione futurista* (Milan: Mondadori, 1968), pp. 321-324; A. James Gregor, *The Fascist Persuasion in Radical Politics*, pp. 162f.; Macciocchi, *La donna "nera,"* pp. 31f.

74. Roberto Michels, *Die Grenzen der Geschlechtsmoral* (Munich: Frauenverlag, 1911).

75. Angelo O. Olivetti, "Fatica senza fatica," *Patria del popolo*, November 1922.

76. Mussolini, "Il programma in materia di organismi rappresentativi," *Opera*, XIX, 12f.

77. Mussolini, "Al congresso dell'alleanza internazionale pro suffragio femminile," ibid., 215f.

78. Mussolini, "Al congresso femminile delle tre Venezie," ibid., 226.

79. Mussolini, "La donna e il voto," *Opera*, XXI, 301-305.

80. Cf. Macciocchi, *La donna "nera,"* pp. 34f.

81. Mussolini, "Introduction," Ricardo Korherr, *Regresso delle nascite*, pp. 7-23.

82. Korherr, *Regresso delle nascite*, pp. 101-104.

83. Ferdinando Loffredo, "Il simbolo più alto," *Difesa della razza*, 3, No. 4 (December 20, 1940), 13-17. Loffredo was the most intransigent spokesman for this position; cf. his *Politica della famiglia*. See also A. M. Tentoni, "Il femminismo e la donna italiana," *Difesa della razza*, 2, No. 10 (March 20, 1939).

84. F. Catasta, "Studentesse d'Italia: GUF femminile e orientamento professionale," in *Almanacco delle donna italiana 1935* (Florence: Bemporad, 1934), pp. 156f.

85. As quoted, Meldini, *Sposa e madre esemplare*, p. 77.

86. Marcello Bolletti, "Sport femminile e la salute della razza," *Difesa della razza*, 3, No. 7 (February 5, 1940) and Luigi Manzi, "Lo sport e la donna," ibid., 3, Nos. 21-22 (September 5-20, 1940).

87. Mussolini, as quoted, Vahdah Jeanne Bordeaux, *Benito Mussolini the Man*, p. 248.

88. Ludwig, *Colloqui con Mussolini*, p. 166.

89. Rocco, "Il valore sociale del femminismo," *Scritti e discorsi politici*, I, 59-62.

90. Rocco, "Che cosa è il nazionalismo e che cosa vogliono i nazionalisti," ibid., p. 71; cf. pp. 83, 88. Cf. also "Lo sforzo necessario," ibid., 267.

91. Mussolini, "Il neomalthusianismo e immorale?" *Opera*, XXV, 25.

92. Ferdinando Loffredo conveniently summarized these minor influences on the development of Fascism's family and

377

racial politics. Ferdinando Loffredo, "Politica della famiglia e della razza," *Difesa della razza* 2, No. 24 (October 20, 1938), 26.

93. Cf. Ibid., 23 as an illustrative example of this argument. Similar arguments abound in the Fascist literature of the period.

94. Cf., for example, Roberto Michels, "Beitrag zur Kritik einer eudaemonistischen Oekonomik," *Festschrift fuer Franz Oppenheimer: Wirtschaft und Gesellschaft* (Frankfurt aM.: Wirtschaft und Gesellschaft, 1924), republished in *Soziologie als Gesellschaftswissenschaft* (Berlin: Mauritius, 1926).

95. Meldini, *Sposa e madre esemplare*, p. 103.

96. "Stato fascista e famiglia fascista," *Critica fascista* 15, No. 8 (February 15, 1937), pp. 113-116.

97. Cf. Manlio Pompei, "La famiglia e il fascismo: un' inchiesta da fare," *Critica fascista*, 11, No. 9 (May 1, 1933).

98. Cf. L. Gozzini, "La donna nel squardo del Regime," *Almanacco della donna italiana 1939* (Florence: Bemporad, 1938), pp. 43ff.

99. Meldini, *Sposa e madre esemplare*, pp. 72f.

100. Cf. Alec Nove, "Social Welfare in the USSR," in Morris Bornstein and Daniel Fusfeld, eds., *The Soviet Economy* (Homewood, Ill.: Irwin, 1962).

101. As quoted, Solomon M. Schwarz, *Labor in the Soviet Union*, p. 309.

102. Ibid., p. 310.

103. Harry Schwartz, *Russia's Soviet Economy*, p. 462.

104. Friedrich Engels, "Umrisse zu einer Kritik der Nationaloekonomie," *Werke*, I, 517.

105. Engels' letter to Nikolai Danielson, January 9, 1895, ibid., XXXIX, 374.

106. Engels, "Umrisse zu einer Kritik der Nationaloekonomie," ibid., I, 520, and Engels' letter to Friedrich Lange, March 29, 1865, ibid., XXXI, 466.

107. Engels, "Kritik der Nationaloekonomie," ibid., I, 520.

108. A convenient collection of Marx's and Engels' judgments on Malthusianism can be found in Ronald L. Meek, ed., *Marx and Engels on the Population Bomb*; cf. August Bebel, "The Population Problem and Socialism," in *Society of the Future*.

109. Ibid., p. 131.

110. Nikolai Bukharin, *Historical Materialism*, pp. 124-126.

111. Nikolai Bukharin and Eugene Preobrazhenskii, *The ABC of Communism*, pp. 178f.

112. Cf. Lenin's comments, "Speech at the First All-Russia Congress of Working Women," *Collected Works* (Moscow: Progress, 1965), XXVIII, 180f.

113. Cf. Schwartz, *Russia's Soviet Economy*, pp. 441ff.

114. As far as the benefits that accrued to women who were liberated to undertake employment equal to men, those benefits must be considered in the context of an almost total absence of social service supports for married women in the urban areas. A married woman was required to work fulltime and also perform all the services characterized as "bourgeois drudgery." Cf. Leon Trotsky, *The Revolution Betrayed* (Garden City, N.Y.: Doubleday, Doran, 1937), pp. 144-159.

115. Cf. Mario Parodi, *Il Bolscevismo si confessa*, pp. 70f.

116. Trotsky, *The Revolution Betrayed*, pp. 150f.

117. Parodi, *Il Bolscevismo si confessa*, pp. 68ff.

118. John Hazard, *Communists and Their Law*, chap. 12.

119. Schwarz, *Labor in the Soviet Union*, pp. 319f. ns. 37 and 41.

120. Tommaso Napolitano, *Le metamorfosi del bolscevismo*, chap. 1.

121. G. Sverdlov, "Family Law," in P. S. Romashkin, ed., *Fundamentals of Soviet Law*, p. 358.

Chapter Nine. Fascism and Development in Comparative Perspective

1. John H. Kautsky, *Patterns of Modernizing Revolutions: Mexico and the Soviet Union*, p. 5.

2. Cf. A. J. Gregor, *An Introduction to Metapolitics* (New York: Free Press, 1971), chap. 5.

3. G. Lowell Field, *Comparative Political Development*, pp. 15f.

4. Kautsky, *Patterns of Modernizing Revolutions*; David Apter, *Some Conceptual Approaches to the Study of Modernization*, pp. 193-232; Mihail Manoilescu, *Die einzige Partei*.

5. Cf. Robert Clark, Jr., *Development and Instability*, chap. 1.

6. In this regard, cf. Cyril E. Black, *The Dynamics of Modernization*, chap. 1.

7. Cf. Robert T. Holt and John E. Turner, *The Political Basis of Economic Development* (Princeton: Van Nostrand, 1966).

8. Alfred Meyer, *The Soviet Political System*, p. 37.

9. Roger Hansen, *The Politics of Mexican Development*, p. 223.

10. Kautsky, *Patterns of Modernizing Revolutions*, pp. 34ff.

11. Cf. Clark, *Development and Instability*, pp. 18-22.

12. In this regard, cf. Jean Lacouture, *The Demigods*.

13. T. Adamafio, *A Portrait of the Osagyefo Dr. Kwame Nkrumah* (Accra: Government Printer, 1960), p. 95.

14. Robert Ward, "Japan: The Continuity of Modernization," in Lucien Pye and Sidney Verba, eds., *Political Culture and Political Development*, p. 56.

15. Walt Whitman Rostow, *Stages of Economic Growth*, chaps. 2 and 3.

16. Cf. in this regard, Robert Dernberger, "The Role of Nationalism in the Rise and Development of Communist China," in Harry G. Johnson, ed., *Economic Nationalism in Old and New States*.

17. Martin Rudner, *Nationalism, Planning and Economic Modernization in Malaysia*, p. 15.

18. Cf. P. T. Bauer, "The Economics of Resentment: Colonialism and Underdevelopment," *Journal of Contemporary History*, 4, No. 1 (1969).

19. J. Spengler, "Economic Development: Political Preconditions and Political Consequences," *Journal of Politics*, 22 (August 1960).

20. Cf. V. Panandiker, "Development Administration: An Approach," in N. Raphaeli, ed., *Readings in Comparative Public Administration* (Boston: Allyn & Bacon, 1967).

21. J.G.H. Fei and G. Ranis, "Economic Development in Historic Perspective," *American Economic Review*, 59 (May 1969), 397.

22. Cf. Lee Sigelman, *Modernization and the Political System*, pt. 2.

23. John H. Kautsky, "From Proletarian to Modernizing Movement," in Kautsky, *Communism and the Politics of Development*.

24. Ibid., pp. 69f.

25. Ernst Otto Schueddekopf, *Revolutions of Our Time: Fascism*, p. 99.

26. Mary Matossian, "Ideologies of Delayed Industrialization: Some Tensions and Ambiguities," in John H. Kautsky, ed., *Political Change in Underdeveloped Countries*.

27. Anthony J. Joes, "Fascism: The Past and the Future," *Comparative Political Studies*, 7, No. 1 (April 1974); cf. A. James Gregor, "African Socialism, Socialism and Fascism: An Appraisal," *Review of Politics*, 29 (July 1967).

28. John H. Kautsky, *The Political Consequences of Modernization*, pp. 203-226.

29. Ibid., pp. 210f.

30. Similar arguments can be found in A.F.K. Organski, *The Stages of Political Development*, "Fascism and Modernization," in Stuart J. Woolf, ed., *The Nature of Fascism*; and Benjamin Moore, Jr., *Social Origins of Dictatorship and Democracy*.

31. Norman Kogan in "Discussion: Fascism and the Polity," in Woolf, *The Nature of Fascism*, pp. 58f.

32. Cf. Paul Corner, "Agricoltura e industria durante il fascismo," *Problemi del socialismo*, 3rd ser., 11/12 (1972) and D. Preti, "La politica agraria del fascismo; Note introduttive," *Studi storici*, 4, No. 4 (1973). See the counterarguments in Jon S. Cohen, "Rapporti agricoltura-industria e sviluppo agricolo," in Pierluigi Ciocca and Gianni Toniolo, eds., *L'economia italiana nel periodo fascista*.

33. Kautsky, *Communism and the Politics of Development*, pp. 43, 48.

34. Ibid., p. 53.

35. Ibid., pp. 48f.

36. Ibid., p. 54.

37. Kautsky, *Patterns of Modernizing Revolutions*, p. 21.

38. For a survey of these differences, cf. Juan Linz, "Some Notes Toward a Comparative Study of Fascism in Sociological Historical Perspective," in Walter Laqueur, ed., *Fascism: A Reader's Guide*.

39. Cf. Zeev Sternhell, "Fascist Ideology," ibid.

40. Alan Milward, "Fascism and the Economy," ibid.

41. Nicos Poulantzas, *Fascism and Dictatorship*, pp. 93f., 116f., 119.

42. In this regard, cf. Organski, *The Stages of Political Development*, the exchange between A. L. Greil, A. J. Joes and myself in *Comparative Political Studies*, 10, No. 2 (July 1977), devoted to the question of the relationship between Fascism, modernity and modernization.

43. Celestina Arena, *L'espansione economica in regime corporativo*, pp. 57, 58, 60, 66, 143, 144-148, 172f., 181.

44. Cf. Gualberto Gualerni, *Industria e fascismo*, pp. 10f.

45. Cf. A. James Gregor, "Lo stato totalitario," *Linee per uno stato moderno* (Rome: Volpe, 1976).

46. Cf. Kautsky, *The Political Consequences of Modernization*, pp. 248f. In this regard it is interesting to note that Kautsky, in alluding to the general similarities that unite modernizing regimes, speaks of Bolshevism, Maoism, and Peron's "Justicialismo" as belonging to the same species or subspecies of regimes. "Justicialismo," of course, has frequently been characterized as a fascist regime.

47. For a review of the discussion to date, cf. A. James Gregor, *Interpretations of Fascism*, chap. 7.

48. Juan Linz, "Totalitarian and Authoritarian Regimes," in Fred I. Greenstein and Nelson W. Polsby, eds., *Handbook of Political Science*, III, 175-411; Leonard Shapiro, *Totalitarianism* (New York: Praeger, 1972).

49. Cf. Gregor, *Interpretations*, pp. 234f., and Linz, "Totalitarian and Authoritarian Regimes," pp. 241f.

50. Linz, "Totalitarian and Authoritarian Regimes," pp. 188f.

51. Cf. Carl Friedrich and Zbigniew Brzezinski, *Totalitarian Dictatorship and Autocracy*.

52. Vincenzo Zincone, *Lo stato totalitario*; J. L. Talmon, *The Origins of Totalitarian Democracy*.

53. My volume *The Ideology of Fascism* was subtitled "The Rationale of Totalitarianism." Alberto Aquarone's *L'organizzazione dello stato totalitario* was concerned with the institutional organization of the totalitarian state.

54. In this regard the best books are those by Piero Melo-

grani, *Gli industriali e Mussolini* and Roland Sarti, *Fascism and the Industrial Leadership in Italy, 1919-1940.*

55. In this regard, the work of Renzo De Felice, including both volumes of *Mussolini il fascista*, and *Mussolini il duce*, is essential. Cf. De Felice's comments in *Le interpretazioni del fascismo*, 5th ed. (Rome: Laterza, 1974), pt. 1, chap. 2, and his *Intervista sul fascismo* (Rome: Laterza, 1975).

56. Linz, "Totalitarian and Authoritarian Regimes," pp. 270ff.

57. J.-Lucien Radel, *The Roots of Totalitarianism.*

58. Cf. Giorgio Rochat, *L'esercito italiano da Vittorio Veneto a Mussolini (1919-1925)*, particularly chap. 9; Carlo De Biase, *L'aquila d'oro.*

59. "Proof of the nontotalitarian nature of the Fascist dictatorship is the surprisingly small number and the comparatively mild sentences meted out to political offenders. During the particularly active years from 1926 to 1932, the special tribunals for political offenders pronounced 7 death sentences, 257 sentences of 10 or more years imprisonment, 1,360 under 10 years, and sentenced many more to exile, 12,000, moreover, were arrested and found innocent, a procedure quite inconceivable under conditions of Nazi or Bolshevik terror." Hanna Arendt, *The Origins of Totalitarianism*, p. 303 n. 8.

60. The list of persons who made the transit is very long and includes such notables as Amintore Fanfani. Cf. Nino Tripodi, *Italia fascista in piedi!*; cf. *Camerata dove sei?* (Rome: B & C, 1976).

61. Alexander Groth, "The 'isms' in Totalitarianism," *American Political Science Review*, 58, No. 4 (1964).

62. Frederic J. Fleron, Jr., "Soviet Areas Studies and the Social Sciences: Some Methodological Problems in Communist Societies," *Soviet Studies*, 19, No. 3 (1968).

63. Jeremy R. Azrael, *Managerial Power and Soviet Politics.*

64. Thus, I take John Kautsky's suggestions concerning the antimodernity and the anti-industrial attitudes of fascism to be mistaken. Whatever might be said of National Socialism, Italian Fascism seems to have been clearly modernizing and industrializing in intention. Cf. Kautsky, *The Political Consequences of*

Modernization, p. 214 and n. 12. In this regard, cf. Arthur L. Greil, "The Modernization of Consciousness and the Appeal of Fascism," and A. James Gregor, "Fascism and the 'Counter-modernization' of Consciousness," in *Comparative Political Studies*, 10, No. 2 (July 1977).

65. Kautsky, *The Political Consequences of Modernization*, p. 243. Kautsky attempts to salvage his analysis of fascism by defining fascism as that system that refuses to undermine the position of the landed aristocracy. Thus Peron is not, by definition, a true fascist. Cf. John H. Kautsky, *Political Change in Underdeveloped Countries*, p. 110.

66. Cf. the discussion in "The Situation in the People's Republic of China" (Report of the Central Committee of the Marxist-Leninist Organization of Britain), *Proletariat*, 1, No. 2 (August-September 1970).

67. Ibid., pp. 29, 49, 77, 95.

68. Cf. the first chapter of Roberto Michels, *Der Patriotismus* (Munich: Duncker & Humblot, 1929). Michels clearly anticipated that all peoples were destined to traverse the various stages of development, and any suggestion that some people were inherently incapable of development was to be rejected. Cf. Roberto Michels, *Lavoro e razza* (Milan: Vallardi, 1924), chap. 8.

69. Ibid., pp. 266, 271; cf. chap. 10.

70. Renzo Bertoni, *Russia*, p. 220; cf. pp. 5f., 184, and chap. 10.

71. Cf. Paul Hayes, *Fascism* (New York: Free Press, 1973) chaps. 16 and 17; Anthony J. Joes, *Fascism in the Contemporary World* (Boulder: Westview, 1978); Walter Laqueur, "Fascism —The Second Coming," *Commentary*, 62, No. 2 (February 1976).

72. Ernst Nolte, *The Three Faces of Fascism*, p. 221.

73. Karl Marx and Fredrich Engels, *The German Ideology* (Moscow: Progress, 1964), p. 47.

74. Marx, "The Future Results of British Rule in India," in Schlomo Avineri, ed., *Karl Marx on Colonialism and Modernization*, p. 131.

75. Avineri, "Introduction," ibid., p. 21.

76. Mussolini, "Il Trentino veduto da un socialista," *Opera*, XXXIII, 191; cf. p. 189.

77. Marx, "Preface to the First German Edition," *Capital* (Moscow: Foreign Languages, 1954), pp. 8f., 10.

78. J. P. Nettl, *Political Mobilization* (New York: Basic Books, 1967), p. 232 n. 1.

79. Thomas H. Greene, *Comparative Revolutionary Movements* (Englewood Cliffs, N.J.: Prentice-Hall, 1974), p. 52.

80. Mao Tse-tung, "On People's Democratic Dictatorship," *Selected Works of Mao Tse-tung*, IV, 411-423.

81. The Soviets have produced an inordinate amount of tendentious anti-Maoist material. The most interesting include F. V. Konstantinov, et al., *A Critique of Mao Tse-tung's Theoretical Conceptions*; V. I. Krivtsov, ed., *Maoism through the Eyes of Communists*; Boris Leibson, *Petty-Bourgeois Revolutionism*.

82. P. Fedoseyev, "Maoism: Its Ideological and Political Essence," in *A Destructive Policy* (Moscow: Novosti, 1972), p. 113; cf. pp. 117, 120.

83. Cf. Y. Mikhailov, *China*; A. Kruchinin and V. Olgin, *Territorial Claims of Mao Tse-tung, What Peking Keeps Silent About* (Moscow: Novosti, 1972), *The Preaching and Practice of the Chinese Leaders* (Moscow: Novosti, 1971); O. Leonidov, *Peking Divisionists*; M. Sladkovsky, ed., *Developments in China*; A. Malukhin, *Militarism—Backbone of Maoism* (Moscow: Novosti, 1970).

84. Malukhin, *Militarism*, p. 33.

85. "The New Tsars and the Degeneration of the CPSU," in *Studies in Comparative Communism*, 2, Nos. 3-4 (July-October 1969), 270. Cf. "New and Old Tsars are Jackals from the Same Lair," ibid., 210.

86. Roberto Michels, "Lineamenti di storia operaia nell' Italia degli ultimi vent'anni," *Educazione fascista*, 11, 10 (1933), 856.

BIBLIOGRAPHY

Addis Sava, Marina. *Gioventù italiana del littorio*. Milan: Feltrinelli, 1973.

Alexandrov, G. F. et al. *Joseph Stalin: A Short Biography*. Moscow: Foreign Languages, 1951.

Amantia, Agatino. *La difesa della lira*. Catania: Moderno, 1935.

————. *Principii di economia politica generale e corporativa*. Catania: Moderno, 1935.

Amoruso, Vincenzo. *Il sindacalismo di Enrico Corradini*. Palermo: Orazio Fiorenza, 1929.

Angelelli, Amleto. *Principi di legislazione del lavoro*. Rome: Nuova Europa, 1938.

Anile, Antonino. *Lo stato e la scuola*. Florence: Vallecchi, 1924.

Antonietti, Carlo. *Il capitalismo di stato*. Rome: SIT, 1934.

Apter, David. *Some Conceptual Approaches to the Study of Modernization*. Englewood Cliffs, N.J.: Prentice-Hall, 1968.

Aquarone, Alberto. *L'organizzazione dello stato totalitario*. Turin: Einaudi, 1965.

———— and Vernassa, Maurizio, eds. *Il regime fascista*. Bologna: Il Mulino, 1974.

Arcari, Paola Maria. *Le elaborzioni della dottrina politica nazionale fra l'unità e l'intervento (1870-1914)*. 3 vols. Florence: Marzocco, 1939.

Ardau, Giorgio. *I poteri discrezionali dell'imprenditore nel rapporto di lavoro*. Milan: Guiffrè, 1940.

387

Arena, Celestino. *L'espansione economica in regime corporativo*. Rome: Diritto del Lavoro, 1929.

―――. *Mussolini e la sua opera: La politica sociale*. Rome: Littorio, n.d.

Arendt, Hannah. *The Origins of Totalitarianism*. New York: Harcourt, Brace, 1951.

Assante, Arturo. *Il nuovo regime economico sociale*. Naples: Morano, 1936.

―――. *Dal sindacato alla corporazione*. Naples: Morano, 1934.

Avineri, Shlomo, ed. *Karl Marx on Colonialism and Modernization*. New York: Doubleday, 1968.

Azrael, Jeremy R. *Managerial Power and Soviet Politics*. Cambridge: Harvard University Press, 1966.

Ballarini, Franco. *Dal liberalismo al corporativismo*. Turin: Einaudi, 1935.

Barni, Giulio et al. *Pro e contro la guerra di Tripoli*. Naples: Partenopea, 1912.

Baron, Samuel H. *Plekhanov: The Father of Russian Marxism*. Stanford: Stanford University Press, 1963.

Battista, Gianni. *Dinamica del sindacato*. Pisa: Nistri-Lischi, 1942.

Bauer, Raymond A. *The New Man in Soviet Psychology*. Cambridge: Harvard University Press, 1952.

Bebel, August. *Society of the Future*. Translated by Don Danemanis. Moscow: Progress, 1971.

Beltrani, Vito. *Il problema delle materie prime*. Rome: Tupini, 1940.

Bergson, Abram. *Planning and Productivity under Soviet Socialism*. New York: Columbia University Press, 1968.

――― and Kuznets, Simon, eds. *Economic Trends in the Soviet Union*. Cambridge: Harvard University Press, 1963.

Berlin, Isiah. *Karl Marx: His Life and Environment*. London: Oxford University Press, 1949.

Bernabei, Marco. *Fascismo e nazionalismo in campania (1919-1925)*. Rome: Storia e litteratura, 1975.

Bernstein, Eduard, ed. *Dokumente des Sozialismus*. 2 vols. Stuttgart: Dietz, 1903.

—————. *Evolutionary Socialism*. New York: Schocken, 1961.

—————. *Der Sozialismus einst und jetzt*. 2d enlarged ed. Berlin: Dietz, 1923.

—————. *Die Voraussetzungen des Sozialismus und die Aufgaben der Sozialdemokratie*. Stuttgart: Dietz, 1899.

—————. *Wie ist wissenschaftlicher Sozialismus moeglich?* Berlin: Sozialistische Monatshefte, 1901.

Bertoni, Renzo. *Russia: Trionfo del fascismo*. Milan: La Prora, 1937.

Biagi, Bruno. *Scritti di politica corporativa*. Bologna: Zanichelli, 1934.

—————. *Lo stato corporativo*. Rome: Istituto Nazionale Fascista di Cultura, 1934.

Black, Cyril E. *The Dynamics of Modernization*. New York: Harper, 1967.

Blackstock, Paul W. and Hoselitz, Bert F., eds. *The Russian Menace to Europe*. Glencoe: Free Press, 1952.

Bonavita, Francesco. *Mussolini svelato*. Milan: Sonzogno, 1924.

Bordeaux, Vahdah Jeanne. *Benito Mussolini the Man*. New York: Doran, 1927.

Bottai, Giuseppe. *La carta del lavoro*. Rome: Diritto del Lavoro, 1928.

—————. *Esperienza corporativa*. 2d enlarged ed. Florence: Vallecchi, 1935.

—————. *La nuova sculo media*. Florence: Sansoni, 1941.

—————. *Politica fascista delle arti*. Rome: Signorelli, 1940.

—————. *Vent'anni e un giorno*. Cernusco sul Naviglio: Garzanti, 1949.

Brown, Emily Clark. *Soviet Trade Unions and Labor Relations*. Cambridge: Harvard University Press, 1966.

Bukharin, Nikolai. *Economia del periodo di trasformazione*. Translated by Claudio Papini. Milan: Jaca, 1971.

Bukharin, Nikolai. *Imperialism and World Economy*. New York: Fertig, 1969.

————. *Historical Materialism: A System of Sociology*. New York: International, 1925.

————. *Lenin*. Translated by Giorgio Meucci. Rome: Savelli, 1969.

Bukharin, Nikolai and Preobrazhenskii, Eugene. *The ABC of Communism*. Ann Arbor: University of Michigan, 1966.

Cafiero, Carlo. *Compendio del capitale*. 4th ed. Rome: Savelli, 1975.

Caizzi, Bruno. *Storia dell'industria italiana*. Turin: UTET, 1965.

Canepa, Antonio. *Sistema di dottrina del fascismo*. 3 vols. Rome: Formiggini, 1937.

Cannistraro, Philip V. *La fabbrica del consenso: Fascismo e mass media*. Rome: Laterza, 1975.

Cantagalli, Roberto. *Storia del fascismo fiorentino, 1919-1925*. Florence: Vallecchi, 1972.

Caracciolo, Alberto, ed. *La formazione dell'Italia industriale*. 5th ed. Bari: Laterza, 1973.

Carlini, Armando. *Filosofia e religione nel pensiero di Mussolini*. Rome: Istituto Nazionale Fascista di Cultura, 1934.

Carocci, Giampiero. *La politica estera dell'Italia fascista, 1925-1928*. Bari: Laterza, 1969.

Cavandoli, Rolando. *Le origini del fascismo a Reggio Emilia, 1919-1923*. Rome: Riuniti, 1972.

Catalario, Franco, ed. *L'Italia verso la seconda guerra mondiale (1936-1940)*. Milan: Moizzi, 1976.

———— and Chieffi, Francesco, eds. *La nascita del fascismo (1918-1922)*. Milan: Moizzi, 1976.

Chapman, Janet. *Real Wages in Soviet Russia Since 1928*. Cambridge: Harvard University Press, 1963.

Chiurco, Giorgio Alberto. *Storia della rivoluzione fascista*. 5 vols. Florence: Vallecchi, 1929.

Clark, Robert, Jr. *Development and Instability*. New York: Holt, Rinehart and Winston, 1974.

Clough, Shepard. *The Economic History of Italy*. New York: Columbia University Press, 1964.

Cohen, Stephen F. *Bukharin and the Bolshevik Revolution*. New York: Vintage, 1973.

Collier, Richard, *Duce!* New York: Viking, 1971.

Conquest, Robert, ed. *The Politics of Ideas in the USSR*. London: Bodley Head, 1967.

Conti, Raffaele, ed. *Il convegno di Pisa e la premesse per un ordine economico nuovo*. Rome: La Prisma, 1942.

Cordova, Ferdinando. *Le origini dei sindacati fascisti*. Rome: Laterza, 1974.

Corner, Paul. *Fascism in Ferrara, 1915-1925*. London: Oxford University Press, 1975.

Corradini, Enrico. *Discorsi politici (1902-1923)*. Florence: Vallecchi, 1924.

―――. *La guerra lontana*. Milan: Treves, 1911.

―――. *La marcia dei produttori*. Rome: L'Italiana, 1916.

―――. *La rinascita nazionale*. Edited by G. Bellonci. Florence: Le Monnier, 1929.

Corridoni, Filippo. *Le rovine del neo-imperialismo italico*. Parma: Tipografia Camerole, 1912.

―――. *Sindacalismo e repubblica*. 2d ed. Rome: SAREP, 1945.

Corsini, Vincenzo. *Il Capo del Governo nello stato fascista*. Bologna: Zanichelli, 1935.

Croce, Benedetto. *Cultura e vita morale*. Bari: Laterza, 1955.

La cultura fascista. Rome: Libreria dello Stato, 1936.

Daniels, Robert V. *The Nature of Communism*. New York: Random House, 1962.

De Begnac, Ivon. *L'arcangelo sindacalista (Filippo Corridoni)*. Milan: Mondadori, 1943.

de Bella, Paride. *Cultura fascista*. 2d ed. Milan: Principato, 1939.

De Baise, Carlo. *L'aquila d'oro*. Rome: Il Borghese, 1969.

―――. *L'impero di "faccetta nera."* Rome: Il Borghese, 1966.

De Felice, Renzo. *Fascism: An Informal Introduction to Its*

Theory and Practice. Edited by M. A. Ledeen. New Brunswick, N.J.: Transaction, 1976.

—————. *Intervista sul fascismo.* Edited by M. A. Ledeen. Bari: Laterza, 1975.

—————. *Mussolini il duce Gli anni del consenso, 1929-1936.* Turin: Einaudi, 1974.

—————. *Mussolini il fascista.* Vol. 1: *La conquista del potore, 1921-1925.* Turin: Einaudi, 1966. Vol. 2: *L'organizzazzione dello stato fascista, 1925-1929.* Turin: Einaudi, 1968.

—————. *Mussolini il rivoluzionario.* Turin: Einaudi, 1965.

—————. *Sindacalismo rivoluzionario e fiumanesimo nel carteggio De Ambris-D'Annunzio.* Brescia: Morcelliana, 1966.

Del Giudice, Riccardo. *Dottrina e prassi corporativa.* Bari: Macri, 1940.

—————. *Problemi del lavoro.* Rome: Unione Editoriale d'Italia, 1937.

De'Stefani, Alberto. *Eventi economici.* Bologna: Zanichelli, 1934.

—————. *Garanzie di potenza.* Bologna: Zanichelli, 1936.

—————. *L'ordine economico nazionale.* Bologna: Zanichelli, 1935.

—————. *La restaurazione finanziaria.* Bologna: Zanichelli, 1926.

Deutscher, Isaac. *Stalin: A Political Biography.* New York: Vintage, 1960.

Di Fenizio, Ferdinando. *L'economia di guerra come economia di monopoli.* Milan: Ambrosiana, 1942.

Dinale, Ottavio. *Quarant'anni di colloqui con lui.* Milan: Ciarrocca, 1953.

—————. *La rivoluzione che vince.* Rome: Campitelli, 1934.

Djilas, Milovan. *The New Class.* New York: Praeger, 1957.

Dobb, Maurice. *Soviet Economic Development since 1917.* New York: International, 1948.

Dobbert, Gerhard, ed. *Economia fascista.* Florence: Sansoni, 1935.

Dresler, Adolf. *Mussolini giornalista*. Rome: Pinciana, 1939.

Dumont, René. *Socialism and Development*. New York: Praeger, 1973.

Einzig, Paul. *Economic Foundations of Fascism*. New York and London: Macmillan, 1933.

Engels, Friedrich. *The Condition of the Working Class in England in 1844*. Translated by Florence Wischnewetzky. London: George Allen & Unwin, 1950.

―――. *The Peasant War in Germany*. Translated by Moissaye Olgin. New York: International, 1926.

Fanelli, G. A. *Idee e polemiche per la scuola fascista*. Rome: Cremonese, 1941.

Fantini, Oddone. *La legislazione sociale nell'Italia corporativa e negli altri stati*. Rome: Dante Alighieri, 1931.

―――. *Politica economica e finanziaria*. Padua: CEDAM, 1943.

―――. *La politica economica del fascismo*. Rome: Tiber, 1929.

Farinacci, Roberto. *Storia della rivoluzione fascista*. 3 vols. Cremona: Cremona Nuova, 1937.

Ferrari, Santo. *L'Italia fascista: Nozioni di cultura fascista*. 4th ed. Turin: Libraria Italiana, 1942.

Ferri, Enrico. *Mussolini Statesman*. Philadelphia: Artcraft, 1927.

―――. *Die revolutionaere Methode*. Leipzig: Hirschfeld, 1908.

Festa Campanile, Riccardo, and Fittipaldi, Romeo. *Mussolini e la battaglia del grano*. Rome: CNSFPA, 1931.

Field, G. Lowell. *Comparative Political Development*. London: Routledge and Kegan Paul, 1967.

―――. *The Syndical and Corporative Institutions of Italian Fascism*. New York: Columbia University Press, 1938.

Finer, Herman. *Mussolini's Italy*. New York: Universal Library, 1965.

Foa, Lisa, ed. *L'accumulazione socialista*. Rome: Riuniti, 1972.

393

Fontanelli, Luigi. *Logica della corporazione*. Rome: Novissima, 1934.

Forti, Raul and Ghedini Giusseppe. *L'avvento del fascismo: Cronache ferraresi*. Ferrara: Taddei, 1922.

Friedrich, Carl and Brzezinski, Zbigniew. *Totalitarian Dictatorship and Autocracy*. New York: Praeger, 1965.

Fueloep-Miller, René. *The Mind and Face of Bolshevism*. Translated by F. S. Flint and D. F. Tait. New York: Harper & Row, 1965.

Gaeta, Franco. *Nazionalismo italiano*. Naples: ESI, 1965.

————, ed. *La stampa nazionalista*. Rocca San Casciano: Cappelli, 1965.

Gangemi, Lello. *La politica finanziaria del governo fascista*. Milan: Sandron, 1929.

Gay, Peter. *The Dilemma of Democratic Socialism: Eduard Bernstein's Challenge to Marx*. New York: Collier, 1962.

Gentile, Emilio. *Le origini dell'ideologia fascista*. Rome: Laterza, 1975.

Gerschenkron, Alexander. *Economic Backwardness in Historical Perspective*. Cambridge: Harvard University Press, 1962.

Gianturco, Luigi E. *Misticiamo eroico*. Veroni: Mondadori, 1941.

Gillman, Joseph M. *The Falling Rate of Profit*. New York: Cameron, 1958.

Gini, Corrado. *Le basi scientifiche della politica della popolazione*. Catarria: Moderno, 1931.

————. *I fattori demografici dell'evoluzione delle nazioni*. Turin: Bocca, 1912.

————. *Nascita, evoluzione e morte delle nazione*. Rome: Littorio, 1930.

————. *Saggi di demografia*. Rome: Poligrafico, 1934.

Giuliano, Balbino. *Elementi di cultura fascista*. Bologna: Zanichelli, 1929.

Goldman, Emma. *My Disillusionment in Russia*. New York: Crowell, 1970.

Goldman, Marshall. *The Soviet Economy: Myth and Reality*. Englewood Cliffs, N.J.: Prentice-Hall, 1968.

Gramsci, Antonio. *Scritti politici*. Edited by Paolo Spriano. Rome: Riuniti, 1967.

Grandi, Dino. *Giovani*. Bologna: Zanichelli, 1941.

Gravelli, Asvero. *Panfascismo*. Rome: Nuova Europa, 1935.

————, ed. *Squadrismo*. Rome: Antieuropa, n.d.

————. *A te giovane fascista*. 2d ed. Rome: IEG, 1928.

————, ed. *Vademecum dello stile fascista*. Rome: Nuova Europa, 1939.

————. *Verso l'internazionale fascista*. Rome: Nuova Europa, 1932.

———— and Campanile, Aristide. *Cultura fascista*. Florence: Vallecchi, 1930.

———— and Campanile, Aristide. *Primi elementi di cultura fascista*. Florence: Vallecchi, 1930.

Gray, Ezio Maria. *Lecturae ducis*. Rome: Latium, 1942.

————, ed. *Il pensiero di Benito Mussolini*. Milan: Alpes, 1927.

Graziadei, Antonio. *La produzione capitalistica*. Turin: Bocca, 1899.

Grechi, Aldo. *Le assicurazioni sociali*. Empoli: Noccioli, 1942.

Greenstein, Fred I. and Polsby, Nelson W., eds. *Handbook of Political Science: Macropolitical Theory*. 5 vols. Reading: Addison-Wesley, 1975.

Gregor, A. James. *The Fascist Persuasion in Radical Politics*. Princeton: Princeton University Press, 1974.

————. *The Ideology of Fascism*. New York: Free Press, 1969.

————. *Interpretations of Fascism*. Morristown, N.J.: General Learning, 1974.

————. *A Survey of Marxism*. New York: Random House, 1965.

Grifone, Pietro. *Il capitale finanziario in Italia*. Turin: Einaudi, 1971.

395

Gualerni, Gualberto. *Industria e fascismo*. Milan: Vita e Pensiero, 1976.

Guarneri, Felice. *Battaglie economiche*. 2 vols. Milan: Garzanti, 1953.

Guerin, Daniel. *Fascism and Big Business*. New York: Pathfinder, 1973.

Gumplowicz, Ludwig. *Grundrisse der Sociologie*. Innsbruck: Wagner'schen Universitaet, 1895.

―――. *Outlines of Sociology*. Translated by Frederick Moore. New York: Paine-Whitman, 1963.

―――. *Die sociologische Staatsidee*. Innsbruck: Wagner'schen Universitaet, 1891.

Haider, Carmen. *Capital and Labor under Fascism*. New York: Columbia University Press, 1930.

Hansen, Richard. *The Politics of Mexican Development*. Baltimore: Johns Hopkins University Press, 1971.

Hazard, John. *Communists and Their Law*. Chicago: University of Chicago Press, 1969.

Horowitz, Irving Louis. *Radicalism and the Revolt Against Reason*. New York: Humanities, 1961.

Jaeger, Nicola. *Le controversie individuale del lavoro*. 3rd ed. Padua: CEDAM, 1934.

―――. *Corso di diritto processuale del lavoro*. 2d enlarged ed. Padua: CEDAM, 1936.

―――. *Principii di diritto corporativo*. Padua: CEDAM, 1939.

Johnson, Harry G., ed. *Economic Nationalism in Old and New States*. London: George Allen & Unwin, 1968.

Kautsky, John H. *Communism and the Politics of Development*. New York: John Wiley, 1968.

―――. *Patterns of Modernizing Revolutions: Mexico and the Soviet Union*. Beverly Hills: Sage, 1975.

―――, ed. *Political Change in Underdeveloped Countries: Nationalism and Communism*. New York: John Wiley, 1962.

―――. *The Political Consequences of Modernization*. New York: John Wiley, 1972.

Kautsky, Karl. *Die materialistische Geschichtsauffassung.* 2 vols. Berlin: Dietz, 1929.

Kofler, Leo. *Stalinismus und Buerokratie.* Berlin: Luchterhand, 1970.

Konstantinov, F. V. et al. *A Critique of Mao Tse-tung's Theoretical Conceptions.* Moscow: Progress, 1972.

Korherr, Ricardo. *Regresso delle nascite: Morte dei popoli.* Preface by Oswald Spengler and Benito Mussolini. Rome: Littorio, 1928.

Krivtsov, V. I., ed. *Maoism through the Eyes of Communists.* Moscow: Progress, 1970.

Kruchinin, A. and Olgin, V. *Territorial Claims of Mao Tse-tung: History and Modern Times.* Moscow: Novosti, n.d.

Labedz, Leo, ed. *Revisionism: Essays on the History of Marxist Ideas.* New York: Praeger, 1962.

Labriola, Antonio. *Essays on the Materialistic Conception of History.* Chicago: Charles Kerr, 1904.

———. *Lettere a Engels.* Rome: Rinascita, 1949.

———. *Scritti politici.* Bari: Laterza, 1970.

———. *Socialism and Philosophy.* Chicago: Charles Kerr, 1934.

Labriola, Arturo. *La conflagrazione europea e il socialismo.* Rome: Athenaeum, 1915.

———. *Contro G. Plekhanov e per il sindacalismo.* Pescara: Abruzzese, 1909.

———. *Manuale di economia politica.* Naples: Morano, 1920.

———. *Pro e contro la guerra di Tripoli.* Naples: Partenopea, 1912.

———. *Riforme e rivoluzione sociale.* 3rd ed. Naples: Partenopea, 1914.

———. *Studio su Marx.* 2d ed. Naples: Morano, 1926.

———. *Le tendenze politiche dell'Austria contemporanea.* Naples: Partenopea, 1911.

———. *Il valore della scienza economica.* Naples: Partenopea, 1912.

Lacoutre, Jean. *The Demigods: Charismatic Leadership in the Third World.* New York: Alfred A. Knopf, 1970.

La Francesca, Salvatore. *La politica economica del fascismo.* 2d ed. Bari: Laterza, 1973.

Laqueur, Walter, ed. *Fascism: A Reader's Guide.* Berkeley and Los Angeles: University of California Press, 1976.

Lazzeroni, Nello. *La rivoluzione delle cosciènze.* Imola: Baroncini, 1922.

Le Bon, Gustave. *The Crowd: A Study of the Popular Mind.* London: Benn, 1952.

———. *The Psychology of Socialism.* New York: Macmillan, 1899.

Leibson, Boris. *Petty-Bourgeois Revolutionism.* Moscow: Progress, 1970.

Lenin, Vladimir I. *Collected Works.* 45 vols. Moscow: Foreign Languages, 1960-70.

Leone, Enrico. *Il sindacalismo.* 2d revised ed. Milan: Sandron, 1910.

Leonidov, O. *Peking Divisionists.* Moscow: Novosti, 1971.

Lessona, Alessandro. *Un ministro di Mussolini racconta.* Milan: Edizioni Nazionali, 1973.

Levine, Louis. *Syndicalism in France.* New York: Columbia University Press, 1914.

Levine, Norman. *The Tragic Deception: Marx contra Engels.* Santa Barbara: Clio, 1975.

Loffredo, Ferdinando. *Politica della famiglia.* Milan: Bompiani, 1938.

Lojacono, Luigi, ed. *Le corporazioni fasciste.* Milan: Hoepli, 1935.

———, ed. *L'independenza economica italiana.* Milan: Hoepli, 1937.

Lowy, Michael. *La teoría de la revolución en el joven Marx.* Translated by Francisco Aramburie. Madrid: Siglo XXI, 1973.

Ludwig, Emil. *Colloqui con Mussolini.* Translated by Tommaso Gnoli. 3rd ed. Verona: Mondadori, 1950.

Lunatscharski, Anatoli. *Die Revolution und die Kunst.*

Translated by Franz Leschnitzer. Dresden: Verlag der Kunst, 1962.

Luxemburg, Rosa. *The Russian Revolution and Leninism or Marxism*. Ann Arbor: University of Michigan Press, 1962.

Lyttelton, Adrian. *La conquista del potere: Il fascismo dal 1919 al 1929*. Translated by Giovanni Ferrara and Iole Rambelli. Bari: Laterza, 1974.

Macciocchi, Maria Antonietta. *La donna "nera": "Consenso" femminile e fascismo*. Milan: Feltrinelli, 1976.

McClosky, Herbert and Turner, John E. *The Soviet Dictatorship*. New York: McGraw-Hill, 1960.

Maddison, Angus. *Economic Growth in the West*. London: George Allen & Unwin, 1964.

Mainardi, Lauro. *Nazionalità e spazio vitale*. Rome: Cremonese, 1941.

Malaparte, Curzio. *Europa vivente: Teoria storica del sindacalismo nazionale*. Florence: Vallecchi, 1961.

Malusardi, Eduardo. *Elementi di storia del sindacalismo fascista*. 3rd ed. Lanciano: Carabba, 1938.

Manacorda, Giuliano. *Letteratura e cultura del periodo fascista*. Milan: Principato, 1974.

Manoilescu, Mihail. *Die einzige Partei*. Berlin: Stollberg, 1941.

Mao Tse-tung. *Selected Works*. 5 vols. Peking: Foreign Languages, 1967-77.

Marchesini, Daniela. *La scuola dei gerarchi*. Milan: Feltrinelli, 1976.

Marescalchi, Mario. *L'agricoltura nell'anno decimo*. Rome: Pinciana, 1933.

Mariani, Filiberto. *Italia fascista: Elementi di cultura fascista*. 4th ed. Milan: EST, 1939.

Mariani, Riccardo. *Fascismo e "città nuove."* Milan: Feltrinelli, 1976.

Marx, Karl. *Capital*. 3 vols. Moscow: Foreign Languages, 1962.

―――. *The Economic and Philosophic Manuscripts*. Translated by Martin Milligan. Moscow: Foreign Languages, n.d.

————. *Grundrisse der Kritik der politischen Oekonomie.* Berlin: Dietz, 1953.

————. *Grundrisse.* Translated by Martin Nicolaus. Baltimore: Penguin, 1973.

————. *The Poverty of Philosophy.* Moscow: Foreign Languages, n.d.

Marx, Karl and Engels, Friedrich. *The German Ideology.* Translated by S. Ryazanskaya. Moscow: Progress, 1964.

————. *The Holy Family.* Translated by R. Dixon. Moscow: Foreign Languages, 1956.

————. *The Russian Menace to Europe.* Edited by Paul Blackstone and Bert Hoselitz. New York: Free Press, 1952.

————. *Selected Correspondence.* Moscow: Foreign Languages, n.d.

————. *Selected Works.* 2 vols. Moscow: Foreign Languages, 1955.

————. *Werke.* 39 vols., plus 2 vols. supplementary materials. Berlin: Dietz, 1961-1968.

Marziali, G. B. *Fascismo educatore.* Palermo: Palumbo, 1939.

Masaryk, Thomas G. *Philosophischen und sociologischen Grundlagen des Marxismus.* Vienna: Konegen, 1899.

Masotti, Tullio. *Corridoni.* Milan: Carnaro, 1932.

Matteotti, Carlo. *Il volto economico della dittatura fascista.* Milan: Avanti, n.d.

Matteotti, Giacomo. *The Fascisti Exposed.* Translated by E. W. Dickes. New York: Fertig, 1969.

Meek, Ronald L. *Marx and Engels on the Population Bomb.* Berkeley: Ramparts, 1971.

Meldini, Piero. *Sposa e madre esemplare: Ideologia e politica della donna e delle famiglia durante il fascismo.* Florence: Guaraldi, 1975.

Melograni, Piero. *Gli industriali e Mussolini.* Milan: Longanesi, 1972.

Merlin, Gianni. *Com'erano pagati i lavoratori durante il fascismo.* Rome: Cinque Lune, 1970.

Merlino, F. Saverio. *Pro e contro il socialismo: Esposizione critica dei principi e dei sistemi socialisti.* Milan: Treves, 1897.

Messineo, A. *Spazio vitale e grande spazio.* Rome: La Civiltà Cattolica, 1942.

Meyer, Alfred. *The Soviet Political System.* New York: Random House, 1965.

Mezzetti, Nazareno. *Alfredo Rocco nella dottrina e nel diritto della rivoluzione fascista.* Rome: Pinciana, 1930.

————. *Mussolini e la questione sociale.* Rome: Pinciana, 1931.

————. *La politica sociale del regime.* Rome: Pinciana, 1933.

Michels, Roberto. *First Lectures in Political Sociology.* Translated by A. De Grazia. New York: Harper, 1965.

————. *L'imperialismo italiano.* Milan: Libraria, 1914.

————. *Italien von Heute.* Leipzig: Fuessli, 1930.

————. *Political Parties.* New York: Dover, 1969.

————. *Probleme der sozialphilosophie.* Leipzig: Teubner, 1914.

————. *Il proletariato e la borghesia nel movimento socialista italiano.* Turin: Bocca, 1908.

————. *Saggi economico-statistici sulle classi popolari.* Milan: Sandron, 1913.

————. *Sozialismus und Fascismus in Italien.* Munich: Meyer & Jessen, 1925.

————. *Storia critica del movimento socialista italiano.* Florence: La Voce, 1926.

————. *Storia del marxismo in Italia.* Rome: Mongini, 1909.

————. *Studi sulla democrazia e sull'autorità.* Florence: La Nuova Italia, 1933.

Mikhailov, Y. *China: Threat of Overpopulation?* Moscow: Novosti, 1971.

Missiroli, Mario. *Cosa deve l'Italia a Mussolini.* Rome: Novissima, 1937.

―――. *Il fascismo e il colpo di stato dell'Ottobre 1922.* Rocca San Casciano: Cappelli, 1966.

Mobilio, Settimo. *Il fascismo in marcia.* Salerno: Spadafora, 1938.

Moore, Benjamin, Jr. *Social Origins of Dictatorship and Democracy.* Boston: Beacon, 1966.

―――. *Terror and Progress—USSR.* New York: Harper, 1954.

Mortara, Giorgio. *Prospettive economiche.* 16th ed. Milan: Bocconi, 1937.

Mussolini, Arnaldo. *Scritti e discorsi di Arnaldo Mussolini.* 5 vols. Milan: Hoepli, 1937.

Mussolini, Benito. *Opera omnia.* 36 vols. Florence: La Fenice, 1951-63.

Nanni, Torquato. *Bolscevismo e fascismo al lume della critica marxista.* Bologna: Cappelli, 1924.

Napolitano, Gaetano. *Premesse economiche dell'espansione corporativo.* Padua: CEDAM, 1941.

Napolitano, Tommaso. *Le metamorfosi del bolscevismo.* Milan: Bocca, 1940.

Nardi, Vincenzo. *Il corporativismo fascista.* Rome: IAT, 1974.

Nicolaus, Martin. *Restoration of Capitalism in the USSR.* Chicago: Liberator, 1975.

Nikolaevskij, Boris and Maenchen-Helfen, Otto. *Karl Marx: La vita e l'opera.* Translated by Jole Lombardi. Turin: Einaudi, 1969.

Nolte, Ernst, ed. *Theorien ueber den Faschismus.* Berlin: Kiepenheuer & Witsch, 1967.

―――. *The Three Faces of Fascism.* Translated by Leila Vennewitz. New York: Holt, Rinehart and Winston, 1966.

Nozzoli, Guido. *I ras del Regime.* Milan: Bompiani, 1972.

Olivetti, Angelo O. *Cinque anni di sindacalismo e di lotta proletaria in Italia.* Naples: Partenopea, 1914.

————. *Per la interpretazione economica della storia.* Bologna: Treves, 1898.

————. *Questioni contemporanee.* Naples: Partenopea, 1913.

————. *Il sindacalismo come filosofia e come politica.* Milan: Alpes, 1924.

Orano, Paolo. *Il capitano di Mussolini.* Rome: Pinciana, 1928.

————. *Il fascismo.* 2 vols. Rome: Pinciana, 1939-40.

————. *Lode al mio tempo 1895-1925.* Bologna: Apollo, 1926.

————. *La logica della sociologia.* Rome: Pensiero Nuovo, 1898.

————. *Il precursore italiano di Carlo Marx.* Rome: Voghera, 1899.

————. *La psicologia sociale.* Bari: Laterza, 1902.

————. *La rinascita dell'anima.* Rome: La fionda, 1920.

————. *La società-organismo ed il materialismo storico.* Rome: Pensiero Nuovo, 1898.

Organski, A.F.K. *The Stages of Political Development.* New York: Alfred A. Knopf, 1965.

Padellaro, Nazareno. *Scuola e rivoluzione.* 3rd ed. Florence: Sansoni, 1933.

Pagano, Giuseppe. *Architettura e città durante il fascismo.* Edited by Cesare De Seta. Rome: Laterza, 1976.

Palme Dutt, Rajani. *Fascism and Social Revolution.* San Francisco: Proletarian, 1974.

Paloscia, Leonardo. *La concezione sindacalista di Sergio Panunzio.* Rome: Gismondi, 1949.

Pantaleoni, Maffeo. *Bolcevismo italiano.* Bari: Laterza, 1922.

Panunzio, Sergio. *Appunti di dottrina generale dello stato.* Rome: 1931.

————. *Il concetto della guerra giusta.* Campobasso: Colitti, 1917.

————. *Consenso e apatia.* Ferrara: Annali dell' Università di Ferrara, 1924.

Panunzio, Sergio. *Il diritto e l'autorità*. Turin: UTET, 1912.

————. *Diritto, forza e violenza*. Bologna: Cappelli, 1921.

————. *Il diritto sindacale e corporativo*. Perugia: La Nuova Italia, 1930.

————. *Che cos'è il fascismo*. Milan: Alpes, 1924.

————. *L'economia mista*. Milan: Hoepli, 1936.

————. *Introduzione alla società delle nazioni*. Ferrara: Taddei, 1920.

————. *Italo Balbo: Profilo*. Milan: Imperia, 1923.

————. *La lega delle nazioni*. Ferrara: Taddei, 1920.

————. *Le legge costituzionali del regime*. Roma: Relazione al 1° Congresso Giuridico Italiano, 1932.

————. *Motivi e metodo della codificazione fascista*. Milan: Giuffrè, 1943.

————. *La persistenza del diritto*. Pescara: Abruzzese, 1910.

————. *Popolo nazione stato*. Florence: La Nuova Italia, 1933.

————. *Principi generali del diritto fascista*. Pisa: Pacini Mariotti, 1940.

————. *Il riconoscimento rivoluzionario dei sindacati*. Rome: Diritto del Lavoro, 1927.

————. *Il sentimento dello stato*. Rome: Littorio, 1929.

————. *Riforma costituzionale*. Florence: La Nuova Italia, 1934.

————. *Rivoluzione e costituzione*. Milan: Treves, 1933.

————. *Sindacalismo*. Turin: UTET, 1928.

————. *Il socialismo giuridico*. Genoa: Moderna, 1907.

————. *Sindacalismo e medio evo*. Naples: Partenopea, 1911.

————. *Il sindacalismo del passato*. Lugano: Pagine Libere, 1907.

————. *Il socialismo, la filosofia del diritto e lo stato*. Città di Castello: Il Solco, 1921.

————. *Lo stato di diritto*. Città di Castello: Il Solco, 1921.

————. *Socialismo, sindacalismo e sociologia*. Lugano: Pagine Libere, 1907.

———. *Stato e diritto*. Modena: Società Tipografica Modense, 1931.

———. *Lo stato fascista*. Bologna: Cappelli, 1925.

———. *Lo "stato giuridico" nella concezione di I. Petrone*. Campobasso: Colitti, 1917.

———. *Stato nazionale e sindacati*. Milan: Imperia, 1924.

———. *Spagna nazionalsindacalista*. Milan: Bietti, 1942.

———. *La "storia" del sindacalismo fascista*. Rome: Quaderni di Segnalazione, 1933.

———. *Teoria generale dello stato fascista*. 2d ed. Padua: CEDAM, 1939.

Paoloni, Francesco. *Sistema rappresentativo del fascismo*. Naples: Rispoli Anonima, 1937.

Parodi, Mario. *Il Bolschevismo si confessa*. Milan: Alfieri, 1943.

Pavoni, Giacomo. *Enrico Corradini nella vita nazionale e nel giornalismo*. Rome: Pinciana, n.d.

Payne, Robert. *The Rise and Fall of Stalin*. New York: Simon and Schuster, 1965.

Pellegrineschi, Arnaldo. *Etiopia: Aspetti economici*. Rome: Istituto Nazionali di Cultura Fascista, 1937.

Pellizzi, Camillo. *Fascismo-aristocrazia*. Milan: Alpes, 1925.

———. *Problemi e realtà del fascismo*. Florence: Vallecchi, 1922.

———. *Una rivoluzione mancata*. Milan: Longanesi, 1949.

Perfetti, Francesco, ed. *Il nazionalismo italiano*. Rome: Borghese, 1969.

Pergolesi, Ferruccio. *Il contratto individuale di lavoro nella nuova codificazione*. Bologna: Zanichelli, 1942.

———. *Diritto sindicale comparato*. Bologna: Zanichelli, 1934.

Petrone, Corrado. *L'ordinamento corporativo dello stato*. Rome: Pinciana, 1933.

Pighetti, Guido. *Sindacalismo fascista*. Milan: Imperia, 1924.

Pitigliani, Fausto. *The Italian Corporative State*. London: King, 1933.

Plekhanov, Georgii. *The Development of the Monist View of History*. Moscow: Foreign Languages, 1956.

———. *The Role of the Individual in History*. New York: International, 1940.

———. *Selected Philosophic Works*. 5 vols. Moscow: Foreign Languages, n.d.

———. *Sindicalismo y marxismo*. Mexico, D.F.: Grijalbo, 1968.

Poulantzas, Nicos. *Fascism and Dictatorship*. London: NLB, 1974.

Preobrazhenskii, Eugenii. *La nuova economia*. Translated by the "Cooperativa traduttori LNT." Milan: Jaca, 1971.

Preziosi, Giovanni. *Cooperativismo rosso piovra dello stato*. Bari: Laterza, 1922.

———. *Uno stato nello stato: La cooperativa Garibaldi della gente del mare*. Florence: Vallecchi, 1922.

Prezzolini, Giuseppe. *Fascism*. Translated by Kathleen Macmillan, 1926. London: Methuen, 1926.

———. *Il tempo della Voce*. Milan: Longanesi, 1960.

———. *La teoria sindacalista*. Naples: Perrella, 1909.

———. *La Voce 1908-1913*. Milan: Rusconi, 1974.

Priester, Karin. *Der italienische Faschismus: Oekonomische und ideologische Grundlagen*. Cologne: Pahl-Rugenstein, 1972.

Pye, Lucien and Verba, Sidney, eds. *Political Culture and Political Development*. Princeton: Princeton University Press, 1965.

Radel, J.-Lucien. *The Roots of Totalitarianism*. New York: Crane, Russak, 1975.

Rastelli, Vito. *Filippo Corridoni: La figura storica e la dottrina politica*. Rome: Conquiste d'Impero, 1940.

Renda, Umberto. *L'autarchia nell'Italia fascista*. Milan: Paravia, 1939.

———. *Realizzazioni del fascismo*. 2d ed. Turin: Paravia, 1940.

Riccardi, Raffaello. *La collaborazione economica europea*. Rome: Italiane, 1943.

————. *Economia fascista*. Rome: Unione Editoriale d'Italia, 1939.

Rizzi, Bruno. *La lezione dello Stalinismo*. Rome: Opere Nuova, 1962.

Rocca, Massimo. *Come il fascismo divenne una dittatura*. Milan: ELI, 1952.

Rocco, Alfredo. *Scritti e discorsi politici*. 3 vols. Milan: Giuffrè, 1938.

Rochat, Giorgio. *L'esercito italiano da Vittorio Veneto a Mussolini (1919-1925)*. Bari: Laterza, 1967.

Roehrich, Wilfried. *Robert Michels: Vom sozialistichsyndikalistischen zum fascistischen Credo*. Berlin: Duncker & Humblot, 1972.

Romanini, Luigi. *I principi del fascismo nel campo dell'educazione*. 2d ed. Rome: Paravia, 1939.

Romashkin, P. S., ed. *Fundamentals of Soviet Law*. Translated by Yuri Sdobnikov. Moscow: Foreign Languages, n.d.

Romeo, Rosario. *Breve storia della grande industria in Italia*. 3rd ed. Rocco San Casciano: Cappelli, 1967.

Ronchi, Ennio. *Dieci anni di politica economica e finanziaria del fascismo*. Rome: Pinciana, 1933.

Ronzio, Romolo. *La fusione del nazionalismo con il fascismo*. Rome: Edizioni Italiane, 1943.

Rossi, Ernesto. *Padroni del vapore e fascismo*. Bari: Laterza, 1966.

Rossoni, Edmondo. *Le idee della recostruzione: Discorsi sul sindacalismo fascista*. Florence: Bemporad, 1923.

Rostow, Walt Whitman. *The Dynamics of Soviet Society*. New York: Mentor, 1954.

————. *Politics and the Stages of Growth*. New York: Cambridge University Press, 1971.

————. *Stages of Economic Growth*. New York: Cambridge University Press, 1968.

Roveri, Alessandro. *Le origini del fascismo a Ferrara (1918-1921)*. Milan: Feltrinelli, 1974.

————. *Dal sindacalismo rivoluzionario al fascismo: Capi-*

talismo agrario e socialismo nel ferrarese. Florence: La Nuova Italia, 1972.

Rudner, Martin. *Nationalism, Planning and Economic Modernization in Malaysia: The Politics of Beginning Development*. Beverly Hills: Sage, 1975.

Ruehle, Otto. *Karl Marx: His Life and Work*. New York: Viking, 1935.

Rumi, Giorgio. *Alle origini della politica estera fascista*. Bari: Laterza, 1968.

Russo, L. Fontana. *Preparazione e condotta economica della guerra*. Rome: Cremonese, 1942.

Salvatorelli, Luigi and Mira, Giovanni. *Storia d'Italia nel periodo fascista*. Turin: Einaudi, 1964.

Salvemini, Gaetano. *The Fascist Dictatorship in Italy*. New York: Fertig, 1967.

———. *The Origins of Fascism in Italy*. Edited by Roberto Vivarelli. New York: Harper, 1973.

———. *Scritti sul fascismo*. 2 vols. Edited by Nino Valeri and Alberto Merola. Milan: Feltrinelli, 1966.

———. *Under the Axe of Fascism*. London: Gollanz, 1936.

Santarelli, Enzo. *Origini del fascismo*. Urbino: Argolia, 1963.

———. *Ricerche sul fascismo*. Urbino: Argolia, 1971.

———. *Storia del fascismo*. 2d ed. 3 vols. Rome: Riuniti, 1973.

Sapelli, Giulio. *Fascismo, grande industria e sindacato: Il caso di Torino 1929-1935*. Milan: Feltrinelli, 1975.

Sapori, Francesco. *L'arte e il duce*. Verona: Mondadori, 1932.

———. *Il fascismo e l'arte*. Verona: Mondadori, 1934.

Sarti, Roland. *Fascism and the Industrial Leadership in Italy, 1919-1940*. Berkeley and Los Angeles: University of California Press, 1971.

Scagnetti, Giulio. *Gli enti di privilegio nell'economia corporativo italiano*. Padua: CEDAM, 1942.

Schmidt, Carl. *The Plow and the Sword*. New York: Columbia University Press, 1938.

Schueddekopf, Ernst-Otto. *Revolutions of Our Time: Fascism.* New York: Praeger, 1973.

Schwartz, Harry. *Russia's Soviet Economy.* New York: Prentice-Hall, 1950.

Schwarz, Solomon M. *Labor in the Soviet Union.* New York: Praeger, 1951.

Schwarzenberg, Claudio. *Breve storia dei sistemi previdenziale in Italia.* Turin: ERI, 1971.

————. *Diritto e giustizia nell'Italia fascista.* Milan: Mursia, 1977.

————. *Il sindacalismo fascista.* Milan: Mursia, 1972.

Sega, Carlo. *Gli accordi collettivi intersindacali.* Padua: CEDAM, 1941.

Sermonti, Alfonso. *Il diritto sindacale.* 2 vols. Rome: Littorio, 1929.

Settembrini, Domenico. *Due ipotesi per il socialismo in Marx ed Engels.* Bari: Laterza, 1974.

Sigelman, Lee. *Modernization and the Political System: A Critique and Preliminary Empirical Analysis.* Beverly Hills: Sage, 1971.

Signoretti, Alfredo. *La Stampa in camicia nera.* Rome: Volpe, 1968.

Sillani, Tomasso, ed. *Lo stato Mussoliniano.* Rome: La Rassegna Italiana, 1930.

————, ed. *What Is Fascism and Why?* New York: Macmillan, 1931.

Sladknovsky, M., ed. *Developments in China.* Moscow: Progress, 1968.

Sorel, Georges. *Les polémiques pour l'interprétation du Marxisme. Bernstein & Kautsky.* Paris: Giard & Brière, 1900.

————. *Reflections on Violence.* Translated by T. E. Hulme. London: Collier-Macmillan, 1950.

————. *Saggi di critica del marxismo.* Edited by Vittorio Racca. Milan: Sandron, 1903.

————. *Sorel a Missiroli: Lettere a un amico d'Italia.* Rocca San Casciano: Cappelli, 1963.

Sorel, Georges. *De l'utilité du pragmatisme*. Paris: Rivière, 1928.

Spilimbergo, Jorge E. *La revolucion nacional en Marx*. Buenos Aires: Coyoacan, 1961.

Spinetti, G. Silvano. *Fascismo e libertà*. Padua: CEDAM, 1941.

————. *Mistica fascista nel pensiero di Arnaldo Mussolini*. Milan: Hoepli, 1936.

Spirito, Ugo. *Capitalismo e corporativismo*. Florence: Sansoni, 1933.

————. *Il corporativismo*. Florence: Sansoni, 1970.

————. *Il pragmatismo nella filosofia contemporanea*. Florence: Vallecchi, 1921.

Spriano, Paolo. *L'occupazione delle fabbriche: Settembre 1920*. Turin: Einaudi, 1964.

Stalin, Joseph. *Collected Works*. 13 vols. Moscow: Foreign Languages, 1954.

————. *Problems of Leninism*. Moscow: Foreign Languages, 1953.

Talmon, J. L. *The Origins of Totalitarian Democracy*. New York: Praeger, 1960.

Tamaro, Attilio. *Venti anni di storia*. 3 vols. Rome: Volpe, 1971-75.

Tarde, Gabriel. *The Laws of Imitation*. Translated by Elsie Parsons. New York: Henry Holt, 1903.

————. *Social Laws*. Translated by Harold Warren. New York: Macmillan, 1899.

Tasca, Angelo. *Nascità e avvento del fascismo*. Florence: La Nuova Italia, 1950.

Teodori, Carlo. *Il fascismo e la casa*. Parma: Fresching, 1938.

Thornton, Judith. *Economic Analysis of the Soviet-Type System*. New York: Cambridge University Press, 1976.

Togliatti, Palmiro. *Lezioni sul fascismo*. 3rd ed. Rome: Riuniti, 1974.

Toniolo, Gianni, ed. *Lo sviluppo economico italiano 1861-1940*. Bari: Laterza, 1973.

———— and Ciocca, Pierluigi, eds. *L'economia italiana nel periodo fascista*. Bologna: Il Mulino, 1976.

Tranfaglia, Nicola. *Dallo stato liberale al regime fascista*. Milan: Feltrinelli, 1973.

————, ed. *Fascismo e capitalismo*. Milan: Feltrinelli, 1976.

Trentin, Silvio. *Dieci anni di fascismo 1926-1936*. Rome: Riuniti, 1975.

Tripodi, Nino. *Il fascismo secondo Mussolini*. Rome. Il Borghese, 1971.

————. *Italia fascista in piedi!* 4th ed. Rome: Il Borghese, 1972.

Trizzino, Antonio. *Mussolini ultimo*. Milan: Bietto, 1968.

Trotsky, Leon. *The Revolution Betrayed*. New York: Pathfinder, 1972.

————. *Terrorism and Communism*. Ann Arbor: University of Michigan Press, 1961.

Turati, Augusto. *Ragioni ideali di vita fascista*. Rome: Berlutti, 1926.

————. *Una rivoluzione e un capo*. Rome: Littorio, n.d.

Turati, Filippo. *Le vie maestre del socialismo*. Rocca San Casciano: Cappelli, 1921.

Ungari, Paolo. *Alfredo Rocco e l'ideologia giuridica del fascismo*. Brescia: Morcelliana, 1963.

Uva, Bruno. *La nascita dello stato corporativo e sindacale fascista*. Rome: Carucci, n.d.

Vallauri, Carlo. *Il governo Giolitti e l'occupazione delle fabbriche (1920)*. Milan: Giuffrè, 1971.

Viali, Leopoldo. *Studi di economia politica amministrazione e finanza*. Florence: Bemporad, 1929.

Vickery, Walter N. *The Cult of Optimism*. Bloomington: University of Indiana Press, 1950.

Vita, Francesco. *I sindacati industriali*. Milan: Vita e Pensiero, 1930.

Von Laue, Theodore H. *Why Lenin? Why Stalin?* Philadelphia: Lippincott, 1971.

von Vollmar, Georg. *Ueber die naechsten Aufgaben der deutschen Sozialdemokratie*. Munich: Ernst, 1891.

411

Webster, Richard A. *L'imperialismo industriale italiano: Studio sul prefascismo 1908-1915*. Turin: Einaudi, 1974.

Welk, William G. *Fascist Economic Policy*. Cambridge: Harvard University Press, 1938.

Woolf, Stuart J., ed. *The Nature of Fascism*. New York: Random House, 1969.

Zhdanov, Andrei A. *Literature, Philosophy and Music*. New York: International, 1950.

Zincone, Vincenzo. *Lo stato totalitario*. Rome: Faro, 1947.

Zolo, Danilo. *La teoria communista dell'estinzione dello stato*. Bari: De Donato, 1974.

INDEX

413

419

Library of Congress Cataloging in Publication Data

Gregor, A   James.
  Italian fascism and developmental dictatorship.

  Bibliography: p.
  Includes index.
    1. Fascism—Italy.   2.   Italy—Politics and government
—1922-1945.   3.   Syndicalism—Italy.   4.   Totalitarianism.
I. Title. II. Title: Developmental dictatorship.
DG571.G733   320.5′33′0945   79-83992
ISBN 0-691-05286-7
ISBN 0-691-10082-9 pbk.